Sociology
for AS Level

Stephen Moore

Dave Aiken

Steve Chapman

Published by Collins Educational
An imprint of HarperCollins *Publishers*
77–85 Fulham Palace Road
Hammersmith
London W6 8JB

www.**Collins**Education.com
On-line Support for Schools and Colleges

British Library Cataloguing-in-Publication Data
A catalogue record for this publication
is available from the British Library.

ISBN 0 00 711314 5

Sociology for AS level is not an official publication of AQA or OCR. All material is the sole responsibility of the publisher and has not been provided or approved by AQA or OCR.

Commissioned by Peter Langley
Project managed by Patricia Briggs and Peter Langley
Edited by Sarah Pearsall
Picture research by Thelma Gilbert
Original artwork by Phillip Burrows and Barking Dog Art
Design and typesetting by Patricia Briggs
Cover design by Blue Pig Design
Printed and bound in the UK by Scotprint

You might also like to visit:

www.**fire**and**water**.com
The book lover's website

Author dedications

Stephen Moore:
Thanks to Pete Langley, who first had the idea for the book and brought it to completion.

Dave Aiken:
Thanks to my darling wife Maggie for her support and encouragement, living proof that men only ever achieved anything in the past because their womenfolk ran the rest of their lives for them. Love also to the kids Leo, Laurie and Amelia.
   I would also like to thank Steve Chapman for his generosity and mentoring role and Pete Langley for his patience, good humour and attention to detail.

Steve Chapman:
To Jake, Joe and especially Leyla for her fantastic support and patience. I couldn't have done it without you. Thanks also to Rose, Frank, Maggie, Alan, Dave and Pete for their professionalism and to all my past and present students at York Sixth Form College and Fulford School.

Contents

Acknowledgements

The publishers would like to thank the following for permission to reproduce photographs, artwork and cartoons in this book:

p. 1   Stone (James Nelson)

p. 2   Mary Evans Picture Library

p. 6   Bubbles (Jennie Woodcock)

p. 18   *left*: Mary Evans Picture Library
          right: Format (Maggie Murray)

p. 22   *top left*: Format (Sheila Gray)
          top right: Network (Homer Sykes)
          bottom left: Format (Jacky Chapman)
          bottom right: Format (Paula Solloway)

p. 29   *top*: The Bridgeman Art Library
          bottom: Rex Features (Steve Wood)

p. 30   *left*: Network (Denis Doran)
          middle top: Rex Features (Jeremy Hibbert)
          middle bottom left: Sally and Richard Greenhill
          middle bottom right: Rex Features
          right: Format (Jacky Chapman)

p. 31   Connect Publications

p. 35   Impact Photos (Andrew Smith)

p. 37   Ronald Grant Archive

p. 40   The Bridgeman Art Library

p. 44   *left*: Popperfoto/Reuter (Colin McPherson)
          right: Format (Paula Solloway)
          bottom: Science Photo Library

p. 52   *top*: Murdophoto.com
          bottom: Christopher Jones

p. 57   *top*: Popperfoto/Reuters (Abed Omar Qusini)
          middle left: John Birdsall Photography
          middle right: Rex Features
          bottom: Popperfoto/Reuters (Yannis Behrakis)

p. 65   Photofusion (Sam Scott-Hunt)

p. 66   *top left*: Bubbles (Lupe Cunha)
          top middle: Impact Photos (Peter Arkell)
          top right: John Birdsall Photography
          bottom left, middle and right: John Walmsley

p. 70   John Walmsley

p. 76   *top*: Network (Michael Abrahams)
          bottom: John Birdsall Photography

p. 77   John Walmsley

p. 82   *top left*: Roger Scruton
          top left: Sally Greenhill
          bottom left: Bubbles (Loisjoy Thurstun)
          bottom left: Stone

p. 86   *top*: Format (Jacky Chapman)
          bottom: John Birdsall

p. 90   *left*: Impact (Chris Moyse)
          right: Format (Sue Darlow)

p. 95   Stone (Michael Rosenfeld)

p. 100   *left*: BBC Picture Archives
          right: Channel 4

p. 108   *top*: The Kobal Collection
          bottom: Rex Features

p. 111   Ronald Grant Archive

p. 112   *top left*: Ronald Grant Archive
          top right: The Advertising Archives
          middle left: Rex Features (Ray Tang)
          middle: Rex Features (Steve Wood)
          middle right: BBC Picture Archives
          bottom: The Kobal Collection

p. 116   The Advertising Archives

p. 120   The Advertising Archives

p. 127   Rex Features

p. 128   Network (Mike Goldwater)

p. 132   *top*: Format (Ulrike Preuss)
          middle: Panasonic
          bottom: Ericsson

p. 140   Format (Brenda Prince)

p. 144   *top left*: Format (Ulrike Preuss)
          top middle: Format (Brenda Prince)
          top right: Format (Ulrike Preuss)
          bottom left: John Birdsall
          bottom right: Format (Paula Glassman)

p. 154   Photofusion (Sam Tanner)

p. 158   *left*: Network (Alex Segre)
          top middle: Format (Joanne O'Brien)
          bottom middle: Network (Barry Lewis)
          right: Format (Joanne O'Brien)

p. 164   *left*: Format (Sally Lancaster)
          right: Science Photo Library

p. 172   *left*: John Frost Historical Newspapers
          right: Format (Joanne O'Brien)

p. 178   Stone (Martin Barraud)

p. 178   Format (Karen Robinson)

p. 194   Anti-Slavery International

p. 197   Stephen Bourne

p. 199   John Birdsall Photography

Introduction

The organisation of the book

The book is divided into a series of units, each linking into AQA and OCR AS-level modules. Each unit consists of a number of topics, which divide the unit into manageable parts. Each topic starts by building on students' prior knowledge, then goes on to provide the knowledge required, before checking understanding and reinforcing key concepts. There is then an opportunity to apply the knowledge, practise an exam-style question and build wider skills. Finally there are research- and internet-based extension activities creating opportunities to explore issues further.

Features of each topic

Getting you thinking

The opening activity draws on students' existing knowledge and experiences to lead in to some of the main issues of the topic. The questions are usually open and, although suitable for individual work, may be more effectively used in discussion in pairs or small groups, where experiences and ideas can be shared.

Main text

The text provides the necessary essential knowledge for the topic, highlighting and explaining key concepts throughout.

Key terms

There are simple definitions of important terms and concepts used in each topic, linked to the context in which the word or phrase occurs. Most key terms are sociological but some of the more difficult but essential vocabulary is also included.

Check your understanding

These comprise a set of basic comprehension questions – all answers can be found in the preceding text.

Exploring …

The *Exploring …* feature presents a set of data-response questions that aim to provide exam practice and help develop skills of analysis and evaluation. The questions in Unit 1: *The individual and society*, reflect OCR questions for this module, the mark total being 90. Every other unit uses AQA-style questions with a mark total of 60. Wherever appropriate, OCR essay questions are provided in the extension activities.

Extension activities

These encourage students to take their knowledge and skills further. The activities include internet-based research, as well as opportunities for small-scale research projects that could form the basis of A2 coursework. Many extension activities are particularly suitable for the collection of Key Skills evidence.

Sociology for AS Level: A guide for AQA and OCR candidates

The table below shows how the units in this book relate to the OCR and AQA AS-level specifications. Turn to Unit 8: *Preparing for the AS exam* (pp. 199–205) for more detail and an explanation of the courses and their assessment.

	AQA AS	OCR AS
Unit 1	Core theme*:	AS module:
The individual and society	Socialisation, culture and identity	The Individual and society
Unit 2	AS module 1:	Option within AS module:
Families and households	Families and households	Culture and socialisation
Unit 3	AS module 2:	Part of Youth and culture option within
Education	Education	AS module: Culture and socialisation
Unit 4	AS module 1:	Option within AS module:
Mass media	Mass media	Culture and socialisation
Unit 5	AS module 2:	
Wealth, poverty and welfare	Wealth, poverty and welfare	
Unit 6	AS module 1:	
Health	Health	
Unit 7	AS module 3:	AS module:
Research methods	Sociological methods	Sociological research skills

* Note that there are two 'core themes' within sociology specifications – 'Socialisation, culture and identity' and 'Social differentiation, power and stratification'. These themes run through all the topics in the specifications and all the units in this book.

The individual and society

Getting you thinking

Feral children

left: Komala, one of the 'wolf children', begins to accept food and drink by hand

Feral or 'wild' children are those who, for whatever reason, are not brought up by humans. One famous example of feral children is that of two infant girls who were lost in the jungle in India, in about 1918. The girls had been found living with wolves, in a cave-like den. The older girl was 6 or 7 years old and the other, who died a year later, perhaps a year younger.

When captured, the girls were like animals. They were naked and ran in a sort of stooped crouch. They were afraid of artificial light. They were afraid of humans and kept a good distance. They did not display any characteristically human qualities. For example, they did not use tools of any kind, not even a stick. They did not know how to make a shelter. They did not walk upright. They did not laugh. They did not sing. They did not show any affection or attraction or curiosity towards humans. But what is especially striking is that the girls used no language. They used no noises or gestures to communicate. They didn't point at things or directions, or nod their head in agreement or disagreement. They preferred to eat with the dogs in the compound, who seemed to accept them. They ate by pushing their faces into the food, the way dogs do, and they drank by lapping from a bowl.

Adapted from J. A. Singh and R. N. Zingg (1942) *Wolf-Children and the Feral Man*, New York: Harper

1 **Make a list of the things that the girls could not do and compare them with what you were capable of at the age of 6 or 7 years.**

2 **In your opinion, what skills were the girls likely to have that you lack?**

3 **What does the extract tell us about the behaviour of human beings?**

Shirbit culture

The Shirbit culture believes that the human body is ugly and that its natural tendency is to feebleness and disease. The Shirbit therefore indulge in rituals and ceremonies designed to avoid this, and consequently every household has a shrine devoted to the body. The rituals associated with the shrine are private and secret. Adults never discuss the rituals and children are told only enough for them to be successfully initiated. The focal point of the shrine is a box built into the wall in which are kept charms and magical potions for the face and body. These are obtained from the medicine men who write down the ingredients in an ancient and secret language which is only understood by the herbalist who prepares the potion. These potions are kept in the charm-box for many years. Beneath the charm-box is a small font. Every day, twice a day, every member of the family enters the shrine room in succession and bows his or her head before the charm-box, mingles different sorts of holy water in the font and proceeds with a brief rite of ablution.

The Shirbit have an almost pathological horror of and fascination with the mouth, the condition of which is believed to have a supernatural influence on all social relationships. Were it not for the rituals of the mouth, they believe their teeth would fall out, their friends would desert them and their lovers would reject them. Finally, men and women indulge in barbaric acts of self-mutilation. Men engage in a daily body ritual of scraping and lacerating their faces with a sharp instrument, whilst women bake their heads in a small oven once a month.

Based on R. Levine (1956) 'Body language of the Nacirema', *American Anthropologist*, vol. 58

1 **What aspects of Shirbit cultural behaviour seem alien to you?**

2 **In what ways might Shirbit behaviour be thought to resemble British culture?**

Defining culture

What would you be like if all human influences were removed from your life? Tragic stories of feral children such as that described above show us very clearly that being human is about contact with other people. Without that contact we are reduced to basic and **instinctive** behaviour. But when humans work together – as they usually do – they create **cultures** that are complex, fascinating and utterly different. Our own culture always appears to be the most 'normal' and other cultures may seem strange, different and even inferior in some cases (a view known as **ethnocentrism**). Did you notice that the odd culture of the 'Shirbit' (described above) was actually a description of 'British' behaviour, especially our obsession with cleanliness, as it might appear to someone from a very different culture? ('Shirbit' is an anagram of 'British'.)

The idea of 'culture' is very important for sociologists. Culture is commonly defined as the way of life of a social group. More specifically, the term refers to 'patterns of belief, values, attitudes, expectations, ways of thinking, feeling and so on' which people use to make sense of their social worlds (Billington *et al.*, 1998).

Some sociologists argue that culture also consists of **customs** and rituals, **norms** of behaviour, **statuses** and **roles**, language, symbols, art and material goods – the entire way in which a **society** expresses itself. Culture brings people together because it is shared and taken for granted. The idea of culture helps us to understand how individuals come together in groups and identify themselves as similar to or different from others.

When societies become larger and more complex, different cultures may emerge in the same society. Think of Britain today, where there are cultures based on different ages, genders, classes, ethnic groups, regions and so on – a situation known as **cultural diversity**. Sociologists refer to these 'cultures within cultures' as **subcultures**. They share some aspects of what we think of as 'British culture' – maybe eating with a knife and fork and speaking English – but they also possess distinctive cultural features that are all their own – ways of dressing, accents and attitudes to the family, for example.

The formation of culture

Culture is made up of several different elements, including values, norms, customs, statuses and roles.

Values

Values are widely accepted beliefs that something is worthwhile and desirable. For example, most societies place a high value on human life – although during wartime this value may be suspended. However, in some societies, and in certain circumstances, suicide, euthanasia and capital punishment may be valued more than the sanctity of human life.

Norms

Norms are values put into practice. They are specific rules of behaviour that relate to specific social situations, and they govern all aspects of human behaviour. For example, norms govern the way we dress, the way we prepare food and how we eat that food, our toilet behaviour and so on.

Customs

Customs are traditional and regular norms of behaviour associated with specific social situations, events and anniversaries which are often accompanied by rituals and ceremonies. For example, in Britain many people practise the custom of celebrating Bonfire Night on November 5th, and this usually involves the ritual of burning a Guy Fawkes effigy and setting off fireworks.

It is also the social custom to mourn for the dead at funerals, and this usually involves an elaborate set of ritualistic norms and a ceremony. For example, it is generally expected that people wear black at funerals in Britain. Turning up in a pink tuxedo would be regarded as **deviant**, or norm-breaking, behaviour.

Statuses

All members of society are given a social position by their culture. These positions are known as statuses. Sociologists distinguish between ascribed statuses and achieved statuses. Ascribed statuses are fixed at birth, usually by inheritance or biology. For example, gender and race are fixed characteristics (which may result in women and ethnic minorities occupying low-status roles in some societies). Statuses over which individuals have control are achieved. In Western societies, such status is normally attained through education, jobs and sometimes marriage.

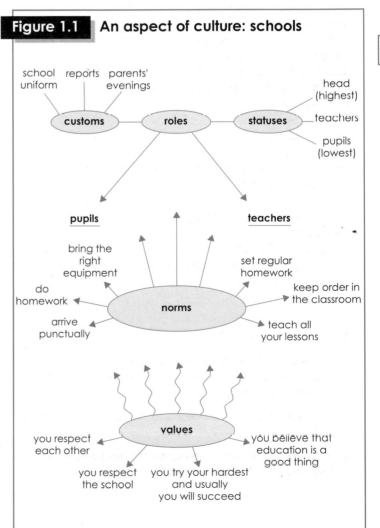

Figure 1.1 An aspect of culture: schools

Roles

Society expects those of a certain status to behave in a particular way. A set of norms is imposed on the status. These are collectively known as a role. For example, the role of 'doctor' is accompanied by cultural expectations about patient confidentiality and professional behaviour.

Culture and biology

Some people, known as **sociobiologists**, believe that human behaviour is largely the product of nature, so we can learn much about humans by studying animals. Most sociologists reject this view. If human behaviour was biologically determined, they argue, we could expect to see little variation in how people behave. However, human behaviour is actually richly diverse. If human behaviour is influenced by biology at all, it is only at the level of physiological need, i.e. we must sleep, eat, go to the toilet, etc. However, when you look more closely you find that even these biological influences are shaped by culture. Cultural values and norms determine what we eat. For example, insects are not popular as a food in Britain, and cannibalism would be regarded with horror.

Cultural norms also determine *how* we eat. For example, eating behaviour is accompanied by a set of cultural norms called 'table manners'; whilst the binge eating associated with bulimia is normally conducted in secret because of cultural disapproval.

Socialisation and the transmission of culture

At birth, we are faced with a social world that already exists. Joining this world involves rapidly learning 'how things are done' in it. Only by learning the cultural rules of a society can a human interact with other humans. Culture needs to be passed on from generation to generation in order to ensure that it is shared. Shared culture allows society's members to communicate and co-operate. The process of learning culture is known as **socialisation**. This involves learning the norms and values of a culture so that ways of thinking, behaving and seeing things are taken for granted or **internalised**.

Primary socialisation♣

The family, and specifically parents, are central to **primary socialisation**, which is the first stage in a lifelong process. Children learn language and basic norms and values. These can be taught formally, but they are more likely to be picked up informally by children imitating their parents. Parents may use **sanctions** to reinforce approved behaviour and punish behaviour defined as unacceptable. Such processes develop children's roles within the family and society so that children learn how they are expected to behave in a range and variety of social situations.

Secondary socialisation✱

Other institutions and groups also participate in the socialisation of children. These are often referred to as agents of **secondary socialisation**. Schools, religion and the mass media all play a role in teaching society's members how to behave in particular situations and how to interact with people of a different status.

Socialisation in all its varied forms involves children interacting with others and becoming aware of themselves as individuals. It is the process through which children acquire both a personal and a social identity.

Culture, socialisation and history

Norbert Elias (1978) argues that the process of socialisation has grown more influential throughout history, so culture exerts a greater civilising influence over our behaviour now than in any other historical age. He points out that in the Middle Ages there were fewer cultural constraints on individual behaviour. People ate with their fingers, urinated and defecated in public, and engaged in explicit sexual behaviour that today would be defined as indecent and obscene. Moreover, burping, breaking wind, spitting and picking one's nose in public were regarded as perfectly normal forms of behaviour.

Culture and society

The concept of 'culture' is often used interchangeably with the concept of 'society', but it is important to understand that they do not mean exactly the same thing. Culture forms the connection between the individual and society – it tells the individual how to operate effectively within social institutions such as the family, marriage, education and so on. Zygmunt Bauman (1990) notes that socialisation into culture is about introducing and maintaining social order in society. Individual behaviour that lies outside the cultural norm is perceived as dangerous and worth opposing because it threatens to destabilise society. Consequently societies develop cultural mechanisms to control and repress such behaviour. This theme will be explored in greater depth in the next topic.

CHECK YOUR UNDERSTANDING ✓ ✓ ✓ ✓

1 Using examples, define what is meant by:
   • values
   • norms

2 Give an example of an ascribed status in Britain.

3 Why do sociologists believe that human behaviour is not biologically determined?

4 What is the difference between primary and secondary socialisation?

5 Identify four agents of secondary socialisation and give an example for each of an important value or norm that each transmits in British society.

Cultural diversity – describes a society in which many different cultures exist.

Culture – the way of life of a particular society or social group.

Customs – traditional forms of behaviour associated with particular social occasions.

Deviance – rule-breaking behaviour.

Ethnocentrism – the belief that one culture is 'normal' and others inferior.

Instinct – a genetic or biological code in animals that largely determines their behaviour.

Internalise – accept something so that it becomes 'taken for granted'.

Norms – rules of behaviour in social situations.

Primary socialisation – socialisation in the very early years of life, normally through parents.

Roles – positions in society such as 'mother' or 'police officer'. Roles are made up of norms (see figure 1.1 on p. 3).

Sanctions – actions that encourage or discourage particular behaviour, such as smiling or frowning at a young child.

Secondary socialisation – socialisation that continues throughout life. Education, the media and religion are all important influences.

Socialisation – the process by which we learn acceptable cultural beliefs and behaviour.

Society – a social system made up of social institutions such as the family, education, law, politics, the media, religion, peer groups, etc.

Sociobiology – the study of similarities between the natural and social worlds.

Status – social position.

Subculture – a group within a larger culture that shares aspects of that culture but also has some of its own values, customs and so on.

Values – widely accepted beliefs that something is worthwhile.

Exploring culture and socialisation

Item A Socialisation is the process whereby the helpless infant gradually becomes a self-aware, knowledgeable person, skilled in the ways of the culture into which she or he is born. Children obviously learn a great deal from their parents but they also learn basic values, norms and language, from a range of people including grandparents (especially grandmothers), childminders and baby-sitters, siblings and neighbours who act as 'aunts' etc. There are other secondary influences such as playgroups and nurseries as well as television, video and computer games and traditional media such as comics or storybooks. Children do not passively absorb these influences. They are from the very beginning active beings. They 'make sense' of their experience and decide for themselves how to react.

Adapted from A. Giddens (1997) *Sociology*, 3rd edn, Cambridge: Polity Press, p. 25 and J. Bernardes (1997) *Family Studies: An Introduction*, London: Routledge, p. 112

1 Briefly explain and illustrate using two examples, the function of the family in regard to socialisation. (12)

2 Briefly explain what social institutions are responsible for secondary socialisation, illustrating your answer with two examples given in Item A. (12)

3 Outline and comment on two ways in which sociologists challenge the idea that culture is socially rather than biologically transmitted. (26)

4 Discuss the view that the socialisation of children is a two-way process and the product of a range of influences. (40)

Extension activities

1 Read about the Shirbit culture in the 'Getting you thinking' activity (p. 2). Write your own account of an aspect of British society from the point of view of a 'stranger' from a very different culture.

2 Use the One World website (www.oneworld.org) or a search engine such as Yahoo to find details of another culture. Compare it with your own by making a list of similarities and differences.

3 Draw up a questionnaire to give to other students which aims to find out the extent to which culture is shared. You might ask about aspects of culture such as meal-times and food customs, leisure activities, values and beliefs, and taste in music. Carry out the survey and analyse your results.

Getting you thinking

Examining the homes in an English suburb, Nigel Barley noticed how organised they are. They begin with front gardens which must be kept in good order but never sat in; it is only permissible to sit in back gardens. Front doors, often elaborately furnished, open into a hall and various public rooms. Rooms are segregated according to functions relating to human bodily functions, such as eating, washing and defecating. Dinner, for example, will only be served in a bedroom if someone is ill. Access to rooms is regulated, so access to the sitting room implies more formality than the kitchen, and lavatories can be used by visitors with permission. Bedrooms, where the most private undressing and sexual functions are performed, are considered to be the most personal rooms, and people knock on bedroom doors. The ideal is for each individual or sexual couple to have their own bedroom, and for new couples to have a new house. Bedrooms are individually furnished or decorated by their inhabitants, but it is never difficult to identify which member of the family owns a particular bedroom or their age or sex.

R. Billington *et al.* (1998) *Exploring Self and Society*, Basingstoke: Macmillan, pp. 38–9

1 **Can Barley's description of the suburban home be applied to your experience of home?**

2 **Do you think this description is typical of most homes in the UK?**

3 **Barley is describing a very ordered and structured world. What do you think is the reason for all this order and predictability? Where does it come from?**

We learn from an early age to see our status as wrapped up with our home, and to see a happy family and home as important goals. In other words, there exists a great deal of agreement in society about how we ought to organise our daily lives. Sociologists refer to this agreement amongst members of society as **consensus**. This consensus means that we have a good idea of how we should behave in most situations. It also means that we can anticipate pretty accurately how other people are going to behave, just as we can guess the layout of their house or flat. Some sociologists see this order and predictability as the key to understanding society. If this order did not exist – if we were always confused and uncertain about our own and others' values and behaviour – then, they believe, chaos and anarchy would be the result. These sociologists are known as **functionalists**.

Functionalism

Functionalism is a **structuralist** theory. This means that it sees the individual as less important than the **social structure** or organisation of society. It is a 'top-down' theory that looks at society rather than the individuals within it. Society is more important because the individual is produced by society. People are the product of all the social influences on them: their family, friends, educational and religious background, their experiences at work, in leisure, and their exposure to the

media. All of these influences make them what they are. They are born into society, play their role in it and then die. But their deaths do not mean the end of society. Society continues long after they are gone.

Social order

Functionalists study the role of different parts of society – **social institutions** – in bringing about the patterns of shared and stable behaviour that they refer to as **social order**. They might study, for example, how families teach children the difference between right and wrong, or how education provides people with the skills and qualifications needed in the world of work. For functionalists, society is a complex system made up of parts that all work together to keep the whole system going. The economic system (work), the political system, family and kinship, and the cultural system (education, mass media, religion and youth culture) all have their part to play in maintaining a stable society from generation to generation.

A major function of social institutions is to socialise every individual into a system of norms and values that will guide their future behaviour and thinking. People need to be taught the core values of their society and to internalise them so that they become 'taken for granted'. Once this is achieved everyone will be clear about their place in society and social order will be the result.

Figure 1.2 Understanding functionalism

Functionalism looks at society as though it were a living thing like a human being.

HOW IS SOCIETY LIKE A HUMAN BODY?

The body

Every part of the body has a function: to keep it alive and healthy

• The human body grows and develops

• All of the parts of the body link together into one big system

• The body fights disease

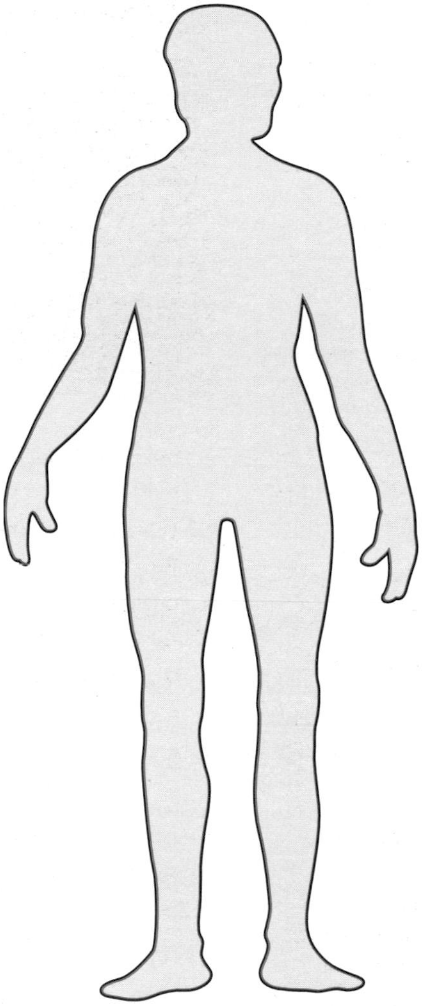

Society

Every part of society helps to keep society going – for example, the family helps by bringing up the next generation

• Societies gradually develop and change

• All of the parts of society work together and depend on each other – they are interdependent

• Society has mechanisms to deal with problems when they occur, such as the police and the legal system

Talcott Parsons

Talcott Parsons (1902–79) was a key functionalist thinker. He argued that socialisation is the key to understanding human behaviour patterns. The role of social institutions such as the family, education, religion and the media is to ensure the passing on, or reproduction, of socially acceptable patterns of behaviour. Social institutions do this in a number of ways:

● They socialise people into key values of society such as the importance of nuclear family life, achievement, respect for authority and hierarchy, and so on. The family, education and the mass media are primarily responsible for this function.

● They give some values and norms a sacred quality so that they become powerful moral codes governing behaviour. Religion and the law primarily perform this function.

● They encourage **social solidarity** (a sense of community) and **social integration** (a sense of belonging). For example, the teaching of history is an important means of achieving this goal because it reminds members of society about their shared culture.

● They control behaviour by reminding members of society about what counts as normality and deviance. This is mainly the job of institutions such as government, the police and the courts, although the media too play a part in publicising crime and punishment.

So our behaviour is controlled by the rules of the society into which we are born. The result is that we don't have to be told that what we are doing is socially unacceptable. We will probably feel inhibited from indulging in such behaviour in the first place because we are so successfully immersed in the common values of society by our experience of socialisation.

Identity

Identity is the way we feel about ourselves. People's identity as fathers, mothers and children, for example, is controlled by a **value consensus**. This defines and therefore largely determines what roles these statuses have to adopt if they are to fit successfully into society. In other words, there is a clear set of expectations about what makes a 'good' mother or father, son or daughter. Our experience of socialisation and social control ensures that most of us will attempt to live up to those social and cultural expectations without question.

Criticisms of functionalism

Functionalism is far less popular in sociology today than it was in the 1950s. Part of its decline in popularity is probably linked to the problems it had attempting to explain all the diversity and conflict that existed from the 1960s onwards. Criticism of functionalism has been widespread.

- Functionalism has been criticised for over-emphasising consensus and order, and failing to explain the social conflicts that characterise the modern world. We see very clear differences in behaviour all around us everyday, and there may be clear cultural differences present in the same society. Some functionalists have attempted to explain this by reference to subculture. This can be defined as a way of life subscribed to by a significant minority who may share some general values and norms with the larger culture, but who may be in opposition to others.
- Functionalism has also been accused of ignoring the freedom of choice enjoyed by individuals. People choose what to do – they do what makes sense to them. Their behaviour and ideas are not imposed on them by structural factors beyond their control. In this sense, functionalism may present 'an over-socialised' picture of human beings.
- There may also be problems in the way functionalists view socialisation as a positive process that never fails. If this were the case then delinquency, child abuse and illegal drug taking would not be the social problems they are.
- Finally, functionalism has been accused by Marxists of ignoring the fact that power is not equally distributed in society. Some groups have more wealth and power than others and may be able to impose their norms and values on less powerful groups. The next few topics focus on this process.

CHECK YOUR UNDERSTANDING

1 Using your own words, explain what is meant by value consensus?

2 What are the key values of society according to Parsons, and what agencies are mainly responsible for their transmission?

3 What agencies are responsible for turning key values into powerful moral codes that guide our most basic behaviour?

4 Why do social agencies such as the law and the media need to regulate our behaviour?

5 How might the teaching of British history encourage a sense of community and integration in British schools?

KEY TERMS

Consensus – a general agreement.

Functionalism – a sociological perspective that focuses on understanding how the different parts of society work together to keep it running smoothly.

Identity – the way we feel about ourselves.

Social institution – a part of society such as education or the family.

Social integration – a sense of belonging to society.

Social order – patterns of shared and predictable behaviour.

Social solidarity – a sense of community.

Social structure – an alternative term for the social organisation of society.

Structuralist theory – a theory that believes that human behaviour is influenced by the organisation of society.

Value, or moral, consensus – an agreement among a majority of members of society that something is good and worthwhile.

Item A   Durkheim believed that the function of social institutions was to promote and maintain social cohesion and unity. The family is one of the key institutions binding the individual into the fabric of social life. It provides society with an orderly means of reproduction and provides physical and economic support for children during the early years of dependence. The child learns the essential ideas and values, patterns of behaviour and social roles (such as gender roles) required for adult life. Education develops both values and the intellectual skills needed by children to perform the role in society to which they had been allocated. The discipline structure and socialisation of children in schools function to maintain consensus and ensure that society operates smoothly. Religion provides a set of moral beliefs and practices which unite people into a common identity and community.

Adapted from K. Chapman (1986) The Sociology of Schools, London: Routledge, p. 38, I. Thompson (1986) Religion, London: Longman, pp. 4-5 and A. Wilson (1991) Family, London: Longman, pp. 9-10

1 Identify and briefly explain the two functions of religion identified in Item A. (12)

2 Identify and briefly explain two ways in which education prepares children for adult life according to functionalists. (12)

3 Outline and comment on two ways in which socialisation into religious values may contribute to social order. (26)

4 Discuss the view that the functionalist theory of society over-emphasises both consensus and the socialisation process. (40)

Extension activities

1 Search for the website 'Dead Sociologists' Society'. Use it to find out about the ideas of the founding father of functionalism, Emile Durkheim.

2 Some functionalist sociologists have suggested that the death of Princess Diana actually brought people together and reinforced a value consensus. Make a list of other events that, it could be argued, bring people together and emphasise their shared values. Explain why you have chosen these events.

3 Interview a sample of people of varying age and gender about their values. To what extent do they share similar values?

Getting you thinking

Imagine that we could illustrate the distribution of income in the UK by getting the population to take part in a parade that will take an hour to pass by. Imagine too that we can somehow magically alter the height of individuals in the parade so that it reflects how much money they have. Those with average income, for example, will have a height of 5ft 8in. Our parade begins with those with the lowest incomes – in other words, the shortest people – and ends with those with the highest incomes – in other words, the tallest people.

The first people to pass by are tiny. For example, after three minutes, a single unemployed mother living on welfare goes by. She is about 1ft 10in high. Six minutes later a single male pensioner, owning his own home and claiming income support, passes by. He is about 2ft 6in high. After 21 minutes, semi-skilled manual workers start to pass by – they are 3ft 9in high. After 30 minutes, there is still no sign of the people earning average incomes. We don't see these until 62% of the population have gone by. After about 45 minutes skilled technicians pass – they are 6ft 10in tall. With ten minutes to go, heights really start to grow. Middle-class professionals pass by – they are 11 feet high. However the real giants only appear in the last minute of the parade. Chief executives of companies over 60 feet high. In the last seconds there are amazing increases in height. Suddenly, the scene is dominated by colossal figures, people as high as tower blocks. Most of them are businessmen, owners of companies, film stars and a few members of the Royal Family. Robbie Williams and Prince Charles are nearly a mile high. Britain's richest man is the last in the parade, measuring four miles high.

Adapted from J. Penn, quoted in P. Donaldson (1973) *A Guide to the British Economy*, Harmondsworth: Penguin

1 **What does this parade tell us about the way income is divided in the UK?**

2 **Give examples of how long it took for people on different incomes to appear in the parade.**

3 **Does the parade surprise you in any way? Is Britain more or less unequal than you thought?**

Lots of students have part-time jobs. Perhaps you have. If so, you sell your time and your ability to work to an employer who, in return, gives you money. But is this a fair exchange? Think about why they employ you. It's not to do you a favour, but because they benefit. They benefit because the work you do is worth more to them than the amount they pay you. They would benefit even more if they paid you less for the same work or got you to do more work for the same pay. Of course it would be better for you if you were paid more for the same work or worked less for the same pay. To put it another way, what is good for your boss is bad for you, and vice versa. There's a very basic conflict of interest between you and your employer. This conflict occurs not because you are unreasonable or your boss is money-grabbing. It occurs simply because the system works that way.

Marxism

This is the starting point for **Marxism** – a sociological perspective based on the ideas of Karl Marx (1818–83). For Marxists, the system we live in (which he called **capitalism**) divides everyone up into two basic classes: bosses and workers. Marx called the bosses the **bourgeoisie** or ruling class (because they controlled society), and the workers he called the **proletariat**. The ruling class benefit in every way from how society operates, whilst the workers get far less than they deserve.

Like functionalism, Marxism is a structuralist theory – i.e. it sees the individual as less important than the social structure of society. In particular, Marxism sees the economic organisation of societies as responsible for the behaviour of individuals. This is because Marxism claims that individuals are the products of the class relationships that characterise economic life.

Society is based on an exploitative and unequal relationship between two economic classes. The bourgeoisie are the economically dominant class (the ruling class) who own the **means of production** (machinery, factories, land, etc.). The proletariat or working class, on the other hand, own only their ability to work. They sell this to the bourgeoisie in return for a wage. However, the relationship between these two classes is unequal and based on conflict because the bourgeoisie aim to extract the maximum labour from workers at the lowest possible cost.

According to Marxists, the result is that the bourgeoisie exploit the labour of the working class. The difference between the value of the goods and services produced by the worker and the wages paid is pocketed by the capitalist class and lies at the heart of the vast profits made by many employers. These profits fuel the great inequalities in wealth and income between the ruling class and the working class.

If society is so unfair, how come the working class go along with it? Why aren't there riots, strikes and political rebellion? Why does society actually appear quite stable, with most people pretty content with their position?

Ideology

Marxists argue that the working class rarely challenge capitalism because those who control the economy also control the family, education, media, religion – in fact all the cultural institutions that are responsible for socialising individuals. Louis Althusser (1971) argued that the function of those cultural institutions is to maintain and **legitimate** class inequality. The family, education, the mass media and religion pass off ruling-class norms and values as 'normal' and 'natural'. Marxists refer to these ruling-class ideas as **ideology**. Socialisation is an ideological process in that its main aim is to transmit the ruling-class idea that capitalist society is **meritocratic**, i.e. if you work hard enough you can get on, despite the fact that the evidence rarely supports this view. This ideological device is so successful that the majority of the working class are convinced that their position is deserved. In other words, they are persuaded to accept their lot and may even be convinced that capitalism has provided them with a decent standard of living.

Marxists argue that capitalist ideology shapes the way of life of a society – its culture. A good example of this, say Marxists, is the way that the mass media convince us through advertising and popular culture – television, cinema, pop music, tabloid newspapers, etc. – that our priority should be to buy more and more material goods. We want to be rich so that we can buy more and more and more, and, somehow, this will make us happy. What is more, while we are all watching soap operas and reading the latest celebrity gossip, we're not noticing the inequalities and exploitation of the capitalist system.

This means that most of us are not aware of our 'real' identity as exploited and oppressed workers. We experience what Marxists describe as **false class consciousness**. Eventually though, Marxists believe, we will learn the real truth of our situation and rebel against the capitalist system.

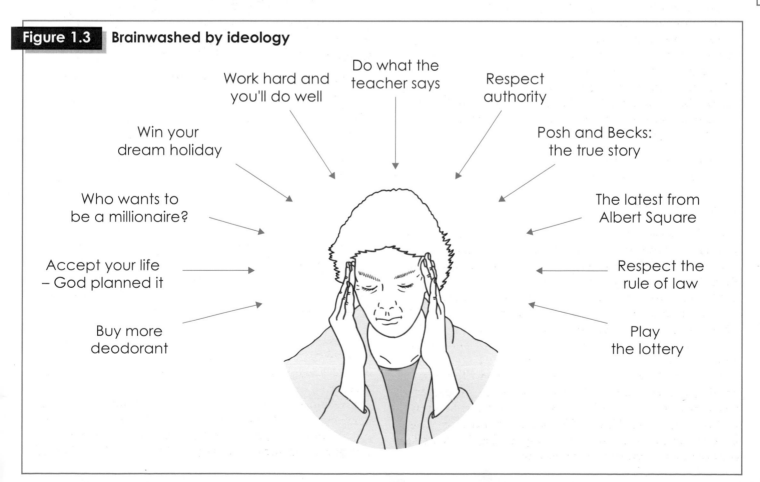

Figure 1.3 Brainwashed by ideology

Criticisms of Marxism

- Like functionalism, Marxism has been accused of ignoring the freedom of choice enjoyed by individuals. People choose what to do and think – they are not 'brainwashed' by ideology. In this sense, Marxism too may present an 'over-socialised' picture of human beings.
- This criticism is not true of all Marxists. Some have argued that **oppositional subcultures** can exist within the capitalist system. For example, Hall and Jefferson (1976) argued that youth subcultures are often a means by which young people can express dissatisfaction with the capitalist system. They argued that the value systems, dress codes and behaviour of groups such as mods, skinheads and punks are a form of symbolic and temporary resistance to society. Their resistance is symbolic in that their behaviour often shocks society, but temporary in that they eventually become passive adults.
- Marxism may put too much emphasis on conflict. After all, despite all its inequalities, capitalism has managed to improve most people's standard of living. Perhaps Marxism also ignores common interests that employers and workers have. If workers work well then the business does well and employers can afford to increase wages.
- Marxism, in general, has been criticised for claiming that all cultural activity is geared to class interests. Consequently Marxists neglect the fact that culture may reflect religious, patriarchal, nationalistic and ethnic interests.

1 What is the relationship between the bourgeoisie and the proletariat?

2 What is the function of ideology?

3 Why do the working class rarely challenge class inequalities?

4 What is the purpose of socialisation according to Marxists?

5 How do youth subcultures challenge capitalism?

KEY TERMS

Bourgeoisie (or capitalists) – the owners of businesses, and the dominant class in capitalist societies.

Capitalism – an economic system associated with modern societies. Based on private ownership of businesses.

False class consciousness – the state of not being aware of our true identity as exploited workers.

Ideology – the norms and values that justify the capitalist system.

Legitimate – make something appear fair and reasonable.

Marxism – a sociological perspective based on the writings of Karl Marx. It believes that societies are unequal and unfair.

Means of production – the land, factories, machines, science and technology, and labour-power required to produce goods.

Meritocratic – based on ability and effort.

Oppositional subcultures – social groups whose value systems and behaviour challenge the dominant capitalist value system.

Proletariat – the working class in capitalist societies.

Exploring conflict, culture and identity

Item A
Marxists believe that social institutions such as the education system, the media, the legal system and religion are agents of capitalism which transmit ruling class ideology. For example, the education system socialises the working class into believing that their educational failure is due to lack of ability and effort when in reality the capitalist system deliberately fails them in order that they continue to be factory workers. Television socialises the working class into believing that consensus is the norm and that serious protest about the way society is organised is 'extremist'. The law socialises the working class into believing that the law is on their side when in reality it mainly supports and enforces the values and institutions of the capitalist ruling class.

Adapted from C. Brown (1979) *Understanding Society: An Introduction to Sociological Theory*, London: John Murray, p. 75 and S. Moore (1987) *Sociology Alive*, Cheltenham: Stanley Thornes, p. 274

1 Briefly explain the term 'ideology', illustrating your answer with two examples taken from Item A. (12)

2 Identify and briefly explain two ways in which the mass media socialise the working-class into a conformist identity. (12)

3 Outline and comment on two effects of ideology on the working class according to Marxists. (26)

4 Discuss the Marxist view that individuals are the products of the class relationships that characterise economic life. (40)

Extension activities

1 Conduct a small survey to see how aware people are of inequalities in income and wealth in Britain.

2 Using the website of the Office for National Statistics (www.statistics.gov.uk), try to find statistics that give an indication of the extent of inequality in Britain. You might look for figures on income, wealth, education and health.

3 Search for the website 'Dead Sociologists' Society'. Use it to find out about the ideas of Karl Marx.

Getting you thinking

DRIVING LICENCE   A030019

1 Surname
PAYNE MR
2 Other names
JAMES
3 Date of birth   Town of birth
24 03 1983   Worcester
4 Permanent Address
14 Roseacre Drive
Worcester WR8 9LA
5 Issued by DVLA SWANSEA

6 Valid from   Valid until
24 03 2000   23 03 2046
7 No
PAYN 785288 B87VU

Signature   James Payne

EUROPEAN COMMUNITY

UNITED KINGDOM OF
GREAT BRITAIN
AND NORTHERN IRELAND

PASSPORT

I have known Rachael for four years. She is a mature young woman who takes her responsibilities seriously. Consequently, she has a conscientious and industrious approach to her academic studies and can be trusted to work independently and with initiative. She also worked well as a member of a team and is well liked and respected by both her peers and teachers. I have no doubt that you will find Rachael to be a thoroughly honest and reliable person. I was aways impressed by her enthusiasm, persistence, motivation and ability to work under pressure. I have no hesitation in recommending her to your institution.

My mother loves me.
I feel good.
I feel good because she loves me.

I am good because I feel good
I feel good because I am good
My mother loves me because I am good.

My mother does not love me.
I feel bad.
I feel bad because she does not love me
I am bad because I feel bad
I feel bad because I am bad
I am bad because she does not love me
She does not love me because I am bad.

R. D. Laing (1970) *Knots*, Harmondsworth: Penguin

1 **What do these documents tell us about a person? What do they not tell us?**

2 **What does the reference tell us about Rachael's identity? What doesn't it tell us?**

3 **What does the poem tell us about this person's identity?**

4 **How does the self-identity apparent in the poem contrast with the picture of the individual in the reference?**

Official documents tell us about the identity we present to the world – our date and place of birth, age, nationality, address, marital status and so on. References, like the example above, give us some insight into **social identity** – how well we perform our social roles such as our jobs. However, poems, like the one above, can tell us about the way we see ourselves – our self-identity – and how this is often the result of how we interpret other people's reactions to us.

Think about a small child. Children try out different sorts of behaviour and then watch other people react. By doing this they learn about themselves and about what is acceptable and unacceptable. In other words, people find out about themselves through the reactions of others.

Social action theory

What has just been described is the view of **social action** or **interactionist** sociologists. They reject the structuralist assumption that social behaviour is determined, constrained and even made predictable by the organisation of society. They see people as having a much more positive and active role in shaping social life. If structuralist theory is a 'top-down' theory, then social action theory is 'bottom-up', as it starts with people rather than society.

Social action theorists argue that society is the product of people coming together in social groups and trying to make sense of their own and each other's behaviour. People are able to work out what is happening because they bring a set of **interpretations** or meanings to social situations which they use to make sense of them. For example, I might interpret drinking and dancing at a party as appropriate yet the same behaviour at a funeral as inappropriate. It is likely that other people will share my interpretations, and it is therefore unlikely that the behaviour described would occur at the funeral.

Socialisation and identity

Socialisation involves learning a stock of shared interpretations and meanings for most given social interactions. Families, for example, teach us how to interact with and interpret the actions of others; whilst education brings us into contact with a greater range of social groups and teaches us how to interpret social action in a broader range of social contexts. The result of such socialisation is that children acquire an identity.

Social action theorists suggest that identity has three components:

1 Personal identity refers to aspects of individuality that identify people as unique and distinct from others. These include personal name, nickname, signature, photograph, address, National Insurance number, etc.
2 Social identity refers to the personality characteristics and qualities that particular cultures associate with certain social roles or groups. For example, in our culture, mothers are supposed to be loving, nurturing and selfless. Therefore women who are mothers will attempt to live up to this description, and consequently they will acquire that

social identity. As children grow up, they too will acquire a range of social identities such as brother, sister, best friend, student. Socialisation and interaction with others will make it clear to them what our culture expects of these roles in terms of obligations, duties and behaviour.
3 The individual has a **subjective** (internal) sense of his or her own uniqueness and identity. Sociologists call this the **'self'**. It is partly the product of what others think is expected of a person's social identity. For example, a mother may see herself as a good mother because she achieves society's standards in that respect. However, 'self' is also the product of how the individual interprets their experience and life history. For example, some women may have, in their own mind, serious misgivings about their role as mother. The self, then, is the link between what society expects from a particular role and the individual's interpretation of whether they are living up to that role successfully.

Labelling theory

Labelling theory is closely linked to the social action approach and helps us to understand how some parts of society may be responsible for socialising some people into identities that may have negative consequences. Take education as an example. Interactionists believe that the social identity of pupils may be dependent on how they interact with teachers. If teachers act in such a way that pupils feel 'labelled', then this will seriously affect their behaviour and progress.

| Figure 1.4 | Master status and the self-fulfilling prophecy: an example |

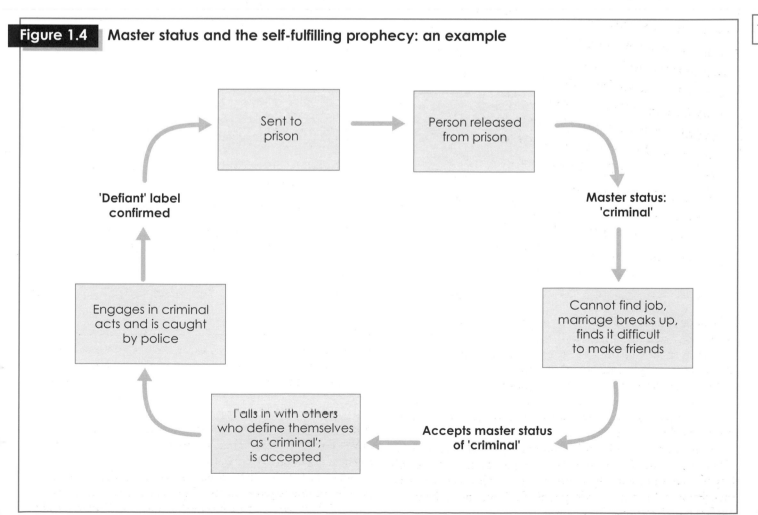

Take streaming, for example. How do pupils who are placed in low streams feel? They may well accept a view of themselves as 'failures' and stop trying – after all, what's the point if you're 'thick'? Or what if a pupil feels 'labelled' a 'troublemaker' because he or she is 'black'? The negative label may be internalised (accepted) and a **self-fulfilling prophecy** may occur. The self sees itself as a 'failure' or as 'deviant' and reacts accordingly. The label makes itself become true.

Recent labelling studies have looked at the ways in which pupils may resist such processes and defend their identities by forming **anti-school subcultures**. Troyna (1978), for example, shows how Afro-Caribbean pupils react to negative treatment by asserting their cultural identity via subcultures influenced by Rastafarianism.

Howard Becker (1963) points out that labels often have the power of a **'master status'**. For example, the master status of 'criminal' can override all other statuses, such as father, son, etc. In other words, deviant labels can radically alter a person's social identity. For example, someone labelled as 'criminal' may be discriminated against and consequently find it difficult to get employment, make new friends and be accepted into their community. They may end up seeking others with similar identities and values, and form deviant subcultures. Again, a self-fulfilling prophecy is the result as the labelling makes itself become true.

Criticisms of social action theory

Social action theories have been criticised because they tend to be very vague in explaining who is responsible for defining acceptable norms of behaviour. They do not explain who is responsible for making the rules that so-called deviant groups break. In this sense, they fail to explore the origin of power and neglect potential sources such as social class, gender and ethnicity. For example, Marxists argue that the capitalist ruling class define how social institutions such as education and the law operate. In other words, social action theories tend to be descriptive rather than explanatory.

1 How is society formed, according to social action theorists?

2 From an interactionist perspective, what is the function of socialisation?

3 What is meant by 'social identity'?

4 Explain the meaning of 'self'.

5 What causes a 'self-fulfilling prophecy'?

6 What is the result of deviant labels becoming master statuses?

KEY TERMS

Anti-school subculture – a group of pupils who band together in opposition to school values, perhaps as a reaction to negative labelling by teachers.

Interpretations – the meanings that we attach to particular objects or situations, e.g. we usually interpret classrooms as learning environments and act accordingly.

Labelling theory – the idea that categorising or stereotyping individuals or groups can seriously affect their behaviour. Used especially in the fields of education and deviance.

Master status – a label or status that can override all others (e.g. criminal, child abuser).

Self – refers to how we see ourselves, usually in reaction to how we think others see us.

Self-fulfilling prophecy – a prediction that makes itself become true.

Social action theory or interactionism – a sociological perspective that focuses on the ways in which people give meaning to their own and others' actions.

Social identity – refers to how society sees us, in terms of whether we live up to the cultural expectations attached to the social roles we play.

Subjective – personal, based on your own view.

Exploring conflict, culture and identity

Item C   Individuals, like actors, are performing for an audience. Speech, acts and gestures all require someone else to be watching or listening. Our identities therefore are the product of how we present ourselves and how others perceive us. For example, you have to persuade your tutor that you have seriously adopted the identity and role of student. Your tutor may respond by according you an 'ideal' student label or identity. If you fail to convince, you may be labelled as a 'deviant' student, i.e. as idle or troublesome. This 'deviant' label is a 'master status' which overshadows other aspects of identity. Often people who are considered deviant in one respect are assumed to be deviant in other respects. For example, other teachers may negatively judge you in staffroom discussions.

Deviants often experience stigma – people behaving differently towards them. In reaction, those labelled may pursue a deviant career by adopting a lifestyle which confirms their deviant status. In other words, a self-fulfilling prophecy results.

Adapted from K. Woodward (ed.) (2000) *Questioning Identity: Gender, Class, Nation*, London: Routledge, pp. 14-15 and H. Croall (1998) *Crime and Society in Britain*, Harlow: Longman pp. 61-2

1 Briefly explain the term 'self-fulfilling prophecy', illustrating your answer using Item A. (12)

2 Briefly explain the term 'identity', illustrating your answer with two examples. (12)

3 Outline and comment on two consequences that might arise from acquiring a deviant activity according to labelling theory. (26)

4 Discuss the view that social identity is largely the product of interaction with others. (40)

Extension activities

1 Observe an everyday situation involving interaction between people. It could be in a library, at a bus stop, in a common room or a pub. What is going on? Does everyone share the same interpretation of the situation? How do people try to manage the impression they give of themselves?

2 Find two groups of students: one group who have experience of being placed in a high stream, and one group who have experience of being placed in a low stream. Give a questionnaire to, or interview, each group in order to find out how streaming affected their self-image, motivation and progress. Compare the responses of the two samples.

Getting you thinking

Try to imagine the life ahead for the woman from the 1930s in the first photograph.

1 What sort of family life do you think she would have had?

2 Might she have had paid employment? What problems might she have faced in pursuing a career?

3 What about the roles played by her and her husband?

Now think about the future for the young woman of today.

4 What sort of family life do you think she is likely to have?

5 Is she likely to have paid employment?

6 What about her relationship with her husband?

You may well have found it fairly straightforward to plot out the future for the young woman of 70 years ago. Attempting the same task for a woman today is much more difficult. Maybe she will choose not to live in a family. Maybe she won't have children. Alternatively, she could devote her life to a family, but then again she might decide to focus on following a career – or she could do both. The choices appear endless. Being a woman today seems much more flexible and uncertain and less predictable than in the past.

Sociologists have watched recent social changes with great interest. Some have reached the conclusion that society has experienced such major upheavals that the old ways of explaining it just won't work any more. They believe that we are entering a new sort of society, which they refer to as the postmodern world or **postmodernity**. But before we can consider this we need to head back to the beginnings of sociology.

Have you ever wondered why sociology came about? History tells us that sociology developed in order to explain the rapid social changes associated with **industrialisation** and **urbanisation** during the nineteenth century. Lives changed so drastically during this period that it is not surprising that people looked for theories and explanations that would help make sense of the bewildering changes taking place. Families left the rural communities where they had lived for centuries, to find work in the new cities. They had to adjust to a different lifestyle, different work, different bosses and different kinds of relationships with family and community.

On the whole, early sociologists approved of these changes and the kind of society they created – now commonly referred to as modernity or the modern world. They set out to document the key features of what they saw as an exciting new order.

The nature of the modern world

Sociologists have identified four major characteristics of the modern world:

1 **Industrialisation** – production is industrial and economic relationships are capitalist. Factories produce goods, bosses own factories, and workers sell their labour to bosses. Social class is therefore the basic source of difference and identity in modern societies.
2 **Urbanisation** – early modernity was associated with great population movement to the cities, known as urbanisation. Twentieth-century theories of modernity have tended to celebrate the bright lights and innovation of the city whilst ridiculing rural culture as living in the past.
3 **Centralised government** – government is characterised by a bureaucratic state that takes a great deal of responsibility both for the economy and for the welfare of its citizens.
4 **Rational, scientific thinking** – what really made modern society stand apart from pre-modern societies was the revolution in the way people thought about the world. Before industrialisation, tradition and superstition had provided the basis for views of the world. The modern world adopted a new way of thinking, shaped by science and reason.

New ideas and theories (referred to by postmodernists as 'big stories' or '**meta-narratives**') competed with each other to explain this constantly changing modern world; and these theories frequently called for more social progress. Some of these theories were political (e.g. **socialism**); some were cultural (e.g. the ideas of feminism). To paraphrase Marx, one of the leading modernist thinkers, their job was not just to explain the world – the point was to change it.

Sociology and the modern world

Sociologists were caught up in this excitement about modernity, and attempted to create scientific theories that would explain the transition from the traditional to the modern. One of the founding fathers of sociology, Auguste Comte, believed that sociology was the science of society. This **positivist** view argued that sociological research based upon scientific **rationality** could rid the world of social problems such as crime.

Marx, too, celebrated modernity, despite his criticism of its economic relationships, because he believed that science had given people the power to change the world. Sociological theories therefore also developed into meta-narratives as they attempted to provide us with knowledge or 'truth' about the nature of modernity.

The postmodern world

In the past 20 years or so, some sociologists have identified trends and developments which, they claim, show that modernity is fragmenting or dissolving. They argue that it is being replaced by a postmodern world in which many sociological ideas and concepts are becoming irrelevant. The following characteristics of postmodernity have been identified.

Work

The nature of work and economic life has changed. Work is no longer dominated by mass factory production in which thousands of people work alongside each other. Work today is mainly located within the **service sector**, and is dominated either by jobs that mainly involve the processing of information (e.g. the financial sector), or by jobs that involve the servicing of **consumption** (e.g. working in a shop).

Our ideas about work have also changed. People today are less likely to expect a job for life, and are more willing to accept a range of flexible working practices, such as part-time work, working from home and job sharing.

Culture

As our society has grown wealthier, so the media and other cultural industries – such as fashion, film, advertising and music – have become increasingly central to how we organise our lives. It is suggested that we are a 'media-saturated' society in which media advice is available on how we can 'make-over' our homes, gardens, partners and even ourselves. Look, for example, at the lifestyle magazines in your local WH Smith, advising you on skin-care, body size and shape, hair colour and type, fitness, cosmetic surgery and so on. What these trends tell us is that consumption is now the central defining feature in our lives.

Postmodern culture is also about mixing and matching seemingly contradictory styles. Think about the way in which different music from different times and different styles is 'sampled', for example.

Endless choice in the postmodern world

IF DISSATISFIED WITH ANY PRODUCT, SIMPLY RETURN IT AND EXCHANGE IT FOR ANOTHER

GENDER ROLES

RELIGIONS

WORK

VALUES

FAMILY LIFE

Identity

Our identities are now likely to be influenced by mainstream popular culture which celebrates **diversity**, consumerism and choice. In other words, the old 'me' was about where I came from in terms of my family and class background, the area I lived in and so on. The new postmodern 'me', however, is about designer labels, being seen in the right places, the car I drive, listening to the right music and buying the right clothes. Style has become more important than substance. As Steve Taylor (1999) argues, society has been transformed into 'something resembling an endless shopping mall where people now have much greater choice about how they look, what they consume and what they believe in'.

Globalisation

The global expansion of **transnational companies** – such as McDonald's, Sony, Coca-Cola and Nike – and the global marketing of cultural forms such as cinema, music and computer games have contributed to this emphasis on consumption. Such globalisation has resulted in symbols that are recognised and consumed across the world. Images of Britney Spears and Eminem are just as likely to be found adorning the walls of a village hut in the interior of New Guinea as they are a bedroom wall in Croydon. Brands like Nike and Coca-Cola use global events like the World Cup and the Olympic Games to beam themselves into millions of homes across the world.

It is therefore no wonder that this global culture is seen to be challenging the importance of national and local cultures, and challenging **nationalism** as a source of identity. Information technology and electronic communication such as e-mail and the internet have also been seen as part of this process.

Knowledge

In the postmodern world, people no longer have any faith in great truths. In particular, people have become sceptical, even cynical, about the power of science to change the world, because many of the world's problems have been brought about by science. In the political world, ideologies such as socialism – which claimed they were the best way of transforming the world – have been discredited in many people's eyes, with the collapse of communism in Eastern Europe. Postmodernists insist that truth is both unattainable and irrelevant in the postmodern world. Instead, postmodernism stresses the **relativity** of knowledge, ideas and lifestyles, such that many different yet equally authentic values are possible.

Postmodernism and sociology

Steve Taylor argues that these developments have three main consequences for sociology:

1 Most sociology is concerned with explaining the nature and organisation of modern societies and their social institutions. However, the key relationships that underpin such societies – class, family, gender – are no longer relevant.
2 Sociologists can no longer claim to produce expert knowledge about society, because in postmodern societies relativity and uncertainty have replaced absolute judgements about what is or should be. As Swingewood (2000) argues, in postmodern societies 'knowledge is always incomplete, there are

no universal standards, only differences and **ambiguity**'. The big sociological stories, such as functionalism and Marxism, are defunct, because 'knowledge' is now judged in terms of its usefulness rather than its claim to be a universal 'truth'.
3 Sociologists can no longer make judgements or claim that they know what is best for societies. Sociology is only one set of ideas competing with others. All have something relevant to offer. If people want to listen to sociologists and act upon their findings, it is up to them. It is equally relevant not to do so.

Criticisms of postmodernism

Critics of postmodernism suggest that it is guilty of making too much of recent social changes. Evidence suggests that aspects of the postmodernist argument – especially the decline of social class, ethnicity and nationalism as sources of identity – are exaggerated. For example, surveys indicate that people still see social class as a strong influence in their lives, and use aspects of it to judge their success and status and that of others. There is no doubting that consumption has increased in importance, especially among young people, but it is pointed out that consumption does not exist in a vacuum. The nature of your consumption – i.e. what and how much you consume – still very much depends upon your income, which is generally determined by your occupation and social class.

CHECK YOUR UNDERSTANDING

1 What term is used by postmodernists to describe theories of society?

2 What was the role of sociology, according to Auguste Comte?

3 Identify two social changes that have led some sociologists to argue that we are entering a postmodern world.

4 How do the media contribute to our sense of identity?

5 What is the relationship between globalisation and postmodernism?

6 How did the collapse of communism in Eastern Europe contribute to people's cynicism about meta-narratives?

7 What is the role of the internet in postmodern society?

KEY TERMS

Ambiguity – the state of being open to a range of interpretations – the meaning is not clear.

Bureaucratic – based on rules and procedures.

Consumption – the use of goods and services, especially as part of forming an identity.

Diversity – variety.

Industrialisation – the transformation of societies from being agricultural to industrial, which took place in the eighteenth and nineteenth centuries. (See Unit 2, Topic 2.)

'Meta-narratives' or 'big stories' – the postmodernist term for theories like Marxism and functionalism which aim to explain how societies work.

Exploring postmodernism

Item A A good deal of postmodern theory in sociology (and popular culture) is an attempt to come to terms with some of the effects of living in a media-saturated society. Postmodernists argue, in opposition to most sociological theories of the media, that the 'information explosion' of the last two or three decades has not led to increasing conformity and acceptance of 'dominant values', but rather, has led to greater choice and diversity. We are now bombarded with a mass of different media images.

The effect of this, according to postmodern theorists, has been to transform society into something resembling an endless shopping mall where people now have much greater choice about how they look, what they consume and what they believe in.

A consequence of this, postmodernists argue, is that what most sociologists call societies, or social structures, have become fragmented and have become much less important in influencing how people think and act. For postmodernists, our sense of identity – that is, our ideas of who we are – comes less from things like where we live, our family, our class and our gender, and much more from the images we consume via the media. In a postmodern world, people define themselves much more in terms of the choices they make about their clothes, cars, football teams and so on.

S. Taylor (1999) 'Postmodernism: a challenge to sociology', 'S' *Magazine*, no. 4, p. 14

1 **Identify and briefly explain two ways in which people define themselves in the postmodern world, according to Item A. (12)**

2 **Identify and briefly explain two sources of identity in modern societies. (12)**

3 **Outline and comment on two ways in which postmodernism may challenge sociological thought. (26)**

4 **Discuss the view that the effects of living in a media-saturated society have led to the emergence of a postmodern society characterised by diversity and choice. (40)**

Extension activities

1 Create a table to compare modernity and postmodernity. Use one column for modernity and another for postmodernity. Compare them using factors such as **work, knowledge, politics, roles, religion and gender.**

2 Use the World Wide Web to search for information on:
- postmodernism – find out about its influence on art, architecture and literature
- Jean Baudrillard, a key postmodern thinker

3 Write a review of any film, novel or piece of music that mixes 'seemingly contradictory' styles. What are these styles, and how does the film, novel or piece of music mix them up? How effective is the end product?

Modernity – period of time starting with the industrial revolution, associated with industrial production, urban living, rational thinking and strong central government.

Nationalism – belief system/political view that stresses shared geographical location, history and culture.

Positivism – the view that sociological research based upon scientific principles could rid the world of social problems such as crime.

Postmodernity – term used by postmodernists to describe the contemporary period which is characterised by uncertainty, media-saturation and globalisation.

Rationality – actions decided by logical thought.

Relativity – the idea that no one example of something (e.g. political view, sociological theory, lifestyle, moral) is better than any other.

Service sector – a group of economic activities loosely organised around finance, retail and personal care.

Socialism – a political belief system based on the idea of collective ownership and equal rights for all.

Transnational companies – companies that produce and market goods on a global scale.

Urbanisation – the trend towards living in towns and cities rather than in rural areas.

Getting you thinking

1 **Examine the photographs above. Put each person in a social class of your choice.**

2 **What differences do you think might exist between these individuals, in terms of values, lifestyle and political attitudes?**

Let's face it: class exists. You were probably able to identify quite different characteristics for the people in the photographs above. Wealth, income and status matter. They influence our educational achievement, our chances of good health or an early death – even our choice of leisure pursuits (how many working-class people go fox-hunting?). So what classes exist, and how does class affect the way we feel about ourselves and the world around us?

The working class

Until the late twentieth century, most people's identities and interests (especially men's) were part and parcel of the type of work they did and the work-based communities they lived in. In particular, the working class had a strong sense of their social class position. Virtually all aspects of their lives – including gender roles, family life, political views and leisure – were a product of their working-class identity.

Workers felt a strong sense of loyalty to each other because of their shared work experience, especially in dangerous jobs. They were also very aware of the fact that they were working-class, and tended to see society in terms of 'them' (the bosses) and 'us' (the workers). Such working-class identity was reflected in mass membership of organisations such as the Labour Party, trade unions and work-/trade-based working men's clubs.

However, more recently, some researchers have claimed that the notion of a working-class identity is less important, particularly because of the decline in manual work in recent years. The numbers employed in traditional heavy industries such as mining and shipbuilding have dropped rapidly since the 1970s and 1980s. Consequently, manual workers now make up considerably less than half of the total workforce.

So the economic basis for class identity and solidarity has weakened. Research has identified a new sort of worker who sees work as a means to an end rather than as a source of identity. Traditional hostility towards capitalism is being abandoned as capitalism is seen to be effective in raising living standards. The new workers therefore have no heightened sense of class injustice. They define themselves through their families and their standard of living, rather than through their work.

The 'underclass'

Pete Saunders (1990) sees the old class divisions based on work as becoming less and less relevant. For Saunders, what you do with your money is more significant than how you get it. He believes that society is now characterised by a major **'consumption cleavage'** (a split based on what people do with their money). In particular, Saunders argues that home ownership has encouraged the more well-off members of the working class to focus their attention on their homes and family lives. This has loosened their ties with other members of the working class. However, there are also those who are dependent upon state benefits – the **underclass**. This consists of groups such as those in badly paid or casual jobs, the unemployed and single parents. Saunders suggests that the culture and identity of this underclass revolve around being work-shy and dependent on the welfare benefits provided by the state.

Unsurprisingly, not everyone agrees with this controversial view. Studies of the poor and long-term unemployed, such as Jordan (1992), suggest that those living in poverty have the same ideas about work and family as everyone else. Surveys of the poor indicate that they often feel shame about getting into debt, guilt about having to ask others for help, insecurity and lack of dignity.

Surveys such as that carried out by Marshall *et al.* (1988) indicate that manual workers are still aware of class-based issues. Many believe that the distribution of wealth and income is grossly unfair. Importantly, in the survey, most workers identified themselves as working-class. Marshall concludes that the working class is still distinctive but more **fragmented** (broken-up) than in the past. For example, divisions exist within the working class based on gender and ethnicity. Female and ethnic minority manual workers earn less than white male manual workers and enjoy less job security.

The middle class

Savage's research (1995) describes four types of middle-class identity:

1 **Professionals** – such as doctors and lawyers – tend to adopt an intellectual identity gained from a long and successful education. They value cultural assets such as knowledge, qualifications, lifestyle and values, and feel it is important to pass these on to their children. Such **cultural capital** is crucial in contributing to the success of children from this background.

2 **Managers in private businesses** define success in terms of their standard of living and leisure pursuits. However, despite high pay and status, they are aware that their jobs are more insecure than those of professionals such as doctors and lawyers. A take-over or reorganisation of the business can mean the disappearance of their job. Consequently they encourage their children to make the most of education in order to follow professional rather than managerial careers.

3 **Self-employed owners of small businesses** have traditionally operated as individuals. However, the insecurity brought about by economic recession has recently led to collective action such as the blockading of fuel depots by farmers and hauliers.

4 The **entrepreneurial group** works mainly in the City or in the media. This group has an identity that revolves around the consumption of a mixture of high and popular culture – they may go to the Royal Opera House as well as going to Premier League football matches or spending a night 'clubbing'.

White-collar or **clerical** workers – clerks and secretaries, for example – have traditionally been seen as having a middle-class identity. However, some sociologists have suggested that their skills are less important today because of the introduction of technology such as computers. Consequently their pay and status are in decline, and they now have more in common with the working class. However, surveys of clerical workers indicate that they still see themselves as middle-class. They rarely mix with manual workers, and spend their leisure time and money in quite different ways.

Members of the middle classes are a very mixed group. They are mainly concerned about ensuring that their standard of living is maintained relative to their peers.

The upper class

There has been limited research into the identity of the upper class. Mackintosh and Mooney (2000) point out that: 'wealth and privilege are not very visible. The wealthy can withdraw into a private world of fee-paying schooling, private transport and health care, and social networks that are largely invisible to the non-wealthy.'

However, it is likely that their sense of identity is powerful. Children born into this class learn distinct ways of speaking, mannerisms, attitudes, values and ways of seeing the world that clearly distinguish them from other groups (this, as already mentioned, is known as cultural capital). They learn that they have security, control, and power over the lives of others. This lifestyle results in self-confidence and a sense of social superiority. All of this is reinforced by kinship and marriage, a public school and Oxbridge education, and 'old-boy' networks. Consequently this is a social class that practises **social closure** – it is **self-recruiting** in that entry to the class is not the result of merit. Rather, entry is restricted to those with a social background deemed 'worthy' by the upper class.

Class today

In recent years some sociologists have argued that class has ceased to be the main factor in creating identity. **Postmodernists** argue that class identity has fragmented into numerous separate identities. Gender, ethnicity, age, region and family role interact with consumption and media images to make up our sense of identity today.

But are postmodern ideas exaggerated? Marshall's research does indicate that social class is still a significant source of identity for many. Members of a range of classes are aware of class differences and are happy to identify themselves using class categories.

Postmodernists also ignore the fact that, for many, consumption depends on having a job and an income. For some, poverty is going to limit any desire to pursue a postmodern lifestyle. In other words, consumption – what we buy – depends on social class.

Figure 1.5 **Social closure: how the upper class self-recruit**

Brown blasts Oxford over Geordie girl

The Government launched a fierce attack last night on selection procedures at Oxford University.

Gordon Brown, the Chancellor, blamed an old-boy network for refusing a place to a girl from a Tyneside state school who is expected to gain five As at A level. The university condemned Mr Brown's remarks as 'a travesty of the truth' made 'without knowledge of the facts behind the headlines'. It accused the Government of using the row to prepare cuts in funding for universities that admitted a high proportion of pupils from independent schools.

Mr Brown, with the backing of Tony Blaire and David Blunkett, the Education Secretary, declared it an 'absolute scandal' that Laura Spence, 18, was not offered a place at Magdalen College. Downing Street said it was a 'shame' that she was taking advantage of a £65,000 scholarship to go to Harvard University instead of studying in Britain.

Mr Brown said that Miss Spence, who had the 'best A-level qualifications you can have', had been 'turned down by an interview system more reminiscent of an old-boy network and the old school tie than genuine justice for society. 'It is about time we had an end to the old Britain, where all that matters is the privileges you were born with, rather than the potential you actually have.'

Source: *The Daily Telegraph*, 26 May 2000

Oxford bias against state pupils 'starts at interview'

New evidence of how Oxford University discriminates against state school pupils was published yesterday by the Oxford Magazine, the don's journal.

Prof. A.H. Halsey and Dr Gerard McCrum analysed the fate of 7,629 pupils who applied to Oxford from state and independent schools between 1994 and 1997. After dividing applicants into four groups on the basis of their A-level scores, they found that in each group independent school pupils were more likely to be offered a place than their state school counterparts.

Of those who achieved three A grades, 60 per cent from the independent sector were given a place, compared to 51 per cent from state schools. Of those who achieved two As and a B, 34 per cent from the independent sector were given a place compared to 27 per cent from the state sector.

Source: *The Daily Telegraph*, 10 November 1999

Entry to Eton

There are some 1,280 boys at Eton, comprising: about 70 King's Scholars, selected by a competitive examination of which details may be obtained from the Registrar; and about 1,210 other boys, called Oppidans, who normally qualify for admission by preliminary registration on the Eton List and subsequent success in the Conditional Place Test and in the Common Entrance Examination.

Registration on the Eton List

Parents who wish their son to come to Eton in due course as an Oppidan should register him with the Eton List Secretary at any time between birth and the age of 10 years and 6 months (the latter a very firm deadline). The appropriate form may be obtained from the Eton List Secretary.

The Conditional Place Test and Interview

At about the age of 11, every boy registered on the Eton List will be invited to Eton for interview and testing. Those who are successful will be given Conditional Places (conditional, that is, on their passing Common Entrance in due course), and some will be placed on the Waiting List.

School fees (payable in advance) Oppidans: £5,496 per half (i.e. per term)

Source: www.etoncollege.com

CHECK YOUR UNDERSTANDING

1 Identify two reasons for the decline in working-class identity.

2 What motivates the 'new' working class?

3 What is the 'underclass'?

4 In what ways could it be argued that the working class is fragmented?

5 What different kinds of middle-class identity exist?

6 Which social class practises social closure? And how?

7 Why might postmodern views of class be 'exaggerated'?

Consumption cleavage – the idea that society is now stratified by spending patterns and habits rather than social class.

Cultural capital – the cultural advantages passed down from middle- and upper-class parents to their children.

Entrepreneurial – a term used to describe people in business who are willing to take risks to make gains.

Fragmented – broken-up.

Postmodernism – a theory that suggests that universal phenomena such as social class have ceased to have any meaning in a world characterised by choice and diversity.

Self-recruiting – describes those groups whose members come only from families who are within the same group.

Social closure – the practice of preventing 'outsiders' from joining a group.

Underclass – a subculture that exists outside mainstream culture, supposedly characterised by welfare dependency, criminal tendencies and single parents.

White-collar, or clerical, workers – people in lower-level office work.

Exploring class and identity

Item A

Social class provides us with a sense of belonging and identity; it can tell us who 'we' are and who 'they' are and, hence, how to relate to the world around us. Many people see the UK as a society sharply divided by class divisions and inequalities. In a 1996 survey, two-thirds of those interviewed agreed that 'there is one law for the rich and one law for the poor' and that 'ordinary people do not get their fair share of the nation's wealth'. However despite this 'class consciousness', individuals may not have a strongly developed sense of class identity anymore because of changing patterns of occupation, income, lifestyle and authority. The old labels 'working' and 'middle class' may be less relevant today because most manual workers now lead a middle-class consumer lifestyle as statistics on everything from videos and home ownership to foreign holidays and school staying-on rates tell us. However, despite these trends, it can be argued that we are a more, not less, divided society. Accents, houses, cars, schools, sports, food, fashion, drink, smoking, supermarkets, soap operas, holiday destinations, even training shoes: virtually everything in life is graded with subtle or unsubtle class tags attached. Snobbery is the religion of England.

Adapted from K. Woodward (ed.) (2000) *Questioning Identity: Gender, Class, Nation*, London: Routledge, pp. 95–6 and A. Adonis and S. Pollard (1997) *A Class Act: The Myth of Britain's Classless Society*, Harmondsworth: Penguin, p. 10

1 **Identify and briefly explain two ways in which social class may provide people with a sense of belonging and identity, illustrating your answer with examples from Item A. (12)**

2 **Identify and briefly explain two changes which may mean that that class labels are less important today. (12)**

3 **Outline and comment on two ways in which the UK might be 'sharply divided by class divisions and inequalities'. (26)**

4 **Discuss the Marxist view that social class is still important as a source of identity. (40)**

Extension activities

1 List five words or phrases that you typically associate with the upper class. Now list five that you associate with the working class. Is this exercise easy to do? What does this tell us about class and culture?

2 Conduct a survey to find out the extent of class identity among a sample of young people. What classes do they think exist? Do they believe that class is still important? Do they feel that they belong to any particular class?

3 Find the website of the polling organisation MORI (Market and Opinion Research International). Use their 'search' facility to find the results of any surveys they have conducted about any aspect of social class. What research has taken place and what are the key findings?

Getting you thinking

Look at the photographs above.

1 List the stereotypical and non-stereotypical masculine and feminine characteristics that come to mind on first seeing these images.

Now read the extract below.

A visit to Isabella Mackay's home in Arlesley, Bedfordshire is like a walk through the pages of *Little Women*. She opens the door wearing a pretty pink blouse, children hiding in her flowing skirt. Isabella has some interesting ideas about motherhood. She says 'I could no more go out to work, abandon my children or disobey my husband than I could grow an extra head. I don't have any of the modern woman's confusion about her role in life. From the day I was born I knew I was destined to be a wife and mother. By the age of 16, 1 knew that all I really wanted from life was to get married, have children and make a lovely home. That was my ambition.'

There are probably many women who feel the same way but few would go as far as Isabella. She not only believes that a mother's place is in the home, but that the feminist movement is a 'dangerous cancer and perversion'. Her words. The world, she says, would be a better place if the Equal Opportunities Commission was shut down and workplace crèches were scrapped. The rape-within-marriage law should be abolished too. She says 'in the rare event of a wife refusing sex with her husband he has every right, perhaps even a duty, to take her as gently as possible. Once a woman is married she loses the right to say no to her husband's advances. The female role is a submissive one. The male role is assertive and aggressive.'

Adapted from *Woman* magazine (1994)

2 What aspects of this view of femininity do you agree or disagree with?

The exercise above should have shown you that our gender identities are strongly influenced by stereotypical ideas about what is masculine or feminine. However, the exercise should also have shown you that there are different types of men and women. Some of the men may have had some typically feminine characteristics, whilst some of the women may have exhibited masculine tendencies.

The Isabella Mackay exercise may have provoked a more emotional response, especially from female students! I suspect that many readers reacted strongly to her ideas. However, only thirty years ago such ideas were very common, and they probably still have some credibility with an older generation of women. Ideas about femininity have certainly changed. One of the reasons for these changes has been the growth of **feminism**.

Feminism

Feminists believe that women are unfairly treated, and they want to change society so that there is equality between men and women. Feminists vary in their views. Some **radical feminists** believe that the oppression and exploitation of women by men are built into every aspect of the way society is organised. They call this situation **patriarchy**. Other feminists are more optimistic. These **liberal feminists** believe that there has been a steady improvement in the position of women, as old-fashioned attitudes break down and more and more women have successful careers.

A key term for most feminists is **gender**. What exactly do they mean by this?

Gender identity

Sociologists often distinguish between '**sex**' and '**gender**':

● Sex refers to the biological differences between males and females. For example, chromosomes, hormones and genitals. These biological differences are not necessarily permanent. Women's body shape, for example, has historically shifted with fashion. The 'beautiful' women in previous centuries were often far larger than 'beautiful' women today.
● Gender refers to the expectations society places on males and females. Gender expectations are transmitted to the next generation through **gender role socialisation**. Because gender differences are the result of society's expectations, they are often described as **socially constructed**, as opposed to being **biologically determined** (fixed by our physical make-up).

Gender role socialisation

From an early age, people are trained to conform to social expectations about their gender. Much of this training goes on in the family during primary socialisation. For example, people use gender-based terms of endearment when talking to children, they dress boys and girls differently, and sex-typed toys are often chosen as presents.

Oakley (1982) identifies two processes central to the construction of gender identity:

● **Manipulation** refers to the way in which parents encourage or discourage behaviour on the basis of appropriateness for the child's sex.
● **Canalisation** refers to the way in which parents channel children's interests into toys and activities that are seen as 'normal for that sex'.

These types of gender reinforcement are extremely powerful. Statham (1986) studied parents who were deliberately trying to avoid gender-stereotyping their children. She found that it was almost impossible for parents to overcome the cultural pressure for their children to behave in gender-stereotyped ways. By the age of 5, most children have acquired a clear gender identity. They know what gender they belong to and they have a clear idea of what constitutes appropriate behaviour for that gender.

Other agencies of socialisation are also involved in gender role socialisation. Schools, children's books and the mass media all have a significant role to play in reinforcing gender roles. McRobbie's study (1991) of girls' magazines in the 1970s observed how girls retreated into a world of media romance and a culture of femininity that centred around finding a boyfriend. Sue Sharpe's survey of working-class girls (1976) concluded that such socialising processes meant that female identity revolved around 'love, marriage, husbands, children, jobs and careers, more or less in that order'.

Other studies of gender identity have focused on the assumption that males and females have different sexual personalities. Males are supposed to be promiscuous predators (they want to have sex with as many women as possible), whereas females are supposed to be passive and more interested in love than sex. Because of this, gender identity for women carries risks. Their identity may be subjected to being labelled a 'slag' or a 'slapper' if they appear to behave in similar ways to men. Lees (1986) found that females in her study conformed to gender expectations in order to protect their reputation.

The way sexual identity is defined in modern societies may mean that women's social identity is dependent upon being seen as physically attractive by men. Their social identity may have little to do with being educated and intelligent. Rather, it may depend on how well they conform to society's definition of women as sex objects.

Criticisms of the idea of gender role socialisation

The idea of gender role socialisation has been criticised on a number of counts:

● The experiences of men and women vary greatly. There are huge differences depending on ethnicity (race), area, class and age. Most accounts of gender socialisation ignore these differences.
● It assumes that women passively accept the gender identity imposed on them. It neglects the choice we have in developing an identity and the fact that many women and men resist attempts to make them conform to gender stereotypes.

Postmodernism and gender

Postmodernists argue that changes in gender roles are having a positive effect on female identity.

The increasing participation and success of women in the world of paid work mean that traditional notions of female identity are being abandoned. Sharpe's study (1994) suggests that young females are becoming more assertive about their rights. Moreover there has been a rise in the number of divorces initiated by women. Surveys indicate that an increasing number of females are electing to pursue careers and forgo marriage and children. All of these trends suggest that female identity is being redefined.

What is more, increasing economic independence means that women are now viewed as significant consumers. There are signs that mass media products are increasingly being targeted at single women. This means that women are more likely to see consumption and leisure as the key factors in their identity. Being a good mother and housewife – the traditional domestic role – is becoming less significant.

Criticisms of postmodernism

Some feminists reject this view. They point out that there is little evidence that men and women are sharing equally in the consumption of goods and services. For example, most media and cultural products are still aimed at men. Consumption in the form of clubbing, buying CDs and so on may only be a temporary phase that young single women go through before they set out on the well-trodden paths of marriage and motherhood.

Masculinity

Connell (1995) argues that, until recently, most British men were socialised into what he calls **hegemonic masculinity**. They expected to be financial providers and authority figures in the home, dispensing wisdom and firm discipline to their wives and children. Men were expected to be individualistic, aggressive, risk-taking and ambitious. They were not expected to participate in domestic work or to express their emotions. This type of masculinity was also responsible for defining what counted as 'feminine'. Ideas about female beauty, 'sexiness', ideal shape and behaviour were all shaped by men; women were either sex objects or mother/housewife figures.

Connell acknowledges that masculinity today is experiencing change. He documents the emergence of three other forms of masculinity:

1 **Complicit masculinity** refers to those men who believe that men and women should share roles within families. Such men still benefit from what he calls 'the patriarchal dividend' because even in these households women are still responsible for the lion's share of housework and especially childcare.

    Some sociologists have even gone as far as suggesting that a '**new man**' has emerged who is more in touch with his feminine and emotional feelings. Others have suggested that this is merely a creation of the advertising industry.

2 **Subordinate masculinity** refers to homosexual men. Although there is greater tolerance and acceptance of homosexuality in society today, it still generally remains a subordinate and stigmatised identity.

3 **Marginalised masculinity** is a response to the fact that the traditional masculine identity of male protector/bread-winner may be changing. Working-class men in particular can see that economic recession has led to the decline of manual work and to large-scale unemployment. They can see that women are taking many of the new jobs. Mac an Ghaill (1996) talks about how this is leading to a '**crisis of masculinity**'. Older men may feel threatened as their wives become the main breadwinners and they are expected to take on more domestic responsibilities. Younger males may see their futures as bleak and therefore view schooling and qualifications as irrelevant to their needs. They may seek alternative sources of status in activities such as delinquency.

CHECK YOUR UNDERSTANDING

1 How are the views of liberal and radical feminists different?

2 Explain in your own words the meaning of 'patriarchy'.

3 What is the difference between the two concepts 'sex' and 'gender'?

4 Explain in your own words what is meant by 'gender role socialisation'.

5 Why does gender identity carry risks for females?

6 Identify three important agencies of secondary socialisation and illustrate how these may reinforce gender roles.

7 Explain in your own words the meaning of 'hegemonic masculinity'?

8 In what ways has masculinity changed in the past 20 years?

KEY TERMS

Biologically determined – fixed by our physical make-up.

Canalisation – the channelling of children's interests into toys and activities traditionally associated with their sex.

Complicit masculinity – refers to those men who believe that roles within families should be shared.

Crisis of masculinity – the view that men who have been socialised into hegemonic forms of masculinity are experiencing anxiety and uncertainty because their patriarchal authority is being challenged by economically successful women.

Feminism – the belief that women are treated unfairly and that society should be changed to create equality between the sexes.

Gender – refers to the expectations society places on men and women.

Gender role socialisation – the process by which boys and girls are socialised (by the family and by secondary agents of socialisation such as education and the mass media) into masculine and feminine modes of behaviour.

Hegemonic masculinity – refers to traditional ideas about the role of men, e.g. that men should be breadwinners and authority figures.

Liberal feminists – feminists who believe in gradual change towards equality for women.

Marginalised masculinity – refers to the decline of traditional masculinity.

'New man' – a type of masculinity that is keen to explore its feminine and sensitive side. Many sociologists believe it to be mostly a media creation.

Patriarchy – a social system in which men oppress and exploit women and children.

Radical feminists – feminists who believe that society is structured in a way that benefits men and exploits women.

Sex – refers to the biological differences between men and women.

Socially constructed – produced by society.

Subordinate masculinity – homosexuality.

Item A

Frank Mort (1988) argues that there were significant changes in male identity in the mid-1980s reflected in the portrayal of men and masculinity in the media and through the marketing and consumption of large quantities of toiletries, such as aftershave, other perfumes and hair gel. However Sean Nixon points to a backlash against the 'new man' phenomenon in the early 1990s with what is popularly termed 'new laddism'. Nixon suggests there has been another shift in cultural norms as young men revert to sexist type as reflected in magazines such as 'Loaded' and 'Maxim'.

Adapted from D. Abbott (2000) 'Identity and new masculinities', Sociology Review, vol. 10, no.1, pp. 5–6

1 Identify and briefly explain two ways in which the images in Item A reflect changes in what is defined as femininity. (12)

2 Identify and briefly explain two ways in which families socialise children into gender roles. (12)

3 Outline and comment on two ways that sociologists distinguish between 'sex' and 'gender'. (26)

4 Discuss the view that there are a variety of feminine and masculine identities in modern society. (40)

Extension activities

1 Get hold of at least two toy catalogues or catalogues that include toys. Analyse any links between gender and the presentation of the catalogues. Are girls or boys pictured playing with toys? Do the pictures reflect or challenge typical gender roles? Are some toys targeted more at girls and others more at boys? Which are targeted at which? How can you tell?

2 Find the website www.feminist.com. What issues are covered and what information is available? Look around the site and identify the key issues that concern feminists today.

3 Ask some parents you know for permission to observe their young children. Compare the language, actions, toys and behaviour of the boys and girls.

4 Conduct in-depth interviews with an adult man and an adult woman about their life history. To what extent have their experiences been influenced by their gender?

Getting you thinking

Examine these images.

1 In your opinion, what characteristics does society generally attach to these ethnic minority groups?

2 Are these characteristics justified or are they stereotypes?

3 How might the way in which these groups are seen by the majority white group affect their chances of being accepted as British?

4 Are some of those pictured above more likely to be accepted than others? Explain your answer.

You may well have decided that society generally attaches negative characteristics to most of the social groups pictured. However, I imagine that most of you recognised Lenny Henry and that you didn't attach negative characteristics to him. This is not surprising: he is a popular comedian and people generally identify him as a comedian and entertainer rather than as a black man. Consequently, it is likely that society has no problem in seeing Lenny Henry as British. However, this may not be true of the other individuals pictured.

What is ethnic identity?

Ethnic identity – or **ethnicity** – revolves around the belief that there are shared origins or traditions within a group. People recognise themselves as part of this group and feel positively about others who share the same culture. However, as Mason (2000) points out, many British people tend to see ethnicity as something other groups have. This involves the use of 'they statements' which usually make stereotypical and imagined assumptions about other ethnic groups. For example, according to Said (1985), the West sees Islam as mysterious, exotic, unpredictable, extreme and fanatical. This reinforces false assump-

tions about both Islam and Western culture – especially the view that Muslim identity means the **subordination** of women, and that Western behaviour is somehow more civilised.

Ethnic minorities

In Britain, ethnicity is mainly associated with minority groups from the former British colonies on the Indian subcontinent, in the Caribbean and in Africa. This kind of categorisation is a problem because it emphasises skin colour rather than common cultural characteristics. In doing so it ignores significant white ethnic groups resident in the UK, such as Greek Cypriots, Jews and Irish people. It also means that differences between these minority groups and the majority white population are exaggerated, whilst differences between ethnic minorities are neglected.

The ability of ethnic minorities in Britain to choose their self-identity is limited by the way in which they are seen by powerful groups. Teacher stereotypes, a National Curriculum based on middle-class white values, negative media representations, policing, the courts, immigration laws, discrimination in jobs and housing allocation, and racial violence may all serve to negatively categorise minority identities. Consequently, Mason points out, many members of Britain's ethnic minority communities experience a sense of exclusion from the identity 'British'. As a result, the family may become a refuge from the problems they experience in the wider community. Studies by Anwar (1981), amongst others, indicate that Asian families – regardless of whether they are Hindu, Muslim or Sikh – socialise children into a pattern of obligation, loyalty and religious commitment, which, in most cases, they accept.

Modood's survey (1997) of ethnic minority groups found that most of his **second-generation** sample thought of themselves as mostly but not entirely culturally and socially British. They didn't feel comfortable with a 'British' identity because they felt that the majority of white people did not see them as British.

Ethnic identities as resistance

There are a number of ways in which ethnic minorities may react to being denied a British identity. Sometimes ethnic identity is used as a means of resisting racism, as the following examples demonstrate:

- Skin colour is an important source of identity to many Afro-Caribbeans, according to Modood's research. Black identity and pride may be celebrated as a response to black people's perceptions of racial exclusion and stereotyping by white people.
- Jacobson (1997) notes that young Pakistanis see Islam as crucial in creating their identity. It has a strong impact on their identity, in terms of their diet, worship, dress and behaviour, and their everyday routines and practices. For many it is a defensive identity, created as a response to being excluded from white society.
- There is some evidence that black-led evangelical churches and the **Rastafarian** movement may provide similar sources of identity for Afro-Caribbeans.
- Ethnic identity may be used to resist racial stereotyping in schools, although it may not be immediately recognised as such. Research by both Fuller (1984) and Mac an Ghaill (1988) has documented how this occurs.
- Young Afro-Caribbeans often adopt identities based on ethnic history, their everyday experiences and popular culture to challenge racism and exclusion. Gilroy (1993) notes that music such as gangsta rap and hip-hop is used as an upbeat reaction to white oppression.

New ethnic identities

New ethnic identities are now emerging, especially among Britain's younger minority ethnic citizens. Charlotte Butler (1995) studied third-generation young Muslim women ('third-generation' means that their parents and grandparents were born in Britain). She found that they choose from a variety of possible identities. Some will choose to reflect their ascribed position through the wearing of traditional dress, while others may take a more 'negotiated' position. This may mean adopting Western ideas about education and careers whilst retaining some respect for traditional religious ideas about the role of women. Some young Islamic women may adopt quite different identities compared with their mothers on issues such as equality, domestic roles, fashion and marriage.

Johal (1998) focused on second- and third-generation British-Asians. He found that they have a dual identity in that they inherit an Asian identity and adopt a British one. This results in Asian youth adopting a 'white mask' in order to interact with white peers at school or college, but emphasising their cultural difference whenever they feel it is necessary.

British national identity

Few people actually ask what exactly 'British' national identity consists of, or whether it exists at all. In fact, the British people are a mix of social and immigrant groups. Nevertheless, as Schudsen (1994) points out, they are socialised into a common national culture and identity through various means:

1 *A common language*
   In the UK, this is obviously English, although the Welsh language is promoted in Wales through the education system and the mass media. However, there are criticisms that other minority languages, such as Gaelic and Cornish, are being suppressed. Ethnic minority groups too have complained that their languages are neglected – by the education system, for example.

2 *Education*
   The teaching of history, English literature and religion aims to promote **nationalism**. The Education Reform Act (1988) stresses Christian worship in schools, despite the fact that the UK is a **multicultural** society.

| **Figure 1.6** | **British culture?** |

Source: Connect Publications

31

Unit 1 The individual and society

3 *National rituals*

Rituals such as the Coronation, the Queen's Jubilee and Remembrance Sunday, and national events of mourning such as the funeral of Diana, the 'people's princess', all promote national unity.

4 *Symbols*

Symbols such as flags, national anthems and passports – often linked to the monarchy in some way – encourage a feeling of 'Britishness'.

5 *The mass media*

Television, magazines and newspapers encourage people to identify with national symbols such as the Royal Family and the England football team.

6 *The mass production of fashion and taste*

Retailers such as Marks & Spencer are seen as 'British' institutions, and we are encouraged to be proud of British products such as the Rolls-Royce.

But perhaps – as the cartoon on the previous page suggests – this is all a bit old-fashioned. Waters (1995) suggests that British national identity may be under threat for a number of reasons.

First, the boundaries between nation-states may become less significant as **transnational companies** and international financial markets increasingly dominate world trade. This may have a number of implications for British culture and identity:

- British identity may be diluted as British companies are taken over by foreign concerns or as multinationals invest in Britain.
- Television programmes, films and music are increasingly being produced for the international market. There are fears that these products may erode national cultures and create a single commercialised culture offering superficial mass entertainment.

Secondly, national or local cultures may be strengthened as they attempt to resist these global influences. Some cultures may adopt **fundamentalist movements** (i.e. a return to tradition). Other societies may exaggerate aspects of their own culture in order to resist global threats. For example, membership of the European Union is seen by some as a threat to British sovereignty.

Thirdly, there is the possibility that national cultures may go into decline. This could be seen as a positive trend because it may result in a decline in xenophobia (fear of foreigners), prejudice and racial discrimination. It may lead to the evolution of multicultural societies, through inter-marriage, or as second-generation members of ethnic minority groups subscribe to values and norms from both their inherited and adopted cultures.

The decline of British identity?

Guibernau and Goldblatt (2000) ask what type of identity will result from the decline of 'Britishness'. They are optimistic that a multicultural and diverse national identity will emerge, although they are realistic enough to acknowledge that racism and Britain's imperial history may prove to be obstacles. They point out that the process of acquiring an English or British identity may involve stereotyping and labelling minorities so that they are discriminated against. There is already evidence that **institutional racism** may be embedded in institutions such as the police, prison and immigration services.

However, there are positive signs that a new sense of 'Britishness' is slowly emerging in the field of popular culture, especially in the worlds of food, fashion and music. This new Britishness has been shaped by the traditional but also, ironically, by multiculturalism and **globalisation**.

CHECK YOUR UNDERSTANDING ✓✓✓✓

1 Define in your own words what is meant by ethnicity.

2 Why is it problematical to associate ethnicity only with racial characteristics such as skin colour?

3 How do religion, culture, ethnicity and nationality affect young Pakistanis' sense of identity?

4 What do Butler and Johal conclude about the relationships between second- and third-generation young Asians, their parent generation, and their white peers?

5 Why is there no such thing as a 'pure' British culture?

6 Identify four ways in which people are socialised into a common national identity?

7 In what way do transnational corporations dilute national identity?

8 Identify two positive effects of the decline of national identities.

KEY TERMS

Ethnicity – a shared identity based on common cultural and religious factors.

Fundamentalism – believing in a return to 'traditional', often religious, values.

Globalisation – a process whereby national boundaries become increasingly irrelevant.

Institutional racism – racism that is built into the 'taken-for-granted', everyday life of an organisation.

Multicultural – based on many cultures.

Nationalism – the belief that your country is the most important source of your identity

Rastafarianism – a religion originating in Jamaica and associated with reggae music.

Second generation – the children of those who migrated to Britain.

Subordination – being dominated.

Transnational (or multinational) companies – companies that have offices or plants in different countries.

Item A

Subscribing to a British identity is not the first priority for most young Muslim women born and brought up in Britain. They often do not want to abandon their parents' way of life in favour of British culture. Most wish to maintain a distinct Muslim identity. Being British is not considered as important as Islam which, contrary to popular media stereotypes, promotes the rights of women and give Muslim women the right to study and work. In terms of feeling British, other ethnic minority groups experience similar feelings. Surveys of British-born Afro-Caribbeans suggest they find it difficult to see themselves as 'British' because they feel that the majority of white people do not accept them as British because of their race or cultural background. They feel that their claim to be British is all too often denied by hurtful jokes, harassment, discrimination and violence. Miri Song's research into the Chinese in Britain found that second generation Chinese see themselves as influenced by both Chinese and British cultures. They aspire to British cultural goals such as educational achievement and careers outside the family business, consequently their cultural identity is less influenced by Chinese culture.

Adapted from C. Butler (1995) 'Religion and gender: young Muslim women in Britain', *Sociology Review*, vol. 4, no.3, pp. 21–2, T. Modood, quoted in N. Abercrombie and A. Warde (2000) *Contemporary British Society*, Cambridge: Polity Press, p. 238 and D. Abbott (1998) *Culture and Identity*, London: Hodder and Stoughton, p. 113

1 Identify and briefly explain two ways in which Item A challenges the idea of a single British national identity. (12)

2 Identify and briefly explain two reasons why people from ethnic minority backgrounds may be reluctant to fully adopt a British identity. (12)

3 Outline and comment on two ways in which ethnic minority identity may be used to resist racism. (26)

4 Discuss the view that the family and religion are the most important agents of socialisation in regard to ethnic minority identity. (40)

33

Extension activities

1 Ask ten people for ten words each that they associate with 'Britain' or 'England'. Compare the lists. What differences or similarities are there? What do the lists tell you about people's images of Britain?

2 Find the following websites to get to know more about ethnicity and racism in Britain:

3 Play Britkids – it's aimed at students a little younger than you but it's still worth a visit. Find it at www.britkids.org.uk

4 Test your knowledge by trying the quiz at the Institute of Race Relations site – www.irr.org.uk/quiz/index.htm

5 The Institute also has excellent pages about current issues. Head for www.irr.org.uk/resources/index.htm

Families and households

Getting you thinking

The family does not feature heavily in the culture of the Ik of Northern Uganda. In fact, as far as the Ik are concerned, the family means very little. This is because the Ik face a daily struggle to survive in the face of drought, famine and starvation. Anyone who cannot take care of him- or herself is regarded as a useless burden by the Ik and a hazard to the survival of the others. Families mean dependants such as children who need to be fed and protected. So close to the verge of starvation, family, sentiment and love are regarded as luxuries that can mean death. Children are regarded as useless appendages, like old people, because they use up precious resources. So the old are abandoned to die. Sick and disabled children too are abandoned. The Ik attitude is that, as long as you keep the breeding group alive, you can always get more children.

Ik mothers throw their children out of the village compound when they are 3 years old, to fend for themselves. I imagine children must be rather relieved to be thrown out, for in the process of being cared for he or she is grudgingly carried about in a hide sling wherever the mother goes. Whenever the mother is in her field, she loosens the sling and lets the baby to the ground none too slowly, and laughs if it is hurt. Then she goes about her business, leaving the child there, almost hoping that some predator will come along and carry it off. This sometimes happens. Such behaviour does not endear children to their parents or parents to their children.

Adapted from C. Turnbull (1994) *The Mountain People*, London: Pimlico

1 How do the Ik define the family?

2 Think of three features of the family that your experience of family life would lead you to expect in all families wherever they are. How do these three features differ from the Ik?

3 In what ways might some British families share some of the characteristics of the Ik?

Many of you probably reacted to the Ik with some horror and shock. It is very tempting to conclude that these people are primitive, savage and inhuman, and that their concept of the 'family' is deeply wrong. However, sociologists argue that it is wrong to simply judge such societies and their family arrangements as unnatural and deviant. We need to understand that such arrangements may have positive functions. In the case of the Ik, with the exceptional circumstances they find themselves in – drought and famine – their family arrangements help ensure the survival of the tribe. Moreover, some of you may have concluded that British family life and the Ik have some things in common. British family life is not universally experienced as positive for all family members. For some members of our own society – for young and old alike – family life may be characterised by violence, abuse and isolation.

The problem with studying the family is that we all think we are experts. This is not surprising, considering that most of us are born into families and socialised into family roles and responsibilities. It is an institution most of us feel very comfortable with and regard as 'natural'. For many of us, it is the cornerstone of our social world, a place to which we can retreat and take refuge from the stresses of the outside world. It is the place in which we are loved for who we are, rather than what we are. Family living and family events are probably the most important aspects of our lives. It is no wonder then that we tend to hold very fierce, emotional, and perhaps irrational, views about family life and how it ought to be organised. Such 'taken for granted' views make it very difficult for us to objectively examine family arrangements that deviate from our own experience – such as those of the Ik – without making critical judgements.

Defining 'the family'

The experiences of the Ik suggest that family life across the world is characterised by tremendous variation and diversity. However, in the UK, we can see that popular definitions of 'the family' are dominated by the traditional view that the **'nuclear family'** is the ideal. We can identify a number of characteristics that are normally associated with this type of family:

- It is small and compact in structure, in that it is composed of a mother, father and usually two or three children, who are biologically related and who share a common residence. **Extended kin** such as grandparents, aunts, uncles and cousins are less important than they were in the past.
- It is assumed that the relationship between the adults is **heterosexual** and based on romantic love. Children are seen as the outcome of that love. Such **procreation** is considered an essential element in the **reproduction of society**.
- The nuclear family is reinforced by marriage. It is assumed that marriage encourages **fidelity** and therefore family stability.
- There is a clear **division of labour** in such families, which is assumed to be the product of biology and therefore natural. It is taken for granted that women want to have children and that this is a biological need determined by a **'maternal instinct'**. Consequently it is assumed that the female function within the family should be primarily concerned with the emotional and **nurturing** roles inherent in motherhood and housework. The male function should be to provide financially for the family, to protect the family and to act as an authoritarian/disciplinary role model for children.

It is now more widely accepted that there may be some overlap between these roles, and men are now taking on more responsibility for childcare and housework than in the past. Nevertheless, the belief that the main responsibility for parenting lies with mothers is still very powerful.

The importance of the traditional view of the family

Traditional beliefs have powerful consequences for family life in the UK. We can see them reflected in government **social policy** – for example, in the assumption that there is no need for state provision of free childcare, because women are happy to give up work to look after children. We can see the same traditional beliefs reflected in the organisation of the economy and labour force – for example, surveys indicate that employers regard women as less reliable because of their family commitments. The same beliefs are reflected in the pronouncements of religious leaders, politicians and editors of newspapers, which regularly state that certain types of relationships (e.g. homosexual ones) and certain types of living arrangements (e.g. broken homes and cohabitation) are not worthy of being called families. We can also see such views reflected in our own everyday behaviour and attitudes, as Jon Bernardes argues:

> Men may hesitate or not know how to engage in certain tasks or, in public, men may be discouraged from comforting a lost child whilst a woman may 'naturally' take up this role.

Bernardes, 1997, p. 31

Figure 2.1 The traditional nuclear family · THE SIMPSONS

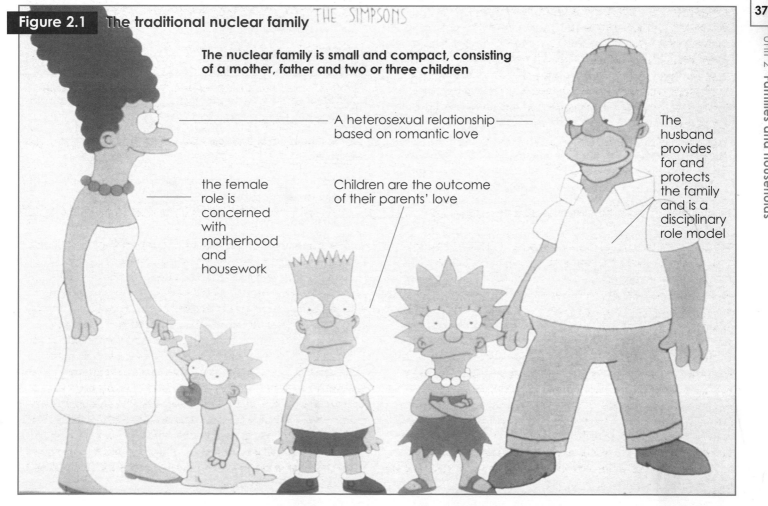

The nuclear family is small and compact, consisting of a mother, father and two or three children

A heterosexual relationship based on romantic love

the female role is concerned with motherhood and housework

Children are the outcome of their parents' love

The husband provides for and protects the family and is a disciplinary role model

Figure 2.2 The 'warm bath' theory

commuting · deadlines · productivity · competition · overtime · promotion · stress · pace of life · budgets · hard work · hiring and firing · money · job insecurity

home and family

Functionalism and the family

The existence of the nuclear family has also been taken for granted by many sociologists. For many years, the sociology of the family was dominated by the theory of functionalism. You may remember from Unit 1 that functionalists see society as a social system made up of interrelated and inter-dependent institutions, such as education, work, religion, law, the family, etc. The overall function of these institutions is to maintain social order. Functionalist sociologists suggest that the nuclear family is the norm in modern industrial societies, and that it has a number of functions that contribute to the well-being of society:

1   The family is the primary agent of socialisation, and socialises new members into the culture of society by teaching them common norms and values. This means that the family is central to the creation of consensus and order. Parsons (1955) argued that families are 'personality factories', producing children who are committed to shared norms and values and who have a strong sense of belonging to society.
2   The family controls society's members on a daily basis, in order to maintain consensus and social order. For example, marriage functions to control sexual relationships. Heterosexual sex within marriage is defined as morally acceptable behaviour, and this functions to prevent the potential chaos and disorder of unregulated relationships.
3   Parsons argued that the family functions to relieve the stress of modern-day living. This is sometimes referred to as the 'warm bath' theory, in that the family provides a relaxing environment for the male worker to immerse himself in after a hard day at work.

Functionalists therefore see the family as an important social institution functioning positively both for society and for the individual.

Criticisms of functionalist views of the family

- The idea that families benefit all the individuals in them has been strongly attacked, especially by feminist sociologists, who argue that the family serves only to exploit and oppress women. Moreover, the rosy and harmonious picture of family life painted by functionalists ignores social problems such as increases in the divorce rate, child abuse and domestic violence.
- Functionalist analyses of the nuclear family tend to be based on middle-class and American versions of family life, and they consequently neglect other influences such as ethnicity, social class, religion, etc. For example, Parsons does not consider the fact that wealth or poverty may determine whether women stay at home to look after children or not.
- Functionalists also tend to see socialisation as a one-way process, and children as passive recipients of culture. However, this view under-estimates the role of children in families – they may have more choice in accepting or rejecting the attempts to mould their personalities than functionalists give them credit for.
- Finally, functionalist thinking on the family suggests that biological needs underpin the nuclear family, despite a lack of scientific evidence to support this view.

CHECK YOUR UNDERSTANDING

1   What role do extended kin play in the traditional model of the family?

2   How influential is biology in shaping the traditional family?

3   What has been the impact of the traditional model of the family on popular thinking?

4   What is the 'warm bath' theory?

5   How have functionalist views of the family been criticised by feminists?

KEY TERMS

Division of labour – the organisation of work.

Extended kin – relations beyond the nuclear family, such as aunts, uncles and grandparents.

Fidelity – faithfulness.

Heterosexual – attracted to the opposite sex.

Maternal instinct – a 'natural' instinct to desire motherhood and want to care for children.

Nuclear family – a family consisting of two parents and their children.

Nurturing – caring for and looking after.

Procreation – having children.

Reproduction of society – passing on society from one generation to the next.

Social policy – the measures the government takes to address social issues.

Exploring ... defining the family

Item A

There are five sentiments that underpin traditional ideas about the nuclear family. First, marriage is regarded as the climax of romantic love, and children are seen as symbolic of the couple's commitment to each other. Secondly, it is assumed that the ultimate goal of women is to have children, stay at home and gain satisfaction through the socialisation of their children. Women who choose not to have children may be viewed as 'unnatural'. Thirdly, it is assumed that the family is a positive and beneficial institution in which family members receive nurturing, care and love. Fourthly, the male is expected to be head of the household and to provide for the family. Finally, it is assumed that the immediate family comes first and all other obligations and relationships come second.

Adapted from S. Chapman and D. Aiken (2000) 'Towards a new sociology of families', *Sociology Review*, vol. 9, no. 3

Item B

The existence of 'the family' has been taken for granted by many sociologists. For functionalist sociologists, in particular, any query over the use of 'the family' appears trivial and tends to be dismissed. The failure to question the idea of 'the family' has allowed all sorts of mistaken ideas to persist, such as the naturalness of monogamy (whereas many societies permit more than one marriage), the inevitability of female inferiority (which many feminists dispute), the right of men to control and abuse women (which many women dispute), and the right of parents to smack children (which is banned in some European countries, including Scotland).

Adapted from J. Bernardes (1997) *Family Studies: An Introduction*, London: Routledge, pp. 4–5

Item C

Functionalism sees the family as playing a key role in helping the individual to learn the social behaviour required by society. There are four core functions that the family performs. It provides society with an orderly means of reproduction. It provides physical and economic support for the child during the early years of dependence. It socialises the child into the essential ideas, values, traditions and patterns of behaviour required for the social roles it will play in adult life. The family provides the emotional support that allows an individual to cope with the pressures of adult life. It can be argued that the family also performs educational, political and religious functions, as well as being a major centre for leisure and recreation.

Adapted from A. Wilson (1985) *Family*, London: Routledge, pp. 9–10

1 **Explain what is meant by 'monogamy' (Item B). (2)**

2 **Suggest two ways in which the traditional family is supposed to benefit adults, according to Item A. (4)**

3 **Identify three ways in which the traditional family may function to bring about social order in society. (6)**

4 **Identify and briefly describe two 'mistaken ideas' that have arisen out of the failure to question the idea of the family, according to Bernardes in Item B. (8)**

5 **Using information from the Items and elsewhere, examine the difficulties in defining the family. (20)**

6 **Using information from the Items and elsewhere, assess the view that the nuclear family constitutes an ideal living arrangement for individuals and society. (20)**

Extension activities

1 Conduct a survey amongst your classmates to find out about other families and their lifestyles. Focus particularly on size of family, whether parents work, who takes responsibility for domestic duties in the home, contact with extended kin such as grandparents, the role and responsibilities of children, etc. How much do their accounts differ from your own experience of family life?

2 Visit websites dedicated to the family such as **www.familyeducation.com** and familylife.shop-smarterkids.com. Look at the content of these sites in terms of advice, news and letters from parents. What functions should families be performing according to these sites? Do such functions support the functionalist theory of the family?

3 Make a list of the functions that your family performs. Think about how family functions change according to how old you are and what gender you are. For example, think about how the family functioned for you as a baby. Compare that with how you think the family will function for you when you are 20.

Question for students taking OCR exam board AS level

4 (a) Identify and explain two ways in which definitions of 'family' are dominated by traditional views about how family life ought to be lived. (20 marks)

   (b) Outline and discuss the view that the family functions for the good of society and individuals. (40 marks)

Getting you thinking

Left and below: Images of work in pre-industrial societies

1 What roles appear to be played by men, women, children and members of the extended family in the pictures above?

2 Compare these with the roles they typically play today.

3 What reasons can you think of to explain the changes in roles?

The pre-industrial family

Parsons (1955) argued that the economic systems of **pre-industrial** societies were largely based on **extended kinship networks**. Land and other resources were commonly owned by a range of relatives extending well beyond the nuclear family unit. For example, it was not uncommon to live with and work alongside cousins. This extended family was responsible for the production of food, shelter and clothing, and would trade with other family groups for those things they couldn't produce themselves. Very few people left home to go to work. Home and workplace were one and the same thing.

Roles in these families were the product of **ascription** rather than **achievement**. What this means is that both family status and job were the product of being born into a

particular extended family known for a particular trade or skill. For example, if the family were pig farmers, then there was a strong likelihood that all members of the family – men and women, old and young alike – would be involved in some aspect of pig farming. Moreover, these roles would be passed down from generation to generation. Few family members would reject the roles, because duty and obligation to the family and community were probably the key values of pre-industrial society.

In return for this commitment, the extended family network probably performed other functions for its members:

- The family equipped its members with the skills and education they needed to take their place in the family division of labour, although this socialisation rarely extended to literacy and numeracy.

- The family functioned to maintain the health of its members, in the absence of a system of universal health care. However, the high infant mortality rates and low life expectancy of the pre-industrial period tell us that this was probably a losing battle.
- The family also provided welfare for its members. For example, those family members who did make it into old age would be cared for, in exchange for services such as looking after very young children.
- The extended family was expected to pursue justice on behalf of any wronged family member.

The effects of industrialisation

Parsons argued that the industrial revolution brought about three fundamental changes to the family:

1 **Industrialisation** demanded a more **geographically mobile** workforce. At the same time, achievement became more important than ascription as mass education was introduced. Nuclear families were formed as people moved away from their extended kin in order to take advantage of the job opportunities brought about by industrialisation.
2 Specialised agencies developed which gradually took over many of the functions of the family. In particular, factories took over the production function. The home and the workplace became separated as people became wage-earners. The state eventually took over the functions of education, health and welfare, and consequently the nuclear family was able to specialise in child-centred functions such as socialisation.
3 The new nuclear unit provided the husband and wife with very clear social roles. The male is the **'instrumental leader'**, responsible for the economic welfare of the family group. He goes out to work and earns money. The female is the **'expressive leader'**, primarily responsible for the socialisation of children and the emotional care and support of family members.

Parsons concluded that only the nuclear unit could effectively provide the achievement-orientated and geographically mobile workforce required by modern societies.

Historical criticisms of Parsons' view

Historians suggest that Parsons was far too simplistic in his interpretation of the history of the family. They point out that the evidence suggests that industrialisation may follow different patterns in different industrial societies. The Japanese experience, for example, has been quite different from that of Britain, and, consequently, extended families have remained important in Japan.

The study of English parish records suggests that only 10 per cent of households in the pre-industrial period contained extended kin. In other words, most pre-industrial families may have been nuclear, and not extended as Parsons claimed. Such small families were probably due to late marriage, early death and the practice of sending children away to become servants or apprentices. It may also be the case that industrialisation took off so quickly because nuclear families already existed – and so people could move quickly to those parts of the country where their skills were in demand.

Michael Anderson's historical study (1971) of the industrial town of Preston, using census records from 1851, also contradicts Parsons' view that the extended unit had been replaced by the nuclear family. Anderson found a large number of households shared by extended kin. These probably functioned as a **mutual support system** in a town in which unemployment and poverty were common.

The British sociologists Young and Willmott (1957) take issue with Parsons over the speed of change. They suggest that the movement towards the nuclear unit was not as sudden as Parsons suggests, but rather that it was more gradual in nature. Their empirical research conducted in the 1950s, in the East End of London (Bethnal Green), showed that extended families existed in large numbers even at this advanced stage of industrialisation. This extended kinship network was based upon emotional attachment and obligation. It was also a mutual support network, offering its members assistance with money, jobs, childcare and advice. Young and Willmott (1973) argue that the extended family unit went into decline in the 1960s, when working-class communities were re-housed in new towns and on council estates after extensive slum clearance. Moreover, the welfare state and full employment in the 1950s undermined the need for a mutual support system. Young and Willmott therefore concluded that the nuclear family only became the universal norm in Britain in the late twentieth century.

Marxist views

Marxists argue that the working-class extended family has been deliberately discouraged by the capitalist ruling class, because its emphasis on a mutual support system and collective action encourages its members to be aware of their social class position. This class consciousness (see Unit 1, Topic 6) may eventually challenge the wealth and power of the capitalist class.

The nuclear family unit is seen to be more capitalism-friendly because it can be used as an **ideological apparatus** to promote capitalist values. For example, consumer advertising is primarily aimed at nuclear families, and it encourages them to pursue capitalist goals by stressing the importance of materialism and 'keeping up with the Joneses'. In addition, the way in which nuclear families are traditionally organised (e.g. the male as the head of the household) encourages passive acceptance of authority, hierarchy and inequality. In other words, the nuclear family benefits the capitalist class, rather than benefiting the whole of society as functionalists suggest.

Marxist-feminist views

Marxist-feminists are sceptical about Parsons' claim that the nuclear family meets the needs of industrial society. They suggest that the nuclear family benefits the powerful at the expense of the working class. Moreover it also benefits men.

Margaret Benston (1972) suggests that the nuclear family is important to capitalism because it rears the future workforce at little cost to the capitalist state. Women's domestic labour and sexual services also help to maintain the present workforce's physical and emotional fitness. Family ideology results in governments practising social policies that support traditional roles within the home.

Some feminists suggest that the nuclear family may also be useful to capitalism because it provides an emotionally supportive retreat for male workers who may be frustrated at their treatment in the workplace. The focus on a comfortable home and standard of living may distract workers from their workplace problems and reduce the possibility of industrial unrest. However, some men may attempt to make up for their lack of power and control in the workplace by exerting control within the family. This may have negative consequences for some females, in the form of domestic violence.

Radical feminist views

Radical feminists argue that the main effect of industrialisation was that women's prime function was defined as mother–housewife, allowing men to dominate paid work. They argue that both men and women are socialised into a set of ideas that largely confirm male power and superiority. The family is the main arena for transmitting this **patriarchal ideology**, through the socialisation of children into gender roles. Such socialisation encourages the notion that the sexual division of labour is 'natural', that women are primarily sexual objects and mothers/housewives, and that violence against women is not a serious social problem.

Feminists therefore suggest that the emergence of the modern nuclear family meets the needs of men rather than the needs of all members of society. The family is essentially a patriarchal institution which exploits and oppresses women.

CHECK YOUR UNDERSTANDING ✓ ✓ ✓ ✓

1 **In Parsons' view:**
   (a) What functions did the pre-industrial family perform?
   (b) What happened to the functions of the family after industrialisation?

2 **In what ways do historians challenge Parsons' ideas about family change?**

3 **From a Marxist perspective, whom does the nuclear family benefit? How?**

4 **Whom does the nuclear family benefit according to radical feminists? How?**

Exploring the family and industrialisation

Item A Until relatively recently it was widely accepted by sociologists that the present form and structure of the modern family had evolved from an earlier extended type that was predominant in pre-industrial societies. The modern nuclear family emerged as a result of the processes of industrialisation and urbanisation.

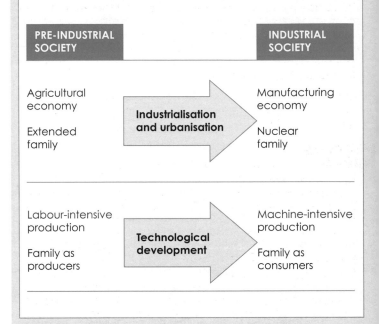

The functionalist view of the evolving family

PRE-INDUSTRIAL SOCIETY		INDUSTRIAL SOCIETY
Agricultural economy	Industrialisation and urbanisation →	Manufacturing economy
Extended family		Nuclear family
Labour-intensive production	Technological development →	Machine-intensive production
Family as producers		Family as consumers

The assumption of a dominant experience of an extended family in the past has been questioned in recent years as a result of the work of a number of family historians.

N. Jorgensen (1995) *Investigating Families and Households*, London: Collins Educational, pp. 14–15

KEY TERMS

Achievement – the allocation of roles and statuses on the basis of individual merit, e.g. through the acquisition of qualifications.

Ascription – the allocation of roles and statuses on the basis of fixed characteristics, e.g. on the basis of gender or what family you are born into.

Expressive leader – Parsons' term for the female function of mother–housewife.

Extended kinship networks – relationships between family members beyond the nuclear family, e.g. grandparents, cousins.

Geographical mobility – the ability to move quickly around the country.

Ideological apparatus – according to Marxists, any institution that is involved in the transmitting of ruling-class ideas, e.g. education, mass media.

Industrialisation – the process (occurring during the eighteenth and nineteenth centuries in Britain) whereby societies moved from agricultural production to industrial manufacturing. It had a huge impact, creating cities (urbanisation), changing the sort of work people did, and fundamentally altering their social experiences and relationships.

Feminists have examined the history of family life and changes in the organisation of families, from the perspective of women. There is some disagreement as to whether or not women have always been subordinated and exploited in the family, or whether their subordination is a result of the growth and development of industrial capitalism. Radical feminists argue that patriarchy in the family existed long before industrialisation. Liberal feminists suggest that before industrialisation every member of the family worked to produce what the family needed. However, after industrialisation, women became associated with the domestic sphere and the care of the home and children. Marxist feminists argue that the resulting economic dependency of women on men and female exploitation benefit capitalism, because women in the home ensure a fit and active workforce.

Adapted from P. Abbott and C. Wallace (2000) *An Introduction to Sociology: Feminist Perspectives*, 2nd edn, London: Routledge, pp. 141–5

Item C

According to functionalists, industrialisation led to greater geographical mobility and loss of regular contact with extended kin. The wider family network was no longer required as emotional and personal needs were met by the nuclear unit. However, a number of sociological studies of the 1950s and 1960s suggested that the isolation of the nuclear family from the wider family had been exaggerated. The study of Bethnal Green in London by Young and Willmott (1957) found extended families with frequent and strong contact between kin. By the late 1960s, studies of new council estates and factory workers with high incomes were suggesting that contact with kin, although not totally severed, was in decline. Research indicated that people were mainly living in nuclear families which were more inward-looking, home-centred and less inclined to be sociable outside the home with kin and friends.

Adapted from N. Abercrombie and A. Warde (2000) *Contemporary British Society*, 3rd edn, Cambridge: Polity Press, pp. 302–9

1 Explain what is meant by 'patriarchy' (Item B). (2)

2 Suggest two ways in which extended kinship networks benefit their members. (4)

3 Identify three ways in which industrialisation affected the family. (6)

4 Identify and briefly explain two reasons why families may have become 'inward-looking, home-centred and less inclined to be sociable outside the home with kin and friends' (Item C). (8)

5 Using information from the Items and elsewhere, examine the view that the nuclear family did not exist in Britain before industrialisation. (20)

6 Assess the view that the nuclear family exists primarily to benefit the powerful rather than society as a whole. (20)

Instrumental leader – Parsons' term for the male breadwinner.

Mutual support system – a system in which family members work to support each other.

Patriarchal ideology – ideas that support and justify male domination of society.

Pre-industrial – before the industrial revolution.

Extension activities

1 Research other functionalist sociologists and historians – such as Ronald Fletcher, William Goode and Edward Shorter – to see whether they agree with Parsons' analysis.

2 Visit your local reference library and ask to see a copy of the 1851 census for your area. Randomly choose a couple of streets and work out how households were organised. Does this evidence support Parsons or Anderson?

Getting you thinking

Far left: a gay family

Left: a working woman

Below: contraceptive pills

Valerie Riches, the founder president of a body called Family and Youth Concern, is a woman of conviction. She is convinced, for instance, that sex education harms the young and undermines the family. She is clear that sending childless housewives out to work means that men's 'masculine role as the provider and father' is being obliterated. She has also criticised the decision of a gay couple to have a child by a surrogate mother. 'It's against the natural order of things', she says. Interestingly, although Ms Riches is second to none in her opposition to single-parent families, she is none the less firmly opposed to the introduction of emergency contraception – the morning-after pill – which might reduce the creation of more such faulty units. 'Taking a morning-after pill will encourage girls to be easy and carefree', she says.

Adapted from C. Bennett (2000) 'Valerie's moral lead', *Guardian*, 14 December

1 Look carefully at the images above. How might some people see them as threatening the traditional family?

2 In the article, five things are identified that Valerie Riches thinks are undermining the family. What are they? Do you agree that these things are harming the family unit?

3 Think of any ways in which the government influences your family life. In your opinion, should it play a greater or a lesser role? What role, if any, should it play?

In Britain, public debate about the family, over the last fifty years, has focused on the changing nature of family life and its impact on society. This debate has often been dominated by those who, like Valerie Riches, take the view that the traditional nuclear family is under attack. Threats to the traditional family are seen as the main cause of the claimed moral decline among young people.

The golden age of family life

Those who claim that the family is in decline can be grouped under the label **'New Right'**, in that they are usually conservative thinkers and politicians who believe very strongly in tradition. These commentators often assume that there was once a 'golden age' of the family, in which husbands and wives were strongly committed to each other for life, and children were brought up to respect their parents and social institutions such as the law.

Many New Right thinkers see the 1960s and early 1970s as the beginning of a sustained attack on traditional family values. In particular, the introduction of the contraceptive pill and the legalisation of abortion in the 1960s have been associated with family decline. The sexual freedom that women experienced as a result of these changes supposedly lessened their commitment to the family; while equal opportunities and equal pay legislation distracted women from their 'natural' careers as mothers. The 1969 Divorce Reform Act was seen as undermining commitment to marriage. And the partial decriminalisation of homosexuality has been interpreted as a particularly important symbol of moral decline, because the New Right see homosexuality as 'unnatural' and deviant.

Familial ideology

New Right views on the family reflect a **familial ideology** – a set of ideas about what constitutes an 'ideal' family. Their preferred model is the traditional nuclear family with a clear sexual division of labour, as described in Topic 1 (see p. 37). This ideology is transmitted by sections of the media and advertising, politicians, religious leaders, and pressure groups such as 'Family and Youth Concern'.

Family decline and the 'New Right'

This familial ideology also makes a number of assumptions about how *not* to organise family life. In particular, it sees the declining popularity of marriage, the increase in cohabitation, the number of births outside marriage, and teenage pregnancy as symptoms of the decline in family morality. Homosexuality, single parenthood, liberal sex education, abortion and working mothers are all seen as threats, both to family stability and to the well-being of society itself.

A good example of the New Right approach to the family can be seen in the view that there exists an underclass of criminals, unmarried mothers and idle young men who are responsible for rising crime. It is argued that this underclass is welfare-dependent, and that teenage girls are deliberately getting pregnant in order to obtain council housing or state benefits. To make things worse, this underclass is socialising its children into a culture revolving around crime and delinquency, and anti-authority, anti-work and anti-family values.

State policy and the family

Britain, unlike other European countries, does not have a separate minister for family affairs. However, three broad trends can be seen in state policy which suggest that the ideology of the traditional nuclear family has had some influence on government thinking:

1   Tax and welfare policies have generally favoured and encouraged the heterosexual married couple rather than cohabiting couples, single parents and same-sex couples.
2   Policies such as the payment of child benefit to the mother, and the government's reluctance to fund free universal nursery provision, have reinforced the idea that women should take prime responsibility for children.
3   The lack of a co-ordinated set of family policies may indicate a reluctance on the part of the government to interfere in what is seen as the privacy of the family.

Nevertheless, New Right thinkers still believe that grave damage has been inflicted on the nuclear family ideal by misguided government policy. For example, they claim that governments have encouraged mothers to return to work, and consequently generations of children have been 'damaged' by **maternal deprivation**. There have been few tax or benefit policies aimed at encouraging mothers to stay at home with their children. The New Right argue that commitment to marriage has been weakened by governments making divorce too easy to obtain. They also claim that 'deviant' family types such as single-parent families have been encouraged by welfare policies.

Criticisms of the New Right

- Government policy has generally been aimed at ensuring that the family unit does not overwhelm the rights of the individuals within it. Therefore legislation has focused on improving the social and economic position of women. For example, the Conservative government made marital rape illegal in 1991. The Labour government introduced the 'New Deal' in April 1998, which aimed to encourage single mothers back to work. The same government also instructed police forces to get tough on domestic violence. The rights of children have also been enhanced through successive Children's Acts – there is even a possibility that a future Labour government will make smacking children illegal. There is no doubt that such legislation has undermined traditional male dominance in families, but many people believe that improved rights for women and children strengthen the family rather than weaken it.
- The traditional nuclear family is still central to government plans. Although New Labour does at least recognise other family types, especially single-parent families, and is sympathetic to improving the rights of gay people, nevertheless key ministers have stated that children are best brought up by married natural parents.

The 'dark side' of family life

Some sociologists have argued that familial ideology has led to the nuclear family being over-**idealised**. The view that the family is a **private institution** has led to the general neglect of severe social problems such as child abuse and domestic violence. Up until the late 1980s, for example, only as a very last resort would social workers break up families in which they suspected abuse. It took a series of abuse-related child deaths to change this policy.

The majority of all recorded murders, serious assaults and abuse are committed by one member of a family on another. Radical psychiatrists have long argued that the experience of being brought up in nuclear family units is psychologically damaging for some individuals.

Feminists generally see the traditional nuclear family as both the source and main agent of women's oppression. They suggest that familial ideology makes problems such as domestic violence worse, because some women believe they should 'stand by their man' through thick and thin. These women may even blame themselves for being 'bad' mothers and wives, and therefore see themselves as deserving of punishment.

The family: in decline or just changing?

New Right politicians strongly believe that the family – and therefore family ideology – is in decline, and that this is the source of all our social problems. However, it may simply be that family ideology is evolving rather than deteriorating, as we realise that the traditional family denies women and children the same rights as men. People today may be less willing to tolerate these forms of inequality and the violence and abuse that often accompany them. Increasing acceptance and tolerance of a range of family types may be healthy for society, rather than a symptom of moral decay.

CHECK YOUR UNDERSTANDING

1 What legislation introduced in the 1960s and 1970s is seen as damaging to the family, according to New Right commentators?

2 What is the attitude of the Labour government towards the family?

3 What are the main symptoms of the decline in family morality, according to the New Right?

4 In what ways has familial ideology had an impact on state policy?

5 What is meant by the 'dark side' of family life?

KEY TERMS

Familial ideology – the view that a particular type of family (e.g. the nuclear family) and particular living arrangements (e.g. marriage, men as breadwinners, women as mothers–housewives, etc.) are the ideals that people should aspire to.

Idealised – presented as an ideal.

Maternal deprivation – the view that if a child is deprived of maternal love for any significant period of time it will grow up to be psychologically damaged.

New Right – a group of thinkers and commentators who believe very strongly in tradition. They tend to be against change and to support the Conservative Party.

Private institution – something that occurs 'behind closed doors', with few links with the wider community.

Exploring the family, morality and the state

Item A

Conservative thinkers have tended to define what the family should be in terms of a heterosexual conjugal unit based on marriage and co-residence. A clear segregation of tasks based on sexual differences is seen as the 'traditional', 'natural' and 'God-given' way of ordering our lives. It is assumed that the man is the 'natural' head of the family. The family's key tasks are the reproduction of the next generation, the protection of dependent children and the inculcation of proper moral values in children. The family also disciplines men and women in economic and sexual terms: it keeps us in our proper place. Order, hierarchy and stability are seen as the key features of the 'healthy' family and the 'healthy' society. However, conservative commentators see this traditional family as under threat and in decline. This is seen as one of the main causes of the claimed wider moral decay in society.

Adapted from N. Sherratt and G. Hughes (2000) 'Family: from tradition to diversity?' in G. Hughes and R. Fergusson (eds) *Ordering Lives: Family, Work and Welfare*, London: Routledge, p. 60

Item B

The state has intervened significantly in families for a considerable length of time, whether by providing support (such as family income credits for those earning low wages and with dependent children) or in overseeing the bringing up of children (if social workers think this is not being done properly, then children may be put temporarily or more permanently into the care of the local authority). This interference has not lessened – indeed as politicians and the media have come together to discuss what they see as the decline of the family, so the extent of that interference has increased. However, conservative thinkers tend to believe that there has not been enough state input into protecting the traditional family, or that state interference has actually contributed to its decline by encouraging the development of 'deviant' living arrangements.

N. Abercrombie and A. Warde (2000) *Contemporary British Society*, 3rd edn, Cambridge: Polity Press, pp. 287–8

Item C

One constantly hears that the traditional family is in trouble, that it doesn't work any more, that we must find new ways to help it. But does it matter if the family is in trouble, if it does not work any more? The traditional family model is essentially a repressive one teaching authoritarianism and hierarchy and a belief in the unchanging rightness of male power. If the family doesn't work, maybe there is something wrong with its structure. Why assume that humans are flawed and that the family structure is fine and good. People must have reasons for fleeing the nuclear family – abuse and domestic violence are well documented.

S. Hite, *New Statesman and Society*, 4 March 1994

1 Explain what is meant by the phrase 'the traditional family' (Items A, B and C). (2)

2 Identify two ways in which the state intervenes in family life (Item B). (4)

3 Suggest three ways in which the traditional family might be seen as being 'under threat and in decline' (Item A). (6)

4 Identify and briefly explain two reasons why the traditional family might be described as 'repressive' (Item C). (8)

5 Using information from the Items and elsewhere, examine the view that the traditional nuclear family is under attack and in decline. (20)

6 Using information from Item B and elsewhere, assess the argument that state policy has largely failed to protect the institution of the family. (20)

Extension activities

1 Visit the websites of the major political parties and find out what their policies are towards the family. Or, alternatively, write to them, or to your local MP.

2 Conduct a mini-survey of teenagers and old-age pensioners to see whether there is any major difference in how they perceive family life, and so-called 'threats' to it such as homosexuality, cohabitation and illegitimacy.

3 Observe the media and other institutions for signs of familial ideology. You could study television commercials at different times of the day, examine the content of specific types of programmes such as soap operas or situation comedies, analyse the content of women's magazines, or stroll through family-orientated stores such as Mothercare, Boots and BHS to see whether familial ideology is apparent in their organisation, packaging, marketing, etc.

Question for students taking OCR exam board AS level

4 (a) Identify and explain two reasons why the traditional family unit is seen by the New Right as being in decline. (20 marks)

(b) Outline and discuss the New Right view that government policy has done little to support the traditional nuclear family. (40 marks)

Getting you thinking

(a) Marriages and divorces in Britain (thousands)

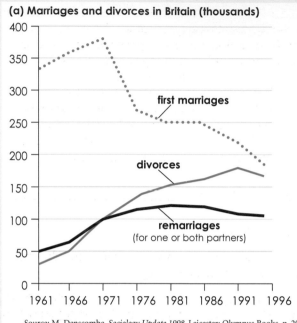

Source: M. Denscombe, *Sociology Update 1998*, Leicester: Olympus Books, p. 20

(b) Divorces in England and Wales (thousands)

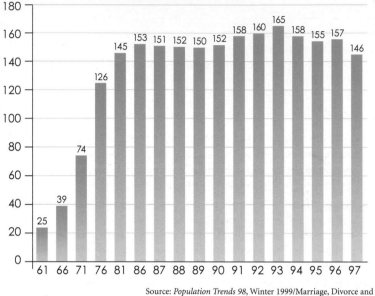

Source: *Population Trends 98*, Winter 1999/Marriage, Divorce and Adoption Statistics 1997, London: The Stationery Office

(c) Divorce rate – proportion of marriages surviving 5–25 years

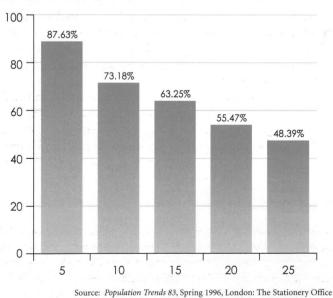

Source: *Population Trends 83*, Spring 1996, London: The Stationery Office

(d) Births outside marriage as a percentage of live births

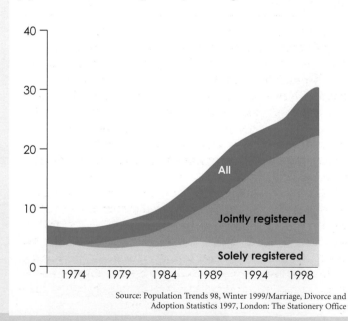

Source: *Population Trends 98*, Winter 1999/Marriage, Divorce and Adoption Statistics 1997, London: The Stationery Office

1 **What has been the general trend for marriage and divorce since 1961?**

2 **What does the barchart (c) tell us about the length of marriages today?**

3 **What does the graph (d) tell us about births outside marriage?**

4 **Identify three trends revealed in the statistics above. Suggest possible explanations for any one of these trends.**

5 **Why might these statistics be alarming for supporters of the traditional family?**

It is not difficult to see why supporters of the traditional family, such as the New Right, are so alarmed by figures like those above. They believe that they indicate a crisis in the family which will inevitably result in increasing anti-social behaviour and moral breakdown. Many postmodernists and feminists look at the figures in a very different way – they see them as indicators of greater personal choice in our private lives, and as evidence of a rejection of patriarchal family arrangements. So who is right?

Marriage

The latest statistics indicate that fewer people are getting married than at any other time in the last 40 years. In 1997 only 200,000 people married for the first time, compared with 330,000 in 1961.

However, New Right fears about what these statistics reveal are probably exaggerated for two broad reasons:

1 People are delaying marriage rather than rejecting it. Most people will marry at some point in their lives. However, people are now marrying later in life, probably after a period of **cohabitation**. Women may delay marriage because they want to develop their careers and enjoy a period of independence.
2 Most people, whether single, divorced or cohabiting, still see marriage as a desirable objective in their lives. For example, remarriages (i.e. in which one or both partners have been divorced) now make up over one-third of marriages. These people are obviously committed to the institution of marriage despite their previous negative experience of it.

Cohabitation

A constant source of concern to the New Right has been the significant rise in the number of couples cohabiting during the last decade. In 1998, 28 per cent of men and 26 per cent of women living in Britain, aged between 25 and 29, cohabited. New Right commentators claim that cohabitation is less stable than marriage. A report by the Institute for the Study of Civil Society, published in August 2000, claimed that cohabiting couples were less happy and less fulfilled than married couples, and more likely to be abusive, unfaithful, stressed and depressed.

However, surveys indicate that few people see cohabitation as an alternative to marriage. It is merely seen as a test of compatibility, and consequently tends to be a temporary phase, lasting on average about five years, before couples eventually marry – usually some time after the first child is born. Cohabitation may also be linked to the rising divorce rate, in that an increasing number of people are not able to get married because they are waiting for a divorce.

Births outside marriage

New Right commentators have been especially disturbed by the fact that one in three babies is now born outside of marriage. In particular, media **moral panics** have focused on the fact that the UK has the highest rate of teenage pregnancy in Europe. For example, in 1998 there were 44,100 pregnancies in the 16–18 age group and 8,400 among the under-16s.

However, according to the National Council for One Parent Families, the under-16 conception rate has fallen considerably, compared with the 1960s, and it remained reasonably stable throughout the 1990s, at 8.9 per 1,000 girls. Only 3 per cent of unmarried mothers are teenagers, and most of them live at home with their parents. Experts are generally sceptical that such teenagers are deliberately getting pregnant in order to claim state housing and benefits. Moreover, four out of five births outside marriage are registered to both parents, and three-quarters of these are living at the same address. Most births outside of marriage, therefore, are to stable cohabiting couples who eventually marry. It should also be pointed out that a significant number of marriages break up in the first year after having a child, so marriage is not always the stable institution that the New Right claim it is.

Some sociologists argue that we should be more concerned about the trend towards childlessness that has appeared in recent years. The Family Policy Studies Centre estimates that one woman in five will choose to remain childless, and this figure is expected to double in the next 20 years.

Marital breakdown

Types of marital breakdown

Marital breakdown can take three different forms: divorce, separation and empty-shell marriages.

- **Divorce** refers to the legal ending of a marriage. Since the Divorce Reform Act of 1969, divorce has been granted on the basis of '**irretrievable** breakdown'; and since 1984 couples have been able to **petition** for divorce after the first anniversary of their marriage. 'Quickie' divorces are also available, in which one partner has to prove the 'fault' or 'guilt' of the other, for matrimonial 'crimes' such as adultery.
- **Separation** is where couples agree to live apart after the breakdown of a marriage. In the past, when divorce was difficult to obtain or too expensive, separation was often the only solution.
- **Empty-shell marriages** are those in which husband and wife stay together in name only. There may no longer be any love or intimacy between them. Today such marriages are likely to end in separation or divorce, although these types of relationships may persist for the sake of children, or for religious reasons.

The divorce rate

Britain's divorce rate is high, compared with other industrial societies. Within Europe, only Denmark has a higher rate. In 1938, 6,000 divorces were granted in the UK. This figure had increased tenfold by 1970, and in 1993 it peaked at 165,000. There are now nearly half as many divorces as marriages. If present trends continue, about 40 per cent of current marriages will end in divorce.

New Right sociologists argue that such divorce statistics are a symptom of a serious crisis in the family. They suggest that, because of the easy availability of divorce, people are no longer as committed to the family as they were in the past. This view was partly responsible for the government abandoning the section of the Family Law Act (1996) that intended to replace existing divorce procedures with a single ground for divorce. Under this new legislation, divorce would be granted to couples with children after a compulsory cooling-off period of 18 months, if both parties agreed after counselling that their marriage had ended. However, fears that this was an easier way out of marriage than the present system prompted the Labour government to abandon it altogether in 2001.

Why is the divorce rate increasing?

Changes in divorce law have generally made it easier and cheaper to end marriages, but this is not necessarily the cause of the rising divorce rate. Legal changes reflect other changes in society, especially changes in attitudes. In particular, sociologists argue that social expectations about marriage have changed. Functionalist sociologists even argue that high divorce rates are evidence that marriage is increasingly valued and that people are demanding higher standards from their partners. Couples are no longer prepared to put up with unhappy, 'empty-shell' marriages. People want emotional and sexual compatibility and equality, as well as companionship. Some are willing to go through a number of partners to achieve these goals.

Feminists note that women's expectations of marriage have radically changed, compared with previous generations. In the 1990s most divorce petitions were initiated by women. This may support the view that women expect far more from marriage than men, and in particular that they value friendship and emotional gratification more than men do. If husbands fail to live up to these expectations, women may feel the need to look elsewhere.

Women's expectations have probably changed as a result of the improved educational and career opportunities they have experienced since the 1980s. Women no longer have to be unhappily married because they are financially dependent upon their husbands. Moreover, divorce may be a reaction to the frustration that many working wives may feel if they are responsible for the bulk of housework and childcare.

Divorce is no longer associated with stigma and shame. This may be partly due to a general decline in religious practices. The social controls, such as extended families and **close-knit communities**, that exerted pressure on couples to stay together, and which labelled divorce as 'wicked' and 'shameful', are in decline. Consequently, in a society dominated by privatised nuclear families, the view that divorce can lead to greater happiness for the individual is more acceptable. It is even more so if divorce involves escaping from an abusive relationship, or if an unhappy marriage is causing emotional damage to children. However, it is important to recognise that such attitudes are not necessarily a sign of a casual attitude towards divorce. Most people experience divorce as an emotional and traumatic experience, equivalent to bereavement.

Divorce trends suggest that **monogamy** (one partner for life) will eventually be replaced by **serial monogamy** (a series of long-term relationships resulting in cohabitation and/or marriage). However, the New Right panic about divorce is probably exaggerated. Four out of ten marriages may end in divorce, but six out of ten succeed. Over 75 per cent of children are living with both natural parents who are legally married. These figures suggest that society still places a high value on marriage and the family.

1 Why have marriage rates declined in recent years?

2 What has been the trend in the number of births outside marriage?

3 Why are teenage mothers not the problem the media make them out to be?

4 Why is cohabitation not a threat to marriage?

5 Why are women more likely to initiate divorce proceedings than men?

KEY TERMS

Close-knit community – a community in which there are close relationships between people (everyone knows everyone else).

Cohabitation – living together as man and wife.

Divorce – the legal ending of a marriage.

Divorce petition – a legal request for a divorce.

Empty-shell marriage – a marriage in which the partners no longer love each other but stay together, usually for the sake of the children.

Irretrievable – unable to be recovered. Broken down for ever.

Monogamy – the practice of having only one partner.

Moral panic – public concern over some aspect of behaviour, created and reinforced in large part by sensational media coverage.

Serial monogamy – a series of long-term relationships.

Item A Disaffected couples should be made to wait longer before they are allowed to divorce, William Hague said yesterday, as he stepped up his efforts to promote the Tories as the party of the family. The Tory leader said he did not believe existing law struck the right balance between allowing people to break free of unsalvageable marriages and ensuring that couples did not rush into divorce because it was easily available. Mr Hague is keen to show that Conservatives still regard marriage as the ideal. Yesterday Mr Hague said: 'I've often thought that it is too easy to divorce.' However, he accepted that 'people live in many different circumstances, that some marriages do break down and often it is better for all involved to bring it to an end'. He said: 'We have to get the balance right and I am not wholly convinced that we have got the balance right at the moment.'

Daily Telegraph, 16 March 1999

Item B The family seems to be dwindling as a social institution. The stark figures would suggest that British society has turned its back on those things normally associated with the idea of 'the family'. Within one generation, we have seen the following changes: only half as many people are getting married, lone-parent families have increased threefold, children born outside marriage have quadrupled in number, and the number of divorces has trebled. However, there is strong evidence that these things indicate a change in the nature of the family rather than its death. The family remains a cornerstone of British society in terms of people's lives and their sense of identity. Families are still a crucial source of care and support for the elderly and the disabled. Nearly two in three working mothers turn to relatives for help with childcare. Most people are in regular contact with relatives and see them at least once a month. At Christmas, more than four in five people join in some form of family gathering.

Adapted from M. Denscombe, *Sociology Update 1998*, Leicester: Olympus Books, p. 20

Item C Marriage is a normal and expected part of women's lives in Western society. However, although the vast majority of women will expect to marry at some time and at least once, in recent years there has been some decline in the popularity of marriage. In 1971 only 4 per cent of women remained unmarried by the age of 50, but by 1987 the proportion had grown to 17 per cent. Women today are marrying older and marrying less. The Family Policy Studies Centre estimates that one in five young women will remain childless. Typically those who defer motherhood are educated women. A recent study showed that women who have qualifications are twice as likely as those with no qualifications to say they expect to have no children.

Adapted from J. Chandler (1993) 'Women outside marriage', *Sociology Review*, vol. 2, no. 4; and N. Jorgensen et al. (1997) *Sociology: An Interactive Approach*, London: Collins Educational, pp. 100–1

1 **Explain in your own words what is meant by the term 'serial monogamy'. (2)**

2 **Suggest two reasons why Mr Hague (Item A) might want to make a couple wait longer for a divorce. (4)**

3 **Identify three ways in which Item B suggests that the family is undergoing change rather than decline. (6)**

4 **Identify and briefly explain two reasons why an increasing number of women are voluntarily choosing childlessness (Item C). (8)**

5 **Using information from the Items and elsewhere, examine the view that the increase in divorce is due to its easy availability. (20)**

6 **Using information from the Items and elsewhere, assess the argument that the decline in marriage and the increases in both cohabitation and births outside marriage are significant threats to the stability of the family. (20)**

Extension activities

1 **Use the archives of either the *Guardian* or the *Daily Telegraph* websites to research the debate about divorce. The latter is excellent for links to relevant sites such as divorceon-line.com, the family law consortium and the Lord Chancellor's Department.**

2 **Carry out a mini survey across three different age groups (e.g. 15–20, 25–30 and 35–40), investigating attitudes towards marriage, cohabitation, childlessness, births outside marriage, etc.**

3 **Interview two males and two females to find out what characteristics they are looking for in a future partner. Do your findings support the view that females set higher standards in relationships?**

Question for students taking OCR exam board AS level

4 **(a) Identify and explain two reasons why marriage rates are in decline. (20 marks)**

(b) Outline and discuss the view that the increase in divorce over the last 30 years is primarily due to changes in women's attitudes. (40 marks)

Getting you thinking

Above: Janet McLean and Aled Murphy

Right: Jasmin Ferguson

Domestic differences

The married couple

Kashif and Sabeen Ashraf are a model nuclear family: a young, happily married couple with a one-year-old son. Sabeen, from Pakistan, joined Kashif in Oldham after their arranged marriage in 1996, and says she would never have dreamed of living with him out of wedlock.

'You hear of people who've cohabited, but none of my friends have', says Kashif, 32, a careers officer. 'It tends to be people in interracial relationships. Maybe a generation down the line it might happen.'

He adds: 'I think marriage is more binding. And also, once I graduated and got a job, the next thing in life was to have a family to complete the circle. I was born in Oldham and have been to university, but I still chose the traditional route.'

The unmarried couple

Janet McLean and her partner Aled Murphy are a typical example of a modern-day white couple. After two years living together in Fife they say marriage is 'not an issue', although they would like to wed if they have children.

The couple see their bond of trust and their practical commitments – a mortgage and joint bank account – as more important than a piece of paper. Forty years ago their families might have disagreed. But what was once condemned as living in sin is now a normal way of life for millions of Britons.

The single mother

Yasmin Ferguson spent 13 years with her childhood sweetheart, but moved out of their shared house in Bristol after their son was born eight years ago.

'I didn't want my son growing up with shouting and I knew it was the fact we were living together that was causing problems', she explains. She continued to see her partner until a year ago.

Yasmin, 29, is a qualified social worker studying for a degree in health and community studies. She believes her self-reliance is partly due to an immigrant work ethic inherited from her parents.

'My mum and dad came over from Jamaica to find a better life for themselves. When we were growing up we were taught we should be independent and self-sufficient', she says. 'Women in general tend to be told you have to go out and find prince charming.'

None of her seven elder brothers and sisters are married, but she still hopes to find a lifelong partner. 'I think that's why I'm single', she says. 'I contribute a lot to relationships and I want my expectations to be met. I do hope one day I will meet someone for ever.

'But I see the disappearance of the image of a nuclear family as a good thing. It will never be seen negatively, but let it be seen as another way of life rather than the way.'

Examine each of the profiles in turn.

1 Which aspects of each profile fit the traditional view of the family?

2 Which profile is closest to the nuclear ideal? Does this surprise you? Explain why.

3 Which aspects of each profile do not fit the nuclear ideal?

4 What do you think Yasmin means when she says, of the nuclear family, 'let it be seen as another way of life rather than *the* way'?

T. Brannigan (2000) 'Domestic differences', *Guardian*, 18 December 2000

The nuclear family is by no means the only way to organise living arrangements. R. N. and R. Rapoport (1982) are very critical of the functionalist and New Right view that the typical family is nuclear. They point out that even back in 1978 only 20 per cent of families fitted this ideal. The Rapoports argue that family life in Britain is actually characterised by **diversity**. A range of family types exist, with diverse internal set-ups which reflect the changing nature of British society.

Organisational or structural diversity

Only 39 per cent of households are made up of couples with dependent children. In other words, the nuclear unit seems to be in the minority. However, household statistics can only give us a static picture of family life. Other categories, such as married-couple and single-person households, may have evolved out of nuclear units, or may evolve into nuclear units in the near future. Therefore it is important not to dismiss the nuclear unit as irrelevant. However, other family structures – such as cohabiting couples with children, one-parent families and **reconstituted families** – are growing in importance.

One-parent families

The number of one-parent families with dependent children tripled from 2 per cent of UK households in 1961 to 7 per cent in 1998. There are now approximately 1.7 million lone-parent families in Britain, making up about 25 per cent of all families. It is estimated that a third to a half of all children will spend some time in a one-parent family.

Ninety per cent of single-parent families are headed by women, and 60 per cent of these are ex-married (divorced, separated or widowed). The fastest growing group of single parents is made up of those who have never married. Most of these are ex-cohabitees, and are probably best described as 'separated'. Contrary to popular opinion, most single mothers are not teenagers – teenage mothers make up just 3 per cent of lone parents. The average age of a lone parent is actually 34.

New Right thinkers see a connection between one-parent families, educational under-achievement and delinquency. They believe that children from one-parent families lack self-discipline and can be emotionally disturbed, because of the lack of a firm father figure in their lives. However, feminist sociologists maintain that the real problem lies with the nuclear family ideal itself. This ideal leads to the **negative labelling** of one-parent families by teachers, social workers, housing departments, police and the courts. Single parents may be **scapegoated** for inner-city crime and educational under-achievement, when these problems are actually the result of factors such as unemployment and poverty. The New Right also rarely consider that single parenthood may be preferable to the domestic violence that is inflicted by some husbands on their wives and children – or that the majority of one-parent families bring up their children successfully.

Reconstituted families

The reconstituted or step-family is made up of divorced or widowed people who have remarried, and their children from the previous marriage (or cohabitation). Such families are on the increase because of the rise in divorce. Reconstituted families are unique because children are likely to also have close ties with the new family of their other natural parent. Children may find themselves pulled in two directions, and they may have tense relationships with their step-parents. These families may be further complicated if the new couple decide to have children of their own.

Kinship diversity

Functionalist sociologists have argued that nuclear families have little need for contact with wider kin. However, McGlone *et al.* (1998) discovered that unemployment and poverty, community care for the elderly, the increasing number of young people electing to live at home for longer periods, and women going out to work all create a greater need for family mutual support systems. Other sociologists note that relatively self-sufficient nuclear families still feel a strong sense of obligation to extended kin in times of family crisis, despite distance.

There is evidence that the **classic working-class extended family** continues to exist. The study *Villains*, by Janet Foster (1990) – of an East End London community – found that

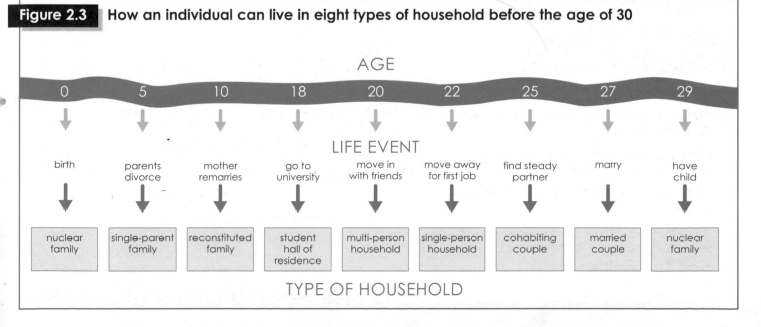

Figure 2.3 **How an individual can live in eight types of household before the age of 30**

AGE

| 0 | 5 | 10 | 18 | 20 | 22 | 25 | 27 | 29 |

LIFE EVENT

| birth | parents divorce | mother remarries | go to university | move in with friends | move away for first job | find steady partner | marry | have child |

| nuclear family | single-parent family | reconstituted family | student hall of residence | multi-person household | single-person household | cohabiting couple | married couple | nuclear family |

TYPE OF HOUSEHOLD

adults were happy to live only a few streets away from their parents and close relatives, and visited them regularly. Ties between mothers and children were particularly strong, and contacts between mothers and married daughters were frequent. Close kinship ties also formed the major support network, providing both emotional and material support.

There is also evidence that extended kinship ties are important to the upper class, in their attempt to maintain wealth and privilege. The economic and political **elite** may use marriage and family connections to ensure 'social closure' – that is, to keep those who do not share their culture from becoming part of the elite.

Cultural diversity

There are differences in the lifestyles of families with different ethnic origins and religious beliefs. Research carried out at Essex University in 2000 indicates that only 39 per cent of British-born Afro-Caribbean adults under the age of 60 are in a formal marriage, compared with 60 per cent of white adults. Moreover, this group is more likely than any other group to inter-marry. The number of mixed-race partnerships means that very few Afro-Caribbean men and women are married to fellow Afro-Caribbeans. Only one-quarter of Caribbean children live with two black parents. There is also a tradition in the Afro-Caribbean community of women living independently from their children's father. Consequently, half of Caribbean families with children are now single-parent.

The Essex study also found that the Pakistani and Bangladeshi communities are most likely to live in old-fashioned nuclear families, although about 33 per cent of Asian families – mainly Sikhs and East African Asians – live in extended families. East African Asian extended families are likely to contain more than one generation, whilst Sikh extended units are organised around brothers and their wives and children.

Marriage in Asian families – whether Muslim, Hindu or Sikh – is mainly arranged, and consequently there is little inter-marriage with other religions or cultures. Relationships between Asian parents and their children are also very different from those that characterise white families. Children tend to respect religious and cultural traditions, and they feel a strong sense of duty to their families, and especially to their elders.

Class diversity

The Rapoports suggest that there may be differences between middle-class and working-class families in terms of the relationship between husband and wife and the way in which children are socialised and disciplined. Some sociologists argue that middle-class parents are more child-centred (see Topic 6) than working-class parents. They supposedly take a greater interest in their children's education, and consequently pass on cultural advantages in terms of attitudes, values and practices (i.e. cultural capital – see Unit 1, Topic 6) which assist their children through the educational system. However, critical sociologists argue that working-class parents are just as child-centred, but that material deprivation limits how much help they can give their children. Therefore, the working-class child's experience is likely to be less satisfactory – because of family poverty, poor schools, lack of material support, greater risks of accidents both in the home and in the street, and so on.

Sexual diversity

An increasing number of single-sex families have appeared in recent years, as homosexual and lesbian couples have children via surrogate mothers and artificial insemination. Studies of children brought up in single-sex families show no significant effects in terms of gender identification or sexual orientation.

Postmodernism and family diversity

Postmodernists argue that postmodern family life is characterised by diversity, variation and instability. For example, women no longer aspire exclusively to romantic love, marriage and children. Pre-marital sex, serial monogamy, cohabitation, economic independence, single-sex relationships and childlessness are now acceptable alternative lifestyles. Men's roles too are no longer clear-cut in postmodern society, and the resulting 'crisis of masculinity' (see p. 28) has led to men redefining both their sexuality and family commitments. Others disagree with this view. They argue that family diversity is exaggerated, and that the basic features of family life have remained largely unchanged for the majority of the population since the 1950s.

There is no doubt that nuclear families are still very common, but the increasing number of other family types – especially single-parent families and reconstituted families – indicates a slow but steady drift away from the nuclear ideal.

CHECK YOUR UNDERSTANDING

1 How might reconstituted family life differ from that experienced in nuclear families?

2 Why do feminist sociologists think that one-parent families are seen as a 'problem'?

3 In what sense might working-class and upper-class families be similar in terms of their contact with extended kin?

4 What differences might exist between working-class and middle-class families?

5 What types of families are Afro-Caribbeans and South Asians likely to be living in?

KEY TERMS

Classic working-class extended family – a family in which sons and daughters live in the same neighbourhood as their parents, see each other on a regular basis and offer each other various supports.

Diversity – difference, variation.

Elite – the most powerful, rich or gifted members of a group.

Negative labelling – treating something as being 'bad' or 'undesirable'.

Reconstituted families – step-families.

Scapegoated – unfairly blamed.

Exploring family diversity

Item A

The Rapoports note that diversity takes a number of forms. Culturally, there is greater diversity of family beliefs and values than used to be the case. The presence of ethnic minorities (such as West Indian, Asian, Greek and Italian communities) has produced considerable cultural variety in family structures and their internal organisation, especially in regard to relations between parents and children. We can also see religious diversity – family structures and domestic arrangements may differ across groups such as practising Catholics, Protestants and Jews. Some religious groups such as Jehovah's Witnesses do not celebrate events such as birthdays and Christmas. Persistent class divisions, between the poor, the skilled working class and the various groupings within the middle and upper classes, sustain major variations in family structure.

Adapted from A. Giddens (1997) *Sociology*, 3rd edn, Cambridge: Polity Press, p. 145

Item B

Fuelled by media moral panics about rising crime, low standards in education, the young lacking a work ethic, and the rise of illegitimacy, divorce and single-parenthood, politicians and other 'opinion formers' appear to give support to the traditional nuclear family. Family diversity, from this view, is a 'social problem' to be solved. However, postmodernists suggest that we cannot say that one type of family is better than another because absolute meaning or truth has collapsed in social life. In postmodern societies we are free to choose the lifestyles we wish since this is the only way to search for meaning in a society that offers choice, fragmentation and diversity. Claims that some family forms are 'better' or more 'natural' or more 'normal' than others are a leftover from modernist thought, which attempted to establish truths about ideal family forms. In a postmodern society we cannot even say what constitutes a 'family'.

Adapted from W. Kidd (1999) 'Family diversity in an uncertain future', *Sociology Review*, vol. 9, no.1

Item C

Controversy surrounds the issue of how children are affected by living in single-parent families. Poorer educational achievement and behavioural problems have been highlighted. However, only a minority of children in separated families experience such outcomes. Above all, such problems are caused by poverty and poor housing rather than inadequate socialisation. In the absence of poverty, children from one-parent families fare no worse than children in other families. Ninety per cent of lone parents say they would like to work at some point, although many find it difficult to combine work with caring for children alone.

Adapted from *One Parent Families Today: The Facts*, National Council for One Parent Families, March 2000

1 **Explain what is meant by the phrase 'cultural diversity in family structures' (Item A). (2)**

2 **Suggest two ways in which family structures or relationships might differ because of religious diversity (Item A). (4)**

3 **Identify three ways in which 'the presence of ethnic minorities ... has produced considerable cultural variety' in the family (Item A). (6)**

4 **Identify and briefly describe two characteristics of the 'postmodern' family (Item B). (8)**

5 **Using material from the Items and elsewhere, examine the view that successful families need two loving heterosexual parents. (20)**

6 **Assess the argument that the basic features of family life have remained largely unchanged for the majority of the population since the 1950s. (20)**

Extension activities

1 **If you know people from other ethnic or religious backgrounds, ask them if you can interview them about their experience of family life. Make sure your questionnaire is sensitive to their background and avoids offending them.**

2 **Use the web to research arranged marriages. There are a number of useful sites dedicated to this topic. Arvi's Punjabi Homepage at www.arvi.pwp.blueyonder.co.uk contains firsthand accounts of how young Asians feel about this arrangement. Other useful sites include prism online at www.journalism.sfsu.ed matrimoniallink.com and interfaith marriage at www.vivaaha.org/interfai.htm**

3 **Research one-parent families, using a range of sources (for example, you could write to organisations such as Gingerbread, the National Council for One Parent Families and the Family Policy Studies Centre). In particular, focus on materials that contradict the view that the one-parent family is a social problem.**

Question for students taking OCR exam board AS level

4 (a) **Identify and explain two ways in which family life is characterised by cultural diversity. (20 marks)**

   (b) **Outline and discuss the view that the increase in one-parent families is a sign of family diversity rather than family decline. (40 marks)**

Getting you thinking

Children dressed like their parents

In the Middle Ages, young and old played together in games and festivals, as in this scene taken from the 'Battle between Carnival and Lent' by Breugel – where the children are depicted as tiny adults

Everyone worked together

At 8 years I put out as an apprentice.

So he could learn his trade from me.

Everyone was held responsible

Tudor law says a seven year old can be hanged for stealing

In many cases, houses were not split up into special rooms, for eating, sleeping, working or cooking

So children could not escape from the adult world

Source: adapted from : 'The invention of childhood', *New Internationalist*, 1978

1 **What does this cartoon tell us about family life in the Middle Ages?**

2 **How does the experience of medieval childhood differ from that of today?**

What is a child? Innocent, cute, funny? That's certainly the popular image suggested by birthday cards, magazines and so on. However, the cartoon and the other images above give a different impression. We can see that ideas about childhood appear to vary between different societies and different historical periods. This means that childhood is a **social construction** – something that is created by society rather than simply a biological stage.

Childhood in pre-industrial society

The social historian Phillipe Aries (1962) suggested that what we experience today as childhood is a recent social invention. He claimed that, in pre-industrial society, childhood as we know it today did not exist. Children were 'little adults' who took part in the same work and play activities as adults. Toys and games specifically for children did not exist. Moreover, Aries argued that children were regarded as an **economic asset** rather than as a symbol of people's love for one another. Investing emotionally in children was difficult when their death rate was so high.

Aries's evidence for this view of childhood has been questioned, but other historians agree that the pre-industrial family was a unit of production, working the land or engaged in crafts. Children were expected to help their parents from a very young age. Those who did not help with domestic production usually left home to become servants or apprentices.

Childhood and industrialisation

After industrialisation these attitudes continued, especially among the working classes, whose children were frequently found working in factories, mines and mills. Aries argued that middle-class attitudes towards children started to change during this period. There was a growth in marital and parental love in middle-class families as the **infant mortality rate** started to fall.

Social attitudes towards children really started to change in the middle of the nineteenth century. Children were excluded from the mines and factories where thousands of them had been killed or injured. Some working-class parents, however, resisted these moves, because they depended on their children's wages.

Many nineteenth-century campaigners were concerned about juvenile delinquency, beggars and child prostitution, and consequently wanted to get children off the streets. However, there is considerable evidence that children continued to be badly treated in this period, and child prostitution and abuse were common features of most cities. It was not until the early 1900s that the age of sexual consent was raised to 16.

Childhood in the twentieth century

The twentieth century saw the emergence of a **child-centred** society. This was probably the result of improved standards of living and nutrition in the late nineteenth century, which led to a major decline in the infant mortality rate. The higher standard of living also meant that having children became more expensive. People chose to have fewer children and invested more in them in terms of love, socialisation and protection.

Childhood and adolescence were consequently seen as separate categories from adulthood. Children were seen as being in need of special attention and protection.

Top: the funeral of a shot Palestinian child

Above left: a typical image of childhood in Britain today

Above: public schoolboys

Left: a child soldier in Sierra Leone

3 **What do these images tell us about the experience of childhood today?**

Children and the state

Concern over the rights of children can be seen in greater state involvement in protecting them. Parents' rearing of children is now monitored through various pieces of legislation, such as the 1980 Child Care Act and the 1991 Child Support Act. The role of social services and social workers is to police those families in which children are thought to be at risk. The state also supervises the socialisation of children through compulsory education, which lasts eleven years; and it takes some economic responsibility by paying child benefit and children's tax credits to parents.

Increasingly, children have come to be recognised as individuals with rights. The Child Support Act (1991) deals with the care, bringing up and protection of children. It protects children's welfare in the event of parental separation and divorce, emphasising that the prime concern of the state should be the child, and what children themselves say about their experiences and needs. Some children have recently used the act to 'divorce' their parents, whilst others have used it to 'force' their separated/divorced parents to see them more regularly.

Theoretical approaches to childhood

The conventional approach

Many functionalists and New Right thinkers tend to subscribe to what has been termed a 'conventional' approach to childhood. This sees children as a vulnerable group – both under threat from and in need of protection from adult society. This approach suggests that successful child-rearing requires two parents of the opposite sex, and that there is a 'right' way to bring up a child. Such views often 'blame' working mothers or single mothers, and/or inadequate parents, for social problems such as delinquency. They also see children as in need of protection from 'threats' such as homosexuality and media violence.

An alternative view

Conventional approaches tend to generalise about children and childhood. This is dangerous because, as we saw earlier, childhood is not a fixed, universal experience. Historical period, locality, culture, social class, gender and ethnicity all have an influence on the character and quality of childhood. This can be illustrated in a number of ways:

- In many less developed nations, the experience of childhood is extremely different from that in the industrialised world. Children in such countries are constantly at risk of early death, because of poverty and lack of basic health care. They are unlikely to have access to education, and may find themselves occupying adult roles – for example, as workers or soldiers.
- Even in a country such as Britain, experience of childhood may differ across ethnic and religious groups. For example, there is evidence that Muslim, Hindu and Sikh children generally feel a stronger sense of obligation and duty to their parents than white children.
- Experiences of childhood in Britain may vary according to social class. Upper-class children may find that they spend most of their formative years in boarding schools. Middle-class children may be encouraged from an early age to aim for university and a professional career, and they are likely to receive considerable material and cultural support from their parents. Working-class childhood may be made more difficult by the experience of poverty.
- Experiences of childhood may differ according to gender. Boys and girls may be socialised into a set of behaviours based on expectations about masculinity and femininity. (See Unit 1, Topic 7.)

We also need to acknowledge that some children's experiences of childhood may be damaging. Different types of child abuse have been re-discovered in recent years, such as neglect and physical, sexual and emotional abuse. The negative effects of divorce have been documented in several surveys of teenagers. There are occasionally reports of child prostitution; and growing numbers of children live rough on city streets. Media reports often focus on cases of bullying and suicide. The recent case of Damilola Taylor, the ten-year-old killed on a housing estate in South London– possibly by other children – illustrates the fragile nature of childhood in the UK.

CHECK YOUR UNDERSTANDING

1 What do sociologists mean when they describe childhood as a social construction?

2 How does Aries believe children were treated in pre-industrial society?

3 What were the main causes of society becoming more child-centred at the end of the nineteenth century?

4 How does the conventional approach to childhood view children?

5 What problems are associated with this approach?

KEY TERMS

Child-centred – treating the needs of children as a priority.

Economic asset – something that brings money in.

Infant mortality rate – the number of babies who die in their first year of life, as a proportion of all live births.

Social construction – something that is created by society.

Exploring childhood

Item A
Most of us tend to think of childhood as a clear and distinct stage of life. 'Children', we suppose, are distinct from 'babies' or 'toddlers'. Childhood intervenes between infancy and the onset of adolescence. Yet the concept of childhood, like so many other aspects of our social life today, has only come into being over the past two or three centuries. In traditional and pre-industrial cultures, the young move directly from a lengthy infancy into working roles within the community. Right up to the start of the twentieth century, in Britain and most other Western countries, children as young as 7 or 8 years old were put to work at what now seems a very early age. There are many countries in the world today, in fact, in which young children are engaged in full-time work, often in physically demanding circumstances (coal-mines, for example). The idea that children have distinctive rights, and the notion that the use of child labour is morally wrong, are quite recent developments.

A. Giddens (1997) *Sociology*, 3rd edn, Cambridge: Polity Press, p. 38

Item B
The changing nature of legislation concerning children has reflected the changing views towards children over time. In the nineteenth century, the idea gradually developed that children were not simply little adults, but were vulnerable members of society who needed care and protection. This concept of the child as vulnerable dominates twentieth-century thinking. For example, the Children Act of 1908 resulted in the criminal justice system treating and punishing criminal adults and children in different ways for the first time. In 1952, local authorities were given the duty to investigate cases of neglect or cruelty in regard to children, whilst the 1989 Children Act made it clear that the child's best interests must be central to any decision made about the welfare of the child. The child's views are therefore sought and taken into account. Such legislation reflects the fact that we are now a child-centred society.

Adapted from S. Moore (1998) *Social Welfare Alive*, 2nd edn, Cheltenham: Stanley Thornes, pp. 366–7

Item C
Childhood is tremendously varied, from the sheltered pre-schooler of Western nations to the maimed street beggar or gun-carrying 'freedom fighter' of less industrialised nations. Even in the UK, children may grow up in a wide variety of different and potentially damaging situations. There are occasional alarming reports of child prostitution linked to runaway children and drug use. We know from recent studies that many children of less than 10 years old may be the main carer in family situations where their parent is chronically ill or disabled. For many children, then, childhood may involve the direct experience of oppression, abuse, exploitation, not to mention parental divorce, poor health and poverty. Childhood experience, then, is extremely diverse by way of region, social class, housing quality, income, culture and ethnicity, prejudice, diet, disease and abuse.

Adapted from J. Bernardes (1997) *Family Studies: An Introduction*, London: Routledge, p. 115

1 Explain what is meant by the phrase 'a child-centred society' (Item B). (2)

2 Suggest two ways in which the experience of being a child in a less developed nation may differ from the experience of a British child (Item C). (4)

3 Identify three ways in which the state protects the rights of children today (Item B). (6)

4 Identify and briefly describe two differences between childhood in pre-industrial society and childhood in contemporary industrial society. (8)

5 Using material from the Items and elsewhere, examine the view that childhood today is not a fixed universal experience. (20)

6 Using information from the Items and elsewhere, assess the argument that Britain has evolved into a successful child-centred society. (20)

Extension activities

1 Visit the website www.child-abuse.com/childhouse. This contains links to a number of excellent sites that look at childhood and children's rights across the world. Alternatively visit the site for Save the Children Fund (UK).

2 Using textbooks, CD Roms and government websites such as those of the Home Office and Lord Chancellor's department (accessible via open.gov.uk), compile a detailed time-line outlining state intervention in children's lives and the rights children now have.

3 As a class, debate the statement 'Only adults know what is best for children.'

Question for students taking OCR exam board AS level

4 (a) Identify and explain two ways in which children experienced childhood prior to the twentieth century. (20 marks)

(b) Outline and discuss the view that the UK is a child-centred society. (40 marks)

Getting you thinking

1 Consider the list of tasks below. Which adult in your home was mainly responsible for each when you were aged 5–7?

(a) Making sure that you had sandwiches for lunch or the money to pay for a school-dinner.

(b) Making sure that your favourite food was in the fridge.

(c) Arranging with other parents for you to go to a party or around to somebody's house for tea.

(d) Making sure that you had a clean swimming costume and towel on the days of school swims.

(e) Changing the sheets on your bed.

(f) Supervising your bath-time.

(g) Picking you up from school.

(h) Buying a present for you to take to another child's birthday party.

(i) Reassuring you if you had a bad dream in the night.

(j) Anticipating that you needed a new pair of shoes because you were about to grow out of your old pair.

Now examine the following table.

	MALE PARTNER	FEMALE PARTNER	SHARED
Plastering	32	4	2
Tidying up	2	67	23
Cooking	4	77	17
Checking car oil	79	9	2
Bathing children	22	44	33

Adapted from A. Warde (1990) 'Domestic divisions of labour', *Social Studies Review*, vol. 6, no. 1

2 What does the table above tell us about the distribution of household tasks?

3 In the light of the first exercise, what do you think are the weaknesses of the table data?

4 What other aspects of power and control in the home are neglected if we only focus on household tasks?

In 1973, Willmott and Young claimed that the traditional **segregated division of labour in the home** – men as bread-winners and women as housewives/mothers – was breaking down. The relationship between husband and wife (the conjugal relationship) was becoming – at least in middle-class families – more joint or '**symmetrical**'. This trend towards **egalitarian** marriage was caused by the decline in the extended family, and its replacement in the late twentieth century by the **privatised nuclear family**, as well as by the increasing opportunities in paid employment for women.

But the exercise above should have shown you that much of women's labour in the home is neglected by studies that focus only on obvious and highly visible tasks. A good deal of what women do in the home is mental and emotional as well as physical, involving anticipating and fulfilling the needs of family members. These more subtle responsibilities tend to be missed by researchers, some of whom have concluded that men and women are becoming more equal in the home – on the basis of their sharing some of the more glamorous domestic tasks, such as cooking. These sorts of surveys can also miss other influences that ensure that power and control in the

home remain firmly in male hands – violence, the lack of status associated with the mother–housewife role, the belief that working mothers damage children, the fact that being a mother limits job opportunities, and so on.

Studies of housework and childcare

The idea that equality is a central characteristic of marriage is strongly opposed by feminist sociologists. Studies of professional couples indicate that only a minority genuinely share housework and childcare. Similarly, studies of unemployed men indicate that, although they do more around the home, their wives, even when working full-time, do the lion's share of housework and childcare. Some sociologists have suggested that unemployed men resist increased involvement in housework because it threatens their masculinity, especially if their wife is the main income-earner.

A survey carried out for the insurance firm Legal & General in April 2000 found that full-time working mothers spent 56 hours per week on housework and childcare, compared with men's 31 hours. This increased to 84 hours if the women had children aged 3 and under. The Future

Foundation survey of October 2000 was more positive. It found that women were receiving more help in the home from husbands and boyfriends. Two-thirds of men said they did more around the home than their fathers. However, even at this rate, women will have to wait until at least 2015 before tasks are shared equally!

The quantifiable evidence therefore indicates that women are still likely to have a '**dual burden**' – they are expected to be mainly responsible for the bulk of domestic tasks despite holding down full-time jobs. Women are also responsible for the emotional well-being of their partners and children. The hard work involved in trying to please all parties in the home may lead to the neglect of their own psychological well-being, and have negative consequences for their mental and physical health.

Decision-making

Some sociologists have focused on the distribution of power within marriages. Edgell (1980) discovered that middle-class wives generally deferred to their husbands in decision-making. Edgell concluded that the men in his sample were able to demand that the interests of their wives and families be subordinated to the man's career, because he was the main breadwinner. Similarly, surveys of young married couples with children conclude that the decision to have children, although jointly reached, dramatically changes the life of the mother rather than the father. However, Gillian Leighton (1992) discovered that the power to make decisions changed when males became unemployed. In her study of professional couples, working wives often took over responsibility for bills and initiated cutbacks in spending.

Fatherhood

In the early 1990s, many sociologists concluded that the role of fathers was changing. For example, men in the 1990s were more likely to attend the birth of their babies than men in the 1960s, and they were more likely to play a greater role in childcare than their own fathers. Burghes (1997) found that fathers were taking an increasingly active role in the emotional development of their children. Beck (1992) notes that in the post-modern age fathers can no longer rely on jobs to provide a sense of identity and fulfilment. Increasingly, they look to their children to give them a sense of identity and purpose. However, it is important not to exaggerate men's role in childcare. Looking after children is still overwhelmingly the responsibility of mothers rather than jointly shared with fathers.

Patriarchal ideology

Feminists have highlighted the influence of patriarchal ideology (see Unit 1, Topic 7) on the perceptions of both husbands and wives. Surveys indicate that many women accept primary responsibility for housework and childcare without question, and believe that their career should be secondary to that of their husband. Such ideas are also reflected in state policy which encourages female economic dependence upon men. Moreover, patriarchal ideology expects women to take on jobs that are compatible with family commitments. Surveys suggest that a large number of mothers feel guilty about working.

Some actually give up work altogether because they believe that their absence somehow damages their children.

The housewife experience

The housewife role has low status compared with paid work, and this may lead to feelings of boredom, loneliness and dissatisfaction. Consequently some housewives may see themselves as worthless or as mere extensions of their husbands and children. They may see themselves as redundant when their children grow up and leave home. Such feelings may be responsible for the high levels of depression experienced by women in modern industrial societies. Feminists would argue that these findings are yet further evidence of inequalities within marriage.

The mother–housewife role and work

Some feminist sociologists have concluded that women's participation in the labour market is clearly limited by their domestic responsibilities. Because of these responsibilities, very few women have continuous full-time careers. Mothers, then, tend to have 'jobs', while their husbands have 'careers'. As a result, women don't have the same access to promotion and training opportunities as men. Some employers may believe that women are unreliable because of family commitments and consequently discriminate against them.

Modern marriages appear far from equal. On all the criteria examined so far – the distribution of housework and childcare tasks, decision-making, and the impact of being a mother–housewife on employment – we see women at a disadvantage compared with men.

Moreover, an important aspect of power within marriage is domestic violence – the power of men to control women by physical force. This type of violence is estimated to be the most common type of violence in Britain. Many women fail to report it because they feel they may not be taken seriously or because they are afraid of the repercussions. Some feminists would argue that so long as men have the capacity to commit such violence there can never be equality within marriage.

Theoretical explanations of inequalities in power and control in families

There are three major theoretical perspectives on the distribution of power and control in the family:

1 Functionalists see the sexual division of labour in the home as biologically inevitable. Women are naturally suited to the caring and emotional role.
2 Marxist-feminists argue that the housewife role serves the needs of capitalism in that it maintains the present workforce and reproduces future labour-power.
3 Radical feminists such as Delphy (1984) believe that 'the first oppression is the oppression of women by men – women are an exploited class'. The housewife role is therefore a role created by patriarchy and geared to the service of men and their interests. Like functionalism, both Marxist and radical forms of feminism see women's exploitation and oppression as rooted in their biological role as mothers.

Criticisms of these theories

- These theories fail to explain why women's roles vary across different cultures. For example, the mother–housewife role does not exist in all societies.
- Feminism may be guilty of devaluing the mother–housewife role as a 'second-class' role. For many women, housework and childcare, like paid work, have real and positive meaning. Such work may be invested with meaning for women because it is 'work done for love' and it demonstrates their commitment to their families. Thus, boring, routine work may be transformed into satisfying, caring work.
- Feminists may under-estimate the degree of power that women actually enjoy. Women are concerned about the amount of housework men do, but they are probably more concerned about whether men show enough gratitude or whether men listen to them, etc. The fact that many women divorce their husbands indicates that they have the power to leave a relationship if they are unhappy with it. Catherine Hakim (1996) suggests that feminists under-estimate women's ability to make rational choices. It is not patriarchy or men that are responsible for the position of women in families. She argues that women choose to give more commitment to family and children, and consequently they have less commitment to work than men have.

Whatever your favoured perspective, it appears that the view that a 'new man' is emerging – sharing domestic tasks, engaging emotionally with women and showing interest in developing his fathering skills – is an over-optimistic picture of life in many **conjugal relationships**.

Exploring power and control in the family

Item A

Working mothers spend more hours a week on housework than on their full-time job, a survey revealed yesterday. The survey of 543 parents of children under 18 was carried out for Legal & General. It found that full-time working mothers spend 56 hours a week on housework, part-time working mothers do 68 hours and housewives put in 76 hours, while fathers do only 31. Mothers spend around 14 hours a week cooking compared with fathers' four hours, and 21 hours washing and ironing compared with eight-and-a-half hours for men. Mothers clean for 13 hours a week compared with their husbands' four hours, and women spend about an hour sewing compared with 10 minutes for men. Fathers do four hours a week of gardening, an hour more than mothers.

Guardian, 10 March 2000

Item B

Relationships of power and intimacy are difficult to research, especially within the family, but there is evidence that, where wives are in full-time employment, there is a tendency towards a more democratic relationship within marriage. However, generally studies indicate that inequality rather than symmetry is the defining characteristic of the majority of present-day marriages. Recent research has focused on an exploration of the perceptions of couples in relation to the fairness of their division of household labour. Hochschild notes that the relative satisfaction with the relationship is less to do with 'who does what' in the home than the giving and receiving of appreciation and gratitude and the sharing of social time together.

Adapted from M. Jones (1997) 'The symmetrical family revisited', *Sociology Review*, vol. 6, no. 3

CHECK YOUR UNDERSTANDING

1 **What did Willmott and Young claim about conjugal roles in the 1970s?**

2 **What have recent surveys concluded about the distribution of domestic tasks between husbands and wives?**

3 **In what circumstances might wives acquire more power over decision-making in the home?**

4 **What do studies generally conclude about women's experience of the mother–housewife role?**

5 **What effect does the mother–housewife role have on women's job opportunities?**

KEY TERMS

Conjugal relationship – the relationship between married or cohabiting partners.

Dual burden – refers to wives taking responsibility for the bulk of domestic tasks as well as holding down full-time jobs.

Egalitarian – based on equality.

Privatised nuclear family – a home-centred family that has little contact with extended kin or neighbours.

Segregated division of labour in the home – a traditional sexual division of labour in which women take responsibility for housework and mothering, and men take responsibility for being the breadwinner and head of the household.

Symmetrical – similar or corresponding.

Item C

Why does such a pronounced division of domestic labour persist? Women who continue to see housework and childcare as an essential part of being a 'good wife and mother' are more likely to be satisfied with an unequal domestic division of labour than women who reject such roles. Baxter and Western (1998) argue that women may deal with situations over which they have little control by defining them as 'satisfactory'. Men may have inflexible and demanding work schedules that make it difficult for them to meet family obligations. However, in criticism of this, men do tend to have greater control and freedom over how they spend their time outside of work. Women are often unable to 'clock on and off' from their caring responsibilities. The most plausible explanation for the persistence of an unequal domestic division of labour is that it suits men and so they resist change.

Adapted from M. Leonard (2000) 'Back to the future: the domestic division of labour', *Sociology Review*, vol. 10, no. 2

Item D

The report 'Fathers and Fatherhood in Britain' by Louie Burghes directly challenges the idea that men are abandoning a role in the family.

The report found that, increasingly, fathers are taking an active involvement in the emotional side of child-rearing. Despite continuing to be the main earner in the family and working long hours, fathers are tending to spend more time with their children. The amount of time fathers spent with children was found to have increased fourfold over a generation between 1961 and 1995.

M. Denscombe (1998) *Sociology Update*, Leicester: Olympus Books

1 Explain what is meant by the phrase 'unequal domestic division of labour' (Item C). (2)

2 Identify two ways in which Item A confirms that a traditional sexual division of labour still exists in the modern family. (4)

3 Identify three reasons why the sexual division of labour continues to persist, according to Item C. (6)

4 Identify and briefly describe two ways in which the mother–housewife role may limit women's employment opportunities. (8)

5 Using information from the Items and elsewhere, discuss the view that the distribution of domestic tasks between husband and wife has become equal. (20)

6 Using information from the Items and elsewhere, assess explanations for inequalities in the domestic division of labour. (20)

Extension activities

1 Conduct a survey of parents using the list of tasks in the 'Getting you thinking' exercise on p. 60. An interesting variation is to ask parents separately whether they think they and their partners are doing enough around the home.

2 Using sources such as *Sociology Review*, newspaper archives and websites such as www.bennett.com/ptv/ – from which you can download *Prone to Violence* by Erin Pizzey – research and prepare a report on the subject of domestic violence.

3 Interview a selection of mothers in different social situations – e.g. full-time mothers, those who have full-time or part-time jobs, those who have children who have left home, etc. Attempt to construct an interview schedule that measures how they feel about the mother–housewife role.

Question for students taking OCR exam board AS level

4 (a) Identify and explain two ways in which fatherhood has changed in the last 20 years. (20 marks)

(b) Outline and discuss the view that the old domestic divisions of labour persist in the twenty-first century. (40 marks)

Education

Getting you thinking

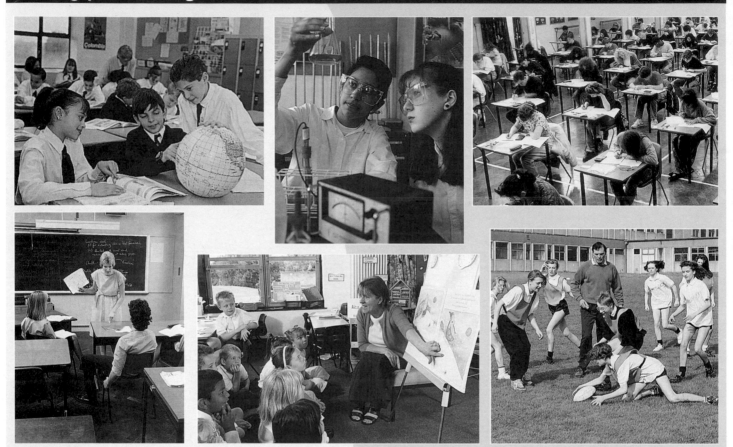

1 **Look at the photographs above. Using these and any other ideas you may have, make a list of the purposes of school for:**
   (a) individuals
   (b) society as a whole

2 **Is there anything that occurs in schools that you feel has no purpose? If so, what?**

3 **What have you really learned at school/college this week? Who will gain from your acquiring this knowledge, set of attitudes or skills?**

4 **Could you learn effectively without school?**

5 **Would society suffer if schools did not exist? Explain your answer.**

The education system is one of the most influential institutions in society. It takes individuals from the age of 4 or 5, for six or so hours per day, over a period of at least eleven years. It bombards them with a vast amount of knowledge, attitudes and skills. These are acquired either formally through set lessons or informally through what is known as the **hidden curriculum** – the processes involved in being 'schooled' and the various interactions that take place whilst in school. By the time they finish compulsory education most pupils will have spent over 15,000 hours in lessons.

So why do modern societies invest so much in **schooling** the next generation? Some of the answers can be found by looking at the introduction of compulsory education over 100 years ago.

The introduction of compulsory education

Children of the upper and middle classes have always had the option of private schooling, but **state education** for all has only been available in Britain since 1880, when it was made compulsory for all children up to the age of 10. There were a number of reasons for the introduction of compulsory education:

● *To create a more skilled workforce*
   Many employers believed that the new industrial society required a numerate, literate workforce able to cope with the complexities of modern industrial production. Britain could then compete with other countries, and employers would maintain and increase their profits.

- ***To improve the effectiveness of our armies***
  The high casualties of the Crimean War (1854–6) were seen as partly due to inexperience and poor tactics. Better-trained, fitter soldiers (who could read, write and count) might have given Britain a better showing.
- ***To re-socialise the feckless (aimless or wasteful) poor***
  Many Victorians felt that the working classes were poor through their own fault – spending unwisely, drinking too much and living immorally. They needed to be taught to lead a more responsible and respectable life.
- ***To reduce the level of street crime***
  Remember *Oliver Twist*? Many felt that compulsory schooling would get young pickpockets 'off the streets', thus reducing the high levels of petty theft.
- ***To ward off the threat of revolution***
  The upper classes feared the 'tide of socialism' that was 'sweeping' through Europe. (After all, Marx himself was writing throughout the period leading up to the introduction of compulsory education.) Free education could, on the one hand, make the ruling classes appear generous, and, on the other, serve to **ideologically control** the masses. They would learn to respect authority, follow instructions and conform to rules.
- ***To provide a 'human right'***
  Many **liberal** thinkers felt that education could improve the life experience of all citizens, including the working class.

Many of the above influences are still shaping the modern education system. The introduction of 'Key Skills', numeracy and literacy in primary schools, and all the developments in **vocational education** (discussed in Topic 6), reflect continuing concern about the skills levels of the workforce. Similarly, the importance of discipline and rules in schools indicates that the social control of young people is still a priority.

Most sociologists agree that education is important, both in teaching skills and in encouraging certain attitudes and values, but they disagree about why this occurs and who benefits from it.

Functionalist approach

Functionalists argue that education has three broad functions:

1 **Socialisation** – education helps to maintain society by socialising young people into key cultural values, such as achievement, individualism, competition, **equality of opportunity**, social solidarity, democracy and religious morality.

2 **Skills provision** – education teaches the skills required by a modern industrial society. These may be general skills that everyone needs, such as literacy and numeracy, or the specific skills needed for particular occupations.
3 **Role allocation** – education allocates people to the most appropriate job for their talents, using examinations and qualifications. This is seen to be fair because there is equality of opportunity – everyone has the chance to achieve success in society on the basis of their ability.

Marxist approach

Marxists challenge the functionalist approach. Althusser (1972) disagrees that the main function of education is the transmission of common values. Rather, he argues that education is an ideological state apparatus (see Unit 2, Topic 2). Its main function is to maintain, legitimate (justify) and reproduce, generation by generation, class inequalities in wealth and power, by transmitting ruling-class or capitalist values disguised as common values. Althusser argues that this is done through the hidden curriculum – conformity to the capitalist system and acceptance of failure and inequality are encouraged in working-class people, through the knowledge that is taught in schools and the way that schools are organised.

Bowles and Gintis (1976) argue that education serves to directly reproduce the **capitalist relations of production** – the hierarchy of workers from the boss down – with the appropriate skills and attitudes. Education ensures that workers will unquestioningly adapt to the needs of the system, without criticism.

Bowles and Gintis suggest that what goes on in school directly corresponds to the world of work. Teachers are like the bosses, and pupils are like the workers, who work for rewards (wages or exam success). The higher up the system the individual progresses, however, the more personal freedom they have to control their own educational or working experiences, and the more responsibility they have for the outcomes.

Bowles and Gintis point out, however, that success is not entirely related to intellectual ability. Those pupils who fit in and conform rise above those who challenge the system. This explains why white middle-class pupils tend to do better. Schools therefore reproduce sets of workers with the appropriate outlook for the position that they come to occupy.

Functionalists see education as turning pupils into model citizens, whilst Marxists argue that it merely turns working-class kids into conformist workers. However, despite their differences, functionalist and Marxist accounts of education do

Bowles and Gintis: the correspondence between school and work

share some similarities – for example, they are both structuralist theories (see Unit 1, Topic 2) in that they see social institutions as more important than individuals. Consequently they do not pay much attention to what actually goes on in classrooms or to the views and feelings of teachers and pupils.

An alternative view: Paul Willis

Paul Willis (1977) provides a major critique of both perspectives when he points out that both theories are **deterministic**. This means that they both see pupils as passive products of the educational system. Both theories, argues Willis, fail to take into account the tendency of many pupils to resist these processes. (After all, are most kids in your experience docile 'teacher's pets'?)

Willis's study identified pro-school and anti-school subcultures (see Unit 1, Topic 4) which were nicknamed the 'earoles' and the 'lads' respectively. 'Earoles' did what teachers expected of them, whereas the 'lads' took little notice of school rules, teachers and work – they substituted their own definitions of what school was about, based on 'having a laff'. However, in developing these strategies to cope with the boredom of school, the 'lads' were also developing a way of coping with the boring and routine type of job that they would ultimately end up in. Even rebellion, says Willis, is reproducing the right type of workforce needed for the capitalist system – a workforce who are uncritical and 'just get on with it'.

Willis's study is a good example of an **eclectic** approach to sociology. He uses an **ethnographic, interactionist** approach to understand the meanings pupils give to their schooling, then applies a Marxist perspective to explain them. Other writers have more recently applied some of Willis's ideas to present-day anti-school subcultures (see Topic 5).

Approaches such as Marxism and functionalism, which relate educational experiences to wider society, as well as interactionism, which focuses more on the actual workings of the school, feature throughout the sociology of education, so it is important to have a basic grasp of these theories. Check Unit 1, Topics 1–4 to remind yourself if you are unsure of them.

Item A

If Britain is ever to achieve industrial and economic prosperity again, schools should encourage competition, discipline, decency, self-reliance and eventually prosperity through a return to hard work, selection, higher standards and biblical morality. We must make it clear to children that there is a distinction between work and play. The playground is the playground, available in short doses for the release of high spirits and horseplay. The classroom, where such are still to be found, is a place where the dominant value is work, labelled as such, and not disguised as anything else. It should be a place where results are expected against a certain time schedule; a place where children should learn, as early and as frequently as possible, the satisfaction, joy and legitimate pride of being stretched to the very limit of their capacity and thereby turning in as faultless a piece of work as they can manage; a place where the teacher gets it across that our second best is not good enough; a place where the shortcomings of even the worst homes are to some extent rectified and not used as a constant excuse for inaction. Schools should get a hard grip on the surly, deceptive and uncooperative, at the earliest possible moment. It is imperative to support the hard-working, the inventive and the original. This means selection, ideally as sophisticated and even-handed as possible. We must toughen up the educational process so that everything else – learning, creativity, technical skills, wealth-creating potential – can flourish properly. Appropriate parts of the Bible should be included in the teaching and examining of English. Children must learn biblical stories such as the Good Samaritan because the stories will speak for themselves.

Adapted from a speech made on 12 October 1984 by Tom Howarth, Senior Tutor, Cambridge University, quoted in R. Burgess (ed.) (1986) *Education, Schools and Schooling*, Walton-on-Thames: Thomas Nelson

CHECK YOUR UNDERSTANDING

1 **Give three of the main reasons why education was made compulsory in 1880.**

2 **According to functionalists, what are the main functions of schools?**

3 **What does Althusser consider to be the main purpose of education, and how is it achieved?**

4 **Why is the theory of Bowles and Gintis called 'correspondence' theory? Give examples.**

5 **Why, according to Bowles and Gintis, do white, middle-class pupils do better?**

6 **Who were the 'earoles' and the 'lads'?**

7 **How does Paul Willis challenge the traditional functionalist and Marxist accounts?**

KEY TERMS

Capitalist relations of production – how members of the workforce are organised in relation to each other under capitalism. (In capitalist industrial societies, this is usually hierarchical, with a few at the top making all the decisions and giving out orders, whilst the majority do what they are told.)

Deterministic – the view that a particular outcome is inevitable.

Eclectic – borrowing freely from various sources; in this context, mixing a range of explanatory approaches.

Equality of opportunity – every person having the same chances.

Ethnography – the study of social groups.

Hidden curriculum – the informal learning of particular values and attitudes in schools.

Extract 1

The space won from the school and its rules by the 'lads' is used for the shaping and development of particular cultural skills principally devoted to 'having a laff'. The 'laff' is of particular importance to the 'lads' – 'We can make them laff, they can't make us laff.' It is used in many contexts – to defeat boredom and fear, to overcome hardship and problems – as a way out of almost anything. The school is generally a fertile ground for the 'laff'. Specific themes of authority are explored, played with and used in their humour. ... When a teacher comes into the classroom he is told 'It's alright, Sir, the deputy's taking us, you can go. He said you can have the period off.' The 'lads' stop second and third years around the school and say 'Mr Argyle wants to see you, you're in trouble, I think.' Argyle's room is soon choked with worried kids.

Extract 2

Joey: On a Monday afternoon, we'd have nothing right? Nothing hardly relating to schoolwork, Tuesday afternoon we have swimming and they stick you in a classroom for the rest of the afternoon, Wednesday afternoon you have games and there's only Thursday and Friday afternoon that you work, if you call that work. The last lesson Friday afternoon we used to go and doss, half of us wagged out of lessons and the other half go into the classroom, sit down and just go to sleep ...

Spanksy: Skive this lesson, just go up on the bank, have a smoke, and the next lesson go to a teacher who, you know, will call the register ...

Bill: It's easy to go home as well. Last Wednesday, Eddie got his mark and went home ...

Eddie: I ain't supposed to be in school this afternoon, I'm supposed to be at college on a link course.

Paul Willis: What's the last time you did some writing?

Fuzz: Last time was in careers, 'cos I writ 'yes' on a piece of paper, that broke me heart 'cos I was going to try and go through the term without writing anything. 'Cos since we've come back, I ain't dun nothing [it was halfway through term].

P. Willis (1977) *Learning to Labour*, Aldershot: Ashgate

1. Explain in your own words what is meant by the 'hidden curriculum'. (2)

2. Suggest two ways in which the writer of Item A might like to see schools 'toughened up'. (4)

3. Suggest three ways in which the 'lads' described in Item B might 'have a laff' at school. (6)

4. Identify and briefly explain two reasons why the 'lads' (Item B) may have rejected the values of the school. (8)

5. Using information from the Items and elsewhere, examine the functionalist argument that schools serve the interests of both the individual and society. (20)

6. Using information from the Items and elsewhere, assess the Marxist view that education benefits the ruling class. (20)

Ideological control – getting people to behave in a desired way by convincing them that it is in their interests to behave in that way.

Interactionism – a sociological perspective that takes a small-scale approach to the study of society, focusing particularly on how individuals react to each other in specific social situations.

Liberals – open-minded people who believe in personal freedom, democracy (the involvement of everyone in decision-making) and the rights of others.

Schooling – the process of compulsory education.

State education – education provided by local and central governments.

Vocational education – education designed to teach the skills needed for particular occupations.

Extension activities

1. What values are the following aspects of school organisation and routine encouraging: assemblies, Speech Days, Sports Days, school uniform, registration, house competitions, school rules, prefects, detention?

2. Search for government educational policy documents and statements at www.dfee.gov.uk. What are the government's stated aims? How do these aims relate to the sociological views you have been introduced to in this Unit?

3. Organise a small research project to discover what people consider the primary purpose of education to be. Compare class, gender and age patterns in terms of the extent to which the wider social purposes are recognised. Which groups see school as most individually beneficial – for example, as helping someone to get a better job?

Getting you thinking

Science

The National Curriculum for England www.nc.uk.net

Key stages 1–4

Chailey School

"Committed to the success of each student"

SECONDARY SCHOOL PERFORMANCE TABLES 2000								
IMPROVEMENT: BLACKPOOL	5 or more grades A*–C				no passes			
	1997	1998	1999	2000	1997	1998	1999	2000
LEA average	-	34.6%	36.5%	36.1%	-	6.9%	7.3%	6.3%
England average	45.1%	46.3%	47.9%	49.2%	7.7%	6.6%	6.0%	5.6%
Arnold School	98%	92%	98%	91%	0%	2%	1%	8%
Beacon Hill High School	22%	25%	23%	21%	17%	5%	2%	3%
Bispham High School – an Arts College	41%	38%	40%	44%	10%	9%	6%	2%
Collegiate High School	32%	28%	34%	29%	7%	5%	9%	6%
Highfield High School	37%	34%	42%	38%	6%	6%	2%	4%
Montgomery High School	48%	54%	55%	55%	2%	1%	1%	6%
Palatine High School	16%	15%	21%	21%	12%	10%	5%	8%
St George's High School	15%	24%	15%	16%	15%	4%	4%	4%
St Mary's Catholic High School	48%	49%	50%	48%	11%	5%	9%	5%

1 **What is the National Curriculum?**

2 **How does the National Curriculum make it possible to test all the pupils of one age in 'SATs' (Standard Assessment Tests)?**

3 **Why do you think the government wants to test pupils?**

4 **Why do so many schools produce glossy brochures? Where does the money to produce these come from? What else could it be spent on?**

5 **Why have recent governments been keen to produce education 'league tables'?**

6 **Apart from improving quality, what can schools do to improve their position in league tables?**

7 **Why do you think the developments discussed here are sometimes referred to as the 'marketisation' of education?**

8 **What arguments can be put forward:**
(a) in favour of marketisation?
(b) against marketisation?

This Topic will examine some of the major changes in the organisation of the education system in England and Wales, and in particular the role that central government has come to play.

1944 to 1965

Until the Second World War (1939–45), children of the working classes attended elementary school up to the age of 14. The school-leaving age was then raised to 15 in 1947. Since its introduction in 1880, compulsory state education had been a fairly haphazard affair, controlled by local administrators who oversaw the provision of basic skills plus religious and moral instruction, with boys and girls often taught separately. Beyond this, the curriculum was different for each sex – girls were usually trained in domestic competence, and boys in technical skills. A small proportion of bright working-class children won scholarships to continue with free education in otherwise fee-paying schools that were mainly attended by the middle classes.

The tripartite system

As part of the aim to create a 'land fit for heroes' after the Second World War, Butler's Education Act of 1944 introduced 'secondary education for all'. The upper classes continued to be educated in the public schools and top universities. The Act had no effect upon their education. But it did aim to abolish class-based inequalities within education. A tripartite system was to be introduced, providing three types of school, each suited to one of three types of ability:

- grammar schools for the academic
- secondary technical schools for the artistic/creative
- secondary modern schools for everyone else

The basic principle underlying this system was 'equality of opportunity for all'. All children would take an IQ test at 11 in order to allocate them to a school suited to their abilities. Only those who 'passed' the 11+ test went to grammar or technical schools. All schools were supposed to have similar standards of provision, known as 'parity of esteem'.

Problems of the tripartite system

- Middle-class children were disproportionately selected for grammar schools, and working-class children for the secondary moderns. Many middle-class children who failed the 11+ were sent into private education by their parents.
- Working-class self-esteem was further damaged by the poor image secondary moderns had. 'Parity of esteem' did not happen, and employers, parents and children themselves generally viewed secondary moderns as inferior to grammar schools.
- It was felt by some that the IQ tests were culturally biased against working-class children.
- Very few technical schools were built, due to the greater cost of equipping them.
- Many were critical of the system because of the unfair way in which it operated. Girls were often sent to secondary moderns even though they had passed the 11+ because schools then were more commonly single-sex and there were fewer girls' grammar schools. Girls' marks were also adjusted downwards because it was assumed that boys

matured later.
- There were also regional variations. It was twice as easy to get into a grammar school in some parts of the country, compared with others, because the percentage of available places varied.

By the mid-1950s it was generally agreed that the tripartite system had failed in its aims. Educational attainment was overwhelmingly class-based – most working-class children left school at 15 and entered work, while middle-class children continued into further and higher education. Twenty per cent of the school population went to grammar schools, 5 per cent to technical schools, and 75 per cent to secondary moderns. A system that failed three-quarters of all schoolchildren was seen as a considerable wastage of talent – although many middle-class parents wanted to retain it. In an attempt to genuinely apply the principle of 'equality of opportunity for all' the tripartite system was abolished (although some areas resisted and continue the system until this day).

1965 to 1979

Comprehensive schools

In 1965, the Labour government instructed all local authorities to submit plans for comprehensive reorganisation. Comprehensive schools educated all children – regardless of class, gender, ethnicity and ability – under one roof. The aim was to promote both social justice and tolerance. A great deal of money was spent on upgrading facilities and on teacher training, so that these schools could not only maintain the standards of the grammar schools but also provide a broader curriculum and greater sporting and recreational opportunities.

The Labour government also embarked on a rapid expansion of higher education, creating more universities, the polytechnics and the Open University. All of these innovations were aimed at increasing working-class access to higher education. However, the public school system and its disproportionate access to Oxbridge (Oxford and Cambridge universities) remained intact.

In 1967, the Labour government set up six Educational Priority Areas (EPAs) in poverty-stricken areas of the UK, which received more cash and more teachers for primary schools. This was known as compensatory education (see Topic 3). The scheme was eventually abandoned in the 1970s having shown little sign of success.

'Progressive education' and mixed-ability teaching

The school-leaving age was raised to 16 in 1972, forcing all pupils to sit exams. Teachers had to find new ways of interesting this sometimes reluctant extra year-group. What was more significant was that many teachers had seen the damage caused by the labelling of pupils according to ability (both in the tripartite system and by streaming in comprehensive schools). Teachers began to experiment with mixed-ability teaching. They wanted to enable all pupils to achieve their maximum potential and, rather than teach all of the class the same thing at the same time, they believed that learning should be a process of guided discovery.

Figure 3.1 The changing educational system

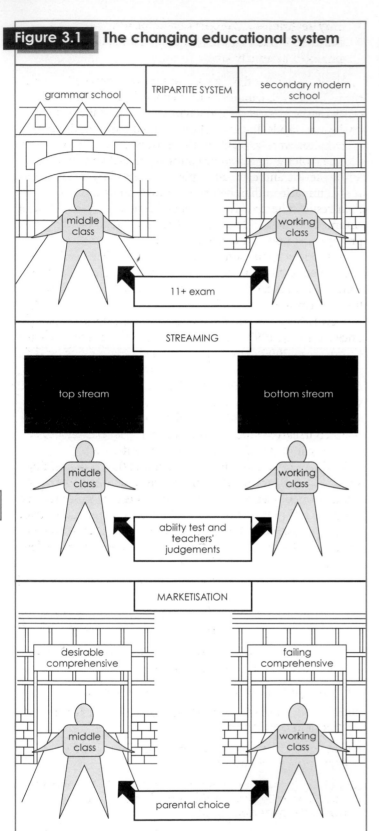

TRIPARTITE SYSTEM

grammar school — secondary modern school

11+ exam

middle class — working class

STREAMING

top stream — bottom stream

middle class — working class

ability test and teachers' judgements

MARKETISATION

desirable comprehensive — failing comprehensive

middle class — working class

parental choice

The education system has been altered in many ways over the last 50 years, usually with the aim of improving standards and increasing opportunities. However, these changes appear to have made little difference to class inequalities in educational achievement, which stubbornly persist.

Why is it that the middle classes always seem to gain the most benefit from educational change? You should get some ideas from both this topic and the next.

In the primary schools this came to be known as **progressive education** – as opposed to **traditional education** which involved strict discipline and teacher instruction. In the secondary schools, mode 3 exams were introduced, which allowed the teachers to write syllabuses that included coursework and to set exams that better reflected their students' background. These were only at CSE level (equivalent to GCSE grades C–G). O levels co-existed for brighter pupils until 1988 (GCSE grades A–C).

By the late 1960s, critics were claiming that progressive education was neglecting the '3 Rs' (Reading, wRiting, aRithmetic), and that standards had fallen. Conservative opposition to what was seen as Labour's educational initiative grew throughout the 1970s.

Comprehensives, especially in the inner cities, were frequently attacked for lack of discipline, poor results, truancy and large class sizes. In 1976, the Labour prime minister, James Callaghan, initiated the 'Great Education Debate', which aimed to address the alleged decline in British education. The opposition education minister, Margaret Thatcher, eventually became prime minister in 1979, and teachers were never to have the freedom to exercise their professional autonomy ever again.

1979 to 1988

Conservative education policy in the 1980s was characterised by:

- An emphasis on preparing young people for work and industry. A number of measures such as the introduction of Youth Training Schemes and work experience in schools became known as the **'new vocationalism'** (see Topic 6 for more details).
- A renewed focus on selection. In 1980 the **Assisted Places Scheme** was introduced, giving bright working-class pupils free places in public schools if they passed the school's entrance exam.

KEY TERMS

11+ – IQ test taken at the age of 11 to determine what sort of school you would attend under the tripartite system.

Assisted Places Scheme – a scheme whereby the government funds bright students from the state sector to attend public schools.

City Technology Colleges – schools funded partly by industry, aimed at giving extra opportunities to inner city pupils.

Compensatory education – making more resources available to schools in poorer areas in order to compensate (make up) for deprivation.

Curriculum 2000 – a complete revision of post-16 education, whereby students in their first year take more subjects and may mix academic and vocational subjects – at a level between GCSE and A level. They then specialise in fewer subjects at full A level in the second year. Additionally, many acquire a Key Skills qualification.

Grant maintained schools – schools funded directly by central government rather than local authority. They do not have to conform to local authority guidelines, e.g. on selection.

IQ tests – supposedly objective tests that establish a person's 'intelligence quotient' (how clever they are).

- Centralisation and a rejection of localised policy and provision. Local funding that reflected social deprivation was felt to have been excessive and wasteful, especially where Labour-controlled local authorities were involved. Other ways of funding schools were introduced, invariably at the expense of poorer areas, but good for the government in terms of middle-class votes.

1988 to the present day

The most influential legislation since 1944 was introduced with the 1988 Education Reform Act:

- The Assisted Places Scheme was expanded.
- All pupils would study the **National Curriculum** – this would involve the same subject content at various key stages from the age of 7 to 16, in maths, English, science, history, geography, technology, music, art, physical education (PE) and a modern language. It would include only 10–20 per cent of optional subjects, with more options allowed at GCSE (the new exam standard to replace CSE and O level).
- Pupils would sit national tests (**SATS**) at 7, 11 and 14, and these would be used to draw up **league tables** which would inform parents of each school's performance.
- Schools could decide for themselves how to manage their budgets or, if they wished, opt out of local authority control altogether, and become **grant maintained** schools, which could make their own decisions about how to recruit pupils. They could select on the basis of ability if they wished.
- **Marketisation** – parents would be allowed to choose which school to send their children to. The restrictions on entry were removed, allowing popular schools to expand, whilst unpopular schools might be closed. Increased competition between schools for pupils would, it was hoped, drive standards up further.

- **City Technology Colleges** were to be introduced, co-funded by industry, to provide special opportunities for pupils in inner city areas.

Many critics felt that the Act was more concerned to reduce the power of the Labour-controlled local authorities; and concerns were expressed over the damaging stressful effects of testing on pupils. **Parental choice** was largely a myth, as few extra places were available in the most popular schools. League tables were felt to be counter-productive by many, as low achievers and difficult pupils were less likely to be entered for examinations than before, because schools did not want their results affected. The National Curriculum has since been slimmed down, and the extent of testing was reduced after protests from overburdened teachers.

In the 1990s, the Conservatives turned their attention to post-16 education. In 1992 they removed further education colleges from local authority control; and a report on curriculum reform was initiated in 1996.

New Labour inherited many of these new initiatives and, once elected in 1997, took forward most of them to introduce **Curriculum 2000.** Post-16 students had long been criticised for being too narrowly specialised in their studies and lacking essential skills for higher education and employment. Also, the **vocational**/academic divide (the lack of 'parity of esteem' between vocational students studying on BTEC, GNVQ and NVQ courses and students studying A levels) was seen to be depriving industry of the brightest students.

With the introduction of Curriculum 2000, more mixing of academic and vocational studies is now possible, and the number of courses has increased. Students now study four or five AS levels (a level between GCSE and A level), rather than three A levels, plus a **Key Skills** qualification. They then continue with the subjects they wish to specialise in at full A level (A2) in the second year.

Key Skills – competence in communication, application of number and information technology as applied to post-16 study and taking the form of both assessed portfolio evidence and achievement in external written tests at a range of levels of difficulty.

League tables – rank ordering of schools according to their test and examination results.

Marketisation – refers to the move towards educational provision being determined by market forces.

Mixed-ability teaching – teaching pupils together, regardless of their ability.

National Curriculum – what every pupil in every state school must learn, decided by the government.

New vocationalism – a series of measures in the 1980s that re-emphasised the importance of work-related education.

Open University – university set up to provide a means of acquiring degree-level education by distance learning, via correspondence, video and TV.

Oxbridge – the collection of colleges forming Oxford and Cambridge universities.

Parental choice – refers to parents being able to choose which schools to send their children to.

Parity of esteem – equal status, equally valued.

Progressive education – child-centred approaches to teaching and learning.

Public schools – the top private fee-paying schools, e.g. Eton, Harrow, Roedean.

SATs (Standard Attainment Tests) – tests for 7-, 11- and 14-year-olds in English, maths and science. Used to compare school performance.

Secondary education – education between ages 11–16.

Social exclusion – term used to describe the situation where people are unable to achieve a quality of life that would be regarded as acceptable by most people.

Streaming – where pupils are taught in groups according to their perceived ability.

Traditional education – teacher-directed approaches to teaching and learning.

Vocational – work-related.

New Labour also introduced many initiatives of their own, including the abolition of higher education grants and the extension of student loans. They tried to tackle **'social exclusion'** by improving educational opportunities for the long-term unemployed and single mothers. Grant maintained schools were re-named 'foundation schools'. They no longer receive grants from central government, but they still retain special status and therefore have a great deal of control over how they recruit pupils.

The general thrust of change has been towards a system that is standardised, measurable, accountable and cost-effective. This has involved the removal of teachers' power to decide what is best for their pupils – this is now decided by central government. At various points in the process, sociological thinking has either informed change or been critical of it. This is especially apparent in sociological explanations of differential educational attainment – i.e. why some social groups do better or worse than others – as the following sections will show.

Exploring how education has changed

Item A

The 1970s and early 1980s witnessed a growing support for mixed-ability teaching in the UK. Studies had highlighted the ways in which setting and streaming created and maintained inequalities, particularly for working-class and ethnic minority students. Schools appeared to be receptive to the results of these and subsequent research studies, which fitted with the more widespread concern for educational equality at that time. However, in the 1990s, large numbers of schools have returned to policies of setting. This turn-around does not seem to have occurred because schools have forgotten about the reported consequences of setting, (i.e. the negative impact of labelling pupils, low self-esteem, anti-school cultures), nor because they have ceased to be concerned about educational equality. Rather, schools appear to be responding to a set of policies, arising directly and indirectly from the Education Reform Act, that have forced them to turn their attention away from equality and towards academic success, particularly for the most able.

The ERA required schools to adopt a National Curriculum, and research has shown that a number of teachers regard this curriculum as incompatible with mixed-ability teaching. This is partly because of its levelled nature and, related to this, the introduction of a tiered examination system. The creation of an educational 'marketplace', which forces schools to compete with each other for students, also means that schools have become concerned to create images that are popular with the parents of 'valued' students. Both setting and streaming appear to be regarded as positive school qualities, particularly amongst the middle-class parents that schools generally want to attract. The establishment of league tables, which position schools in order of their GCSE results, also forces schools to pay more attention to potential high achievers than other students. This has impacted upon setting policies via a widespread belief that setting enhances achievement for high ability.

Adapted from J. Boaler (1996) 'Setting, social class and survival of the quickest', a paper presented at the Annual British Educational Research Association Conference, University of Lancaster

Item B

The parents who chea for their children

Faced with the reality that 1 in 5 children is now denied their first choice of school (1 in 2 in London), parents desperate to squeeze their children into schools with high league table positions will resort to desperate measures. Their tactics include: claiming that they are on the verge of moving to an area; using a relative's address; or even temporarily splitting up, renting a flat for one partner close to the preferred school, and registering as the child's address, and then getting back together once the child has been secured a place. Others are prepared to pay up to £2,500 a month in rent, or to move permanently to a usually smaller house in the 'better' are of the school. Such tactics are clearly only possible for certain social classes.

Adapted from L. Ward, *Independent*, 17 April 1997

Item C

Ex-private [fee-paying] school students hold upwards of 75 per cent of the top jobs in British institutions, including the government, the civil service, the church, the legal system, the armed forces and the financial system in the City. Yet, they make up only about 7 per cent of the school population. Furthermore, those who control these institutions come overwhelmingly from a few exclusive schools – for example, Eton, Harrow, Winchester and Westminster – and have attended Oxford or Cambridge universities (the so-called Oxbridge connection).

Those who occupy the top jobs perpetuate these inequalities in two ways:
- by sending their own sons and daughters to these same schools;
- by appointing new recruits to top jobs from these schools.

This restrictive elite self-recruitment is known as the old boy (or school tie) network.

(Public schools don't have to follow the National Curriculum, nor are their teachers inspected by central government officers.)

Adapted from M. Denscombe (1993) Sociology Update, Leicester: Olympus Books

1 How was the education system organised prior to 1944?

2 Why was Butler's Education Act introduced?

3 Why did the idea of 'parity of esteem' not work?

4 What were the aims of progressive education?

5 How did the 1988 Education Reform Act seek to create a uniform and more efficient system?

6 Why would critics argue that the Act was more concerned to curb the influence of Labour-controlled local authorities?

7 Why was post-16 education reformed?

1 Explain what is meant by 'labelling pupils' (Item A). (2)

2 Identify two reasons why many schools have moved away from mixed-ability teaching (Item A). (4)

3 Suggest three ways in which someone in a 'top job' can attempt to ensure that their sons and daughters attain a position of similar status (Item C). (6)

4 Identify and briefly explain two reasons why it is more likely that middle-class parents will get their children into their first-choice school (Item B). (8)

5 Using material from the Items and elsewhere, examine the sociological arguments and evidence in favour of the view that changes to the education system have resulted in greater equality of opportunity for all pupils. (20)

6 Using material from the Items and elsewhere, assess the view that the main thrust of educational reform has been to increase the control of education by those outside the education system. (20)

Extension activities

1 Conduct a survey on a sample of adults over the age of 45, including ex-grammar and ex-secondary modern school pupils. Compare their experiences in terms of teacher expectations, personal feelings, attitudes to school, the curriculum, examination success, age at leaving education, final job/career.

2 Interview an experienced member of your school or college staff. Ask them to describe the impact that the following changes had upon their educational career and experiences:
   (a) The introduction of the National Curriculum, school/college inspections, league tables, competition between schools/colleges, parental choice
   (b) The introduction of Curriculum 2000, including new AS levels and Key Skills

Getting you thinking

Children from working-class backgrounds:

- are less likely to be found in nursery schools or pre-school play-groups
- are more likely to start school unable to read
- are more likely to fall behind in reading, writing and number skills
- are more likely to be placed in lower sets or streams
- are more likely to get fewer GCSEs or low grades
- are more likely to leave school at the age of 16
- are less likely to go on into the sixth form and on to university

It seems obvious: our educational success or failure is simply the result of our ability and motivation. When sociologists look at educational achievement, however, they find that there are distinct patterns. It seems that ability and motivation are closely linked to membership of certain social groups.

Ethnicity and class: patterns of achievement

Differential educational attainment refers to the tendency for some groups to do better or worse than others in terms of educational success. The issue was initially considered by sociologists solely in terms of class, but some ethnic minorities share the same experiences because they tend also to be working-class. Research by Drew (1995) examined the relative impact of class, gender and ethnicity on educational attainment. Whilst class was clearly the most important factor, Afro-Caribbean males were still at the bottom of each class group in terms of attainment. However, West Indian females, although they suffer from initial disadvantages in school, tend to do even better than white pupils by the time they take their GCSEs. Fuller (1984) suggests that they may appear 'cool' in order to present a positive self-image to boys and teachers, but that they recognise the importance of getting good qualifications.

Indian, Chinese and African-Asian children also do very well within the education system. There is a strong emphasis on self-improvement through education within these cultures, and many of the children have professional backgrounds, providing support, appropriate role models and material advantages. Their culture is perceived more positively by teachers than that of West Indian males. In addition to all of the points listed above (for children from working-class backgrounds), West Indian males:

- tend to get fewer GCSEs and poorer grades than any other group
- are over-represented in special schools for children with behavioural or learning difficulties
- tend to get expelled or suspended up to four times more often than their white counterparts

Some Pakistani and Bangladeshi children do relatively badly in school, but recent research has shown these groups to be catching up. The length of time Asian immigrant groups have lived in Britain varies. Those who have been here longer achieve more highly in the education system, because older siblings, educated here, are able to help their younger brothers and sisters. Also, reflecting changes within the white community, females generally tend to perform better than males (see Topic 4).

Explanations of differential educational attainment

Differential educational attainment has been explained in a number of ways.

Material deprivation

Certain groups have less money than others and so are not able to make the most of their educational opportunities. They may not have the time and space at home to do schoolwork; they

1 Make a list of possible explanations for the points in the list on the left. Use the photographs to help you.

2 Compare your list with those of others. Rank the explanations you have identified in order, with the most important first.

3 Explain why you have ranked some explanations higher than others.

may not be able to raise money for educational trips; and they may not have access to educational materials such as books, computers and the internet. They may experience ill health, have to work part-time to support their studies, or have to care for younger siblings. As most ethnic minorities tend to be working-class, these material disadvantages translate into educational disadvantages in the same way as for the working class.

Governments have attempted to reduce the material disadvantages faced by working-class pupils through **positive discrimination**. This takes the form of programmes of compensatory education which plough more resources into poorer areas. The Conservative government in the 1990s allocated up to 25 per cent more money to local authorities in poor areas; and the introduction of **Educational Action Zones** by the Labour government in the late 1990s was also an attempt to raise standards by compensating for deprivation.

Cultural disadvantages

The education system is mostly controlled by middle-class people, many of whom are white. Those who share these characteristics may well be viewed more positively and be more likely to succeed in the tests and exams created to assess their abilities. The 11+ test (see Topic 2) was criticised for middle-class bias. Being able to unscramble an anagram (a jumbled-up word) such as 'ZOMRAT' to form the name of a famous composer (MOZART) is much easier for a child familiar with anagrams (because their parents do crosswords) and classical composers (because they have seen their names on CD covers in their parents' music collection). Many working-class and ethnic minority pupils may feel under-valued and demotivated by an educational system that does not recognise *their* qualities, which are based on their class and ethnic culture.

West Indian under-achievement has been blamed on the high numbers of one-parent families in Afro-Caribbean communities. Some politicians have suggested that, because many of these families are female-headed, West Indian boys, in particular, lack the discipline of a father-figure, and this, they suggest, may account for the high percentage of West Indians in special schools. For girls, on the other hand, the role model provided by a strong, independent single mother is a motivating influence, and this helps to explain their relative success in education. However, although a slightly higher number of West Indians do live in one-parent families, it should be noted that most West Indian children live in nuclear families.

Much (now dated) research into language has identified class differences in spoken and written language which disadvantage working-class children. The middle classes succeed not because of greater intelligence but merely because they use the preferred way of communicating. Language has also been seen as a problem for West Indian children, who may speak different dialects of English; and children from other ethnic groups may come from homes where a language other than English is spoken. This language difference may cause problems in doing schoolwork and communicating with teachers, leading to disadvantage at school.

Cultural capital

The idea of cultural capital (see Unit 1 Topic 6) is used by Marxists to explain cultural influences on educational success. Bordieu (1977) suggested that middle-class culture (cultural capital) is as valuable in educational terms as material wealth (economic capital). Schools are middle-class institutions run by the middle class. The forms of knowledge, values, ways of interacting and communicating ideas that middle-class children possess are developed further and rewarded by the education system. Working-class and ethnic minority children may lack these qualities and so do not have the same chances to succeed.

Ball *et al.* (1994) showed how middle-class parents are able to use their cultural capital to play the system so as to ensure that their children are accepted into the schools of their choice. The strategies they use include attempting to make an impression with the headteacher on open day, and knowing how to mount an appeal if their child is unsuccessful in their application to a particular school. Ball also shows how ethnic minority parents are at a disadvantage when trying to get their children into the better schools. The parents, especially if born abroad, may not have much experience of the British education system and may not be able, or confident enough about their English language skills, to be able to negotiate the system.

The influence of the school: interactionist explanations

Interactionist explanations of differential educational achievement – based on 'labelling theory' (see Unit 1 Topic 4) – look at what goes on in schools themselves, and, in particular, teacher–pupil relationships. These theories had a major impact on the development of both the comprehensive system and the idea of 'progressive' education. Labelling theories suggest that teachers judge pupils not by their ability or intelligence but by characteristics that relate to class, gender and ethnicity, such as attitude, appearance and behaviour. Becker (1971) showed how teachers perceive the 'ideal pupil' to be one who conforms to middle-class standards of behaviour.

In a classic study by Rosenthal and Jacobsen (1968), the two researchers reported pupils' 'results' in intelligence tests to their teacher. The names of the 'high flyers' were in fact picked at random and bore no relation to any test results. However, the pupils' real performance by the end of the school year equated with their 'fake' test success. Teachers had somehow communicated their expectations to the pupils and the pupils had responded, creating a 'self-fulfilling prophecy' (see Unit 1 Topic 4). The teachers also perceived such pupils as happier, better-adjusted and more interesting than the rest. Interestingly, those pupils who were not named as the high flyers, but who improved in performance against expectations, were described as showing 'undesirable' behaviour.

Labelling and racism in schools

Afro-Caribbean boys often have the label 'unruly', 'disrespectful' and 'difficult to control' applied to them. Gillborn (1990) found that Afro-Caribbean pupils were more likely to be given detention than other pupils. The teachers interpreted (or misinterpreted) the dress and manner of speech of Afro-Caribbean pupils as representing a challenge to their authority. In perceiving their treatment to be unfair, the pupils responded, understandably, in accordance with their labels.

Whilst few would argue that teachers display overt racism, Wright (1992) found that there is considerable discrimination in the classroom. She observed Asian and Afro-Caribbean children in primary schools. She found that teachers paid Asian pupils, especially girls, less attention. They involved them less in discussion, and used simplistic language, assuming that they had a poor command of English. Teachers also lacked sensitivity towards aspects of their culture and displayed open disapproval of their customs and traditions. This had the effect of making the girls feel less positive towards the school, and also attracted hostility from other pupils who picked up on the teachers' comments and attitude towards the Asian pupils. Despite this, teachers did have high expectations of Asian pupils, with regard to academic success.

The same was not true of Afro-Caribbean pupils, who were expected to misbehave and who were more harshly treated than white pupils who exhibited similar 'bad' behaviour. Teachers also made little effort to ensure that they pronounced names correctly, causing embarrassment and unnecessary ridicule. Finally, both Asian and Afro-Caribbean pupils were victims of racism from white pupils.

The curriculum

Some sociologists have argued that what is taught in schools – the curriculum – actually disadvantages the working class and ethnic minorities. The knowledge that they encounter at school does not connect with their own cultural experience. Working-class experience is almost invisible in the school curriculum. History, for example, tends to deal with the ruling classes – such as kings, queens and politicians – rather than with the vast majority of ordinary people.

Coard (1971) showed how the content of education also ignored black people. The people who are acclaimed tend to be white, whilst black culture, music and art are largely ignored. Coard argued that this led to low self-esteem among black pupils. However, this assertion was refuted by both the Swann Report (1985) and Stone (1981), who noted that, despite feeling discriminated against by some teachers, West Indian children had been able to maintain an extremely positive self-image.

Since the 1970s some effort has been made to address the neglect of other cultures in the curriculum. **'Multicultural' education**, which acknowledges the contribution of all of the world's cultures, has become more common, although it has been criticised for focusing only on external factors ('saris and samosas') and failing to address the real problem of racism. Ethnic minority languages still do not have the same status as European languages; and schools are still required to hold Christian assemblies. The National Curriculum has also been criticised for being ethnocentric – emphasising white middle-class culture at the expense of other cultures – especially in its focus on British history and literature.

Problems of categorisation

Classifying according to ethnic origin is by no means simple. The term 'ethnic minorities', for example, includes many different groups and does not take account of class and gender differences within those groups. Gillborn and Gipps (1996) argue that terms such as 'white', 'black', 'Asian' and 'other' actually prevent any real understanding of differences in achievement. Postmodernists go further: they argue that the increasingly diverse nature of contemporary societies makes it impossible to explain educational achievement (or anything else) in terms of broad categories such as class or ethnicity, and that the generalisations that are made actually do more harm than good. They suggest that a conscious attempt needs to be made to understand the complexities of cultural difference and identity in modern society.

1 Briefly describe the educational outcomes of Afro-Caribbean males and females.

2 Explain why some ethnic minorities do well within the education system.

3 How has recent government policy attempted to address material deprivation?

4 Give three examples of ways in which cultural differences may affect both class and ethnic achievement in education.

5 How does Ball argue that cultural capital helps middle-class children to gain a place in the school of their choice?

6 Using examples, explain how labelling can affect educational success.

7 How might the curriculum itself disadvantage ethnic minority pupils?

Exploring class, ethnicity and educational achievement

Item A

Children still class-bound

Children from working-class homes are no more likely to get educational qualifications than they were 20 years ago, writes Geraldine Hackett. Research from the Institute of Education's centre for longitudinal studies suggests that social class remains a major factor in determining life chances. According to the study, 'Obstacles and Opportunities on the Route to Adulthood', for those born into poverty, there remains persistent under-achievement. The report says education provides an avenue for children from disadvantaged backgrounds but their peers from advantaged families gain even more from school.

The report says: 'Class of origin and childhood poverty make educational attainment more difficult even for children of similar test scores.' For children from disadvantaged backgrounds, the die is cast by the time they reach the third year of secondary school, when they may have already started to truant.

Times Educational Supplement, 23 December 2000

Item B

A class apart?

Despite efforts from many sides, social class still dictates educational prospects.

Student applicants from the upper social classes are more likely to be admitted to the London School of Economics than any other university, the latest official statistics reveal. The LSE leads a batch of elite London academic institutions, including King's College and University College London, where a much larger proportion of students from posh backgrounds have successful applications than students from poorer households.

The figures have emerged as two Oxford academics reiterate their calls to abolish the interview system at the Oxbridge universities, after research showed that half of all independent school students attaining three A grades at A level ended up at Oxbridge universities, compared to just under a third of those with the same grades from state schools.

Adapted from Times Educational Supplement, 16 November 1999

Item C

PERCENTAGE REACHING A LEVEL/VOCATIONAL EQUVALENT STANDARD, BY ETHNIC GROUP

	1988	1997
All ethnic minorities	31%	39%
White	38%	46%
16–19-year-olds in full-time education		
All ethnic minorities	56%	63%
White	37%	50%

Adapted from P. Trowler (1995) *Investigating Education and Training*, London: Collins Educational, p. 113; and M. Haralambos and M. Holborn (2000) *Sociology: Themes and Perspectives*, 5th edn, London: Collins Educational, pp. 869–70

Cultural disadvantage – this term has been used in two ways: 'cultural deprivation' theory suggests that some pupils' backgrounds are in some way deficient or inferior (e.g. in not placing sufficient emphasis on the importance of education). 'Cultural difference' explanations suggest that pupils' backgrounds are simply different, and that the mismatch with the culture of the school places them at a disadvantage.

Differential educational attainment – the extent to which educational achievement differs between social groups.

Educational Action Zones – set up by Labour in 1998 and spread to 25 areas of high deprivation and low achievement. Money from the government and private sector sponsors is used to attract teachers (through more pay) and to set up 'homework clubs'.

Material deprivation – lack of money leading to disadvantages such as an unhealthy diet and unsatisfactory housing.

Multicultural education – education that celebrates cultural differences.

Positive discrimination – treating a disadvantaged individual or group positively in order to make up for their disadvantages.

---

1 Explain what is meant by the term 'under-achievement' (Item A). (2)

2 Suggest two possible reasons why 'half of all independent school students attaining three A grades at A level ended up at Oxbridge universities, compared to just under a third of those with the same grades from state schools' (Item B). (4)

3 Identify three patterns in the data in Item C. (6)

4 Identify and briefly explain two possible reasons why, despite greater staying-on rates than whites, ethnic minorities still achieve fewer post-16 qualifications than whites (Item C). (8)

5 Using information from the Items and elsewhere, discuss the view that social class differences in educational achievement are the result of cultural factors. (20)

6 Assess the view that it is schools themselves that are the cause of differences in achievement amongst social classes and ethnic groups. (20)

Extension activities

1 Conduct a survey among a representative sample, involving a range of schools, to determine which pupils have been given detentions. (You could, for example, distribute a questionnaire via a sibling/younger friend/relative.) Present your data statistically in terms of age, gender and ethnicity. Summarise your key findings.

2 Examine the data below and discuss how useful it is in showing ethnic and gender differences in educational attainment.

HIGHEST QUALIFICATION HELD, BY GENDER AND ETHNIC GROUP, 1997–8 (PERCENTAGE OF ALL THOSE OF WORKING AGE)							
	Degree or eq.	HND or eq.	A level or eq.	GCSE A–C	Other qual.	No qual.	All %
Males							
Indian/Pakistani Bangladeshi	18	5	16	14	25	22	100
Black	14	6	22	18	24	16	100
White	14	8	32	18	14	15	100
Other	20	5	17	15	27	15	100
Females							
Indian/Pakistani Bangladeshi	9	5	11	18	25	33	100
Black	9	12	14	27	22	16	100
White	11	9	16	29	15	20	100
Other	12	8	15	17	33	15	100

Source: Department for Education and Employment (1998) Labour Force Survey, London: HMSO

3 Search for statistics about ethnic groups and education at the Department for Education and Employment website (www.dfee.gov.uk/statistics/). What statistics and reports are available? Do they tell us anything about the government's priorities?

4 Use the UCAS website (www.ucas.ac.uk) to investigate class and ethnic differences in higher education applications. What patterns can you find and how do they appear to be changing? Has the reduction in government financial support for students in the last few years had any effect on applications?

Getting you thinking

'It is my view that boys are simply not socialised in a way that suits the process of being educated. The over-stimulating, action-packed and exciting world they are now able to choose to belong to outside more than ever conflicts with the relatively confined and passive nature of the classroom environment.'

Ray O'Neil, deputy headteacher of a primary school in Gravesend, Kent

1 What do the pictures suggest are the key differences in the socialisation of boys and girls?

2 What features of schooling might seem more in line with girls' experiences outside school?

3 What features of schooling might seem to conflict with boys' experiences outside school?

4 What, according to Ray O'Neil, has increased the mismatch between boys' socialisation and schooling?

Until the late 1980s there was much concern about the under-achievement of girls. They did not do quite as well as boys in exams, and were also less likely to take A levels and enter higher education. However, since the early 1990s, girls have begun to out-perform boys at most levels of the education system. For example, they do better at every stage of the National Curriculum SAT results in English, maths and science, and in all subjects at GCSE and A level, except physics. However, there are still concerns about the subject choices made by girls. For example, they are still less likely than boys to apply for degree courses in the 'hard' sciences (chemistry and physics) and information technology. This may impact negatively on post-educational opportunities in terms of training and jobs.

Why has girls' achievement improved?

The job market

There are increasing job opportunities for women in the **service sector** of the economy. Many girls have mothers in paid employment who provide positive role models. As a result, girls recognise that the future offers them more choices – economic independence and careers are now a real possibility.

Female expectations

Many women are now looking well beyond the mother–housewife role. In a 1976 survey, Sue Sharpe discovered that girls' priorities were 'love, marriage, husbands, children, jobs and careers, more or less in that order'. When the research was repeated in 1994, she found that the priorities had changed to 'job, career and being able to support themselves'.

Feminism

The work of feminist sociologists in the 1970s and 1980s led to a greater emphasis on equal opportunities in schools. Teaching approaches and resources were monitored for sex bias to ensure more 'girl-friendly schooling', especially in the sciences. Consequently, teachers are now more sensitive about avoiding gender stereotyping in the classroom. Various anti-sexist initiatives have raised both teachers' and girls' consciousness. Single-sex classes in some subjects, projects such as **Girls into Science and Technology**, and the exploration of sexism through **PSE** and citizenship classes have all made a difference.

Behaviour

There is mounting evidence that girls work harder and are more motivated than boys. Girls put more effort into their work and spend more time on homework. They take more care with presentation of their work, they are better organised, and consequently they meet deadlines more successfully than boys.

Changes in the organisation of education

The National Curriculum emphasis on science means that girls cannot avoid doing some 'hard' science. Also, the course-work involved in GCSE, GNVQ and some A levels requires organisational skills and sustained motivation – skills that girls seem to be better at than boys.

Better socialisation for schooling

Research shows that girls spend their leisure time differently from boys. Whereas boys relate to their peers by *doing* (e.g. being active in a range of ways), girls relate to one another by talking. This puts girls at an advantage because school is essentially a language experience, and most subjects require good levels of comprehension and writing skills. Other research indicates that girls like reading, but that boys prefer more active communication media, such as computers and video.

Why is there concern about boys' achievement?

Changes in the job market/status frustration

Some commentators, notably Mac an Ghaill (1994), suggest that working-class boys are experiencing a 'crisis of masculinity' (see Unit 1, Topic 7). They are socialised into seeing their future male identity and role in terms of having a job and being a 'breadwinner'. However, the decline of **manufacturing industry** and the rise in long-term unemployment make it increasingly unlikely that males will occupy these roles. Moreover, new jobs in the service sector are often part-time, desk-based, and suited to the skills and lifestyles of women. In some families, females may be the primary breadwinners. Consequently, traditional masculine roles are under threat. Working-class boys' perception of this may influence their motivation and ambition. They may feel that qualifications are a waste of time because there are

only limited opportunities in the job market. They may see their future as bleak and without purpose. Consequently, they don't see any point in working hard at school.

Peer group status

Some boys may gain 'street cred' and **peer group status** from not working. These boys may create subcultures in some schools, which are both anti-education and anti-learning. These subcultures are explored in more depth in Topic 5. Their members may well see schoolwork as 'uncool' and unmasculine. In particular, reading may be regarded as boring, feminine and to be avoided at all costs. This may explain why boys are less conscientious and lack the application for coursework skills. The following quote from a school headmaster illustrates this well:

'It is better to be famous for being a clown or a toughie than working hard and being a failure.'

Bob Perris, headteacher, Hedworthfield Primary School, Jarrow

Social control differences

There is also some evidence that teachers are not as critical with boys as with girls. They may have lower expectations of boys, expecting work to be late, rushed and untidy, and expecting boys to be disruptive. Some research suggests that boys are less positively influenced than girls, or even turned off, by primary school environments which are female-dominated and may have an emphasis on neatness and tidiness.

Unrealistic attitudes

There are signs that boys' over-confidence may blind them to what is actually required for educational success. Research indicates that they are surprised when they fail exams, and tend to put their failure down to bad luck rather than lack of effort; whereas girls are more realistic, even self-doubting, and try that much harder in order to ensure success.

What about the future?

- Some feminist researchers are concerned that girls are still under-achieving because of disruptive boys. Teachers may be so tied up with controlling boys that girls don't get the attention they deserve.
- Feminists are also still concerned about the narrow subject choices that females are making at further and higher education level. Females are still more likely to take arts subjects, and males are more likely to take scientific and technological subjects. Such gender stereotyping may be the result of gender socialisation in early childhood (e.g. different toys and activities around the home), teacher advice on subject choice, and a continuing perception that the sciences are masculine subjects.
- The debate may be influenced by social class and gender. Although middle-class girls out-perform all other groups, working-class girls constitute a significant number of under-achievers in the school system, and should not be neglected. Moreover, girls from some ethnic backgrounds perform significantly worse than all other groups.
- Many feminists believe that the current concern about boys and achievement is simply a 'moral panic' which reflects anti-female sentiments and a patriarchal society. (Why, instead, aren't girls praised for their improvements?)

Figure 3.2 Gender and education: some figures

Boys/girls candidates getting A*–C in selected GCSE subjects in 1999 (percentage)

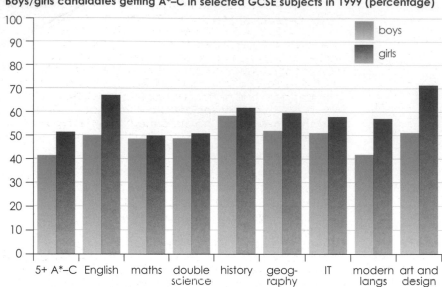

Additional data

Number of A-level subject entries by gender (thousands)

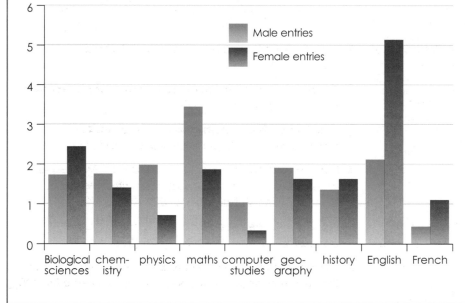

Look at these figures.

- Identify what you think are the key trends in each.
- Where are the significant gender differences?
- Suggest explanations for these differences.
- What might be their consequences?
- Are there some areas where the gender differences are not very significant?

Source: *Department for Education and Employment, 2000*

CHECK YOUR UNDERSTANDING

1 **What have been the overall trends in male and female achievement in the last 20 years?**

2 **How might changes in the economy affect both female and male attitudes towards education?**

3 **How have changes in both the organisation of the education system and classroom practices benefited the education of females?**

4 **What characteristics do male anti-school cultures possess that undermine educational success for boys?**

5 **Explain how class and ethnicity may be just as important as gender in explaining the current achievement patterns of boys.**

KEY TERMS

Girls into Science and Technology – a pre-National Curriculum initiative designed to encourage females to opt for science and technology.

Manufacturing industry – industries that actually make goods. Most of the work in such industries is manual and based in factories.

Peer group status – being seen as 'big' or important in the eyes of friends and other people around you.

PSE – Personal and Social Education. Sometimes known as PSHE (including Health Education) or PSME (including Moral Education).

Service sector – a group of economic activities loosely organised around finance, retail and personal care.

Item A

*Are girls now
really on top?*

The recent concern expressed in the media about the under-achievement of boys has put equal opportunities back on the agenda. But, as before, we need to take a closer look at the figures before being able to suggest effective strategies for dealing with the situation. Which boys are under-achieving? Some boys are actually doing very well.

What is happening to girls in school and after they leave? They are still not doing so well in some subject areas and, regardless of their actual ability, girls tend to have less confidence in their academic achievement and self-report their ability lower than boys. What happens to girls when they get into the workplace? Women who work full-time earn an average 80 per cent of men's hourly pay, and latest figures show this gap widening.

Adapted from *Times Educational Supplement*, 21 January 2000

Item B

Debates about boys and schooling take three main forms. There are stories about 'poor boys' who are victims of feminism or teachers, about schools which fail them and about their laddishness. 'Poor boys' stories call for alterations to the curriculum and teaching to favour boys. 'Failing schools' stories lead to punitive inspection processes, hit squads and action zones. Like 'poor boys' the 'boys will be boys' stories call for alterations to teaching to favour boys and, in addition, seek to use girls to police, teach, control and civilise boys. But these responses are based on over-simplified explanations of what is happening in schools. Not all boys are doing worse than girls. The picture is far from simple. Rather than spending our time in hand-wringing, we must try to understand the complexity of the situation. If we ask 'which boys, in which areas, are doing badly?' we find that the impact of class and ethnicity on achievement is greater than that of gender.

Adapted from D. Epstein *et al.* (eds) (1999) *Gender and Achievement*, Milton Keynes: Open University Press

Item C

*Forget gender, class
is still the real divide*

Reports of girls' GCSE success obscure the true picture, says Gillian Plummer. Yet another simplistic, statistical interpretation of gender differences in examination results makes the national news: 'Boys are out-performed by girls in GCSEs.' As a result the government wants all education authorities to take action in raising the academic performance of boys.

But beware: simplistic statistical analyses are dangerously misleading. We do not have a hierarchy in which girls are positioned in the top 50 per cent and boys in the bottom 50 per cent at GCSE. It is social class, not gender or race differences, which continues to have the single most important influence on educational attainment in Britain.

The majority of boys and girls from socially advantaged families do much better in all subjects at GCSE than the majority of girls from socially disadvantaged families.

While, overall, girls do out-perform boys at GCSE, working-class girls only do marginally better than working-class boys in public examinations.

The desperate need for detailed research on the educational failure of the majority of working-class girls has been hidden by:
• statistics recording the admirable rise in the achievements of middle-class girls, who are taken to represent 'all girls';
• serious concerns about the deviant behaviour and particularly poor exam performance of working-class boys.

It is dangerous and inaccurate to imply that all boys under-perform and that all girls do well.

The real question is: what action is being taken to raise the academic performance of working-class girls (as well as other under-achievers)?

Adapted from *Times Educational Supplement*, 23 January 1998

1 **Explain what is meant by the phrase 'laddishness' (Item B). (2)**

2 **Suggest two ways in which 'teaching might be altered to favour boys' (Item B). (4)**

3 **Identify the three explanations for the 'under-achievement' of boys described in Item B. (6)**

4 **Identify and briefly explain two reasons why the writer of Item C believes that social class differences are more significant than gender differences. (8)**

5 **Account for the recent improvements in the educational achievement of girls. (20)**

6 **Using information from the Items and elsewhere, assess the view that boys are under-achieving in education. (20)**

Extension activities

1 **The government's concern about gender and achievement is demonstrated by their creation of a website devoted to the issue. Visit it (at www.standards.dfee.gov.uk/genderandachievement) for statistical data and summaries of research.**

2 **Conduct a content analysis of two science and technology textbooks used at your school or college. One should be significantly older than the other, if possible. Count the number of times that males and females appear in diagrams, photographs, etc., and record how they are shown. Find examples that are gender-specific. What roles do they suggest as typical for each gender? Is there a change over time?**

3 **Interview a sample of boys and girls. Try to find out if they have different expectations about future success. Are there differences in the amount of time they spend on homework?**

Question for students taking OCR exam board AS level

4 **(a) Identify and explain two ways in which boys' and girls' achievements in school may differ. (20 marks)**

(b) Outline and discuss the view that the influence of male culture disadvantages boys in education. (40 marks)

Getting you thinking

1 Look at the photographs. Compare the pupils in the two photographs in terms of their likely:
   (a) attitudes to education
   (b) home background
   (c) educational achievement

2 Identify one occasion from your own education where most pupils seemed positive about their school experience.

3 What was it about the school, teachers or pupils that contributed to these feelings?

4 Identify one occasion from your own education where most pupils seemed negative about their school experience.

5 What factors do you think caused this? Was the negativity confined to particular pupil groupings, such as specific class, gender or ethnic groups?

6 Why do you think that some groups are pro-school (in favour of school) whilst others are anti-school (against it)?

Pupils respond to their schooling in different ways. Some groups accept the rules and the authority of teachers without question, while others may devote all their attention to rule-breaking and avoiding work. You have probably encountered examples of both during your compulsory education. Sociologists are interested in these subcultures. Why do they form, and what effect do they have on their members, other pupils, teachers and schools?

In the 1970s a great deal of media concern was directed at inner city comprehensives and the alleged misbehaviour of their pupils. This prompted sociologists such as Paul Willis (see Topic 1) to examine the possible reasons for the development of these mainly male, working-class groups of 'undisciplined' school pupils, or anti-school subcultures. As we saw in Topic 1, Willis identified a group of 'lads' – whose main aim at school was to have a 'laff' by rejecting the values of the school – and a more conformist group, referred to by the 'lads' as 'earoles'.

On a general level, all subcultures have things in common. Their members gain status, mutual support and a sense of belonging from the subculture. According to Hargreaves (1967), anti-school working-class subcultures are predominantly found in the bottom streams of secondary schools. In fact, he argued, they are caused by the labelling of some pupils as 'low stream failures'. Unable to achieve status in terms of the **mainstream values** of the school, these pupils substitute their own set of **delinquent values** by which they can achieve success in the eyes of their peers. They do this by, for example, not respecting teachers, messing about, arriving late, having fights, building up a reputation with the opposite sex, and so on.

Writers such as Hargreaves and Willis refer to the pro- and anti-school cultures as **homogeneous**, coherent groups, sharing their own uniform set of values. Peter Woods (1983), however, argues that this is too simplistic. He argues that pupils use a variety of **adaptations**, depending upon the ways in which the values of the school are accepted or rejected. Some pupils may partially accept aspects of the school's values but reject others. It is now recognised that responses will also differ within and between the different categories of pupils, and in different school situations. The study of school subcultures is therefore a lot more complex than it used to be.

Male subcultures

The anti-school male subcultures of the early 1970s made a degree of sense in that their members nearly all got jobs, despite their lack of qualifications. Their **coping strategies** – what the 'lads' in Willis's study called 'having a laff' – also equipped them for the monotony of the work they were destined for.

The economy has changed, however, and very few working-

**The Bash Street Kids
– an example of anti-school subculture**

class jobs remain in manufacturing. Has this changed the anti-school subculture of the 'lads'? There is concern that some working-class boys are stuck in a time-warp. That is, they imagine that work will be available whatever happens to them in school, and so they make little effort. In a sense the 'laff' is on them when they find that this is not the case and they are forced to join training schemes. Riseborough (1993) describes how boys on **YTS** schemes show some awareness and resentment of their predicament. They quickly realise that there is little likelihood of a job at the end of the scheme, and that they are being exploited.

Mac an Ghaill (1994) illustrates the complexity of subcultural responses by examining the relationship between schooling, work, masculinity and sexuality. He identifies a range of school subcultures.

The 'macho lads'

This group was hostile to school authority and learning, not unlike the lads in Willis's study. Willis had argued that work – especially physical work – was essential to the development of a sense of identity. By the mid-1980s much of this kind of work was gone. Instead, a spell in youth training, followed very often by unemployment, became the norm for many working-class boys.

The academic achievers

This group, who were from mostly skilled manual working-class backgrounds, adopted a more traditional upwardly mobile route via academic success. However, they had to develop ways of coping with the stereotyping and accusations of effeminacy from the 'macho lads'. They would do this either by confusing those who bullied them, by deliberately behaving in an effeminate way, or simply by having the confidence to cope with the jibes.

The 'new enterprisers'

This group was identified as a new successful pro-school subculture, who embraced the 'new vocationalism' of the 1980s and 1990s (see Topic 6). They rejected the traditional academic curriculum, which they saw as a waste of time, but accepted the new vocational ethos, with the help and support of the new breed of teachers and their industrial contacts. In studying subjects such as business studies and computing, they were able to achieve upward mobility and employment by exploiting school–industry links to their advantage.

'Real Englishmen'

These were a small group of middle-class pupils, usually from a **liberal professional** background (their parents were typically university lecturers, or writers, or they had jobs in the media). They rejected what teachers had to offer, seeing their own culture and knowledge as superior. They also saw the motivations of the 'achievers' and 'enterprisers' as shallow. Whilst their own values did not fit with doing well at school, they did, however, aspire to university and a professional career. They resolved this dilemma by achieving academic success in a way that appeared effortless (whether it was or not).

Gay students

Finally, Mac an Ghaill looked at the experience of a group neglected entirely by most writers – gay students. These students commented on the **heterosexist** and **homophobic** nature of schools, which took for granted the naturalness of heterosexual relationships and the two-parent nuclear family.

Female subcultures

Mac an Ghaill refers to the **remasculinisation** of the vocational curriculum. By this he means the higher-status subjects such as business studies, technology and computing, which have come to be dominated by males. Girls are more often on lower-level courses – doing stereotypical work experience in retail or community placements, for example. In Mac an Ghaill's study, although girls disliked the masculinity of the 'macho males', most sought boyfriends. Lower-class girls, in particular, even saw work as a potential marriage market. More upwardly mobile girls saw careers more in terms of independence and achievement.

Griffin (1985) studied young white working-class women during their first two years in employment. Rather than forming a large anti-authority grouping, they created small friendship groups. Their deviance was defined by their sexual behaviour rather than 'trouble-making'; and, most importantly, there was not the same continuity between the school's culture and that of their future workplace as there had been for the lads in Willis's study. Instead there were three possible routes for the girls, which they could follow all at the same time:

- **the labour market** – securing a job
- **the marriage market** – acquiring a permanent male partner
- **the sexual market** – having sexual relationships, whilst at the same time maintaining their reputation so as to not damage marriage prospects

Ethnic subcultures

O'Donnell (1991) showed how the various ethnic subcultures have distinctive reactions to racism, prejudice and discrimination, which may have different effects on educational performance. Afro-Caribbean males often react angrily to and reject the white-dominated education system, gaining status and recognition through other means. Indians show their anger, but do not tend to reject the education system. Instead, they succeed because they use the education system to their advantage.

Other studies point out that Afro-Caribbean females resent negative labelling and racism in schools. They particularly resent the fact that many teachers expect them to fail. Like males, they develop resistance to schooling. However, they do not form totally anti-school subcultures – they realise that these lead to educational failure. Instead, they adopt strategies that enable them to get what they need from the system, that allow them to maintain a **positive self-image**, obtain the qualifications they desire, and above all prove their teachers wrong.

Mirza (1992) found that the black girls in her study, whilst rarely encountering open racism, were held back by the well-meaning but misguided behaviour of most of the teachers. The teachers' 'help' was often patronising and counter-productive, curtailing both career and educational opportunities that should have been available to the black girls. For example, the girls were entered for fewer subjects to 'take the pressure off', or they were given ill-informed, often stereotypical, careers advice. The girls therefore had to look for alternative strategies to get by, some of which hindered their progress – such as not asking for help. Alternatively, they helped each other out with academic work, but were seen to resist the school's values by refusing to conform through their dress, appearance and behaviour.

It is clearly the case that membership of subcultures in school has an impact on pupils' experience of schooling and their achievement, in a variety of ways. But the situation can be highly complex and it is difficult to generalise about the nature of school subcultures and their impact on educational experience.

CHECK YOUR UNDERSTANDING

1 How, according to Hargreaves, did 'low stream failures' respond to their label?

2 Explain in your own words why the work of early writers on pupil cultures has been criticised.

3 How has the economic situation for working-class males changed since the 1970s?

4 Which of Mac an Ghaill's male subcultures were pro-school, and which anti-school? What were the reasons for this?

5 Give three examples of the ways in which the experience of female subcultures is said to be different from that of male subcultures.

6 Why, despite their generally positive identification with school, do black girls remain disadvantaged in the education system?

Exploring how pupils respond to education

Item A

PERMANENT EXCLUSIONS, BY ETHNIC GROUP, 1998/9

Ethnic group	Number of exclusions	Exclusions per 1,000 pupils
White	7,234	2.7
Black African	126	4.1
Black Caribbean	502	11.9
Black other	216	9.6
Indian	69	0.8
Pakistani	157	2.0
Bangladeshi	41	1.4
Chinese	5	0.4
Other	265	4.8

Source: DfEE Exclusions 1998/9, data from Annual Schools' Census, January 2000

Item B — *Youth culture blamed as pupils fail*

A respected black academic last night sparked a furious debate after he claimed his community was 'not interested' in intellectual activity and blamed black youth culture for the poor school record of Afro-Caribbean boys and girls. Tony Sewell, a university lecturer who has just finished an inquiry into soaring levels of exclusions among black pupils from a London school, claimed that too much concern with money and consumer goods was almost as damaging to black pupils' chances as racism.

He warned that fashionable black youth culture inevitably crossed over to white teenagers, and said tackling it would benefit all pupils. 'What we have now is ... not only the pressure of racism, but black peer grouping has become another pressure almost as big as institutional racism was.'

Black children had gained much-needed self-esteem from their youth culture becoming part of the mainstream, he conceded. 'But that culture is not one that, for example, is interested in being a great chess player, or intellectual activity. It is actually to do with propping up a big commercial culture to do with selling trainers, selling magazines, rap music and so on.'

Sewell's comments provoked an angry response from others in the black community and ignited an acrimonious debate about the real causes of under-achievement in British schools. Black community leaders accused him of encouraging a 'blame the victim' culture. 'But I would never attack black culture. ... Black youths need something: they

KEY TERMS

Adaptations – refers here to different ways of responding to compulsory schooling (e.g. by being a teacher's pet, by going through the motions but not trying to achieve anything, or by doing your own thing).

Coping strategies – ways of 'getting by' in an unpleasant situation.

Heterosexist – biased against homosexuals.

Homogeneous – the same throughout, undifferentiated.

Homophobic – fearing that homosexuals pose a threat of some kind.

Liberal professional – university-educated (usually in the arts/humanities) people who tend to be open-minded and encourage personal freedom and self-expression, and who tend to work in areas that enable this outlook to thrive.

Positive self-image – feeling good about yourself.

Remasculinisation – making something male-orientated again.

YTS – Youth Training Scheme (see Topic 6).

feel debased, they need something to identify with.'

Sewell, a lecturer at the University of Leeds who investigated black parents' allegations of unfair exclusions from Malory comprehensive school in Lewisham, south-east London, said he was telling a truth that liberal white researchers dare not.

He admits he was one of the lucky few blacks to succeed academically: 'I teach 400 trainee teachers and there is not one black face.'

G. Hinsliff and M. Bright, writing in the *Observer*, 20 August 2000

Item C   *Young money*
– the three marketeers

Despite being fresh out of Torquay Boys' Grammar, Adrian Bougourd, 18, Will Rushmer, 19, and Ryan Hayward, 18, look set to beat the other five teams on the Channel 4 fantasy share game show, Show Me The Money, at the end of the ten-week series next Friday. The youngest contestants [on the show] have made a profit of over £55,000 on an imaginary £100,000 lump sum in only eight weeks.

The teenagers, who have all recently started university, with 11 A level A grades between them, are not new to stocks and shares. They started taking an interest in the stock market last year when their school entered the ProShare national investment programme. That competition for school pupils ended in May, and was won by a group of girls from Haberdashers' Aske's School, who were still doing GCSEs at the time.

Both Will, who is studying economics at Warwick, and Ryan are hoping for a career in the City in either fund management or investment banking once they have finished their degrees. Adrian, who is studying finance, accounting and management at Nottingham University, is toying with the idea of financial journalism. The Three Freshers, as they called themselves for the show, are just one of thousands of investment clubs in the UK. The number of investment groups increased by 3,800 last year, pushing the total to more than 9,000, according to ProShare, which promotes share ownership.

The Times, 11 November 2000

Item D   Negative labelling by teachers is often blamed for the relative under-performance of African-Caribbean boys. But there is remarkably little research evidence of significant racial prejudice – conscious or unconscious – among schoolteachers. Although individual African-Caribbean teenagers differed as much from each other as did boys from other ethnic groups, their anti-school cultures are probably as deeply rooted as those of working-class boys in the 1960s and 1970s.

The African-Caribbean boys we questioned as part of our research into masculine identities often found school boring and irrelevant. One group ironically labelled itself 'the under-achievers', and some of the boys had developed a defensive, aggressive peer culture – hardly surprising given the historical and contemporary reality of white racism. Many were sensitive to racism and resentful or angry about it. But they often managed to appear confident and 'cool'.

Our findings illustrate why schools alone cannot change embedded ethnic identities and patterns of interaction. It is therefore unjust to blame either the teachers or the boys.

Understanding, rather than criticism, is what is required. The relative educational success of Indian children and the relative failure of African-Caribbean children clearly owe something to how their cultures interact with the British school system and dominant culture.

Adapted from M. O'Donnell, 'Research focus: peer group downsides', *Times Educational Supplement*, 1 December 2000

---

1 Explain in your own words what is meant by 'anti-school cultures' (Item D). (2)

2 Suggest two ways in which the writer considers Afro-Caribbean under-achievement to be affected by peer group membership (Item B). (4)

3 Identify three trends in school exclusions in the table in Item A. (6)

4 Identify and briefly explain two ways in which the pro-school subculture described in Item C differs from the anti-school subcultures referred to in Items B and D. (8)

5 Using information from the Items and elsewhere, assess the extent to which subcultures are a response to the problems faced by different groups of school pupils. (20)

6 Assess the view that some studies of school subcultures before the 1990s were over-simplified. (20)

Extension activities

1 Conduct a participant observational survey of your school or college to identify pro- and anti-school subcultures. (Use Mac an Ghaill's categories as well as some of your own.)

2 Design a questionnaire to examine the relationships between class, ethnicity and gender and subcultural membership.

Question for students taking OCR exam board AS level

3 (a) Identify and explain two differences between pro-school and anti-school subcultures. (20 marks)

    (b) Outline and discuss the view that pupil subcultures are a significant influence on pupils' experience of school. (40 marks)

Getting you thinking

Left: Andrew Simmons was partly responsible for the creation of the Blue Water shopping centre, the biggest in Europe, expected to provide for over 10 million customers per year

Far right: A degree from Oxbridge is a sure route to the top professions

1 Which of your experiences, both in school and out of school, have been helpful in developing knowledge and skills that may prove useful in your working life?

2 Which of the individuals in the photographs do you most admire? Why?

3 Do you think that vocational education is perceived less positively than academic education? Why do you think this might be the case?

4 Do you think that this may have had a bearing on Britain's lack of economic success relative to other countries?

5 Might the Oxbridge route, as the perceived height of success, be in any way to blame for the lower status of other routes to jobs in British society? If so, how?

The 'new vocationalism'

Ever since the introduction of compulsory education, successive governments have recognised that the low status of work-related (or vocational) education is a problem. In Topic 1 we saw how these concerns helped to justify the introduction of compulsory state education in the first place. These arguments reappeared in the 1980s. It was claimed that the British workforce lacked appropriate technical skills because schools had lost touch with the needs of industry. Individuals who left school at 16 or 18 were ill-equipped for work. Even those with higher qualifications tended to enter professions such as law or medicine rather than engineering or manufacturing. Consequently, Britain was viewed as being at a disadvantage in relation to international competition; and it was suggested that this 'skills crisis' was a significant factor in Britain's industrial decline.

It was felt that education had been dominated for too long by the **liberal humanist tradition** and the academic concerns of the universities, which emphasised a critical appreciation of subject knowledge for its own sake. This was fine for developing a nation of critics, but no help in developing the economy – in fact, it was a barrier, according to the New Right.

Although people interested in industry have for a long time studied vocational courses – such as City and Guilds qualifications or BTECs in colleges of further education – these were mostly post-school courses. It was felt that school pupils had not got enough experience of industry to make proper decisions about what jobs they wanted to do. Whilst the more able school-leavers may have been denied an industrial future due to lack of awareness, the less able needed the proper knowledge and skills to make them more employable. So, a number of schemes were developed, which were grouped together under the 'new vocationalism'.

These training and education schemes aimed to make young people more familiar with the world of work. They included courses such as **General National Vocational Qualifications** (now renamed Vocational A levels) and **National Vocational Qualifications** (job-specific qualifications which demonstrate 'on the job' competencies such as 'production machine sewing'), which are often studied part-time in college in the evening, or on day release, alongside full-time work.

Vocational education involves industry-related studies, mainly based in school or college. **Vocational training**, on the other hand, is designed to develop job-specific knowledge and skills in mainly work-like situations. Key developments in vocational training are outlined in the table on the next page.

DEVELOPMENTS IN VOCATIONAL TRAINING

Date	Development	Issues
1980	The Conservative government extended the powers of the Manpower Services Commission (MSC – the national organisation responsible for providing youth training, later renamed the Training Agency).	In order to get school-leavers to accept YTS (see below), the MSC embarked on lavish advertising campaigns which stressed the contrast between the 'interest and creativity' of YTS work and what the MSC described as the boredom, monotony and stagnation of being on the dole.
1983	The Youth Training Scheme (YTS) was introduced (a one-year training scheme for school-leavers, combining work experience with education). In 1986 YTS was extended to a two-year scheme.	YTS was presented as something that could open up exciting new opportunities for enthusiastic and talented trainees. After 1987 young people could be denied benefit if they refused to take part in this scheme.
1990	The government replaced YTS with YT (Youth Training). Trainees were now offered a programme that varied in length according to their needs, and they were also able to work towards National Vocational Qualifications (NVQs).	The greater direct involvement of training providers in the further education sector undermines the sector's freedom to be self-determining, as TECs and local employers have more and more say.
1992	Management of YT was passed to 82 Training and Enterprise Councils (TECs).	TECs were local organisations run mainly by business people with limited influence from educationalists.
1993	Training for Work was intro-duced. This is a 20-week college or workplace-based programme designed to improve the skills and attitudes of unemployed adults and make them more employable.	Despite the name, the provision of training by the work placement is not a requirement of the scheme, and, unsurprisingly, the take-up of places has been slow and the drop-out rate high.
1997–8	The New Deal was introduced for those under 25 receiving benefits. They are now required to accept a subsidised job, do voluntary work, clean up the environment, or take up full-time education or training.	The scheme was extended to over-25s who had been out of work for more than two years, including single parents and the disabled. The latest figures show that, by March 1999, of the 250,000 who started the scheme, almost half had left or finished, with about 40 per cent gaining 'real' jobs.

Source: Adapted from Heaton, T. and Lawson, T. (1996) *Education and Training*, Basingstoke: Macmillan, pp. 22–5

Criticisms of the 'new vocationalism'

Vocational education and training have had many critics:

● Finn (1987) argues that there is a hidden political agenda to vocational training. It provides cheap labour for employers, keeps the pay rates of young workers low, undermines the bargaining power of the unions (because only permanent workers can be members), and reduces politically embarrassing unemployment statistics. It may also be intended to reduce crime by removing young people from the streets.

● Critics such as Phil Cohen (1984) argue that the real purpose of vocational training is to create 'good' attitudes and work discipline rather than actual job skills. In this way, young people come to accept a likely future of low-paid and unskilled work. Those young unemployed who view training schemes as cheap labour, and refuse to join them, are defined as irresponsible and idle, and are 'punished' by the withdrawal of benefits.

● It is not proven that young people lack job skills. Many have already gained a lot of work experience from part-time jobs. Youth unemployment is the result not of a shortage of skills, but of a shortage of jobs.

● Critics also point out that the sorts of skills taught to YTS trainees are only appropriate for jobs in the **secondary labour market**. This consists of jobs that are unskilled, insecure, and pay low wages – such jobs offer little chance of training or promotion, employer investment is very low, and labour turnover is consequently very high.

● In practice, it is lower-ability students who tend to be channelled into vocational courses. The new vocationalism thus introduces another form of selection, with working-class and ethnic minority students being disproportionately represented on these courses.

Youth training: a critical view

Welcome to Spraggett Engineering. You're here to learn important technical skills and experience the latest in high-technology engineering.

Excellent! Someone to clean out the toilets and make the tea – and we hardly have to pay them anything.

- Training schemes do not appear to be breaking down traditional patterns of sex-stereotyping found in employment and education; nor are they encouraging girls to move into non-traditional areas. In fact, they are structured so as to reproduce gender inequality.
- Buswell (1987) points out that the types of schemes into which girls are channelled, such as retail work, lead to occupations where they are low-paid when young, and work part-time when older, reflecting women's position in the labour market.

Many sociologists are sceptical about the claims for vocationalism. They argue that the central aim of giving students skills is fine in theory, but has been difficult to achieve in practice. **Competence-based learning** and assessment often become more about getting the right boxes ticked, rather than developing real skills. However, there have been some benefits arising from the new vocationalism – although it may be that these are simply the result of the extra resources being pumped into education to support all of the initiatives.

Curriculum 2000

The changes brought about in post-16 education and training by Curriculum 2000 should, in theory, enable students to mix and match vocational and academic qualifications. Vocational A levels can be studied alongside traditional subjects, and all students have been encouraged to achieve 'Key Skills' qualifications. However, there is, as yet, little evidence of this happening. Most middle-class white students are still opting for the traditional academic curriculum, as before; whilst vocational courses continue to be dominated by working-class and ethnic minority students.

CHECK YOUR UNDERSTANDING

1 In your own words explain why Britain was seen to be at a disadvantage in terms of equipping people for industry.

2 What was the 'new vocationalism'? Give examples.

3 What is the difference between vocational education and vocational training?

4 What is Youth Training?

5 What did the 'New Deal' mean for those who were unemployed and under 25?

6 What do you consider to be the three most serious criticisms of vocational training?

7 What is meant by the vocational–academic divide, and how has the government tried to remove this divide?

KEY TERMS

Competence-based learning – type of learning where the aim is to demonstrate that a particular skill has been acquired.

General National Vocational Qualifications (GNVQs) – broad vocational courses/qualifications enabling students at Foundation, Intermediate and Advanced level to get a taste of the occupational sector and the range of work within it.

Liberal humanist tradition – the belief in education for its own sake, to enrich the life of the learner and develop their sense of personal worth.

National Vocational Qualifications (NVQs) – courses/qualifications that improve trainees' skills in particular occupations.

Secondary labour market – employment involving second-class jobs, poor wages, and little job security or promotion prospects.

Vocational education – work-related courses offered in schools and colleges (usually with a small amount of work experience).

Vocational training – work-related courses offered through work experience (usually with a small amount of time in college).

Item A

PARTICIPATION OF 16-YEAR-OLDS IN EDUCATION AND TRAINING (IN ENGLAND)

Year	Males (%)	Females (%)	Total (% of age group)
1988	80.9	80.6	80.8
1989	82.7	81.0	81.9
1990	82.3	84.1	83.1
1991	84.8	88.0	86.3
1992	84.9	89.0	86.9
1993	87.2	90.2	88.6
1994	87.6	89.8	88.7
1995	85.4	88.0	86.7
1996	84.1	87.5	85.7
1997	82.3	86.1	84.2
1998	82.8	88.7	85.6

Source: Department for Education and Employment (1999)

Item B

There is often a gap between the image promoted of youth training and its reality. The literature of YT often suggested that it could open up exciting and creative opportunities for young people regardless of social background. However, youth trainees have long complained that they are being trained for 'Noddy jobs'. Certainly there is evidence that the majority of YT places are provided by the big retailers such as the supermarkets and department stores such as BHS and Marks and Spencer. Consequently YT trainees have generally found themselves trained in a narrow range of skills such as working on the till, shelf-filling and stock-taking which are common to most retail jobs. One study found that 80 per cent of the jobs that YTS trainees went into required no entry qualification. There is also evidence that some employers are using YT as a screening device. If the trainee is uncomplaining, docile and flexible about the mundane tasks they are allocated, there is a good chance that they will be offered a post. Finally, whilst YT schemes emphasise equal opportunities for females and ethnic minorities there is evidence that female training places reinforce traditional gender roles, whilst in some areas youth training places with major employers have been monopolised by white youth.

Adapted from S. Maguire (September 1993) 'Training for a living? The 1990s youth labour market', *Sociology Review*, vol. 3, no. 1.

1 Explain what is meant by the term 'youth training' (Item B). (2)

2 Identify two trends in the table in Item A. (4)

3 Identify three examples of the gap between the image promoted of youth training and its reality (Item B). (6)

4 Suggest and briefly explain two reasons why the percentage of 16-year-olds in education and training increased between 1988 and 1998 (Item A). (8)

5 Using information from the Items and elsewhere, describe and explain the view that the 'new vocationalism' was necessary and has been a success. (20)

6 Using information from the Items and elsewhere, assess sociological criticisms of the 'new vocationalism'. (20)

Extension activities

1 Survey a group of post-16 students at your school or college. Choose a sample that includes students following both academic and vocational courses. Why did they stay on at the age of 16? What is motivating them, and what do they hope to achieve from their qualifications? Are there differences in the motivations of students following academic or vocational courses?

2 Conduct interviews with 'New Deal' students in college, or students who have undertaken work experience. Find out about their experiences and whether they feel that these experiences will better equip them for a future job.

3 Find out about government policies on training at the Department for Education and Employment website (www.dfee.gov.uk). Do you think that these will be successful? Do they represent real opportunities for young people, or might there be other motives behind the policies?

Topic 1 Who controls the mass media?

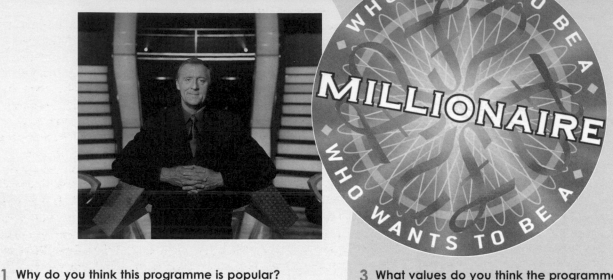
Before answering the question in the title of this topic, we need to think why it is being asked. The mass media have clearly become a very influential part of our society. Virtually every household has one TV, or more, which the average person spends 25 hours per week watching. Over 20 million people read a daily newspaper. We rely on the media for information about everything from the latest DVD releases to the current state of politics. Whoever controls this output has potentially a lot of power and influence over how society operates.

First of all, we need to know a bit about trends in ownership.

Trends in ownership

Media companies have become huge multinational or global concerns, worth billions of pounds. This has been achieved through a number of developments in the way that they are owned.

- **Concentration** – media companies are bought and sold at an alarming rate, with smaller companies being swallowed up by larger ones. Over the last 20 or 30 years the media have become more and more concentrated into fewer and fewer hands. If the USA's media were owned by separate individuals, there would be 25,000 owners. Instead, only ten huge corporations own everything.
- **Vertical integration** – one way to maximise profit is to own all the stages in the production, distribution and consumption of a media product. This is known as vertical integration. For example, a newspaper owner might own

the sawmills that produce the wood, the paper mills that produce the paper, newspaper offices, printing facilities, lorries and newsagents. This cuts out all of the middlemen, cutting costs and increasing profits.

- **Cross-media ownership** – this occurs where more than one form of media – say, radio and TV stations – come to be owned by the same company, creating what is known as a **media conglomerate**, such as NewsCorp.
- **Diversification** – to increase their profitability, many companies move into areas outside the media, so that when one part of the business is struggling another area can prop it up until things improve. Granada, for example, owns TV studios, TV and computer rental outlets, and motorway service stations. Sony owns film studios and music recording studios, although its main source of income is through electronic consumer goods.
- **Transnational ownership** – media companies are no longer restricted by national boundaries. They buy up smaller companies all over the world. There is some concern that this could undermine national and local production.
- **Technological convergence** – digital technology has enabled previously separate forms of media production to combine, such as the internet and mobile phones (WAP), web TV and publishing on CD-Rom. This is causing media companies in previously separate fields to merge. The even bigger companies that emerge, such as Time Warner/AOL, have more power to promote their products to a wider audience.

Ownership and control

So do the owners of the media actually control its content? Is our information about the world distorted through the eyes of a few, very wealthy, media barons? The extent to which this occurs is an area of intense debate, which centres around the interconnected roles of media proprietors (owners), media professionals (those who work for them) and us, the consumers.

Sociologists have come up with three basic theories to explain the links between ownership and control.

Traditional Marxism

According to this view, the media help maintain the unfair and exploitative capitalist system by 'brainwashing' the public. Media owners are rich and successful people who benefit considerably from capitalism and therefore have a vested interest in ensuring its survival. Because of this, they directly manipulate media output so that it reflects their interests. The media encourage us to support the system and to hold values that enable capitalism to thrive. Marxists call these values 'ideology'.

There is considerable evidence of direct manipulation. Rupert Murdoch, who owns and controls NewsCorp (a huge media corporation which owns, or has a controlling interest in, the *Sun*, *The Times*, the *News of the World*, Sky and Fox, as well as over 1,000 other media concerns in five continents), has been accused of manipulative practices on many occasions. When Sky made a bid for Manchester United, for example, all of the press except the *Sun* and *The Times* condemned the move. Murdoch has even been dubbed 'the Phantom Prime Minister'.

Critics of the traditional Marxist view highlight the wide range of views in society, which, they claim, would not exist if media manipulation was as powerful as is suggested. Also, they point out, it is impossible for owners to be directly involved in all aspects of their business to the extent that they have any real influence. Their businesses are too immense and they could not possibly find the time.

In addition, media owners are not free to act totally as they wish because they are governed by a number of laws and other regulations – for example, the Official Secrets Act and libel law. Their activities are also monitored by a number of **'watchdogs'** such as the Press Complaints Commission.

Because of these criticisms, many Marxists do not agree with the traditional view. They still believe that the media reflect the views of the powerful, but they have a slightly different explanation.

Hegemonic Marxism

This view is similar to the traditional Marxist view in that it believes that the media provide the public with ideology – views and information that support the capitalist system. However, this group of Marxists does not believe that the content of the media is under the direct control of the owners. Instead they believe that ideology is transmitted constantly via institutions such as schools and churches, as well as via the media. Eventually nobody even notices it – the views of the ruling class have become 'common sense'. Of course, it's always easier to dominate and control people if they are happy to go along with you, and the media have played a key role in bringing about this situation, which is known as **hegemony.**

But why, ask hegemonic Marxists, do the media present views that support the unfair capitalist system? Because of their background, journalists and broadcasters (who tend to be white, middle-class and male) usually subscribe to a 'middle of the road', unthreatening set of viewpoints, which will, they believe, appeal to the majority of readers. Anyone outside the consensus is seen as an extremist. Alternative views are sometimes represented but usually ridiculed.

Agenda-setting

Meetings usually have an **agenda** – a list of issues to be discussed. The media provide an agenda for discussion in society. How often do you hear people talking about the latest news stories, scandals or soap operas? Hegemonic Marxists argue that the media present us with a fairly narrow agenda for discussion. We talk about Posh and Becks but don't often discuss the massive inequalities that exist in society. We are more likely to be outraged by the latest events in Albert Square than by the number of people living in poverty. In this way the public are distracted from really important issues, and we never question the workings of capitalist society because its worst points are rarely presented.

But, you may ask, don't we get different political views presented to us so that we can make real choices about how society should be run? In the run-up to the 1997 General Election, only two national newspapers supported the Labour Party, and six supported the Conservatives (although the *Express* and *Sun* switched their allegiance to Labour in the final weeks). People frequently argue that, since New Labour emerged, there has, in any case, been very little difference between the parties, so the agenda for discussion has narrowed even further.

Both of the positions we have looked at argue that the media support the capitalist system by controlling – consciously (traditional Marxism) or unconsciously (hegemonic Marxism) – media output so that it benefits those in power. The final position is the one that, unsurprisingly, the media themselves tend to support.

Pluralism

From a **pluralist** viewpoint the media are seen as offering a wide selection of the views of the various groups in society. Modern society is democratic and people have freedom of choice. If they did not like the output of the media they would not buy it or watch it. The media have to give the public what they want – otherwise they would go out of business.

Pluralists raise a number of points in support of their view:

- The media are not all-powerful – governments have tried at various times to legislate against media owners having too much power. For example, vertical integration has been considered unfair for two reasons: first, it doesn't allow competition to survive because smaller companies can't compete with the cheaper costs of the conglomerates; and second, it reduces customer choice, because one person's or group's views or products can become too dominant.
- In the USA, the huge film studios have on more than one occasion been prevented from owning film production, film distribution and cinemas at the same time. Many countries have cross-ownership rules preventing companies from owning more than one media form in the same area.
- Journalists and editors often refuse to go along with what their owners want of them.

- Finally, the media have a strong tradition of **investigative journalism** which has often targeted those in power. For example, two reporters on the *Washington Post* forced the President of the USA – Richard Nixon – to stand down after they exposed him for authorising the bugging of his opponent's offices at Watergate in 1972.

Whether direct manipulation goes on or not, pluralists claim that there is no proof that audiences passively accept what is being fed to them. Audiences are selective and at times critical. To suggest that the audience can be manipulated is to fail to recognise the diversity of the audience or the ways in which they use the media. This will be considered more fully in later topics.

Figure 4.1 Advertising: increasing consumer choice, or 'brainwashing'?

CHECK YOUR UNDERSTANDING

1 How have recent developments in media increased the power of media owners?

2 How does traditional Marxism view the influence of media owners on media output?

3 Give two examples of Rupert Murdoch's direct manipulation of media output.

4 How would hegemonic Marxists challenge the view that the media present us with a wide range of opinion?

5 What are the differences between traditional Marxism and hegemonic Marxism?

6 Give examples of three arguments put forward by pluralists to show that the media do not just represent the views of the powerful but cater for everyone in society.

KEY TERMS

Agenda-setting – controlling what issues come to public attention.

Cross-media ownership – occurs where different types of media – e.g. radio and TV stations – are owned by the same company.

Diversification – the practice of spreading risk by moving into new, unrelated areas of business.

Hegemony – domination by consent (used to describe the way in which the ruling class project their view of the world so that it becomes the consensus view).

Investigative journalism – journalism that aims to expose the misdeeds of the powerful.

Media concentration – the result of smaller media companies merging, or being bought up by larger companies, to form a small number of very large companies.

Media conglomerate – a company that owns various types of media.

Pluralism – a theory that society is made up of many different groups, all having more or less equal power.

Technological convergence – the tendency for once diverse media forms to combine as a result of digital technology.

Vertical integration – owning all the stages in the production, distribution and consumption of a product.

Watchdog – an organisation created to keep a check on powerful businesses.

Exploring control of the mass media

Item A

'These cost accountants or their near clones are employed by new kinds of media owners who try to gobble up everything in their path. We must protect ourselves and our democracy, first by properly exercising the cross-ownership provisions currently in place, and then by erecting further checks and balances against dangerous concentrations of the media power which plays such a large part in our lives. No individual or company should be allowed to own more than one daily, one evening and one weekly newspaper. No newspaper should be allowed to own a television station and vice versa. A simple act of public hygiene, containing abuse, widening choice and maybe even returning broadcasting to its makers.'

Dennis Potter: excerpt from the James MacTaggart memorial lecture, Edinburgh Film Festival, 1993 (reproduced in D. Potter (1994) *Seeing the Blossom: two Interviews and a Lecture*, London: Faber and Faber)

Item B

Blair gives pledge on cross-media ownership

A Labour government would not impose further restrictions on cross-media ownership, Tony Blair has confirmed. The Labour leader is to call for the likes of News International proprietor Rupert Murdoch merely to behave 'responsibly', he has told the *New Statesman*.

'But let me make it clear: we've never traded policies with Rupert Murdoch in return for the support of his papers.' ... Mr Blair tells the *New Statesman* that there would be no legislation to restrict Mr Murdoch's expanding media empire. He says: 'It's not a question of Murdoch being too powerful. He's got a strong position and whatever authority or power he has needs to be exercised responsibly.' But his comments prompted Conservative sources to claim that this was evidence that he had struck 'a private commercial agreement' with Mr Murdoch in order to win the backing of his *Sun* newspaper during the election.

(The *Sun* did back Labour and they won the 1997 General Election with a massive majority.)

Adapted from *New Statesman*, Thursday, 20 March 1997

Item C

Could 1999 be the year of the multinational media merger? On January 2, Time Warner and AT&T joined forces to form one of the most powerful forces in the global media system.

This alliance of the world's largest media corporation with the world leader in telecommunications follows a growing trend in global communications towards cross-media ownership, with a handful of media multinationals assuming worldwide control. Time Warner, Disney, Bertelsmann, Viacom, and News Corporation already have a stranglehold on the world media market. For Rupert Murdoch, head of News Corporation, that is not enough. According to Murdoch's rivals, 'he basically wants to conquer the world. And he seems to be doing it.'

The political power of these multinationals cannot be under-estimated. It has been said that the likes of Murdoch and Bill Gates (head of Microsoft) have more global influence than the President of the USA.

Excerpt from Syndication News International webpage, January 1999

1 Explain the term 'cross-media ownership' (Items A and B). (2)

2 Identify two measures to control cross-media ownership that Dennis Potter would like to see. (4)

3 Suggest three reasons why Tony Blair might have made promises to Rupert Murdoch regarding media regulation in the future (Item B). (6)

4 Identify and briefly explain two reasons why Dennis Potter is against cross-media ownership (Item A). (8)

5 Discuss the view that 'the likes of Murdoch and Bill Gates (head of Microsoft) have more global influence than the President of the USA' (Item C). (20)

6 Using information from the Items and elsewhere, assess the pluralist theory of the media. (20)

Extension activities

1 Use the following websites to discover the extent of diversification, vertical integration, cross-media ownership, and transnational ownership in one or more of the newspaper groups in the chart opposite:

www.westherts.ac.uk/publishing/News/news_gen.htm

www.westherts.ac.uk/publishing/News/newslink.htm

Question for students taking OCR exam board AS level

2 (a) Identify and explain two changes in the nature of media ownership over the last 30 years. (20 marks)

(b) Outline and discuss the view that media owners have little control over media output. (40 marks)

Newspaper groups

	Market share
News International (*Sun, Times, Sunday Times, News of the World*)	35%
Mirror Group (*Mirror, Sunday Mirror, People, Daily Record*)	26%
United News & Media (*Express, Express on Sunday, Star*)	13%
Associated Newspapers (*Mail, Mail on Sunday*)	12%
Telegraph (*Daily Telegraph, Sunday Telegraph*)	7%
Guardian (*Guardian, Observer*)	3%
Pearson (*Financial Times*)	1%

Source: Pears Cyclopaedia, 98–99

Getting you thinking

1 Which aspects of the above screen shots suggest that the news:
- is 'up to the minute'?
- comes from around the world?
- employs the latest technology?

2 Think of the music that introduces news broadcasts. What impression does it give?

News: a 'window on the world'?

For most of us, TV news is the most important source of information about what is going on outside our day-to-day experiences. We rely on TV news to help us make sense of a confusing world. As you probably worked out from the introductory activity, news broadcasts are carefully managed to give an impression of seriousness and credibility. But do they really represent a 'window on the world'? How do TV journalists and editors decide which of the millions of events that occur in the world on any day will become 'news'?

Critics of the media have pointed out that the news is most certainly not a 'window on the world'. Instead, they argue that it is a manufactured and manipulated product involving a high degree of selectivity and bias. What causes this?

Three important factors are:

1 Institutional factors both inside and outside the newsrooms (such as issues of time and money).
2 The culture of news production and journalism (how news professionals think and operate).
3 The ideological influences on the media (the cause and nature of bias).

Institutional factors

The 'news diary'

Rather than being a spontaneous response to world events, many news reports are planned well in advance. Many newspapers and TV news producers purchase news items from press agencies (companies who sell brief reports of world or national news 24 hours per day). They also receive press releases from pressure groups, government agencies, private companies and individuals, all of whom wish to publicise their activities.

Schlesinger (1978) highlighted the influence of the **news diary**. This is a record of forthcoming social, political and economic events which enables journalists and broadcasters to plan their coverage, and select and book relevant 'experts'. It also allows them to make practical arrangements – which could include anything from liaison with local authorities and the police over outside broadcasts, or organising satellite link-ups, to sorting out the catering for location staff. Such events might include the Chancellor of the Exchequer's speech on budget day, royal birthdays, the release of a notorious prisoner or the arrival of a famous entertainment personality.

Financial costs

Financial considerations can also influence the news. Sometimes so much has been spent on covering a world event (sending camera crews, flights, accommodation for journalists, pre-booked satellite links, etc.) that it will continue to get reported on even though very little that is new has happened.

The point at which the news company's financial year-end falls can also affect how, and even whether, costly news items are covered. ITN had spent most of their 1991 overseas budget covering the Gulf War when news of the protests in Tiananmen Square broke (in which unarmed pro-democracy demonstrators in China faced tanks in their demands for less state control). The BBC, who had a different financial year, still had the budget to send crews, who were able to capture some of the most memorable images of the decade.

Competition

This highlights another factor: competition. News producers are desperate to be the first to 'break the news'. This can cause them to cut corners – for example, accepting 'evidence' from sources without properly checking it, or relying on official sources because they are more easily accessed. This can lead to a biased view in favour of the official side of the argument (see the work of the Glasgow University Media Group below).

Time or space available

News items have to be selected from the thousands that flood into the newsroom every day, and they then need to be fashioned into a coherent and recognisable product. The average news bulletin contains 15 items which must take exactly the same amount of time to put across each day. Similarly, a newspaper has a fixed amount of space for each news category. Sometimes stories are included or excluded merely because they fit or don't fit the time or space available.

Figure 4.2 Gatekeeping and news values

Spice Girls to split

Soap star attacked

England lose again

Mother of ten wins lottery

Madonna in new baby shock

Ten dead in Chilean earthquake

Share prices crash

Homelessness at all time high

New figures show gap between rich and poor widening

Is it extraordinary?
Is it a human interest story?
Is it about a top person or rich country?
Is it dramatic?

Audience

The time of a news broadcast (and who is perceived to be watching), or the readership profile of a paper, will also influence the selection of news. A lunchtime broadcast is more likely to be viewed by women, and so an item relating to the supermarket price war might receive more coverage than it would in a late-evening news bulletin.

The culture of news production and journalism

Various studies have been conducted that have attempted to identify what makes an item 'newsworthy' for journalists. Galtung and Ruge (1973) identified several key **news values** that might be used to determine the 'newsworthiness' of events. These included:

- extraordinariness: events that are considered 'out of the ordinary'
- events that concern important or elite persons or countries
- events that can be personalised to point up the essentially human characteristics of sadness, humour, sentimentality and so on
- events that are dramatic, clear and negative in their consequences

Different media have different ways of prioritising news values. TV news would see picture values as an important consideration, whilst the tabloid press would tend to prioritise stories based on 'human interest' or famous personalities.

Journalists thus make decisions about what is and what is not 'newsworthy'. Their work has been referred to as **'gatekeeping'**: they only let a tiny minority of events through the 'gate' to become news.

Ideological influences on the media

As we saw in the previous topic, traditional Marxists argue that all of the news selection described above is deliberate and the result of conscious manipulation. News producers have a vested interest in maintaining the capitalist system, and so they help maintain that system by being directly supportive of the ruling class. The news is biased in favour of the powerful in society, and against those who are a threat to that power. While this view may overstate the case, it is certainly true that the ruling classes are appreciative of the role that the media play. Many newspaper proprietors and TV news producers have received recognition through knighthoods or other honours.

For hegemonic Marxists the way in which journalists learn what makes a good story is governed by their common white, male, middle-class background. Their lifestyle and standard of living are such that they see little wrong with society and rarely adopt a critical stance. This essentially attunes them to taken-for-granted, common-sense assumptions that maintain the system.

In contrast to these views, pluralists would argue that the news reflects the full diversity of viewpoints in society. Certain views will dominate in each situation, but the direction that the bias takes is not consistent, and so there is no overall slant towards a particular viewpoint.

Owners and controlling companies	Certain owners directly manipulate the media. Owners and controllers have interests that they wish to promote or defend – Rupert Murdoch made sure that his bid for Manchester United was reported in a positive light in his papers.
Media institutions (and their identities)	Media institutions have a public image which they need to maintain. This affects their decisions about what to include and how to present it. The News of the World, for example, over-reports sex and scandal as this is what its readers want and expect.
The law	The media are subject to legal controls such as the Official Secrets Act and the Prevention of Terrorism Act, as well as the laws of libel and contempt of court. Contempt of court means that the media cannot report in a way that might affect the verdict in an ongoing court case.
Constitutional constraints	Media organisations are governed by written 'contracts', such as the BBC charter, which they agree to in order to gain the right to publish or broadcast.
Media regulation and self-regulation	The media have their own standards and regulatory bodies which monitor content. Examples are the Press Complaints Commission and the Broadcasting Standards Council. Professional practices are also an influence. Journalists often censor their own work by taking out what they know will not be published.
Economic factors	The amount of money and resources available will inevitably influence the media. Look back at the example of coverage of the Gulf War and Tiananmen Square, for example.
Advertisers	Most of the media need advertising to survive. This means that the needs of advertisers will be taken very seriously when decisions are made about the content of the media. For example, there were suspicions that the link between smoking and lung cancer was slow to be reported because of the importance of tobacco companies' advertising.
Audiences	It is assumed that different kinds of people watch, listen and read at different times of the day. A lunchtime TV programme is likely to be aimed at women or pensioners, and early evening programming is likely to be aimed at schoolchildren.
Media personnel (class, race, gender, socialisation)	The media may reflect a white, male, middle-class viewpoint, as many people in the media are drawn from these social backgrounds.
Sources	With news coverage in particular, certain groups – such as the government – are believed to be more reliable, honest and objective.

The Glasgow University Media Group (GUMG)

The GUMG have studied news broadcasts for many years. They use a technique called **content analysis** which involves detailed analysis of the language and visual images used by the media. They have found that the media consistently reflect the common assumptions of the powerful in society, whilst **marginalising** the views of others.

During the Gulf War of 1991, the GUMG analysed the language used to describe the Allies and the Iraqis. The former were described as 'professional', 'loyal' and 'heroes', whilst the latter were 'brainwashed', 'blindly obedient' and 'cowardly'. In an analysis of industrial disputes the GUMG discovered that managers were often interviewed in the orderly, calm environment of their offices, whilst strikers were interviewed above the noise of the picket lines. The former were seen as the representatives of order and reason, the latter as unreasonable.

The work of the Glasgow Media Group shows that the media do not just reflect public opinion but that they also provide a framework (or agenda) for the public, so that people think about issues in a way that benefits the ruling class. In this respect the media are a powerful ideological influence. (See also Item A in the 'Exploring' activity.)

Class bias is not the only area of misrepresentation that critics of the pluralist position point to. Women, ethnic minorities, the disabled and the young may also be victims of media bias. The following topics will examine these issues in more detail.

CHECK YOUR UNDERSTANDING

1 How does the use of a news diary demonstrate that news is not a spontaneous response to world events?

2 Give two examples of the impact of financial factors on news production.

3 Explain in your own words how the format and intended audience for a news programme affect news output.

4 What are 'news values'?

5 Explain in your own words how the process of gatekeeping affects the form that news output eventually takes.

6 Use the work of the Glasgow University Media Group to show how the media influence the way the public thinks about issues.

KEY TERMS

Content analysis – a detailed analysis of media content.

Gatekeepers – people within the media who have the power to let some news stories through and stop others.

Marginalising – making a group appear to be 'at the edge' of society and not very important.

News diary – a record of forthcoming events that will need to be covered.

News values – assumptions that guide journalists and editors when selecting news items.

Item A *Ten conclusions from the Glasgow University Media Group*

1 News is reported in a simplified and one-sided way.
2 The effects of events tend to be reported rather than their causes. There is no sense of their development.
3 There is biased use of words in TV news – e.g. 'miners' strike' rather than 'coal dispute'.
4 There is biased use of images in TV news. During the Liverpool council workers' strike, the piles of rubbish and unburied bodies reinforced the effects rather than the causes of the dispute, and put the viewer on the side of the management rather than the strikers.
5 Stories are reported selectively – only certain facts are presented and others are left out.
6 Protesters' tactics are more likely to be reported than their views.
7 There is a hierarchy of access to the media – experts and establishment figures are more likely to get their views heard than ordinary people.
8 There is a hierarchy of credibility whereby only certain groups are asked for their opinion, as they are seen to be more reliable and their remarks more valid.
9 The media have an agenda-setting function. Journalists have a 'middle of the road', consensual outlook informed by their common background and experience. They frame events within a very narrow range, limiting the breadth of possible discussion.
10 Personnel in the media act as 'gatekeepers' – they exclude some stories from the news and include others.

Adapted from *Bad News* (1976), *More Bad News* (1980), *Really Bad News* (1982), *War and Peace News* (1985), London: Routledge

Item B We do our best to give a clear picture of what is going on. In that sense the news is 'a window on the world'. Of course we can't include every detail, or interview every person involved – that's just not possible. We try to be balanced but we do make judgements about what our viewers' opinions are likely to be on the issue and try to cover stories in a way that will interest and inform them.

An anonymous journalist, 2000

1 In your own words, explain what is meant by the term 'hierarchy of access' (Item A). (2)

2 Identify two of the groups who 'are asked for their opinion, as they are seen to be more reliable and their remarks more valid' (Item A). (4)

3 Identify and briefly explain three reasons why the role of 'gatekeeper' (Item A) is important. (6)

4 Identify and briefly explain: (a) the perspective reflected by the journalist's views in Item B, and (b) one criticism of this perspective. (8)

5 Using material from Item A and elsewhere, examine the view that the news is biased in favour of the powerful. (20)

6 Using information from the Items and elsewhere, assess the sociological arguments *against* the view that the news is a 'window on the world' (Item B). (20)

Extension activities

1 List the first ten news items from an edition of the BBC evening news. Do the same for ITN news on the same evening. What are the differences? Can they be explained in terms of 'news values'?

2 Tape one news programme. Analyse the lead story in terms of the sources that are used, e.g. newscaster's script, live film footage, location report from a reporter at the scene, interview – taped, live or by satellite – archive footage (old film), amateur film, etc. Then brainstorm a list of all the people who must have been involved, e.g. reporters, photographers, editors, companies buying and selling satellite time, drivers, outside broadcast crews, film archivists, etc. Discuss how practical problems may have served to structure the story in a particular way.

3 Look at the web pages of the following daily newspapers on the same day: the *Sun*, the *Daily Telegraph* and the *Guardian*. Compare their main stories and the way they are presented. Why do you think they are different?

Question for students taking OCR exam board AS level

4 (a) Identify and explain two ways in which journalists may decide that a story is newsworthy. (20 marks)

   (b) Outline and discuss the view that the news is a manufactured product. (40 marks)

Topic 3 How do the media affect people?

104

Getting you thinking

The passage on the right is adapted from an advice leaflet for teachers, produced by a Catholic teachers' group in Australia.

1 What is the writer concerned about?

2 What sort of music and TV programmes do you think the writer might object to?

3 What do you think is the writer's view of TV audiences and of young people in particular?

4 To what extent do you agree with the views expressed in the extract? What arguments could be presented against these views?

TV and music have a great influence on our students. You only have to hear them sing at a disco to realise they learn lyrics of very sensuous songs off by heart but find it difficult to recite Our Father. It may be useful to discuss as a class the frequency of sexual innuendo and references in shows they commonly watch.

What would God say to the following if He appeared before them today?

- Authors of corrupt novels, newspapers, plays, films, and indecent styles.
- Those who display eroticism (openly sexual behaviour) in modern music, television, dance and dress.
- Those who distribute condoms and other contraceptives to the youth of today, knowing full well what behaviour this encourages and knowing full well that 100 per cent 'safe sex' is a myth.
- Parents who allow their children to watch suggestive and lustful TV shows.

Adapted from a Teachers for Life Association leaflet
(Western Australia)

Groups such as the Christian Right in the extract above, the old-fashioned clergy, and many Conservative politicians, as well as pressure groups such as the National Viewers' and Listeners' Association, blame the media for corrupting the morals of society – especially the young. According to such groups, the media are responsible for family breakdown, crime, abortion, under-age sex and even homosexuality!

But concern about the media is not just limited to these kinds of groups. Many feminists and Marxists also feel that media messages can be corrupting – for example, by encouraging male violence against women, or by brainwashing viewers into being passive consumers.

Most ideas about media effects start by setting out an overall relationship between the media and their audience. For this reason they are often called **models** of media effects.

'Hypodermic syringe' model

In 1957 Vance Packard wrote a famous book about advertising called *The Hidden Persuaders*. He described how ordinary people were persuaded to consume goods without being aware of the techniques being used. His view appeared to be that the mass media were so powerful that they could directly 'inject' messages into the audience, or that, like a 'magic bullet', the message could be precisely targeted at an audience, who would automatically fall down when hit.

This view has become known as the **'hypodermic syringe' model**. According to this model, the audience is:

- passive – weak and inactive
- **homogeneous** – all the same
- 'blank pages' to be written on – with the media exerting a powerful influence that provokes an immediate response from the audience

Sociologists are generally very critical of this model. They believe that it fails to recognise the different social characteristics of audience members. They also believe that people are not as vulnerable as the hypodermic syringe model implies. Nevertheless, it has been very influential in **media regulation** in Britain. The 9 p.m. watershed and age restrictions on video hire, along with a range of other controls, have made censorship of the British media among the most restrictive in the free world.

Cultural effects model

The **cultural effects model** also sees the media as a very powerful influence, but it recognises that the media audience is very diverse. People have different backgrounds and experiences and this means that they interpret what they see, read and hear in different ways. A programme about life in an inner-London borough, for example, may be interpreted as evidence of racial conflict and deprivation, or as evidence of interesting cultural diversity, depending on who is watching.

But those who produce the media do expect the audience to respond to their work in a particular way. This anticipated response is known as the **preferred (or dominant) reading**. Those who lack direct experience of the issue presented by the media (in many cases the majority of the audience) are likely to accept this preferred reading.

In the Marxist version of this model, the ideas of the dominant groups in society – i.e. ruling-class ideology (see Unit 1, p. 11) – continually bombard audiences from every direction. It becomes difficult for anyone to retain a critical viewpoint. In the end most people come to believe that ruling-class ideas are right. They consent to the dominance of the powerful without even realising it. Many elderly people, for example, are so taken in by the media portrayal of social

Figure 4.3

security claimants as 'scroungers' that they don't even claim the benefits that are rightfully theirs.

Rather than having an immediate, direct effect, like the hypodermic syringe model, this model suggests that there is a slow, 'drip-drip' process taking place over a long period of time. Eventually, dominant values come to be shared by most people – values such as 'happiness is about possessions and money', 'you must look like the models in magazines', or 'most asylum seekers are just illegal immigrants'.

Active audience approaches

Other theories of media effects see the media as far less influential. They believe that people have considerable choice in the way they use and interpret the media. There are various versions of this view.

Selective filter model

Think of a sieve: some things pass through while others stay in the sieve. The **selective filter model** holds that media messages are similar: some get through, while others are ignored or rejected by the audience.

Klapper (1960) suggests that, for a media message to have any effect, it must pass through the following three filters:

- **Selective exposure** – a message must first be chosen to be viewed, read or listened to. Media messages can have no effect if no one sees or hears them! Choices depend upon people's interests, education, work commitments and so on.
- **Selective perception** – the messages have to be accepted. For example, some people may take notice of certain TV programmes but reject or ignore others.

- **Selective retention** – the messages have to 'stick'. People have a tendency to remember only the things they broadly agree with.

Uses and gratifications model

Blumler and McQuail (1968) point out that people get what *they* want from the media. Old people may watch soaps for companionship or to experience family life, whilst young people may watch soaps for advice on relationships or so that they have something to talk about at school the next day. In other words, the media satisfy a range of social needs, and different people get different pleasures – or gratifications – from the media.

Structured interpretation model

This view suggests that the way people interpret **media texts** differs according to their class, age, gender, ethnic group and other sources of identity. Those who hold this view analyse how and why different groups receive media messages. The methods they use are called **reception analysis**.

This is a more optimistic view than the cultural effects model. Media messages may be interpreted in a variety of ways, and even though one interpretation is dominant (the preferred reading) it is not always accepted.

Morley (1980) argues that people choose to make one of three responses:

- Dominant – they go along with the views expressed in the media text.
- Oppositional – they oppose the views expressed.
- Negotiated – they reinterpret the views to fit in with their own opinions and values.

For example, let's say the news contains a report about the Notting Hill Carnival. The report focuses on 12 arrests for drug dealing. A preferred (or dominant) reading might be that black people can't enjoy themselves without breaking the law. An **oppositional reading** might be that the police or the media are racist, focusing on drug-related crime unnecessarily. After all, 12 arrests are nothing, considering the millions who attend. A **negotiated reading** might be that there is probably a lot of drug use among Afro-Caribbeans, but that it's mostly cannabis use, which should, in the viewer's opinion, be legalised anyway.

These **'active audience' approaches** see the audience as interpreting media messages for themselves, and this makes it difficult to generalise about the effects of the media. Some of the most recent postmodern approaches go even further. Rather than seeing the audience as an undifferentiated mass, or as divided into cultural or other groupings, they argue that generalisations about media effects and audiences are impossible, since the same person may react to the same media message in different ways in different situations. Postmodern thinking on the media will be examined more fully in Topic 7 (p. 122).

1 How can the hypodermic syringe model be supported by people of very different views, e.g. Conservative politicians as well as some Marxists and feminists?

2 Why is the hypodermic syringe model also known as the 'magic bullet' model?

3 How has this model been influential?

4 Give two similarities and two differences between the cultural effects model and the hypodermic syringe model.

5 'It is no coincidence that Hollywood films were at their height of popularity during the war years.' How does this statement illustrate the uses and gratifications model?

6 In the example of the Notting Hill Carnival above, would the following people be most likely to have dominant, oppositional or negotiated responses? Give reasons for your answers:
  (a) an 18-year-old Afro-Caribbean male
  (b) a sociologist
  (c) a white, middle-aged, village dweller
  (d) the majority of people
  (e) young, white, inner-city kids

KEY TERMS

Sociology for AS Level

Active audience approaches – theories that stress that the effects of the media are limited because people are not easily influenced.

Cultural effects model – the view that the media are powerful in so far as they link up with other agents of socialisation to encourage particular ways of making sense of the world.

Homogeneous – the same throughout, undifferentiated.

Hypodermic syringe model – the view that the media are very powerful and the audience very weak. The media can 'inject' their messages into the audience, who accept them uncritically.

Media regulation – control of what we see, hear and read in the media from outside bodies.

Media text – any media output, be it written, aural or visual, e.g. magazine article, photo, CD, film, TV or radio programme.

Negotiated reading – an interpretation of a media text that modifies the intended (preferred) reading so that it fits with the audience member's own views.

Oppositional reading – an interpretation of a media text that rejects its intended (preferred) reading.

Preferred (or dominant) reading – the intended messages contained within the text.

Reception analysis – research that focuses on the way individuals make meanings from media messages.

Selective exposure – the idea that people only watch, listen or read what they want to.

Selective filter model – the view that audience members only allow certain media messages through.

Selective perception – the idea that people only take notice of certain media messages.

Selective retention – the idea that people only remember certain media messages.

Structured interpretation model – the view that people interpret media texts according to their various identities, e.g. class, gender, ethnic group.

Uses and gratifications model – the view that people use the media for their own purposes.

Item A
An incident that became a classic example of the powerful influence of the media was the radio broadcast in 1938 of H. G. Wells's book *The War of the Worlds*. The dramatised adaptation was so convincing that it generated mass hysteria in many American states. What is significant, though, is that not all of the six million listeners responded in the same way. The broadcast was a dramatisation of an invasion of Martians into a rural area of New Jersey, USA.

'Long before the broadcast had ended, people all over the US were praying, crying, fleeing frantically to escape death from the Martians.'

Research on the audience response was undertaken by Cantril (1940), who found that several factors affected the extent to which people believed the broadcast to be true. For example, listeners who had not heard the beginning of the programme were more likely to be taken in by it, and those who were not able to check out the story with neighbours, to 'reality test' it, were convinced by the broadcast and reacted accordingly. Radio news was at that time the only source of immediate knowledge about the world at large. As the programme was broadcast in the style of a news programme, listeners were more likely to treat it as real.

Adapted from M. Haralambos (ed.) (1986) *Sociology: New Directions*, Ormskirk: Causeway Press

Item B
The Coal Dispute of 1984 (referred to as the 'miners' strike' by the media) occurred as a result of the decision by the Coal Board to close pits much earlier and in greater number than had been agreed in writing. The police and miners were involved in well-publicised confrontations. The media blamed the miners for both the strike and the resulting violence. They also greatly exaggerated the alleged lack of solidarity among the miners by constantly referring to the 'drift back to work', which, in fact, was the case for only a small minority of miners.

In order to expose the main messages received by the audience, Philo asked audience members, in groups, a year later, to write their own media stories based on photographs. The respondents were shown pictures of violence and asked to put together a news item. This was then followed up by interviews where the respondents were given the opportunity to explain their thinking. Philo found that many of the audience members produced very similar stories, focusing on the violence of the picket-lines and on the phrase 'drift back to work' (implying that the strike was failing).

Taken at face value this would seem to suggest that the audience were all passive victims of the media, as the hypodermic syringe model suggests. However, through interviews, Philo discovered that the respondents were perfectly able to create stories 'in the style of a biased media', while not actually believing these stories.

While all believed in the media's view that violence is wrong, there was not common agreement on who should be blamed. Working-class trade unionists blamed the police, whilst middle-class professionals were more likely to blame the pickets for starting the trouble.

Adapted from G. Philo (ed.) (1990) *Seeing and Believing: The Influence of Television*, London: Routledge

1 In your own words, explain what is meant by the 'hypodermic syringe' model. (2)

2 Suggest two ways in which the *War of the Worlds* example (Item A) appears to support the hypodermic syringe model. (4)

3 Suggest three reasons why the media may have blamed the miners for the strike (Item B). (6)

4 Identify and briefly explain two cultural factors that may have influenced those who fled the 'Martian attack' (Item A). (8)

5 Examine sociological criticisms of the hypodermic syringe model. (20)

6 Using material from the Items and elsewhere, assess the view that, rather than having a uniform effect, the media mean different things to different people. (20)

Extension activities

1 There is a great deal of concern about lack of control of the internet. Search the web using the keyword 'censorship' to find out arguments for and against regulation of the internet.

2 Find the website of the Advertising Standards Authority. Look up some of its adjudications (decisions about complaints), and see to what extent you agree with them.

3 Complete a media grid for each member of your household, detailing one day's media use. Follow this up by asking each person to state, for each viewing/listening slot, which of the following needs or gratifications it satisfied:
• Diversion (escape from routine)

• Interaction with others (companionship, conversation, etc.)
• Learning (information-seeking, education)
• Advice (personal development etc.)

Annotate the grid using the letters D, I, L and A to indicate their responses. At the end, count up the letters, and compare the uses and gratifications of the media for different household members.

Question for students taking OCR exam board AS level

4 (a) Identify and explain two ways in which media audiences may use the media. (20 marks)
(b) Outline and discuss the view that media content has an immediate and direct effect on audiences. (40 marks)

Getting you thinking

Above: Anthony Hopkins as Hannibal Lecter

Right: Rock performer, Marilyn Manson

An investigation by the Justice Department and the Federal Trade Commission into the marketing of violent films and games commented that, by the age of 18, the average American had seen 40,000 screen murders and 200,000 acts of violence on television and in films.

The cold-blooded murder of 12 Columbine High School students and a teacher by two fellow students, who then killed themselves, generated revulsion and soul-searching among millions of Americans. The incident in Littleton, Colorado, on April 20, 1999 was the sixth and worst such school-based 'massacre' in less than two years. Much of the analysis and criticism focused on guns and their easy availability and the possible de-sensitising [making people less concerned about real violence] effects of video games, violent films and rock lyrics.

Adapted from C. Cozens, writing in the *Media Guardian*, Tuesday, 12 September 2000

1 **Can you think of any specific examples of violent video games, films and rock lyrics?**

2 **Do you think that these might have a dangerous effect on some members of the audience? If so, what possible effects might they have?**

3 **What sorts of viewers do you think are most vulnerable? Why?**

4 **Do you agree that screen violence may have a de-sensitising effect?**

On the 12th of February 1993, two 10-year-old boys abducted toddler James Bulger from a shopping mall. They tortured and killed him, according to the tabloid press, by mimicking scenes from a video – *Child's Play 3*. Later that year, the judge, in sentencing the boys, speculated on the significant role that the film had played. An obvious example of the dangerous effects of screen violence, you may think. However, things were not quite that simple. The police stated that there was no evidence at all that either of James's killers had seen the video.

This case illustrates the controversy and confusion that surround the 70 years of debate and research about violence and the media. In the main, researchers have fallen into one of two major camps:

1 The **effects approach** – those who think that everyone is affected in much the same way by screen violence.
2 Alternative approaches – those who think that the media's effect depends on who is viewing and the situation in which that viewing takes place.

The effects approach

The main model underpinning the effects approach is the hypodermic syringe model (see Topic 3). The audience is seen as a homogeneous (similar) mass who interpret the media in the same uncritical way and are powerless to resist its influence. A direct **correlation** (connection) is believed to exist between screen violence and violence in society. The following are three examples of the possible effects of media violence.

1 *'Copycat' violence*

In 1963, Bandura, Ross and Ross showed three groups of children real, film and cartoon examples of a self-righting doll (bobo doll) being attacked with mallets, whilst a fourth group saw no violent activity. After being introduced to a room full of exciting toys, the children in each group were made to feel frustrated by being told that the toys were not for them. They were then led to another room containing a bobo doll, where they were observed through a one-way mirror. The three groups who had been shown the violent activity – whether real, film or cartoon – all behaved more aggressively than the fourth group.

2 *De-sensitisation*

A more subtle approach was adopted by Hilda Himmelweit (1958). She accepted that viewing one programme was not going to affect behaviour in everyone – only in the most disturbed. She suggested, however, that prolonged exposure to programmes portraying violence may have a 'drip drip' effect such that individuals are socialised into accepting violent behaviour as normal.

3 *Catharsis*

Not all effects research focuses on negative effects. Fesbach and Sanger (1971) found that screen violence can actually provide a safe outlet for people's aggressive tendencies (known as catharsis). They looked at the effects of violent TV on teenagers. A large sample of boys from both private schools and residential homes were fed a diet of TV for six weeks. Some groups could only watch aggressive programmes, whilst others were made to watch non-aggressive programmes. The observers noted at the end of the study that the groups who had seen only aggressive programmes were actually less aggressive in their behaviour than the others.

Criticisms of the effects approach

- Most effects studies have been conducted using a scientific approach. Some critics say that this makes their findings questionable, as people do not behave as naturally under laboratory conditions as they would in normal life.
- Effects studies often ignore other factors that may be causing violent or anti-social behaviour, such as peer-group influences.
- Effects theorists do not always distinguish between different kinds of screen violence, such as fictional violence and real-life violence in news and current affairs programmes.
- Recent research (see Morrison's work below) shows that the context in which screen violence occurs affects its impact.
- Effects studies often take a patronising view of children, seeing them as vulnerable to the damaging effects of the media. Recent work, such as that of Buckingham (see below), shows that children are much more **media literate** than researchers have assumed.

Despite these criticisms, the effects approach remains an influence on government policy. A report by Professor Elizabeth Newsom (1994) presented a strong case for greater controls over the renting of videos and, despite a wave of criticism of its use of the effects approach, led directly to the Video Recordings Act which gave videos certificates and restricted their availability to children.

Alternative approaches

These approaches focus on the audience as a heterogeneous (diverse) and active group, with different social characteristics and different ways of using and interpreting the media. They draw on 'uses and gratifications', 'cultural effects' and other 'active audience' theories (see Topic 3). The following are three examples of recent research using alternative approaches.

1 Buckingham (1993) looked at how children interpret media violence. He criticises effects research for failing to recognise that gender, class and ethnic identities are crucially important, as is the changing identity of the child as he/she grows up. Buckingham does not accept that children are especially vulnerable to TV violence. He argues that children are much more sophisticated in their understanding and more media literate than previous researchers have assumed.
2 Julian Wood (1996) conducted a small-scale study of boys' use of video. He attended an after-school showing of a horror video in the home of one of the boys (the boy's parents were away). Wood describes the boys' comments in detail, and is able to demonstrate that, in this situation, the horror film is used almost as a rite of passage. The boys can prove their heterosexuality to each other, behave in a macho way, swear and, above all, demonstrate their fearlessness. Rather than being a corrupting influence, video violence is merely a part of growing up.
3 Morrison (1999) showed a range of clips – including scenes from *Brookside*, news footage, and excerpts from violent films – to groups of women, young men, and war veterans. All of the interviewees felt that the most disturbing clip was a man beating his wife in *Ladybird, Ladybird*, a film by Ken Loach. It caused distress because of the realism of the setting, the strong language and the perceived unfairness, and also because viewers were concerned about the effect on the child actors in the scene. By contrast, the clip from *Pulp Fiction* – in which a man is killed out of the blue during an innocent conversation, spraying blood and chunks of brain around a car – was seen as 'humorous' and 'not violent', even by women over the age of 60, because there was lighthearted dialogue.

Where are we now?

So, over 1,000 studies later, we have not really made much progress and many questions remain. Are some people less able to distinguish between artificial and real violence? Is some censorship justified in order to protect us? But would more censorship push violence underground, so that even more disturbing material might become available? Does the way in which violence is depicted make a difference to its impact – for example, if there are differences in power between the participants, or if humour is involved?

The more we seek to find the answers to questions about the effects of media violence, the more questions seem to be generated.

1 Explain in your own words what is meant by the claim that there is a correlation between screen violence and violence in society.

2 How might the media de-sensitise their audience to violence?

3 Explain in your own words three limitations of the effects approach.

4 What evidence is there that the effects approach still has its supporters today?

5 Identify and explain three insights into the nature of the audience that critics of effects approaches have put forward.

KEY TERMS

Correlation – a relationship between two or more things, where one characteristic is directly affected by another.

'Copycat' violence – violence that occurs as a result of copying something that is seen in the media.

Media literate – an intelligent, critical and informed attitude to the media.

Effects approach – an approach based on the hypodermic syringe model (see Topic 3) which believes that the media have direct effects on their audience.

De-sensitization – the process by which, through repeated exposure to media violence, people come to accept violent behaviour as normal.

Catharsis – the process of relieving tensions – for example, violence on screen providing a safe outlet for people's violent tendencies.

Exploring violence and the media

Item A A study by Hagell and Newburn for the Policy Studies Institute compared young offenders' viewing habits with those of non-offending teenagers. They found that there were very few differences between the two groups in terms of what they watched, with hardly any having seen the films that were causing concern at the time. Few members of either group had a particular interest in violent output. The young offenders, in fact, generally had had less access to TVs, video, cable or satellite TV. Other factors beyond the media must be causing the differences in behaviour.

FAVOURITE TV PROGRAMMES (TOP FIVE)

Male offenders	Male schoolchildren
The Bill	Home and Away
EastEnders	Neighbours
Neighbours	The Bill
Home and Away	Quantum Leap

FAVOURITE FILMS (TOP FIVE, CERTIFICATE IN BRACKETS)

Male offenders	Male schoolchildren
Terminator 2 (15)	Terminator 2 (15)
New Jack City (18)	Point Break (18)
Scarface (18)	Aliens (18)
The Bodyguard (15)	White Men Can't Jump (15)
Absent Without Leave (18)	Blood Sport (18)

Adapted from A. Hagell and T. Newburn (1994) *Young Offenders and the Media: Viewing Habits*, London: PSI

Item B In responding to the observation that his new movie *The Phantom Menace* shouldn't contain so much gunfire, especially given the recent high school massacres, George Lucas commented:

'It really has to do with context. I definitely think that hurting people for fun and enjoyment is not the issue here. You have to fight for freedom, you have to fight for your rights, you have to fight in self-defence. You have to stand up for yourself.'

Samuel L. Jackson, who plays the Jedi Master, Windu, in *Phantom Menace*, is also featured in one of the films that was targeted after the Columbine massacre [see the 'Getting you thinking' activity on p. 108]. He played the Bible-quoting hit-man in the very violent *Pulp Fiction*. He also has a 17-year-old daughter, and he's happy to explain why he's not worried about what she sees on the big screen.

'It's not about the images that they're being bombarded with', he says. 'If you have some people at home who are looking at you and asking you every day what's going on and how your life is, you don't have to worry about them saying, "I hate everybody at my school and I'm going to kill them today." One of those guys had a sawn-off shotgun on his dresser and his parents didn't even notice. What the hell is that?'

Jackson, who is 50, reminds us that on-screen violence isn't exactly a new phenomenon, even if it has become more common and more graphic.

'When I was a kid, I lived in front of the television', says Jackson. 'There were people dying every hour, on the hour, on all those cowboy series – *Have Gun Will Travel*, *Wanted Dead or Alive* – and Christmas wasn't Christmas unless I got a toy gun. But none of my friends went out and killed anybody. We had people at home who cared about us. We had real guns in my house, but I never went outside and played with them. I understood what guns were.'

Adapted from C. Vognar, writing in the *Dallas Morning News*, 22 May 1999

1 In your own words, explain what is meant by 'de-sensitisation'. (2)

2 Suggest two reasons why the PSI study concludes that 'other factors beyond the media must be causing the differences in behaviour' between the young offenders and the schoolchildren (Item A). (4)

3 Give three reasons why George Lucas and Samuel L. Jackson are not concerned about the violence in *The Phantom Menace*. (6)

4 Identify and briefly explain two other factors that might be responsible for the differences in behaviour of the two groups studied in Item A. (8)

5 Discuss the view that the social situation of audience members affects the way in which media messages are received and understood. (20)

6 Using material from the Items and elsewhere, assess the view that violence in the media should be subject to stricter controls. (20)

Extension activities

1 Using the internet and/or newspaper CD-Roms, investigate one dramatic act of violence that has been reported in the press over the last few years – perhaps the murder of James Bulger or Stephen Lawrence, the Dunblane massacre or the Littleton shootings. To what extent is screen violence blamed ? What actual evidence is put forward to link media violence to the murders?

2 Investigate what types of violence different age, gender, class or ethnic groups consider to be disturbing. Present your findings quantitatively.

3 Using a library or the internet, find out about any one study of the media and violence. Present the key findings and an account of the research to the rest of your class.

Question for students taking OCR exam board AS level

4 (a) Identify and explain two ways in which violence on screen may have a positive effect on audiences. (20 marks)

   (b) Outline and discuss the view that violence on screen can cause violence in society. (40 marks)

Getting you thinking

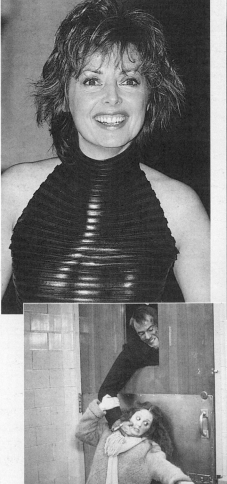

Look at these images of women.

1 Which of these women are playing stereotyped female roles? What are these roles?

2 What do these photographs tell us about the way in which women are portrayed in the media?

3 To what extent do you think that images of women in the media are changing?

As women have begun to achieve more visibility outside the home and to compete on a more equal basis with men in the workplace, you might expect this to be reflected in the mass media. Sociological research suggests, however, that, although there is some recent evidence of greater equality, the roles allocated to the sexes across a range of media – such as advertising, television and film – have been restricted in the following ways:

- Women have been allocated a limited range of roles
- Women are less visible in the media than men.
- Women have been presented as ideals.
- Women have been selected to appeal to men.
- Men have been seen as aggressors, women as victims.
  Let's look at these issues in more detail.

A limited range of roles

Women are represented in a narrow range of social roles in the media, whilst men perform the full range of social and occupational roles. Women are especially found in domestic settings – as busy housewives, contented mothers, eager consumers and so on. Tuchman (1978) adds sexual and romantic roles to this list. Whilst these are still the primary **representations**, there has recently been an increase in the number of 'stronger' roles for women – for example, in TV dramas such as *Prime Suspect and Ally McBeal*. Soap operas also tend to promote independent and assertive female characters, whereas male soap characters tend to be weaker. This may be because soaps focus on domestic issues, the only legitimate (accepted) area for female authority.

Women are rarely shown in high-status occupational roles such as doctors or lawyers. If they are, they are often shown to have problems in dealing with their 'unusual' circumstances. For example, they are portrayed as unfulfilled (motherhood is sometimes offered as the answer to this), as unattractive, as unstable, or as having problems with relationships. If they have children, successful women are sometimes shown as irresponsible, with their children getting into trouble due to their emotional neglect. Men are rarely portrayed in this way.

Visibility

In 1990, 89 per cent of voice-overs for television commercials were male, because the male voice is seen to represent authority. Women were the main stars of only 14 per cent of mid-evening television programmes in the 1990s. Analysis of Hollywood films indicates that few women stars are seen by the major studios as being able to carry a film by themselves, although women are slowly moving into lead roles in traditionally masculine areas such as science fiction.

Female issues may be **marginalised** by the media. Most newspapers have 'women's pages' which focus on women as a special group with special – often emotional – needs. Such pages tend to concentrate on beauty and slimming. Tuchman uses the term **'symbolic annihilation'** to describe the way in which women in the media are absent, condemned or trivialised.

Women are also absent from top jobs in the media. An analysis of powerful positions generates the following facts: the majority of media owners are men, as are the higher position holders within media empires. For example, out of 30 top BBC executives in 1996, only four were female. In newspapers, in 1995–6 only 20 per cent of positions of significant decision-making power were held by women. In 1992 there were no female sports editors on national or Sunday newspapers. Women made up only 17 per cent of journalists on national newspapers, and only 35 per cent of all journalists in the UK in 1996.

Women as ideals

Ferguson (1983) conducted a content analysis of women's magazines from between 1949 and 1974 and 1979 and 1980. She notes that such magazines are organised around 'a cult of femininity' which promotes an ideal where excellence is achieved through caring for others, the family, marriage and appearance. Modern female magazines, especially those aimed at teenagers, are moving away from these stereotypes – although Ferguson argues that even these tend to focus on 'him, home and looking good (for him)'. Winship (1987), however, stresses the supportive roles such magazines play in the lives of women, especially as many women are largely excluded from the masculine world of work and leisure. She argues that such magazines present women with a broader range of options than ever before, and that they tackle problems that have been largely ignored by the male-dominated media, such as domestic violence and child abuse.

Most women in films and on television (especially presenters) tend to be under 30. Physical looks, sex appeal and youth seem to be necessary attributes for women to be successful in television and in the cinema. The same is not true for men. Wolf (1990) points out that the media, especially advertising, present a particular physical image as the 'normal' or 'ideal' body image for women to have, even though this image may be unattainable for the majority of women. Some commentators, such as Orbach (1991), have linked such images to anorexia and bulimia in teenage girls.

Sex appeal

Women are often presented as sexual objects to be enjoyed by men. The most extreme media version of this is pornography and 'Page 3 girls' in newspapers. Mulvey (1975) argues that film-makers employ a 'male gaze', whereby the camera lens essentially 'eyes up' the female characters, providing erotic pleasure for men. This is more blatant in films such as *Striptease, Basic Instinct* and *Showgirls*.

Men's style magazines – such as FHM, Maxim and Loaded – encourage young men to dress, smell and consume in particular ways. There is, however, less of a burden on men to change themselves to conform to this ideal. Whilst women may feel that they need to conform in order to ensure that they are desirable, it is more of an option for men.

Buckingham (1993) argues that many boys and probably most men fear being labelled 'effeminate'. The apparent **feminisation of masculinity** (obsessiveness around fashion, men wearing perfume, etc.) has therefore to be offset by more conspicuous and 'macho' behaviour. The 'new lad' that has emerged is supposedly counter-balanced by the 'ladette' (e.g. Sara Cox and Denise Van Outen), who leers at males through an alcoholic haze and is also aggressively sexual.

Male aggressor, female victim

Many people are concerned about the media's presentation of sexual violence against women. A Channel 4 series, *Hard*

News, analysed more than 600 articles in ten national newspapers in early 1990. They found that, despite the fact that such crime only makes up 2 per cent of all recorded crime, almost 70 per cent of crime stories focused on rape. Such stories were often distorted in their reporting. Rape victims were often stereotyped as either 'good' women (e.g. virgins, mothers) who had been violated, or 'bad' women who led men on. Newspapers often **sensationalised** cases and focused on what they saw as the most 'titillating' aspects – usually the details of the defendant's evidence.

Joan Smith (1989) notes how the female fear of violent assault is used as a basis for many films. These films may add to the stock of fear that already exists in society. They contribute to the notion of women as 'vulnerable and potential victims' of the superior strength of men. Yet women are also presented as needing the protection of males. 'Female fear sells films. It's a box office hit. ... Terror, torture, rape, mutilation and murder are handed to actresses by respectable directors as routinely as tickets on a bus. No longer the stock in trade only of pornographers and video-nasty producers, they can be purchased any day at a cinema near you' (Smith, 1989).

During the 1980s, action films such as *Commando*, *Die Hard* and *Predator* paraded the bodies of their male heroes in advanced stages of both muscular development and undress. One film in particular, *Rambo: First Blood Part II*, starring Sylvester Stallone, became a particular focus for concern. The figure of Rambo has been taken to represent the re-emergence of a threatening, physical form of masculinity. In an overview of the period, Jonathan Rutherford (1998) put forward the idea that there existed two key images of masculinity in the late 20th century. He termed these images, 'new man' and 'retributive man'. For Rutherford, images of the new man attempt – partly in a response to feminism – to express men's repressed emotions, revealing a more feminised image. Against this, the face of retributive man represents the struggle to reassert a traditional masculinity; a tough authority.

More recently, male violence in cinema has acquired a glamour and stylishness that seems to celebrate the more traditional representations of masculinity. Films like *Lock Stock and Two Smoking Barrels*, *Face Off* and *Snatch* present men who gain admiration by solving their problems through violence. These kinds of films are currently outnumbering those that represent alternative views of masculinity, such as *The Full Monty*.

Explanations of gender representations

Feminists have been very critical of the representations of men and women in the media. However, they differ in their emphasis. (See Unit 1, Topic 7 for explanations of the different types of feminism.)

- **Liberal feminists** believe that media representations are lagging behind women's achievements in society. However, they also believe that the situation is improving as the number of female journalists, editors and broadcasters increases.
- **Socialist and Marxist feminists** believe that stereotypical images of men and women are a by-product of the need to make a profit. The male-dominated media aim to attract the largest audience possible, and this leads to an emphasis on the traditional roles of men and women.
- **Radical feminists** feel strongly that the media reproduce patriarchy. Traditional images are deliberately transmitted by male-dominated media to keep women oppressed in a narrow range of roles.

Not everyone accepts these kinds of feminist analysis. Critics argue that they under-estimate women's ability to see through stereotyping. Pluralists (see Topic 1, p. 97) believe that the media simply reflect social attitudes and public demand. They argue that the media are meeting both men and women's needs – although the question remains: to what extent are the media actually creating those needs in the first place?

CHECK YOUR UNDERSTANDING ✓ ✓ ✓

1 What might be the reason why women often have independent and assertive roles in soap operas?

2 Describe the differences in gender representation in top positions in the media.

3 How does Winship argue that women's magazines can be supportive?

4 What problems are associated with the 'ideal' body image for women?

5 How does Buckingham explain the emergence of the 'new lad'?

6 According to Joan Smith, what are the effects of media representations of women as victims?

7 How do feminists explain the representations of women in the media?

KEY TERMS

Feminisation of masculinity – refers to men adopting behaviour traditionally associated with women, e.g. wearing make-up, showing concern over fashion.

Marginalised – forced out of the mainstream.

Representation – the way in which people are portrayed by the media.

Sensationalise – exaggerate something in order to excite an audience.

Symbolic annihilation – term used by Tuchman to describe the way in which women in the media are absent, condemned or trivialised.

Exploring gender and the media

Item A

Item B

LEVEL OF APPEARANCE BY GENDER (TERRESTRIAL TELEVISION)

Level of appearance	Male No.	%	Female No.	%	Total No.	%
Major role	1,482	16	1,080	23	2,562	18
Minor role	1,475	16	693	15	2,168	16
Incidental/interviewer	6,217	68	2,922	62	9,139	66
Total	9,174	100	4,695	100	13,869	100

Source: Broadcasting Standards Commission Report 1999, p. 100

Item C

The presentation of women in the media is biased because it emphasises women's domestic, sexual, consumer and marital activities to the exclusion of all else. Women are depicted as busy housewives, as contented mothers, as eager consumers and as sex objects. This does indeed indicate bias because, although similar numbers of men are fathers and husbands, the media has much less to say about these male roles; men are seldom presented nude, nor is their marital or family status continually quoted in irrelevant contexts. Just as men's domestic and marital roles are ignored, the media also ignore that well over half of British adult women go out to paid employment, and that many of both their interests and problems are employment-related.

J. Tunstall (1983) *The Media in Britain*, London: Constable

1 Explain what is meant by the term 'presentation of women in the media' (Item C). (2)

2 Compare the covers of the two magazines in Item A. Identify two assumptions that they make about the interests of young men or young women. (4)

3 Identify three patterns in the data in Item B. (6)

4 Identify and briefly explain two reasons why more men appear on TV than women. (8)

5 '... the media has much less to say about ... male roles; men are seldom presented nude, nor is their marital or family status continually quoted in irrelevant contexts' (Item C). Discuss how helpful this statement is in understanding the representation of men in the media. (20)

6 Using material from the Items and elsewhere, assess the view that women's representation in the media is distorted and limited. (20)

Extension activities

1 Individually or in groups, conduct a content analysis of a soap opera, a news broadcast, a game show and a TV drama. How many men and women appear? How much time does each gender spend on screen? What roles do they play? How typical is each programme of others of its kind? What conclusions can you draw about men and women in the media?

2 Compare the views of young men and young women about the representation of women in the media. You could do this by conducting in-depth interviews or by using a questionnaire. Try showing respondents examples of men's and women's magazines to get them talking.

Question for students taking OCR exam board AS level

3 (a) Identify and explain two ways in which women have been misrepresented by the media. (20 marks)

(b) Outline and discuss the view that the representation of women in the media today is an accurate reflection of their role in society. (40 marks)

Getting you thinking

1 **What do you think most people's interpretation of what is happening in this photograph is likely to be?**

2 **Why will they think this?**

3 **What other possible interpretations can you think of?**

In the photograph above a black, plain-clothes police officer leads some of his uniformed colleagues in chasing a suspect. However, many people are likely to interpret the photograph differently, believing that the black man is being chased by the police. This mistake should come as no surprise, as many people do associate young black men with criminality. Why is this? Perhaps the explanation lies with the representation of ethnic minorities in the media. Ethnic minorities tend to be either ignored by the media or, when they do actually appear, portrayed in distorted ways that owe more to **stereotypes** than to reality. But ethnic minorities are not the only groups who have reason to be concerned about their portrayal in the media. This topic will look at media representations of various groups.

Ethnic minorities

Old films, comics and adventure stories that portrayed black people as happy, dancing savages with a brutal streak have, thankfully, largely disappeared from modern television and films. However, the media still have a tendency to associate black people with physical rather than intellectual activities, and to view them in stereotypical ways. Some of the most common stereotypes and myths are described below.

Black people are portrayed in the media in the following ways:

- **As criminal** – van Dijk (1991) conducted a content analysis of tens of thousands of news items across the world over several decades. He found that black crime and violence are one of the most frequent issues in ethnic coverage. Black people, particularly Afro-Caribbeans, tend to be portrayed, especially in the tabloid press, as criminals – and more recently as members of organised criminal gangs. The word 'black' is often used as a prefix if an offender is a member of an ethnic minority, e.g. 'a black youth'. The word 'white' is rarely used in the same way. The truth is that a black person is 36 times more likely to be the victim of a violent attack than a white person.

- **As a threat** – tabloid newspapers are prone to panic about the numbers of ethnic minorities in Britain. It is often suggested that immigrants are a threat in terms of their 'numbers', because of the impact they might have on the supply of jobs, housing and other facilities. The same newspapers are also concerned about refugees and asylum seekers, who are allegedly coming to Britain to abuse the welfare state and take advantage of a more successful economy than their own.

- **As abnormal** – some sections of the media are guilty of creating false cultural stereotypes around the value systems and norms of other cultures. For example, tabloid newspapers have run stories that suggest that Muslims have negative attitudes towards women. They claim that they 'force' daughters into arranged marriages against their will. The distinction between 'forced' marriage – an extremely rare occurrence, strongly disapproved of by Asian communities – and arranged marriage, which is based on mutual consent, is rarely made.

- **As unimportant** – some sections of the media imply that the lives of white people are somehow more important than the lives of non-white people. News items about disasters in other countries are often restricted to a few lines or words, especially if the population is non-white. The misfortunes of one British person tend to be prioritised over the sufferings of thousands of foreigners.

- **As dependent** – as the government report *Viewing the World* (2000) points out, stories about less developed countries tend to focus on the 'coup-war-famine-starvation syndrome'. The implication of such stories, both in newspapers and on television, is that the problems of developing countries are the result of stupidity, tribal conflict, too many babies, laziness, corruption and unstable political regimes. It is implied that the governments of these countries are somehow inadequate because they cannot solve these problems. Such countries are portrayed as coming to the West for help time and time again. The idea that the poverty of developing countries may be due to their exploitation by the West is often ignored and neglected.

Under-representation

Surveys of television, advertising and films indicate that black people are under-represented. When they do appear, the range of roles they play is very limited. Black people are rarely shown as ordinary citizens who just happen to be black. More often they play 'black' roles, their attitudes and behaviour being heavily determined by their ethnic identity. Some soaps such as *EastEnders* have in fact included black characters as ordinary members of the community. However, its main rival on ITV, *Coronation Street*, has had only one leading black character in its 40-year history, despite being set in what would be a multicultural area of Manchester. It seems that, for every positive observation, there is a negative equivalent, as the table below demonstrates.

REPRESENTATION OF ETHNIC GROUPS IS BECOMING MORE POSITIVE	REPRESENTATION OF ETHNIC GROUPS IS NOT IMPROVING
Images of race found on television or in advertising show that a conscious effort has been made to counter the negative stereotypes of the past. For example, Downing (1988) points to the positive role models offered by shows such as The Cosby Show and The Fresh Prince of Bel-Air.	Jhally and Lewis (1992) are critical of shows such as The Cosby Show because they depict an extremely unrepresentative group of black people, who are isolated from and who ignore the problems of racism, deprivation and under-achievement that disproportionately affect black people in the USA.
Others point to the positive portrayal of black athletes and musicians.	The constant depiction of blacks as athletes and musicians restricts the role models open to young blacks, and reinforces a stereotype in white people's minds.
Black presenters are much more common, with some in positions of considerable authority, e.g. Trevor MacDonald, Moira Stewart	Whilst the number of black presenters has increased, this is merely 'window dressing', as the numbers of black producers, researchers and writers are disproportionately low, and most black people in the media are working 'behind the scenes' in the catering and cleaning departments.
Some parts of the media that cater for ethnic minorities are on the increase, and their representations of race are very different from those found in the wider media.	Black media such as *The Voice*, *Ebony* and *Network East* effectively marginalise ethnic issues, because the mainstream media do not bother to include such issues, knowing that coverage is already 'taken care of'.

What are we to conclude from all this? Have the media begun to recognise the needs, interests and experiences of ethnic minorities in Britain? It is certainly true that the media have been very positive in their exposure of problems such as racism. The murder of the black teenager Stephen Lawrence by white racists in 1993 received high-profile coverage, both on television and in the press. Even the *Daily Mail* presented a front-page story highlighting police racism, and attempted to 'name and shame' the racists who committed the murder.

An interesting recent development is media recognition of the influence of ethnic cultures on white culture. The comedian Ali G **satirises** the cultural mix of modern British youth. But there is an irony here: Ali G is played by a white man.

The disabled

Ten per cent of the UK population are disabled, yet disabled people make up only 1.5 per cent of the characters we see on television. The table below shows that disabled characters who do appear tend to be subjected to negative emotional responses.

ATTITUDES SHOWN TOWARDS CHARACTERS IN TELEVISION DRAMA		
Attitude	Able-bodied characters %	Disabled characters %
Sympathy	7	34
Pity	2	12
Patronising	14	30
Sadness	3	16
Fear	7	16
Avoidance	3	9
Attraction	43	33
Respect	51	39
Mocking	8	10
Abuse	13	15

Source: G. Cumberbatch and R. Negrine (1992) *Images of Disability on Television*, London: Routledge

There have, however, been recent improvements, particularly in the cinema. Films such as *My Left Foot* (1987), *Children of a Lesser God* (1989), *The Piano* (1992) and *Four Weddings and a Funeral* (1997) had disabled characters – with conditions as diverse as cerebral palsy, deafness, dumbness and blindness – leading fulfilling and independent lives.

The elderly

Whilst old age is generally represented as undesirable in the media, significant numbers of older middle-class males are portrayed in prominent social positions. In films and television, older men such as Michael Douglas are still seen as sexual partners to young women. Females, however, must match up to a youthful ideal all their lives. Even in non-fiction programming, such as news broadcasts, younger women tend to complement older men.

Soap operas tend to feature older people, but this reflects the perceived market for such programmes. Sitcoms tend to show the elderly as feeble, vague or cantankerous – just think of Victor Meldrew. The very old are under-represented in all aspects of the media, and the problems of ageing, such as decline and dependency, are generally ignored.

Class

The upper class are often seen in nostalgic representations which paint a rosy picture of a time when Britain was great, and honour, culture and good breeding prevailed. Wealth and social inequality are rarely critically examined. Examples of this type of representation include TV costume dramas such as *Pride and Prejudice*, and films such as *A Room With a View*.

The middle classes are over-represented in the media, possibly because most of the creative personnel in the media are themselves middle-class. In news and current affairs the middle classes dominate in positions of authority – the 'expert' is invariably middle-class.

Jhally and Lewis (1992) found that, on American TV between 1971 and 1989, 90 per cent of characters were middle-class, whilst the percentage of working-class characters over the period fell from 4 per cent to only 1 per cent. In Britain the working class tend to appear as criminals, single parents, 'welfare scroungers' or delinquent children. Soaps in Britain have tended to show working-class life in a more positive, if unrealistic, light – presenting an ideal of a tight-knit community with a shared history and mutual obligations.

Homosexuals

Until recently, gay people have generally been either invisible in the media or represented in a negative light – being stereotyped as either 'camp' gay men or 'butch' lesbian women.

Gay men were heavily stigmatised in the wake of the initial AIDS reporting, but, since then, sexuality has been more openly discussed. Several celebrities have recently 'come out' (declared their sexual orientation publicly). These include Michael Barrymore, Elton John, George Michael and Stephen Gateley. In such cases, their appeal to female audiences has suffered little from the publicity given to their sexual orientation.

It appears that homosexuality is now much more acceptable within the media. Graham Norton, the openly gay presenter of a popular TV chat show, has a huge following of mainly heterosexual viewers. The runner-up in the *Big Brother* reality game show in 2000 was a lesbian whose sexuality was perceived as normal by both viewers and the other *Big Brother* housemates. Mainstream television dramas now explore the lives of homosexuals, while *Brookside*, another soap, has had two main storylines featuring gay characters.

Youth and 'moral panics'

Young people are often presented as a problem by the media. By identifying groups of young people as 'football hooligans' and 'ravers', the media can create a **'moral panic'** – in which the behaviour of such groups is seen as a threat to the moral order and stability of society. The media play a key role in creating moral panics by sensationalising and grossly exaggerating the threat that these groups pose. They soon become **'folk devils'** – evil people who are threatening our ordinary, everyday lives.

Ironically, the media's desire to produce sensational stories about youth, sometimes out of nothing, can help create the very behaviour they are attacking. For example, many young people are actually attracted by sensational coverage of youth groups (which they otherwise might not have heard about or recognised). They begin to conform to media stereotypes in order to acquire status and recognition in the eyes of their peers, and some notoriety in the wider society. The prejudiced attitude of the general public and the police drives them further towards deviance (a process known as **deviance amplification**). Thus a real problem is created out of something that would probably have remained fairly small-scale had it not been for the media's sensational coverage.

MORAL PANICS AND 'FOLK DEVILS' – SOME EXAMPLES

Date(s)	Moral panic – the perceived problem	'Folk devil' – the group to blame	Potential victims
Late 1940s–1980s	violent youth – civil unrest; threat to public order/decency/safety	most youth subcultures, such as 'mods and rockers'	ordinary citizens and their property
Every decade	football hooliganism – street violence; vandalism; damage to life/property	organised, 'mindless' hooligans who are not 'real' fans	innocent bystanders; 'real' football fans
Late 1960s	hippies – a threat due to their alternative lifestyle, drug-taking and sexual freedom	long-haired, young middle classes	all decent; hardworking people
1960s and 70s	sex on screen – corruption of children and offence to the unwitting viewer	irresponsible film and TV producers	the impressionable young; decent folk
1970s	mugging – threat to peace in the streets and personal security	black youths	the vulnerable on the street
mid 70s	'scroungers' – social security fraud	undeserving, fraudulent claimants (often non-white)	everyone who pays taxes
Early 1980s	Aids – death through deviant sexual practices	mainly homosexuals	all the sexually active, especially young, single people
1980s, 90s	glue-sniffing – out of control youth; premature death	youth underclass	all lower working class youth
1990s	female violence – breakdown in social values and gender roles; threat to family life	girl gangs the family as an institution	the vulnerable on the street;
Late 1980s–1990s	club culture , ecstasy – drug deaths; threats to public order	clubbers; ravers	all young people; the general public
Mid 1990s	Satanic ritual abuse – widespread sexual abuse of children by parents	mostly incestuous fathers and overzealous social workers	children and the family unit
Mid 1990s	children, violence and the family (plus video nasties) – moral decline; family breakdown; corruption of young	children of 'underclass' families	toddlers; small children
Late 1990s	paedophilia, child pornography	middle-aged men, organised through the internet	every child

CHECK YOUR UNDERSTANDING

1 What does van Dijk's study tell us about media representations of ethnic minorities?

2 What do the media suggest is the main motivation for refugees and asylum seekers in coming to Britain?

3 How is the relationship between developing countries and the West portrayed in the media?

4 How have representations of the disabled improved recently?

5 Compare media representations of the upper, middle and working classes.

6 How is the media's attitude to gay people changing?

7 Explain in your own words the terms 'moral panic' and 'folk devils'.

8 How can media coverage of deviant youth groups actually make the 'problem' worse?

Item A

Item B — *Improving media relations: a view from the Muslim News*

There isn't a day that goes by without seeing shrieking headlines in newsprint against Islam or Muslims. Muslims respond in various ways.

In September, the *Express* ran a front-page Islamophobic headline, 'Moslem plot to bomb London'. It implied that Muslims in Britain were involved in a plot to bomb London. The news item in question was about the raids and subsequent arrest of seven Muslims from the Middle East who were residing in Britain. The allegation in the news item was that they were intending to carry out bombings in London, targeting American institutions. However, until now no evidence has been found to support such allegations. All were released without charge (one was re-arrested after the US requested extradition to the US – Britain is still waiting for the 'evidence' from the US).

When the *Express* published the offending headline, the Muslim Council of Britain (MCB) immediately contacted the newspaper, and as a result an apology was published in the editorial column on the following day, September 25. The editorial accepted that 'it is wrong to suggest all Moslems are Islamic extremists linked to Osama bin Laden'. It concluded: 'it was not our intention to cause offence to the Moslem community. We're sorry.'

However, the editorial still used the term 'Islamic extremists'. It never uses the equivalent term 'Christian extremists' when it reports or comments on the terrorism perpetuated by Christians in Northern Ireland or in Bosnia or Kosovo.

A. Versi, writing in the *Muslim News*, 27 November 1998

Item C — *Over-50s rail at TV stereotyping*

Just days after Victor Meldrew was killed off and Inspector Morse had a fatal heart attack, a new survey has found that older people resent being stereotyped as either grumpy or sweet in TV comedy and drama. The study of the over-50s also found a lack of interest among older audiences in programmes specifically aimed at them, and it found that older viewers believe that over-50s are under-represented on TV programmes aimed at mass audiences.

The advertising industry in particular is criticised by 50-somethings for portraying a narrow, idealised version of consumers. People in the 50–60 age group felt strongly that advertisers should change their attitudes and the images they use during the next five to ten years, to reflect the profile of their changing market.

The survey, *Age in the Frame*, which was drawn from the results of focus group sessions, is published today by the Independent Television Commission and Age Concern England.

While many over-50s enjoyed *One Foot in the Grave*, they found it unfortunate that Victor Meldrew's grumpy character was the best-known old person on TV. *Last of the Summer Wine* also came in for criticism, though again some older people said they still found it funny. But one focus group participant described the long-running sitcom as 'patronising'. He said: 'It's just a bunch of daft old gits running around and fancying a woman with wrinkled stockings around her ankles.'

The report found that older viewers resent being pigeon-holed as the *Songs of Praise* generation, when they have a wide range of interests and viewing habits.

Left: an infamous Benetton advert of the 1990s, depicting a man dying of Aids

D COLORS
NETTON.

Deviance amplification – the reinforcing of a person's or a group's deviant identity, as a result of condemnation by agencies of social control such as the media.

Folk devils – groups seen by the media as evil and a threat to the moral well-being of society.

Moral panic – public concern, created by the media, about the behaviour of certain groups of people who are seen as a threat to the moral order and stability of society.

Satirise – ridicule something or somebody in order to make a point.

Stereotype – a typical or 'shorthand' picture of a certain group.

Extension activities

1 Find the websites of the Refugee Council and the Campaign against Racism and Fascism. What do they have to say about media coverage of refugees and asylum seekers?

2 Watch a range of television programmes one evening. Conduct a content analysis by counting the numbers and types of roles taken by older and younger people. What conclusions can you reach about media representations of age?

3 Find the report, *Viewing the World*, at the website of the Department for International Development. This can be accessed from the main government website (www.open.gov.uk). What methods does the study use and what are its key conclusions about media coverage of development issues?

Question for students taking OCR exam board AS level

4 (a) Identify and explain two ways in which ethnic minorities have been misrepresented by the media. (20 marks)

(b) Outline and discuss the view that the representation of ethnic minorities in the media has significantly improved over the last 20 years. (40 marks)

One respondent said: 'we like the same things we liked when we were younger. I like *The Royle Family* and *Have I Got News For You* just like my grandson.' A lady in her 60s added that she liked 'a good violent American thriller. The type of thing with Al Pacino in it.' Over half of over-65s, and 40 per cent of over-50s, thought there should be more older people on TV, and that older women are particularly under-represented.

Guardian, 27 November 2000

1 Explain what is meant by the term 'Islamophobic' (Item B). (2)

2 Suggest two reasons why Benetton selected the image in Item A. (4)

3 Identify three stereotypes associated with older people (Item C). (6)

4 Identify and briefly explain two reasons why the author of the article in Item B may not have been satisfied with the apology from the *Express*. (8)

5 Discuss the problems – for individuals and society – created by stereotyping in the media. (20)

6 Using material from the Items and elsewhere, assess the view that stereotyping in the media is declining. (20)

Getting you thinking

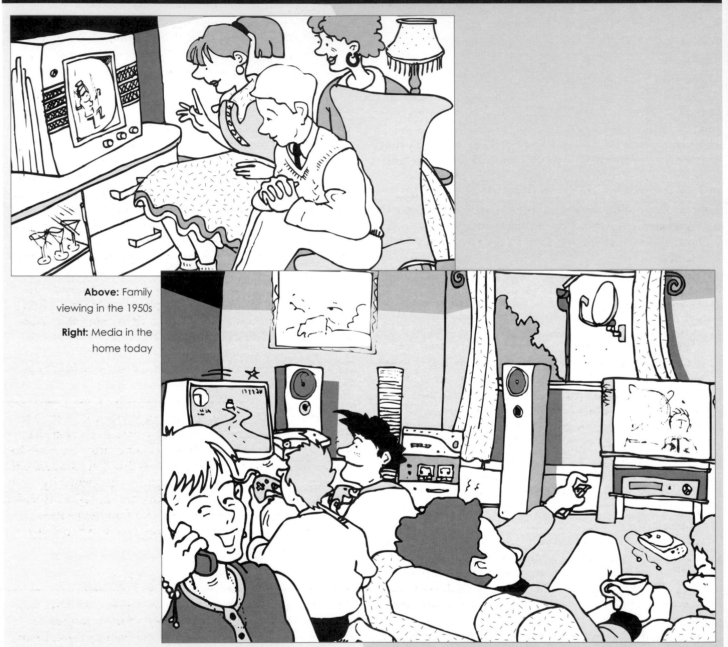

Above: Family viewing in the 1950s

Right: Media in the home today

Look at the cartoons above.

1 In what ways do they show that our use of the media is changing?

2 How do they show that the media themselves have changed?

3 What effect might these changes have on family life?

4 To what extent may changes in the media have reduced social interaction?

5 To what extent may changes in the media have increased social interaction?

6 'Media output was once highly structured for us, now we structure it to suit ourselves.' How far do you consider this statement to be true?

People – at least those who can afford the technology – are now exposed to an ever-increasing range of media. Once part of a whole family experience, **media consumption** has become a more individual affair (just look at the cartoon). But it can also involve a worldwide community, through technology such as the internet. Viewers take in a much wider range of programming and images, often flicking from channel to channel and producing their own viewing schedules through the use of video, DVD and other emerging technologies. How has this all come about and what are the implications for societies and their cultures?

Postmodernism and the media

As we saw in Unit 1, Topic 5, it has been suggested that societies have entered a new stage of development known as postmodernism. In economic life, information technology is increasingly becoming more important than manufacturing technology. White-collar workers, who specialise in the production of information and knowledge, now outnumber industrial workers. And the globalisation of mass media, information technology and electronic communication, such as e-mail and the internet, has led to the decline of national cultures and the growing importance of cultural diversity in our lifestyles.

Dominic Strinati (1995) argues that the mass media are centrally important in the development of postmodern society, for the following reasons:

- The part people played in the manufacture of goods once determined their social, national and local identities. These identities were further structured by factors such as social class, gender and ethnicity. In postmodern society, however, identities are increasingly being structured and interwoven through **consumption patterns**. Now, the media are responsible for providing most of our experience of social reality. What we take as 'real', therefore, is to a great extent what the media tell us is real. Consequently our lifestyles and identity are defined for us by the media. For example, TV programmes and lifestyle magazines tell us what our homes and gardens should look like. Advertising tells us what products we need to buy to improve the quality of our lives. Magazines tell us how we can become attractive to the opposite sex. The news tells us what issues we should be thinking about. Fly-on-the-wall documentaries reassure us that other people share our anxieties, and so on.
- Image and style have more significance than form or content. In the postmodern world we learn through the media that the consumption of images and signs for their own sake is more important than the consumption of the goods they represent. In other words, style is often more important than substance. We buy the labels and packaging rather than the clothes or goods themselves. People are judged negatively because they wear the wrong trainers rather than because of some fault in their character or lack of ability.
- In the past a **cultural hierarchy** existed. Classical music, for example, was considered to be more 'serious' and 'important' than pop music. But in the postmodern

world there are constant crossovers between '**high culture**' and '**popular culture**'. The classical musicians Luciano Pavarotti, Vanessa Mae and Nigel Kennedy have all attempted pop music projects, whilst pop artists such as Paul McCartney have experimented with classical music. Time and place have also become confused and **decontextualised**. For example, Fatboy Slim sampled a few lines from a protest song of the American Civil Rights Movement of the 1960s, 'Praise you', and turned them into a number one record (the result was brilliant dance music devoid of political meaning). Shakespeare's *Romeo and Juliet* was re-presented as a teen movie set in late twentieth-century LA.

The popular media themselves have become the subject of heated intellectual debate. For instance, you can now study towards an honours degree in *Star Trek*. The 'cultural expert', whose views have more weight than those of ordinary consumers, no longer exists. Now we are all experts.

According to postmodernists, it is the constant bombardment of media imagery in this **media-saturated society** that has caused all of this, transforming not only individual societies but even national identities – to the extent that, as some claim, we now live in a '**global village**'. People all over the world share many of the same consumption patterns and the same image-conscious outlook. Companies such as Disney, Levi Strauss, McDonald's, Sony and Coca-Cola target their products at a global audience. People across the world have real-time access to world news from CNN, while their kids argue about switching over to MTV.

Criticisms of the postmodern view of the media

Postmodernists are criticised for exaggerating the extent to which wider social influences have subsided. Their critics argue that they underplay the continuing importance of class, gender and ethnicity in our lives, and that they exaggerate the changes that the media have brought about. Inequality remains a key issue, as access to the internet, digital television and so on is denied to many millions of poorer people worldwide. How can a 'global village' exist when so many cannot enter it?

Resistance to globalisation

The growing influence of the global corporations and media giants has not gone unnoticed. They are often accused of eroding national cultures or even undermining them. Islamic countries denounce the Western media for using degrading images of women. Eastern political regimes (e.g. China, Malaysia), fearing undesirable political and moral messages, have boycotted Western-owned satellite broadcasters. Even Rupert Murdoch has realised that the promotion of local culture, through the Star satellite that he owns (which broadcasts to Asia), will gain more government approval, and ultimately bigger audiences, than would the imposition of Western programmes on Eastern audiences.

In parts of Europe, resistance to '**McDonaldisation**' (the American take-over of culture) has had a reverse effect. New broadcasting technology is being used for the development of more local and regional programming, aimed at preserving distinctive European cultural traditions and outlooks.

The explosion of satellite, digital and internet technologies has transformed the way in which most of us organise our lives. Families, communities, and national life have all been affected. There is no doubt that – whatever the exact nature of their influence – the media have had an immense impact on modern societies throughout the world, and that, in the process, the world has become a smaller place.

CHECK YOUR UNDERSTANDING

1 **Identify three changes associated with the shift towards a postmodern society.**

2 **What is the relationship between consumption and identity? Give an example of your own.**

3 **What is meant by the phrase 'style is more important than substance'?**

4 **Why might postmodernists argue that Fatboy Slim's version of 'Praise you' is just as valid as the original?**

5 **Explain in your own words the term 'globalisation'.**

6 **Give examples of two positive and two negative outcomes of globalisation.**

Sociology for AS Level

124

Exploring postmodernism and the media

Item A

The internet is no longer the preserve of the young and the nerds. It is rapidly approaching critical mass. A survey last week found that people spent more time with their computer than with most other domestic activities including cooking, eating and reading. One in three schoolchildren do their homework electronically (girls more than boys). And the over-60s spend more time on computers than anyone else. The way the internet has turned the world into a global village has been well charted. It is now a universal source of knowledge on any subject and the medium for instant communication through e-mail. You can do live video-conferencing, listen to radio stations from anywhere, download music or create your own website. Soon there will be an explosion of electronic web commerce. PA Consulting Group reckons that the onset of Web-TV (full internet access via the TV) will see today's on-line population expand from 50 million to more than a billion in five years, causing the opening of hitherto closed networks to customers and suppliers.

V. Keegan, *Guardian*, 23 November 1998

Item B

In 1981, American films accounted for 94 per cent of foreign films broadcast on British TV, 80 per cent of those broadcast on French TV and 54 per cent on West German TV. In Western Europe as a whole, American imports represented 75 per cent of all imports. The share represented by US-originated programmes in other parts of the world is even greater. These media products depict Western (often idealised) lifestyles. This *cultural imperialism* is transnational. More recently, there has been some debate as to whether the US dominance is slipping, with increased competition at regional, national and local levels. However, what has happened to replace American programming is in many cases a local adaptation of American television formats. Local cultures are re-presented in an Americanised form.

Adapted from S. Taylor (1999) *Sociology Issues and Debates*, London: Routledge

KEY TERMS

Cultural hierarchy – term used to describe the way in which the opinions and tastes of particular individuals and groups, who are seen to have more cultural expertise, are valued above the tastes of others.

Decontextualised – used to describe something that has been taken out of the situation in which it arose.

'Global village' – the idea that the world has become much smaller as the media allow us all to communicate easily with each other and to share ideas and lifestyles.

High culture – cultural forms, such as opera, that are associated with high-status or elite sections of society and considered 'superior' to other forms of culture.

McDonaldisation – the idea that American culture has overwhelmed other national cultures – literally that McDonald's has taken over the world.

Media consumption – use of the media.

Media-saturated society – a society in which every aspect of social life is influenced by the media.

Popular culture – cultural forms, such as soap operas, that are preferred by the majority of the population.

Item C

In 1984, the rich industrialised countries (USA, Canada, Western Europe, Japan and Australia) owned 96 per cent of the world's computer hardware. Of the world's 700 million telephones 75 per cent can be found in the 9 richest countries. In 39 countries there are no newspapers, while in 30 others there is only one. Japan has 125 dailies and the US has 168. In 1997, the world's average TV ownership was 240 per 1,000 – in Europe and America this was 436 per 1,000, whilst in the poorest countries ownership dropped to 23 per 1,000.

Inequalities also exist within countries. In the UK in the mid-1990s, 52 per cent of professional households had a home computer compared to 21 per cent of unskilled households.

Office of Science and Technology (1995) *Technology Foresight Panel 14: Progress through Partnership – Leisure and Learning*, London: HMSO

Item C

A theologian [scholar of religion] asked the most powerful supercomputer 'Is there a God?' The computer said it lacked the processing power to know. It asked to be connected to all the other supercomputers in the world. It still didn't have enough power. So, it was hooked up to all of the mainframes in the world, and then all the PCs, then laptops and eventually to all the computers in cars, microwaves, VCRs, domestic appliances and so on.

The theologian asked the final time 'Is there a God?' And the computer replied: 'There is now!'

J. Naisbitt (1995) *Global Paradox*, New York: William Morrow, p. 80

1 Explain what is meant by the term 'cultural imperialism' (Item B). (2)

2 Suggest two reasons why 'the over-60s spend more time on computers than anyone else' (Item A). (4)

3 Suggest three ways in which the internet may help create a 'global village' (Item A). (6)

4 Identify and briefly explain two possible consequences of the inequalities of access to the media described in Item C. (8)

5 Using information from the Items and elsewhere, examine the effects of new media technologies on societies. (20)

6 Outline and assess the postmodernist view of the media. (20)

Extension activities

1 Use the website of the United Nations Social and Cultural Organisation (http://unescostat.unesco.org/) to explore trends in the worldwide distribution of media forms. Re-present the data graphically and summarise, in your own words, the key trends for particular countries.

2 Design a questionnaire and conduct a survey within your school or college to assess the differences in access to and consumption of the new media, in relation to class, gender, ethnicity and age. Consider both household ownership and personal consumption of the following media forms: PCs, web TV, cable TV, games consoles, WAP phones, DVD players, videos, MP3 players, digital cameras.

3 When you next visit your local high street or shopping centre, make a note of all of the transnational companies that you see. Use the World Wide Web to identify their country of origin. Which country's cultural influences are most apparent?

4 Draw up a list of the top five terrestrial TV programmes amongst your peer group. What proportion show signs of American influence? How many are reflective of British culture? Do the same for cable/satellite TV.

Question for students taking OCR exam board AS level

5 (a) Identify and explain two ways in which use of the media has changed in the last 20 years. (20 marks)

(b) Outline and discuss the view that we now live in a media-saturated society which defines our lifestyle and consumption patterns. (40 marks)

Wealth, poverty and welfare

Topic 1 Wealth and income

Getting you thinking

Most people were keen to use up their financial assets during their retirement and were not planning to leave substantial amounts as bequests. But those who owned homes hoped to pass these on to their children.

The distribution of wealth is highly unequal – much more so than the distribution of income ... income and wealth are very closely related – those with a gross annual income of less than £5,000 had median total wealth (including state pension wealth) of only about £3,000. Those on incomes of over £35,000 a year had median total wealth of about £110,000.

K. Rowlinson, C. Whyley and T. Warren (1999) *Wealth in Britain: A Lifecycle Perspective*, London: Policy Studies Institute

1 Do you think that people should have a right to pass wealth on to their children, or does it give some people an unfair advantage in life?

2 Do you think that we ought to have much higher rates of tax for the better off, to ensure that there is less inequality in society?

3 What do you think are the advantages and disadvantages of having a great deal of inequality in society?

Wealth

Problems of definition

Wealth is defined as the ownership of property, shares, savings and other assets. However, within that overall definition, there is some debate about exactly what constitutes property and 'assets'. Does a person's house constitute wealth? On the one hand, if a person were to sell their house, they would have a considerable amount of money – but, on the other hand, they would then have nowhere to live.

A similar debate surrounds **pensions** – some argue that pensions must be defined as wealth, because they are savings, whilst others argue that pensions are essential and so they do not actually constitute wealth.

Problems of measurement

A further problem with wealth is actually measuring it. Unlike income, which we discuss later, the **Inland Revenue** does not conduct a yearly assessment of wealth. So researchers obtain their information in one of the following two ways:

1 Looking at the assessment of wealth made for tax purposes when someone dies.

2 Asking a sample of rich people the extent of their wealth.

Some pretty obvious problems arise with both methods.

Inland Revenue statistics based on inheritance tax
Using information obtained from wills usually only provides us with out-of-date figures. What is more, wealthy people will attempt to limit the amount of wealth that they declare for tax

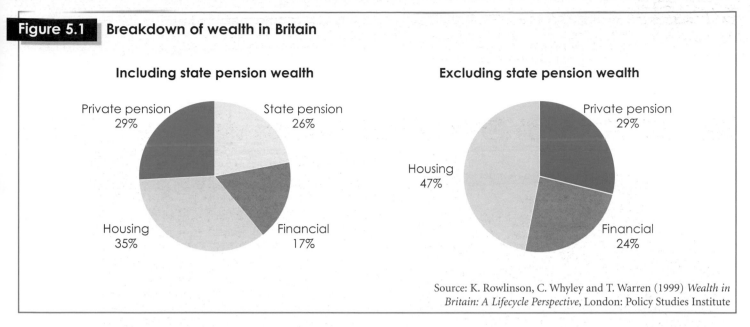

Figure 5.1 Breakdown of wealth in Britain

Including state pension wealth

Private pension 29%
State pension 26%
Housing 35%
Financial 17%

Excluding state pension wealth

Private pension 29%
Housing 47%
Financial 24%

Source: K. Rowlinson, C. Whyley and T. Warren (1999) *Wealth in Britain: A Lifecycle Perspective*, London: Policy Studies Institute

purposes. Charitable trusts, early distribution of wealth to younger family members before death, and financial holdings abroad are all common ways to avoid tax. All of this means that the wealth of the rich may be under-estimated. On the other hand, poorer people who do not pay **inheritance tax** are excluded from Inland Revenue statistics, so their wealth may be under-estimated too.

Surveys

Because of these problems, sociologists turn to surveys, but rich people (understandably enough) are extremely reluctant to divulge their true wealth. Either way the figures will probably be inaccurate.

Changes in wealth distribution over time

We have just seen some of the difficulties of trying to define wealth. However, even bearing in mind the differences that occur if we include such things as house values and occupational pensions, we can still make the simple, clear statement that wealth is distributed very unequally in British society.

In the 1920s, one per cent of the population owned over 60 per cent of all **marketable wealth**. A further 9 per cent owned 29 per cent, leaving 90 per cent of the population with about 11 per cent of marketable wealth.

By the 1970s, however, the share of the top one per cent had halved to about 30 per cent; and the wealthiest 10 per cent (including the top one per cent) owned about 50 per cent of wealth. Since the 1970s, there appears to have been little change – so that, in the mid-1990s, the wealthiest 10 per cent still owned about 49 per cent of wealth.

The composition of wealth

Personal wealth more than doubled in the period between 1980 and the mid-1990s. This reflects the growth in home ownership. As house prices have increased faster than inflation, those who own homes (over 70 per cent of householders) have become 'richer'.

However, if we look only at personal marketable wealth – which consists largely of property, shares and other savings/investments – the situation is very different. Shares in companies are now held by a relatively high proportion of the population, as a result of the 1980s government sell-off of public utilities such as water, electricity and gas – and more recently as a result of some building societies 'giving' shares to their account-holders, when they became banks.

Despite this increase in share ownership, a very large proportion of shares is owned by very few people. The wealthiest one per cent of the population own about 20 per cent of total marketable wealth, and the wealthiest 10 per cent own 50 per cent of all marketable wealth – mainly in the form of company shares.

Income

Defining income

Like wealth, income is difficult to measure. Once again, those with large amounts of income (who are of course often 'the wealthy') will seek to minimise their income levels on their income tax returns, and will employ accountants and tax experts to do just that.

But there are also methodological problems that sociologists face in trying to measure income levels. They have to decide whether to calculate income by household or by individual (poverty statistics, for example, are increasingly based on households). They must decide which is more important, income before tax, or income after tax? And what about people who work for 'cash-in-hand'? Finally, many people receive state benefits, but also receive some services free (bus passes, for example) which others have to pay for – is this income?

Income distribution

Overall, income is much more evenly distributed than wealth, but that does not mean there is any great amount of equality. Families with children are much more likely than other groups to have low incomes – for example, about 40 per cent of couples with dependent children are in the lowest 10 per cent of income earners. At the other extreme, the highest 10 per cent of income earners tend to be middle-aged without dependent children.

Income and the life cycle

These differences suggest that income is closely related to the **life cycle** – people's earnings gradually rise over their lifetime, when their children leave home, and then, when they reach pensionable age, income declines sharply again.

Changes over time

Income inequality is actually increasing, and has been doing so since the early 1980s. On average, income has risen by 44 per cent since 1979, with the wealthiest 10 per cent of the population experiencing an increase of 70 per cent in real terms. On the other hand, the poorest 10 per cent have had an income *decrease* of 9 per cent.

Redistribution and the impact of taxation

If we start by looking at incomes before tax, then the richest 10 per cent earn about 30 times more than the poorest 10 per cent. However, the richest must pay income tax on what they earn, and the poorest will receive state benefits. The result is that the ratio drops to 8 to 1. However, there are still some adjustments to be made. Most goods have **VAT (value-added tax)** charged on them, and this has a greater proportional impact on poorer families (because more of their income is spent, and less is saved). As a result, the actual ratio of incomes between the richest and poorest is about 11 to 1.

The tax and social security systems, therefore, do have an impact – they reduce inequalities by about two-thirds – but this still leaves considerable inequality.

Explanations for increases in income inequality

Government policy
Changes in taxation and state benefits have actually lowered taxes on the rich in real terms; whilst state benefits have declined relative to the increase in average earnings for those employed.

Two-earner households
Pahl (1988) has pointed out that there is an increasing division between households. On the one side there are households in which there is no adult worker at all; on the other side, the number of two-earner households is rising. The divide is increasing because there is a decline in single-earner households, whilst the other two household types are growing – and as they do so the differences in earnings are also growing.

Growth of lone-parent families
This links to the point above. The fastest growing type of family is the one-parent family. Because of childcare responsibilities, the parent (usually a woman) is more likely to work part-time or to have no employment.

Job insecurity
Employment patterns are changing, and the job-for-life is gradually being replaced by job insecurity. People are now expected to perform a range of jobs in their working careers. A Joseph Rowntree Foundation survey in 1999, for example, found that 40 per cent of people who had lost their jobs in the previous six months had been unemployed in the previous two years – showing that unemployment is now a normal expectation for some employees, as employers demand more 'flexible' labour. The impact on income is that those with more reliable work can expect a regular income, whilst the increasing numbers in 'flexible' employment experience peaks and troughs of income.

Explanations for the retention of wealth

- **The global economy** – most economies in the world are now linked. If a democratically elected government were to seek to take wealth away from the very richest, the rich would move their money out of the country. This would have a huge impact on the British economy. Governments are therefore very cautious about upsetting the very rich.
- **The nature of capitalism** – capitalist societies such as Britain are based on inequalities of wealth and income. It is regarded as everyone's right to pass their wealth on to their children. This means that inequalities carry on over generations, because some start life with many more opportunities than others.
- **Entrepreneurial talent** – it is possible for very clever (and possibly fortunate) people, from relatively humble backgrounds, to become rich – although, in practice, very few do so.

CHECK YOUR UNDERSTANDING

1 What three different definitions of wealth are most commonly used?

2 Why might the statistics we have on wealth be inaccurate?

3 What changes in wealth distribution have taken place since the 1970s?

4 Which is more evenly distributed across the nation, income or wealth?

5 In your own words describe any two reasons for the continuing inequalities in income.

6 How does the 'global economy' have an impact on wealth distribution within the UK?

KEY TERMS

Global economy – refers to the way in which investment and trading now span the entire world. This hinders individual governments' control of the economy, because companies can simply move to other countries.

Inheritance tax – tax on wealth when a person dies.

Inland Revenue – the government department responsible for taxes on earnings and wealth.

Life cycle – refers to the changes in a person's economic and social situation over their lifetime.

Marketable wealth – all a person possesses (does not include their pension).

Item A — Distribution of household income in the UK, 1971–97

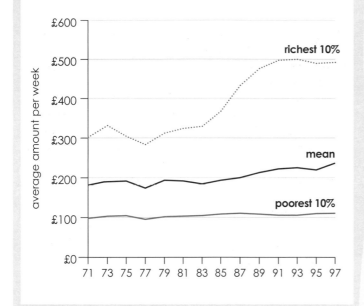

Source: *Social Trends 30*, London: Office for National Statistics, 2000

Item B

Several explanations have been put forward to account for both shifts in individual earnings and the overall growth in inequality of earnings since the mid-1980s. The growth of unemployment, changing forms of work, the decline of the male 'breadwinner' and the increase in women's labour-force participation, the decline of trade union influence and national collective bargaining structures, and changes in the taxation and benefit systems are amongst the factors that have influenced the rapid growth of income inequality in Britain.

N. Abercrombie and A. Warde (2000) *Contemporary British Society*, 3rd edn, Cambridge: Polity Press, p. 119

Item C

● In 1995–6, half of all families in Britain had total wealth of at least £53,000 (the sum of financial savings, accumulated state, occupational and personal pension wealth and net housing wealth). Wealth increased with age, peaking at an average (median) of £133,000 for 60–69-year-olds, then declining for older groups.

● Pensioner couples had the highest levels of wealth of all life-cycle groups, followed by middle-aged couples without dependent children. Young single people (under the age of 35) and lone parents had very little wealth.

● Four factors were found to affect wealth accumulation. The most important was ability to accumulate wealth – those with higher incomes and lower outgoings were most likely to put money into financial savings, mortgages and occupational or personal pension schemes. Attitudes towards saving and knowledge about different schemes also had an effect on wealth accumulation. Finally, the availability of suitable savings and investment schemes was also a key factor.

Joseph Rowntree Foundation, 'Findings', July 1999

1 Explain in your own words the term 'distribution of income'. (2)

2 Identify two trends from the graph in Item A. (4)

3 Identify three sources of wealth (Item C). (6)

4 Identify and briefly explain two reasons why income inequality in Britain has increased (Item B). (8)

5 Discuss the view that statistics on income and wealth are always inaccurate. (20)

6 Using material from Item C and elsewhere, assess the factors that influence the accumulation and distribution of wealth. (20)

131

Pension – a regular payment made to someone when they retire from paid employment.

Personal wealth – wealth owned by individuals. This can be compared with institutional wealth, which is wealth owned by companies.

Redistribution – the transfer of wealth from the rich to the poor. In theory, the taxes the rich pay are used to fund services for the poor.

VAT (value-added tax) – a tax charged on most goods and services. It is an indirect tax because it is not taken direct from people's wages.

Wealth – the ownership of property, shares, savings and other assets.

Extension activities

1 Ask a sample of people to estimate the amount of wealth owned by the richest one per cent and the richest 10 per cent of people in Britain. Compare their responses with the actual figures. What do the results tell you about people's perceptions of wealth?

2 Access the website of the Joseph Rowntree Foundation (www.jrf.org.uk). Search the site for their latest research on income and wealth. What does it tell us about the changing distribution of income and wealth?

Getting you thinking

A national survey was carried out in order to find out how 'ordinary people' defined poverty. The respondents were offered the following three definitions and asked which one(s) they agreed with (they could agree with more than one). The (cumulative) percentage agreeing with each definition is given below.

PUBLIC DEFINITIONS OF POVERTY	
Someone in Britain was in poverty if ...	Percentage agreeing
They had enough to buy things they really needed, but not enough to buy the things that most people take for granted	28%
They had enough to eat and live, but not enough to buy other things they needed	60%
They had not got enough to eat and live without getting into debt	90%

British Social Attitudes Survey 1995, ed. R. Jowell, S. Witherspoon and L. Brook, Aldershot: Gower

Top: a children's party

Above: a television

Left: a mobile phone

1 **If someone could not afford to buy the items pictured, which of the definitions of poverty in the table (if any) would you consider applied to them? Look at each item separately.**

2 **Which definition of poverty do you agree with? Explain your answer.**

3 **According to the figures above, to what extent does the public agree with your definition?**

4 **Why do you think that people have different views about the definition of poverty?**

Each time there is an election, the political party in government will announce all that they have achieved in combating poverty. They manage to produce convincing statistics to show that poverty has decreased under their government. The opposition parties will angrily denounce these statistics as biased, and produce a completely different set, which show, quite clearly, that poverty has increased during the governing party's time in office.

How do we make sense of this? The answer lies, quite simply, in the different definitions and measurements that can be used.

Sociologists have defined poverty in two different ways:
● absolute poverty
● relative poverty

Absolute poverty

This definition is usually traced back to the nineteenth-century anti-poverty campaigner Seebohm Rowntree. Rowntree was concerned that politicians refused to recognise the sheer extent of poverty in Britain. Therefore, in the 1890s, he conducted a 'scientific' survey to discover the real extent of poverty. Part of this survey involved constructing a clear definition that distinguished the poor from the non-poor. The definition was based on deciding what resources were needed for a person to be able to live healthily and work efficiently.

To find the amount of income a person needed, Rowntree added together:

● the costs of a very basic diet
● the costs of purchasing a minimum amount of clothes of minimum quality
● the rent for a basic level of housing

The 'poverty line' was then drawn at the income needed to cover these three costs.

Advantages of an absolute definition of poverty

An absolute definition provides us with a clear measure of who is in poverty at any one time. It also allows us to compare different societies, and the same society over time.

Disadvantages of an absolute definition

An absolute definition fails to take into account the fact that what is regarded as poverty changes over time. What is a luxury today may be a necessity tomorrow, as fashion, acceptable standards of housing and general standards of living change. This makes it very hard to decide exactly what constitutes a 'minimum' standard of clothes or an 'acceptable' diet. The absolute definition of poverty is in fact a measure of **destitution** – that is, the failure to obtain the absolute necessities to keep life going. But poverty is not actually destitution – someone can be poor, but still able to struggle on.

The 'budget standard measure'

A contemporary version of the absolute definition is the 'budget standard measure', which is a rather more sophisticated version of Rowntree's original work. One version of this was developed by the Family Budget Unit, led by Bradshaw (1990). Bradshaw used detailed research information on the spending patterns of the poorest to construct an income that would provide a 'modest but adequate budget'. According to this measure, any family living below this income would be regarded as poor by any reasonable person.

Relative poverty

Critics such as the famous poverty researcher Peter Townsend suggest that poverty should be seen in terms of the *normal expectations* of any society. As societies change and become more (or less) affluent, so the idea of what is poverty will change too. Central heating and colour televisions were at one time luxuries – yet today the majority of homes have them. Already, mobile phones and home computers are becoming part of a 'normal' standard of living.

Relative poverty places poverty in relationship to the 'normal' expectations of society. If a person, or family, is unable to achieve a moderate standard of living, then they are poor.

Advantages of the relative definition of poverty

The relative definition links poverty to the expectations of society – reflecting the fact that people do measure their own quality of life against that of other people. It also broadens the idea of what poverty is – from lacking basic necessities to lacking a range of other 'needs', such as adequate leisure.

Disadvantages of the relative definition

The relative definition does have a number of disadvantages, however. First, it can only be used *within* any one society; it does not help with cross-cultural comparisons. (You are measuring poverty by asking people what is acceptable within their society – not across the world.) Its second disadvantage is the difficulty of deciding what is or is not a 'normal' standard of living.

Furthermore, it does have the rather absurd implication that, no matter how rich people become, there will always be poverty, as long as not everybody is equally rich. This is because relative poverty is as much a measure of inequality as poverty. As long as there is a degree of inequality, it could be argued, there is poverty.

Measuring relative poverty

There are two ways of **operationalising** (measuring) the concept of poverty within the relative approach:

● the relative income measure
● the consensual measure

The relative income measure
This approach measures income as a proportion of typical household income – the idea being that, if a family has a lower than average income, they cannot afford an acceptable standard of living. The most commonly used measure is that a household is in poverty if it receives less than half the average British income, although figures as high as 80 per cent have been suggested. This approach is increasingly being used by the government, and is known as the HBAI (Households Below Average Income) approach.

A consensual measure of poverty
A second approach is to measure the extent of poverty in terms of what possessions and services the majority of people think are necessary in a society. The measure is constructed by asking people to rank in order a list of possessions and services which they consider to be necessities. The resulting list is used as the basis to work out what most people regard as an unacceptable level of deprivation. This approach was used originally by Mack and Lansley in *Breadline Britain* (1993), and developed later by Gordon *et al.* in *Poverty and Social Exclusion in Britain* (2000).

Poverty and social exclusion

The concept of poverty is closely linked to that of **social exclusion**, and there is some debate over whether the term social exclusion should replace 'poverty'.

Poverty is usually seen as lack of income to purchase the goods and services that allow people to fully participate in society. In many ways it is a 'static' concept, based on inability to purchase a socially accepted standard of living. Social exclusion, on the other hand, widens the horizon of analysis, and looks at a range of interconnecting disadvantages from which certain groups in society suffer. These groups have the worst housing, health, education and job prospects in society, whilst suffering from the highest levels of stress, crime victimisation and unemployment.

Measuring social exclusion

The New Policy Institute (a social policy research institute) has suggested that 50 indicators can be identified which measure every aspect of people's lives, from childhood to old age. They cover a wide range – from education to being a victim of crime – and can provide us with a real sense of who is socially excluded.

CHECK YOUR UNDERSTANDING

1 Explain the difference between an absolute and a relative measure of poverty.

2 What criticisms have been made of absolute definitions?

3 Relative definitions of poverty have been criticised by campaigners against poverty in developing countries – why might this be?

4 Give two examples of how researchers have actually 'operationalised' the relative poverty concept.

5 Why has there been criticism of the concept of poverty and a move towards the use of the term 'social exclusion'?

KEY TERMS

Absolute definition of poverty – a person is in poverty if they are unable to afford the most basic necessities of life. Poverty is seen as destitution.

Consensual measure (of poverty) – a form of the relative definition of poverty, based on lack of the goods and services deemed necessary by most people in society.

Destitution – failure to obtain the absolute necessities to keep life going.

Operationalise – refers to how sociologists go about finding a way to measure a concept (e.g. poverty).

Relative definition of poverty – a person is in poverty if they are unable to afford the standard of living considered acceptable by the majority of people.

Relative income measure (of poverty) – a form of the relative definition of poverty, based on having only a certain proportion of the average income in a society.

Social exclusion – term used to describe the situation where people are unable to achieve a quality of life that would be regarded as acceptable by most people.

Exploring ... defining and measuring poverty

Item A

In 1999, David Gordon and colleagues updated a famous study on poverty (*Breadline Britain* by Mack and Lansley) to find out the extent of poverty in 1999. The study concluded that, according to its definition of poverty:

Roughly 9.5 million people in Britain today cannot afford adequate housing conditions. About 8 million cannot afford one or more essential household goods. Almost 7.5 million people are too poor to engage in common social activities considered necessary by the majority of the population.

They used the following methods to define poverty. (Please note that the table shown below is a much shortened version of the full table used in the research and referred to in the quote below.)

[The following table] ranks the percentage of respondents identifying different adult items as 'necessary, which all adults should be able to afford and which they should not have to do without' in 1999. ... People of all ages and walks of life do not restrict their interpretation of 'necessities' to the basic material needs of a subsistence diet, shelter, clothing and fuel. There are social customs, obligations and activities that substantial majorities of the population also identify as among the top necessities of life.

D. Gordon *et al.* (2000) *Poverty and Social Exclusion in Britain*, York: Joseph Rowntree Foundation

ESSENTIAL REQUIREMENTS (1999)

	Necessary	Not necessary
Bed and bedding for everyone	95	4
Heating to warm living areas of the home	94	5
Damp-free home	93	6
Visiting friends or family in hospital	92	7
Two meals a day	91	9
Medicines prescribed by doctor	90	9
Refrigerator	89	11
Fresh fruit and vegetables daily	86	13
Warm waterproof coat	85	14
Replacement or repair of broken electrical goods	85	14
Visits to friends or family	84	15
Celebrations on special days such as Christmas	83	16

Item B

Poverty means going short materially, socially and emotionally. It means spending less on food, on heating and on clothing than someone on an average income.

C. Oppenheim, quoted in P. Alcock (1993) *Understanding Poverty*, Basingstoke: Macmillan, p. 3

Item C

The evidence of improving living standards over this century is dramatic, and it is incontrovertible. When the pressure groups say that one-third of the population is living in poverty, they cannot be saying that one-third of people are living below the draconian [severe] subsistence levels used by Rowntree.

C. Moore (1989) 'The end of the line for poverty', speech to Greater London Area CPC, 11 May, quoted in P. Alcock (1993) *Understanding Poverty*, Basingstoke: Macmillan, p. 3

1 Explain what is meant by the phrase 'subsistence levels' (Item A). (2)

2 Suggest two other items that might be added to the list in Item A. (4)

3 Item A refers to necessities such as 'social customs, obligations and activities'. Suggest one example of each of these. (6)

4 Identify and briefly explain two criticisms of an absolute definition of poverty. (8)

5 Discuss the difficulties faced by sociologists in operationalising a relative definition of poverty. (20)

6 Using material from the Items and elsewhere, assess the view that the word 'poverty' should not be used because there is no agreed definition. (20)

Extension activities

1 Find more information on poverty and the latest research on the Joseph Rowntree website: **www.jrf.org.uk**. Go to the site and search for 'poverty'. You will find the complete version of the Item A table in the research findings section, under the heading 'D. Gordon et al. (2000) Poverty and Social Exclusion in Britain'. Detailed working papers which give you an insight into the research project are available at **www.bristol.ac.uk/poverty/pse**

2 Draw up your own list of ten essential items for an AS level student today. Ask a representative sample of students which items they agree are necessary: 'which all [AS level students] should be able to afford, and which they should not have to do without' (see Item A above).

Getting you thinking

In a study of 1,211 couples, Vogler (1994) found that 'women bore the brunt of both an inadequate total household income and an inadequate distribution of income within the home', with only one-fifth of households having income shared equally between partners.

We tend to think that poverty hits family members equally, yet research indicates that this is not the case. There can be affluence for some and poverty for others, within the same household. A household with a high income could in fact contain a number of poor people, because the main income earner might not want to share 'his' (it is usually the male) wages. Even where both parents earn adequately, they may decide not to spend much on their children.

In most families, the higher earner is the male, and there is some evidence to show that this wage is not shared equally in about 20 per cent of cases. In these families the male keeps a higher proportion of 'his' wages.

1 **In your opinion, does the person who earns the 'family' income have the greatest right to say how it is spent?**

2 **Should the husband hand over the wages for the wife to spend, or should they have equal control over spending?**

3 **What rights should the children have to decide how the money is spent?**

4 **If the parents have low incomes, should the children take on a part-time job?**

5 **If they do, should the children keep the money they earn?**

Above: Husbands are often breadwinners, but do they share income equally with the rest of their family?

As we saw in Topic 2, the numbers of people living in poverty will vary according to which definition and measure are used. But if we take the measure most commonly used by the government – that is, the number of households with incomes below average income (HBAI) – then the figures indicate that about 25 per cent of the population have an income at or below 50 per cent of the average British income.

Poverty, then, is very widespread in Britain, and not just restricted to a few 'unfortunates'. The poor are simply those people who are the least powerful in society, and who are unable to persuade (or force) others to let them have a greater proportion of society's wealth.

Who is at risk of being in poverty?

The answer to this question depends upon how you want to classify people. For example, one useful approach is to ask

what sorts of households are most likely to be poor. The answer is simple: lone-parent households with young children, followed by single pensioners living alone.

Another way of classifying people is by employment/economic status – that is, whether people are employed or not, and what their wage levels are. This classification produces the answer that the unemployed and low-paid are the most likely to be living in poverty.

We could also classify by social group – for example, by ethnicity or gender. This tells us that ethnic minorities are likely to be poorer than the majority of society, and that women are more likely to be poor than men.

Finally, we could look at groups by age. This tells us that young people and old people are the most likely to be living in poverty.

But just to confuse you even further, all of these groups overlap. For example, lone parents are more likely to be unemployed than the population average; and certain ethnic minority groups have higher levels of lone parents than the population as a whole. This means that a lone parent is more likely to come from an Afro-Caribbean background; lone parents are more likely to be unemployed; the majority of lone parents are women; it is likely that the lone parent who is unemployed will be young, and so on.

Whichever classification you use, though, there are about 14 million people in Britain who are living in households with incomes below half the national average. Below we look at a range of groups who have a high risk of living in poverty – drawing examples from all of the classifications above.

Lone-parent families

The number of lone parents – the overwhelming majority of whom are women – has grown from just over half a million at the beginning of the 1970s, to about 1.7 million today. Over 60 per cent of lone parents in Britain live in poverty.

Lone-parent families are more likely to be poor for two, possibly overlapping, reasons. First, there is a higher risk of women from poorer backgrounds actually becoming lone parents in the first place. So they are already more likely to be at risk of poverty before they have children. Second, any lone parent is likely to be poorer because they have to combine childcare with employment. This means that they are more likely to work part-time, so their incomes on average will be lower. But it is important to remember that not all lone mothers are poor – it is just that they are more at risk of poverty.

Children

Forty per cent of children are 'born poor' – that is, they are born into low-income families. In 1998/9 there were 4.5 million children in Britain living in poverty. Child poverty is usually linked to the unemployment of their parents – in fact, the majority of poor children come from households where there is no working parent at all. In 1998/9, 10 per cent of all children of two-parent families had neither parent in employment, and 58 per cent of children of lone parents had no working parent.

The unemployed

We have just seen that 10 per cent of all children come from households with no parent in employment – this adds up to over two million children. But it is not just children who are hit by unemployment. About 63 per cent of those with incomes below half the average (that is, poor according to the HBAI measure) are not working.

Those who are unemployed for a long time face much greater problems than those who are out of work for a short period. These problems include a lower level of income, the gradual exhaustion of savings, and deterioration in the condition of clothing, furniture and general possessions. After three months of unemployment, the average disposable income of a family drops by as much as 59 per cent. It is not just financial losses that occur as a result of long-term unemployment – there are psychological effects too, such as lack of confidence, stress and depression. These further undermine people's ability to obtain work.

The low-paid

In 1999, there were two million employees over the age of 25 who earned less than half the average male hourly wage. People who are low-paid tend to be those with fewer skills, and they often live in areas where there are relatively few jobs, so competition keeps wages low. As we have seen, there is a link between **low pay** and lone parenthood, in that lone parents usually have to take part-time jobs because of childcare responsibilities – and part-time work is typically low-paid.

Figure 5.2 **Causes of poverty**

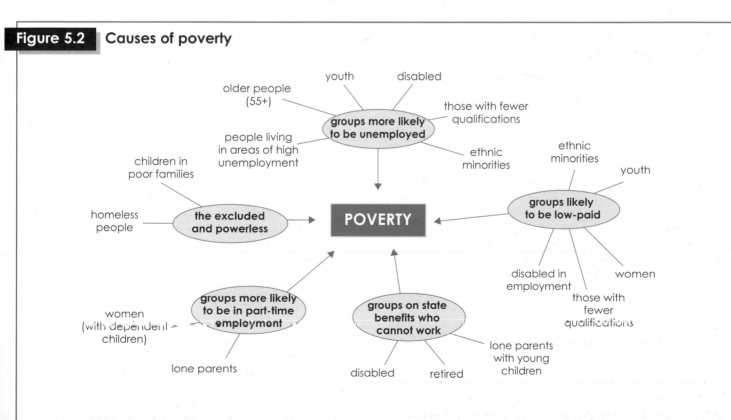

Sick and disabled people

According to government statistics, there are 6.2 million adults (14 per cent of all adults) and 36,000 children (3 per cent of all children) who suffer from one or more disabilities. Of these, 34 per cent are living in poverty. The average income for a disabled adult, under pensionable age, is 72 per cent of that for non-disabled people.

There are several reasons for the poverty of people with disabilities. They may be unable to work, or the work they can do may be limited to particular kinds of low-paid employment. At the same time, people with disabilities often have higher outgoings, such as having to pay for a special diet, or having to pay for heating to be on all day.

Older people

About 18 per cent of the population – over 11 million people – are over retirement age; and over 65 per cent of **older people** are women. With the gradual rise in life expectancy, the number of older people in the population is likely to continue to increase.

Older people are often dependent upon pensions for their income. For those 1.3 million who only receive the state pension, this means living in poverty. The state pension is less than 20 per cent of average male weekly earnings.

Being old does not necessarily make people poor – it is just that the risk increases. Those people who are poor in old age are most likely to be those who have earned least in their working lives.

Ethnic minorities

People of Afro-Caribbean and Asian origin have substantially higher rates of unemployment than the majority of the population. This holds true even if the Afro-Caribbean or Asian person has the same educational qualifications as the majority population. Those of Afro-Caribbean origin and a majority of those of Asian origin have a greater chance of earning lower wages than the majority population, and they are more likely to work in the types of employment where wages are generally low.

Exploring the extent and causes of poverty

Item A
• The value of Income Support (the main government benefit for the unemployed) is at its lowest level, compared with general wage levels, for 17 years, at approximately 20 per cent of average earnings. In 1983, it was worth nearly 30 per cent of average wages.

• 36 per cent of children live in a family without a full-time worker.

Poverty (2000) no. 105, p. 20

Item B
The sheer numbers involved demonstrate the gravity of the problems we face. Millions of children are living in low-income households. One in six people – over seven million – are in working-age families without anyone in work. We've a long way to go. We have a lot to do. But we are committed to a sustained attack on poverty and its causes.

Alistair Darling MP, Secretary of State for Social Security, quoted in *Poverty* (2000) no. 105, p. 21

Item C

NUMBERS OF PEOPLE IN POVERTY IN THE UK

	All people Total population (millions)	Number in poverty (millions)	% of total population	Children Total population (millions)	Number in poverty (millions)	% of total population
1979	54.0	5.0	9%	13.8	1.4	10%
1994/5	55.8	13.3	24%	12.7	4.0	31%
1998/9	56.6	14.3	25%	12.8	4.5	35%

Source: 'Poverty: facts and figures', Child Poverty Action Group website, 2001 (www.cpag.org.uk)

Item D

Table (a) on the right gives us the percentage of each social group (e.g. pensioner couples, couples with children, etc.) who are living in poverty.

Table (b) gives us the total number of people in poverty in each social group, and, for 1998/9, the percentage they comprise of all people in poverty (e.g. there were 1,554,000 single pensioners living in poverty, comprising 11 per cent of all poor people).

THE PERCENTAGES AND NUMBERS IN POVERTY, BY FAMILY TYPE

	Table (a) % of group in poverty 1979	1994/5	1998/9	Table (b) Number in poverty (000s) 1979	1994/5	1998/9	% of total
Pensioner couples	21%	23%	25%	1,020	1,219	1,350	9%
Single pensioners	12%	32%	37%	520	1,376	1,554	11%
Couples with children	8%	23%	24%	2,220	4,784	4,872	34%
Couples without children	5%	12%	12%	490	1,380	1,464	10%
Single with children	10%	55%	62%	460	2,310	2,914	20%
Single without children	7%	23%	22%	530	2,231	2,178	15%

Source: 'Poverty: facts and figures', Child Poverty Action Group website, 2001 (www.cpag.org.uk)

Women

The majority of the poor in Britain are women – most of the groups we have discussed above are likely to have a majority of women members. For example, 95 per cent of lone parents on state benefits are women; and the number of women of pensionable age who have to ask for additional state support is over three times that of men. This is because they are less likely to have savings, as a result of low earnings throughout their lives.

Poverty: a risk not a state

When we talk about poor people, it is rather misleading, because it gives the impression that there is a group of people who live in poverty all their lives. This is true for some people, but the majority of the poor are people who live on the margins of poverty, moving into poverty and out again, depending upon a range of economic factors, government decisions, family responsibilities and their earning possibilities.

1 Explain what is meant by the term 'low-income households' (Item B). (2)

2 Suggest two reasons why a high proportion of the 'single with children' group are in poverty (Item D). (4)

3 Identify three trends from the tables in Item D. (6)

4 Identify and briefly explain two reasons why government benefits have not eliminated poverty. (8)

5 Describe and account for changes in the numbers and types of people at risk of poverty between 1979 and the present day. (20)

6 Using information from the Items and elsewhere, assess the view that poverty exists in the UK. (20)

1 According to the text, how many people in Britain are living in poverty?

2 What percentage of the population is this?

3 There are four ways of classifying those who are at risk of poverty – what are they?

4 What are the implications of the fact that these classifications overlap?

5 Why is long-term unemployment so much worse a problem than shorter-term unemployment?

6 Are all old people poor? What does poverty in old age reflect?

7 Poverty is 'a risk not a state'. Explain what this means in your own words.

KEY TERMS

Low pay – defined as earning less than half the average male wage (women's average wages are lower than men's).

Older people – refers to people of pensionable age, currently 60 for women and 65 for men.

Sick and disabled people – 'sick' refers to chronic illness, where people are unwell on a long-term basis. 'Disabled' refers to people officially classified by the government (on the basis of a medical report) as suffering from some form of disability.

Extension activities

1 Find out the latest figures on 'households below average income', and the latest figures for the 'poverty line'. Search the website of the Child Poverty Action Group (www.cpag.org.uk) to find this and much more information.

2 What particular problems are faced by groups who run a high risk of poverty? Why do they often find it hard to break out of poverty? Search the World Wide Web to find out more about the disabled, single-parent families, child poverty, ethnic minorities, the unemployed, older people and the low-paid.

3 Ask a sample of people to estimate the numbers of the various groups 'at risk of poverty' who are actually living in poverty. Then show them the actual figures (Item D). How closely do their estimates match the figures? Are they surprised at the figures?

Getting you thinking

1 Write down the first six words that come into your head when you see the scene on the left.

2 Compare your words with those of other people. Is it pity or annoyance that you mainly feel?

3 Why do you think these homeless people are there? Is it their own fault? Bad luck? The fault of an unjust society?

4 How would you resolve their problems?

Arguments about the causes of poverty can be traced back as far as we have written records. Most intriguingly, it seems that, although the terminology has changed, the actual explanations for the existence of poverty are pretty much the same. On the one side there are those who claim that affluence is a combination of natural ability and hard work; and on the other side there are those who argue that the poor are unfortunate, or that the 'system' is against them. So one argument lays the blame at the feet of the poor themselves, whilst the other blames the society that condemns some people to poverty.

● **Dependency-based explanations** argue that poverty is the result of individual or cultural deficiency. Such explanations include the belief that there is a specific section of the working class that does not want to work, called the 'underclass'.
● **Exclusion-based explanations** focus on the way in which some people are 'made to be poor' by the economic and political system.

Dependency-based explanations

These sorts of explanations argue that the poor are, in some way, the cause of their own poverty. At their most extreme, they suggest that the welfare system in Britain actually makes people dependent on it by providing an attractive alternative to work.

Three different approaches exist, based on:

● **individual deficiency**
● the **culture of poverty**
● the **underclass**

Individual deficiency

Explanations that centre on the concept of **dependency** stress that people who are poor are in that state because of some personal or cultural deficiency. Essentially, it is their fault if they are poor.

The individual as scapegoat

This is the approach that many nineteenth-century writers took, and it remains, to some extent, in the idea of the '**scrounger**'. There is little evidence that this could explain any more than a tiny proportion of poverty. However, the myth of the scrounger was used powerfully in the 1980s as a justification for cutbacks in welfare.

The dependent individual

This idea was developed by Marsland (1996) who argued that the individual's will to work was undermined by excessively generous state welfare benefits, and that the need to look after other family members was weakened by the extensive provision of state services. The result was a high level of dependence on the state.

The culture of poverty

This idea was originally suggested by Oscar Lewis (1966) in his study of poor people in Mexico. Lewis argued that poor people in a 'class-stratified and highly **individualistic** society' were likely to develop a set of cultural values that trapped them in their poverty. It is important to stress the ideas of class and **individualism**, for Lewis is not arguing that these people are necessarily deficient. He believes that they are caught in a society that really does put barriers in their path – but that the poor themselves help ensure that they are trapped by developing a set of values that prevent them from breaking out of poverty. These cultural values include a sense of **fatalism** and acceptance of their poverty, an inability to think long term, and a desire for immediate enjoyment.

Critics of this approach argue that there is no such thing as a culture of poverty – rather, such cultural values are a perfectly rational reaction to conditions of hopelessness. In the USA, the poorest groups really are excluded, and they are unlikely to be allowed to break out of their poverty. In such a situation the poor may feel that there is no point in planning long term.

The underclass

The underclass approach is a development of the cultural explanations for poverty, but it extends the analysis much further and introduces a very radical critique of the US and UK welfare systems. Whereas the 'cause' of poverty in the culture of poverty thesis lies in a cultural adaptation to a highly class-stratified society, in the underclass approach, poverty is a response to cultural, economic and welfare changes.

The argument, first developed by an American writer, Charles Murray, is that an 'underclass' (see Unit 1 Topic 6) exists, consisting of people who are lazy and make no effort to work or look after themselves. These people prefer to live off the state rather than work. By underclass, Murray means a significant and self-reproducing group who form a distinctive bottom element of the class structure in British and US societies.

Murray accepts that there are poor people who are poor through no fault of their own. Nevertheless, he believes that the bulk of poverty is caused by those who do not make the effort to earn a living, and/or waste what they do have. Murray's analysis (1994) is slightly different for the USA and Britain. His analysis of the USA focuses heavily on 'American blacks' as the source of the underclass; in Britain his analysis is not race-based.

Murray argues that a clear segment of the working class distinguishes itself through:

- **Crime** – Murray points out that a very high proportion of violent and property crime is carried out by a small proportion of the population
- **Illegitimacy** – there are very high levels of children born outside marriage (and in particular to never-married women). These children are the outcome of casual sex, and the fathers have no interest in supporting the child or mother.
- **Economic inactivity** – here Murray is referring to the high levels of long-term unemployment that characterise the same relatively small group of people. Murray argues that it is not that they are unemployed in any traditional sense, but that they prefer to collect state benefit and to work in the **'hidden' economy**. Poverty is a way of life and is chosen by members of the underclass.

Murray's work has been fiercely attacked by a wide range of writers. The consensus amongst critics is that Murray is, quite simply, factually wrong. There is no evidence from social surveys that a group exists that rejects the work ethic. Research shows that the majority of lone parents would like a stable relationship; and there is no evidence of an automatic overlap between lone-parent families and crime.

Exclusion-based explanations

Exclusion-based explanations argue that the poor are poor because they are prevented from achieving a reasonable standard of living by the actions of the more powerful in society.

This approach stresses differences in power between the various groups in society. Those who have least power – the disabled, older people, women, ethnic minorities and, of course, children – have significantly higher chances of living in poverty. Within this approach we can distinguish three strands:

1 Poverty, powerlessness and the **labour market**
2 **Citizenship** and exclusion
3 Poverty and capitalism: the economic system approach

Figure 5.3 The underclass

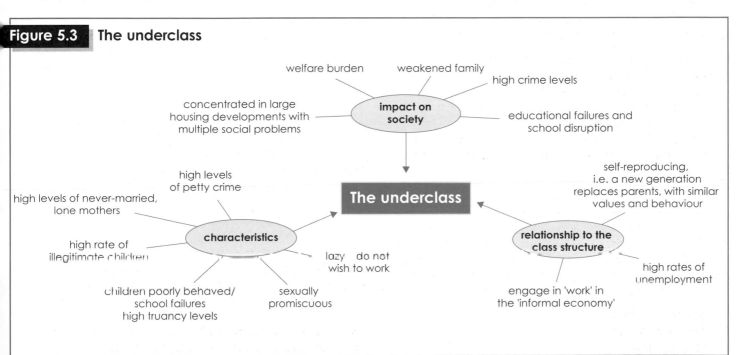

Poverty, powerlessness and the labour market

In all societies the least powerful groups are the most likely to lose out economically and socially, and they will form the bulk of the poor. Indeed, poverty and powerlessness go hand in hand. The powerless include women, lone parents (usually women), the very young and the very old, as well as those with disabilities. When these powerless groups do get employment, it is likely to be in short-term, low-paid, temporary and possibly 'unofficial' work. For many supporters of the welfare state, it is these groups who deserve help, because they are blameless 'victims' of the economic system.

Citizenship and exclusion

Field (1989) has developed this argument, and linked it to the idea of 'citizenship'. Field argues that three groups in society have, over the last 20 years, been excluded from the rights citizens should enjoy, including the right to a decent standard of living. These are:

- the long-term unemployed
- lone-parent families
- those on state retirement pensions

Together these groups comprise what he calls (rather confusingly) the 'underclass'. Field argues that these groups have been particularly hit by government policies which have increased the gap between rich and poor; by increases in the core number of long-term unemployed; and, finally, by an increasing tendency to **stigmatise** and blame the poor for their poverty, rather than look at wider economic and social factors. Once again, the answer to the problem of poverty lies in a better-organised and comprehensive welfare state.

Poverty and capitalism: the economic system approach

The final, and most radical, explanation for poverty is provided by those in the Marxist tradition (see Unit 1 Topic 3). They see poverty as an inevitable outcome of the capitalist system. According to Marxist theory, the economy is owned and run by a small ruling class who exploit the majority of the population who work for them. Poverty emerges from three main causes:

1 The wealth of the ruling class is created from paying the lowest possible wages to people – because it is the profits that produce the wealth.
2 The poor act as a warning – having a group in poverty provides a direct warning to the rest of the workforce of what could happen to them if they didn't work hard.
3 Poor people provide a 'starting point' against which other workers can measure their own income (rather than against the income of members of the ruling class).

For Marxists, the welfare state is a means of hiding exploitation, and it is used by the rich and powerful to provide just enough in the way of health care and income support benefits to prevent a serious challenge to their authority.

CHECK YOUR UNDERSTANDING

1 Explain how, according to some writers, the welfare state can actually be the cause of poverty?

2 What is the 'culture of poverty'? Give two examples of the values of the 'culture'.

3 According to Charles Murray, what is the 'underclass'?

4 Identify three distinguishing features of the underclass.

5 What do sociologists mean by 'exclusion-based approaches'?

6 What three groups have been excluded from the rights of citizenship, according to Field?

7 From a Marxist perspective, how does capitalism cause poverty?

KEY TERMS

Citizenship – refers (in this particular case) to the belief that people living in British society have certain 'rights', including the right to have a decent standard of living.

Culture of poverty – a set of values that some poorer people in society share, which they pass on to their children. The result is that they get trapped in poverty.

Dependency – the state of being dependent. It is used to refer to the idea that some people live off the hard work of others.

Exclusion – the idea that some people are prevented from being able to get on in life and enjoy the benefits of an affluent society.

Fatalism – acceptance that what happens is the result of luck or 'fate'.

Item A

So, let us get it straight from the outset: the underclass does not refer to a degree of poverty, but to a type of poverty.

It is not a new concept. I grew up knowing what the underclass was; we just didn't call it that in those days. ... One class of poor people was never even called poor ... they simply lived with low incomes. ... Then there was another set of poor people ... these poor people didn't lack just money. They were defined by their behaviour. Their homes were littered and unkempt. The men in the family were unable to hold a job for more than a few weeks at a time. Drunkenness was common. The children grew up ill-schooled and ill-behaved and contributed a disproportionate share of the local juvenile delinquents.

C. Murray (1990) *The Emerging British Underclass*, London: IEA (Health and Welfare Series), p. 1

Item B

At one extreme there is a severely deprived group whose behaviour is predictably influenced by their abject poverty but who still do not resemble an underclass in any sociological sense. The only reason they, in Murray's words, 'live in a different world' is that they have no choice. ...

At the other extreme are a growing number of very wealthy people. As an act of social policy, gross inequalities, unknown in Britain for at least 100 years, have been created. ... These two extremes have been openly engineered by government policy, and the massive inequalities underlying them are two parts of the same problem. To paraphrase Tawney, 'what thoughtful rich people may refer to as the problem of poverty, thoughtful poor people may call the problem of wealth'.

A. Walker (1990) 'Blaming the victims' in C. Murray, *The Emerging British Underclass*, London: IEA (Health and Welfare Series), pp. 55–6

1 Explain in your own words what is meant by an 'underclass'. (2)

2 Suggest two characteristics that Murray might associate with the underclass. (4)

3 Suggest three ways in which the poor may live in 'a different world' (Item B). (6)

4 Identify and explain two ways in which government policy could create 'gross inequalities' (Item B). (8)

5 Explain and discuss the statement: 'what thoughtful rich people may refer to as the problem of poverty, thoughtful poor people may call the problem of wealth'. (20)

6 Using material from the Items and elsewhere, assess the extent to which the existence of an underclass is a key cause of poverty. (20)

'Hidden' economy – all of the 'cash-in-hand' and casual work that is never reported to authorities such as the Inland Revenue.

Individual deficiency – refers to a person's specific faults or weaknesses which make them unable to get on in society and be successful.

Individualism – the belief that individuals are far more important than social groups.

Labour market – refers to the sorts of jobs and employment conditions that people have.

'Scrounger' – someone who claims welfare benefits they are not entitled to, and/or who manipulates the benefits system to their own advantage.

Stigmatise – to mark something out as bad.

Extension activities

1 Conduct a series of in-depth interviews, or design a questionnaire, to find out what the public think are the main causes of poverty. Compare their views with the sociological explanations. Which explanation has most public support? Why might this be the case?

2 Find out the current government's views about social exclusion. Go to their website at www.open.gov.uk and search for 'social exclusion'.

Getting you thinking

Clockwise from top left: a homeless young person; a pensioner; a single-parent family; a job seeker; low-wage employment

1 What is causing the people above to be in poverty?

2 Suggest different ways in which the people in each situation might be taken out of poverty.

3 What are the advantages and disadvantages of these approaches? Which do you favour, if any? Explain your answer.

We have seen in earlier topics that there is considerable debate over the definitions, causes and even the extent of poverty in Britain. Clearly, if there is no agreement on any of these, then finding one programme to eradicate poverty that is acceptable to all is, to say the least, difficult. This topic explores the various solutions to poverty that have been put forward, and gives some examples of actual policies that have been tried.

There are four main approaches to solving the problem of poverty:

- the New Right approach
- the social democratic approach
- the 'Third Way'
- the Marxist approach

The New Right approach

The New Right have developed a series of arguments which attack the **welfare state** and see it, both directly and indirectly, as one of the main causes of poverty. New Right theorists argue that, in a democratic, capitalist society, wealth is created by those people who successfully run companies, and by others who innovate, have entrepreneurial ideas and start new companies. Everyone else relies upon these people for jobs, and therefore incomes. These entrepreneurs (see Unit 1 Topic 6) are motivated by money, and it is therefore up to government to make sure that entrepreneurs and owners of successful companies are able to earn well.

Welfare as an indirect cause of poverty

In order to ensure that entrepreneurs are well rewarded, taxation must be kept as low as possible. The welfare state – including provision of state benefits for those without employment – is the largest area of government spending, and without it taxes could be much lower. The welfare state is therefore an indirect cause of poverty, because it discourages the efforts of entrepreneurs to start new companies which would create new jobs; and because it hinders successful, established companies by burdening them with taxes.

Welfare as a direct cause of poverty

Welfare also has a direct role in causing poverty. This is because the welfare state actually undermines the will to work. It does this by providing free health and care services, plus financial support for those who do not want to work. So those who prefer to live on state benefits can do so, thus placing a huge burden in the form of increased taxes and lost productivity on the rest of the population.

Poverty and inequality

According to the New Right approach, there must always be inequality, because only a few can be successful. However, their success can generate enough employment to eliminate poverty. (By 'poverty', they usually mean the absolute definition – see Topic 2.)

Criticisms of the New Right approach

The New Right approach has been heavily criticised on a number of grounds. The first of these is that poverty would actually increase if the welfare state were abolished. The welfare state and the **minimum wage** help to protect workers from exploitative employers. If there were no welfare state, society would be split between a wealthy minority, and a mass of the poor who would have little stake in society.

The New Right approach has been very influential in the USA and there is little evidence that it has helped to eliminate poverty – quite the reverse in fact.

The social democratic approach

This approach to combating poverty underpins the current welfare state. Social democrats argue that in any society there will be some groups who are in poverty through no fault of their own.

Some people may be disabled or retired, others may be unable to work because of childcare responsibilities – or the economy may be passing through a crisis and there may not be enough jobs. The role of the welfare state is to ensure that these people are cared for and are guaranteed a decent standard of living.

Although this approach seems quite uncontroversial nowadays, the idea of a welfare state that guaranteed health care, pensions and financial benefits for the unemployed was very radical in the 1940s when it was first introduced. Before that time, those in need had to rely on charity for health care; and the unemployment benefits that were available were extremely basic.

In this model of welfare, then, poverty is eliminated by means of **welfare benefits/state benefits** provided by the state, which are paid for out of general taxation.

Criticisms of the social democratic approach

The social democratic approach – although broadly supported by many sociologists – has not developed its analysis as society has changed. In particular, it has failed to respond to the growth in single parenthood and the changing position of women in society. Traditionally, benefits had gone to families, with the assumption that there was a working husband/father (or a husband/father who wanted work). By the 1990s this was no longer typical of families in poverty. There were large numbers of single mothers who wanted to work, but who were caught in a **poverty trap** – where the state benefits they lost when they began to work outweighed the income they received. As a result, there was an incentive not to work.

At the same time, the costs of the welfare state were becoming too great for the government to bear, as expectations of health care, housing and standards of living grew. The original welfare state had been based on the costs of providing a very basic living standard. As the relative definition of poverty became more widely accepted, so this basic living standard seemed increasingly out of touch with what people expected.

Figure 5.4 Solutions to poverty

Approach	View of welfare state	View of poor people	Strategy to eliminate poverty	Role of government
New Right	BAD – wasteful and inefficient; undermines will to work	Lazy or less able than successful people	To let entrepreneurs create wealth for themselves, and therefore jobs for others	To create the conditions for successful commerce, e.g. low taxes, few regulations
Social democratic	GOOD – role is to ensure a fair society	Unfortunate people	An all-encompassing welfare state paid for through tax	To organise, provide and fund a 'free' welfare state
Third Way	Essentially good, but too expensive and inefficient	Most poor people could work but they are either unable to (the majority) or do not want to (the minority)	Make a society in which all people can get employment with adequate income to live on	To overcome the barriers that prevent people working
Marxist	Hides the true exploitation of the majority of the population by the few rich	Exploited by the ruling class	Revolution! Take over control of the economy and state	Governments in capitalist societies are just there to represent the interests of the ruling class

The 'Third Way'

From the 1940s until the 1980s, the social democratic approach, with its emphasis on a comprehensive welfare state, was seen as the only way to combat poverty. But there were many criticisms of the system. On the political right there were those who said that it was too expensive and that it undermined self-help. On the left there were those who argued that the system was not generous enough, and that the levels of state benefit simply maintained people in poverty without actually doing anything radical to eliminate poverty.

The Conservative governments during the 1980s and 1990s began a slow process of cutting back on welfare provision. This turned out to be unpopular with the electorate. Since the late 1990s, the Labour administrations have moved towards what they call a 'Third Way' model of welfare.

The Third Way responds to a number of the criticisms that were made of the social democratic approach. It accepts the fact that poverty cannot be eliminated simply by increasing benefits for the poor. Instead it argues that more people should be encouraged into employment, and that the wider context of poverty needs to be taken into account.

Employment and poverty

The Third Way model sees the costs of combating poverty through welfare benefits alone as simply too high, and it argues that the aim of a welfare state is to ensure that all those who can possibly be working are in employment. Rather than the government paying the full costs of unemployment, people without jobs should be strongly encouraged into employment, and the government's role is to provide incentives to work. Consequently, there are now compulsory skills training programmes for youth and long-term unemployed, and payments for childcare so that lone parents can work.

When people are in employment, the wage levels should be high enough to raise them out of poverty. In order to ensure that this is the case, the Labour government introduced a minimum wage, which all employers must pay.

The wider context of poverty

The Third Way also sees poverty as just one element in a broader context of social disadvantage. Poverty refers to lack of financial resources, but just giving poor people more money in the form of better state benefits does not solve the problem. Instead, the Third Way focuses on social exclusion (see Topic 4), which sees poverty as linked to poor health, bad housing, anti-social behaviour, school failure, and a range of other disadvantages. The Third Way has therefore introduced a range of programmes to combat all of these disadvantages – the idea being that only when *all* of these are overcome will poverty itself be eliminated.

Criticisms of the 'Third Way'

The welfare system that the Third Way proposes is really an extension of many of the values of the social democrats. However, many people have noticed a **disciplinary tendency** underpinning the Third Way approach. Whereas in the social democratic approach, welfare benefits were seen very much as a right, the Third Way argues that people must accept work or training for work, or they will lose their rights to benefits. So young people who refuse to go on training courses, for example, can have their benefits suspended; and lone mothers of older children are expected to find employment. Critics have also pointed out that the minimum wage, as it stands, is simply too low for anyone to live on.

The Marxist approach

The Marxist approach to combating poverty sees little place for the welfare state – not because it costs too much, nor because it fails to alleviate poverty, but because it believes that poverty is 'built into' capitalism, and that it is only through radical changes in society that poverty can ever be eliminated.

This approach argues that capitalism survives on exploiting the majority of the working population. Those who own the commercial institutions can only make a profit as long as they can pay the lowest possible wages. The existence of a pool of unemployed people serves to keep wages down by acting as a 'threat' to the employed, because the unemployed will always be there to take the employed people's jobs if their wage demands are too great.

For Marxists, the welfare state merely helps to maintain capitalism, by providing a minimum standard of living which dampens down opposition to the system. Marxists would prefer a radical change in society, such that the rich were forced to give up their ownership of the commercial institutions, and wealth was more evenly distributed across society.

According to this model, therefore, poverty can only be eliminated by radical political and social changes.

Criticisms of the Marxist approach

Critics of this approach have argued that, in a world of global capitalism, if any government did try to take the wealth from the richest members of society, the rich would simply move it elsewhere, and the result would be fewer jobs and even greater poverty. Where governments did take over the commercial institutions, as in Eastern Europe, the result was **authoritarian** government and relatively low standards of living.

CHECK YOUR UNDERSTANDING

1 According to the New Right:
   (a) How do entrepreneurs help to solve the problem of poverty?
   (b) How can the welfare state undermine the 'will to work'?

2 Which approach is associated with the introduction of the welfare state?

3 What is the role of the welfare state, according to social democrats?

4 What is the role of the welfare state, according to Marxists?

5 Explain in your own words what the term 'disciplinary tendency' means, and give one example.

Exploring ... solving poverty

Item A The government's aim is to rebuild the welfare state around work. ... Our ambition is nothing less than a change of culture among benefit claimants, employers and public servants – with rights and responsibilities on all sides. Those making the shift from welfare into work will be provided with positive assistance, not just a benefit payment.

DSS (1998) *New Ambitions for our Country*, London: The Stationery Office, pp. 23–4

Item B Under the slogan of 'Making work pay', it is intended that the minimum wage and a partial fusing of the tax and benefit system will ensure that people who move from welfare to work should be financially better off. ... However, in contrast to earlier opposition, Labour will introduce new financial penalties against the 'workshy'.

M. Powell (2000) 'New Labour and the Third Way in the British welfare state: a new and distinctive approach?' *Critical Social Policy*, vol. 20, no. 1, p. 45

Item C Taxpayers, if not in open revolt over the burden of maintaining expensive and inefficient welfare systems, support political parties that pledge to do something about it. In an era where governments are concerned about their ability to maintain the tax base, particularly in the case of corporate taxes, this is a pressure that has to be taken seriously. Ageing populations, the emergence of a growing, welfare-dependent underclass and the sapping effects of modern welfare states on incentive, initiative and enterprise, also point the way clearly to the need for reform.

D. Smith (2000) 'Editor's introduction' in D. Smith (ed.) *Welfare, Work and Poverty*, London: ISCS, p. 1

Item D Thus, in contrast to the social democratic view, it is insisted that, under capitalism, the functioning and management of state welfare remain part of a capitalist state. ... The benefits of the welfare state to the working class are not generally denied, but they are seen to be largely the by-product of securing the interests of [the ruling class].

Adapted from C. Pierson (1991) *Beyond the Welfare State?* Cambridge: Polity Press, p. 53

1 Explain what is meant by the phrase 'welfare to work' (Items A and B). (2)

2 Suggest two examples of 'positive assistance' that the government might give to help people move from 'welfare into work' (Item A). (4)

3 Identify the perspective represented by Item D. Suggest two criticisms of this view of the welfare state. (6)

4 Identify and explain two reasons why the author of Item C believes that the welfare state is in need of reform. (8)

5 Outline and discuss the New Right approach to poverty and the welfare state. (20)

6 Using material from the Items and elsewhere, assess the effectiveness of the welfare state in eliminating poverty. (20)

KEY TERMS

Authoritarian – 'bossy' and controlling.

Disciplinary tendency – where people are forced into certain patterns of behaviour – e.g. the unemployed are forced to undertake skills training or lose their rights to state benefits.

Minimum wage – the lowest legal wage an employer can pay.

Poverty trap – where a person who gets a job experiences a drop in income, because their wages are lower than the welfare benefits they were receiving when unemployed.

Welfare benefits/state benefits – refers to the financial support that the government gives people as part of the welfare state – e.g. disability benefits and pensions.

Welfare state – a system of welfare benefits and services provided by central or local government.

Extension activities

1 Find out the minimum wage. You can do this by either telephoning the Department of Trade and Industry Minimum Wage Helpline (0845 6000678) or going to the website: www.tiger.gov.uk. Conduct a small survey. Find out what people think the minimum wage is. Do people think it is lower or higher than it really is? Tell them the correct minimum wage – ask them if they think it is 'reasonable'. Calculate the weekly rate, by multiplying the hourly rate by 40 (representing 40 hours' work a week). Do you think it is possible to live 'decently' on this? (You may need to find out about rents/cost of food/clothing, etc. in order to answer this.)

2 Use the websites of the main political parties to compare their approaches to welfare and poverty (and remember that each party is going to be biased in the information it gives you).
Conservative Party www.conservatives.com
Labour Party www.labour.org.uk
Liberal Democrats www.libdems.org.uk

3 Interview a small sample of people to discover their opinions on eliminating poverty. Do they think it can be achieved, and, if so, how? What are their different views? How do these link to sociological views and the policies of the different political parties?

Getting you thinking

This advertisement is seeking to persuade people to take out insurance to cover themselves for private health care.

1 If you had to choose just one of the following statements as the nearer to what you believe, which would it be?
   (a) That health care should be available solely on the basis of a person's need.
   (b) That a person has the right to buy private health care if that is how they decide to spend their money.

2 Make a list of reasons for your choice.

3 Make a list of reasons why the other view is mistaken.

4 Now discuss the two statements with others and see what agreement or disagreement there is. You could take a vote at the end.

STOP!

Don't renew your private health plan until you call PPP healthcare on 0800 33 55 55

Lines open 8am-8pm weekdays, 9am-1pm Saturdays

PPP healthcare

Member of the Global AXA Group

The development of welfare

Before the introduction of the welfare state, there had been a variety of forms of welfare provision, dating back as far as 1601, when the government introduced what we might now call a 'minimum wage'.

In 1834 the Poor Law (Amendment) Act introduced the workhouse system – which meant that the poor and the old had to go and live in workhouses if they were destitute. In order to ensure that people did not 'abuse' the system, the conditions inside the workhouses were deliberately made worse than the conditions outside. As the life of the poor was quite horrific by modern standards, you can imagine what

life was like inside these workhouses!

Workhouses remained in various forms until 1928, although in 1908 and 1912 the Liberal governments introduced sickness benefits (for males only) and old age pensions, which meant that the workhouses were no longer needed.

The welfare state

The welfare state developed from a government report of 1942: the Beveridge Report. Beveridge identified a number of 'social evils' which he felt the government needed to wipe out. The resulting policies became known as the 'welfare state'.

SOCIAL EVIL	WELFARE STATE
Want (poverty)	Poverty was to be tackled by payment of unemployment and sickness benefits, and a 'safety net' benefit that would cover everyone not covered by these other benefits. Today, this safety-net benefit is known as 'income support'.
Ignorance	Free schooling was to be extended (to age 15), and new schools were to be built.
Disease	A National Health Service (NHS) was to be set up whereby everyone would have a right to free health care. Before this, people either paid for their health care, or applied to charitable hospitals.
Squalor (poor housing)	A massive programme of house-building was to be undertaken to get rid of poor-quality housing ('slums').
Idleness (unemployment)	The government was to commit itself to ensuring that never again would there be a return to mass unemployment.

The debate over universal and selective benefits (targeting)

Philosophical arguments

One debate that has dogged the provision of welfare has been the question of who should receive state benefits. Those who support the idea of universal benefits (**universalism**) argue that state benefits – such as free health care, pensions and child allowances – should be given to all those who need them, irrespective of their income. The thinking behind this is that it helps to draw society together and promotes social harmony.

Those who support **selectivism/targeting** argue that universalism simply wastes resources on those who have no need of them. It also undermines people's desire to look after themselves, their family and other members of the community. Universalism thus weakens rather than strengthens social harmony and any sense of community.

Practical arguments

The debate between those who support the universal provision of welfare and those who support selective provision also involves arguments about practicality.

It is true that universalism does provide help to those who have no need of it. However, because everyone gets the same benefits, and there is no complex bureaucratic mechanism to assess who is eligible, the costs of providing the benefits are actually quite low. Furthermore, universal provision ensures that everyone who needs help gets it (because *everyone* does), and it also eliminates the stigma attached to claiming state benefits.

Selectivists point out that universal benefits are wasteful. By targeting the more needy, the levels of benefit could be

higher and the quality of services could be better. It is true that for some benefits the administrative costs of targeting are expensive, but, despite this, overall, money would be saved on most benefits.

The 'mixed economy' of welfare

The **'mixed economy' of welfare** refers to the move away from a state **monopoly** of health and care provision, to having a number of different providers, including:

- **for-profit/private organisations**
- **voluntary (charitable) organisations**
- **informal care** provided by family and friends

Before the introduction of the welfare state, many services we now associate with it, such as health care, were provided either by profit-making organisations or by charities. In the last 20 years there has been a resurgence both of private companies, and of charitable (or non-profit-making) organisations.

The main reason for this has been the influence of the New Right on Conservative governments during the 1980s and 1990s, and the subsequent acceptance of many of their arguments by succeeding Labour governments, which have incorporated these ideas into their 'Third Way' ideology (see Topic 5).

The New Right has argued that the state provision of welfare is both inefficient and of a poor standard, because there is no incentive for the providers of welfare either to attract 'customers', or to save money. The employees of the NHS, for example, continue to receive their salaries no matter how inefficient the system, or how rude they are to the people who use their services. This is because the NHS has been, until recently, the only provider of health services. Supporters of the New Right argue that, if the NHS had to make a profit, the employees would certainly have to act differently. The term used to describe this is the 'discipline of the market'.

Since the 1980s, governments have partially accepted these arguments, and a number of reforms have been introduced that attempt to bring the 'discipline of the market' into the provision of health and welfare.

These changes include:

- Handing over some areas of welfare and health care provision (e.g. housing and the care of older people) to private or charitable organisations.
- Encouraging the NHS to sub-contract certain activities to private organisations (e.g. private hospitals may undertake routine operations such as removal of cataracts and hip replacements).
- The NHS builds new hospitals that are shared with private health care organisations.
- Voluntary organisations are given grants to help support their activities.
- Local health care trusts are required to operate to stringent financial and customer care standards.

Another area of this 'mixed economy' of welfare is the growing emphasis on informal care by family members. The government strongly supports this form of care, primarily because it is cheap. For example, grants are available to enable family carers to stay at home to look after family members with disabilities.

Figure 5.5   Provision of welfare

Informal sector

Care provided by family and friends,
who do so out of love
Pros: • often very high standard of care – only they
           could put in the amount of work needed
         • can strengthen the family
Cons: • carers (who tend to be women) become
           'trapped' and spend their life caring

Private/for profit

Companies that seek to profit from providing
health and care services
Pros: • efficient and usually high standards
Cons: • only for those who can afford it

**Mixed economy
of welfare provision**

Voluntary sector/non-profit

Groups who wish to provide
services that complement the state services
Pros: • address areas of need
         • may have great expertise
         • actions based on care for others
Cons: • if not well-organised, can provide
           poor-quality, possibly harmful service

Public sector services

Provided by national or local government
Pros: • free to use and available on the
           basis of need
Cons: • long waiting lists for most in-demand services

Criticisms of the 'mixed economy' of welfare

Critics of the 'mixed economy' of welfare argue that the state is abandoning its responsibilities, and that it is a step back to the time before the welfare state. The main criticisms are:

● The growth of private health care and its funding by government means that a two-tier system has developed in which the more affluent are able to buy better health care, while the majority of the population have to make do with second-class services.

● Charitable organisations, which are often staffed by volunteers, may have less expertise than professionals.

● Feminist sociologists, in particular, have pointed out that the burden of informal care usually falls upon the women in families.

CHECK YOUR UNDERSTANDING

1 When, and after what report, was the welfare state introduced?

2 What are the advantages of:
   (a) the universal provision of benefits?
   (b) the selective provision of benefits?

3 Explain the meaning of the term 'the mixed economy of welfare'.

4 How has the New Right attacked the welfare state?

5 Which members of the family are most likely to provide 'informal care'?

KEY TERMS

For-profit/private organisations – organisations that provide services in order to make a profit.

Informal care – care provided by family or friends.

'Mixed economy' of welfare – refers to the fact that welfare is provided not just by the state, but also by private and voluntary organisations.

Monopoly – a situation in which there is only one provider of goods or services and, therefore, no competition.

Selectivism/targeting – the belief that only those with limited financial resources should receive welfare services and benefits.

Universalism – the belief that everyone should be entitled to free welfare services and benefits.

Voluntary (charitable) organisations – independent organisations that provide health or welfare services, but do not seek to make any profit.

Exploring welfare provision

In a report – *The End of Altruism?* – Graham Leach, chief economist at the Institute of Directors, blames the excessive intrusion of the state for a collapse in British traditions of philanthropy. ...

'Government is actually part of the problem, and the New Labour ethos does not provide any indication of fundamental change', says Mr Leach. 'Younger age groups in particular are driven by the belief that it is the Government's responsibility to deal with social problems and that this should be paid for out of taxation. Older age groups may be more inclined towards altruism, but also be resentful about paying twice, via tax and giving.'

He adds: 'The Good Samaritan philosophy that the first line of response should be the individual, has been subsumed within the welfare state. Altruism has been crowded out by taxation and the welfare state.'

P. Johnston (1999) 'Welfare state undermines the spirit of giving', *Daily Telegraph*, Monday, 31 May (internet issue 1466)

Surveys suggest that, overall, one-third of the income of the charitable voluntary sector comes from the state. Some are almost totally state-funded, such as the Shaftesbury Society, which receives 90 per cent of its funds from the Government to help the disabled and poor.

[According to the author of the research, Mr Whelan]: 'In the years following the post-war welfare state legislation, politicians found themselves committed to providing a range of services which were vastly expensive to deliver', he says. 'By sub-contracting to charities, the Government could fulfil its obligations on the cheap because voluntary bodies will almost inevitably be able to supply a given service at a lower cost.'

Even the National Council for Voluntary Organisations derives 40 per cent of its income from the state.

P. Johnston (1999) 'Charities "rely too much on state aid"', *Daily Telegraph*, Monday, 2 August (internet issue 1529)

1 Explain the meaning of the term 'philanthropy' (Item A). (2)

2 Suggest two reasons why the government funds charities (Item B). (4)

3 Give three examples to illustrate how the government 'deals with social problems' (Item A). (6)

4 Identify and explain two reasons why some people may believe it is the government's responsibility to deal with social problems. (8)

5 Examine the sociological arguments for and against the universal provision of welfare benefits. (20)

6 Using information from the Items and elsewhere, assess the view that it is the responsibility of the government to provide a 'welfare state'. (20)

Extension activities

1 Find the websites of three charitable organisations. Compare their work. To what extent do they duplicate or work alongside government welfare services? How are they funded?

2 Conduct an opinion survey to find out what the public think about universal and selective benefits, and the welfare state in general. Do the public support the welfare state? Which do they favour, universal or selective benefits? Why?

3 Which voluntary organisations operate in your area? Go to your local public library and find out how many voluntary organisations there are offering help or support with health or caring issues. What do they do?

Getting you thinking

When can an illness be labelled an illness?

Very ill .... Not ill

Migraine symptoms (*severe headache, nausea, impaired vision*)   1 — 2 — 3 — 4

Anorexia nervosa (*severe eating disorder*)   1 — 2 — 3 — 4

Hangover (*severe headache, nausea*)   1 — 2 — 3 — 4

Leukaemia (*cancer of the blood*)   1 — 2 — 3 — 4

Cirrhosis of the liver (*caused by consistent alcohol abuse*)   1 — 2 — 3 — 4

Smoker's cough   1 — 2 — 3 — 4

Lung cancer (*patient is a heavy smoker*)   1 — 2 — 3 — 4

Severe lack of energy   1 — 2 — 3 — 4

Venereal disease due to a holiday romance   1 — 2 — 3 — 4

Source: M. Senior with B. Viveash (1998) *Health and Illness*, Basingstoke: Macmillan

1 Using the scale 1–4 mark how serious you think the 'illness' is.

2 Compare your answers with those of other people. How similar are they?

3 What ways are there of telling that you are not feeling well?

4 When you do not feel well or you think you have some medical problem, do you always go straight to the doctor? Probably not. Who do you ask first for advice?

5 How do you respond to the advice/diagnosis? What happens if you do not agree with the advice/diagnosis?

6 What do you think this tells us, if anything, about our medical knowledge and our certainty as to what is illness or not?

Some days we wake up in the morning and just *know* that we feel ill. However, it may be more difficult to persuade suspicious parents that we really are too ill to go to school or college. It is only when we produce some real evidence, such as vomiting or a rash, that we are believed. Our parents may also be more suspicious when it turns out that we have been drinking pretty heavily the night before. Ill or just hung over? And anyway, why is being hung over not being ill – after all, we feel awful? The answer from disapproving parents might well be that being hung over is the price we pay for a night's drinking, and that it therefore does not count as a 'real' illness.

The same problem is encountered by sociologists in their attempts to agree definitions of health and illness. It would seem that both concepts have very different meanings to different individuals and groups in society. The consequences of the different definitions are quite significant in terms of presenting oneself for treatment at a **general practitioner's** (GP's) surgery, receiving serious attention from the GP, and later receiving support and sympathy from friends and family.

To unravel this complex issue, we will look first at how ordinary people construct their definitions of health and illness, then move on to the competing models amongst health practitioners.

Public definitions of health and illness

In the survey *Health and Lifestyles*, Mildred Blaxter (1990) found that, when she asked almost 10,000 people how they defined health, three clear categories emerged:

1 Positive definitions – health is defined as feeling fit and able to undertake any reasonable task.
2 Negative definitions – health is defined in terms of being free from pain and discomfort.
3 Functional definitions – where people define health in terms of being able to perform a range of tasks.

These different definitions mean that a particular level of discomfort for one person may well indicate that they are ill, whilst, for another person, it may have no such meaning at all.

Factors influencing the public's definitions

A number of factors appear to influence the way in which individuals define their sense of being healthy or ill.

Cultural differences

Different social groups have differing ideas of what constitutes illness. Krause (1989) studied Hindu and Sikh Punjabis living in Bedford, and their illness called 'sinking heart' (dil ghirda hai) which is characterised by physical chest pain. According to Krause, this illness is caused by a variety of emotional experiences – most importantly, public shame of some sort.

Age differences
Older people tend to accept as 'normal' a range of pains and physical limitations, which younger people would define as being symptoms of some illness or **disability**. As we age, we gradually redefine health and accept greater levels of physical discomfort.

Gender differences
Men have fewer consultations with doctors than women. This is partly due to the greater number of complications associated with childbirth and menopause which women face, but it is also partly due to the fact that men are less likely to define themselves as ill, or as needing medical attention. The idea of 'masculinity' includes the belief that a man should be tough and put off going to the doctor.

Men are also more likely to smoke and drink excess alcohol than women – despite being aware of the medical risks.

Social class differences
People from lower social classes are less likely to consult a GP than the more wealthy. This may be because they have a higher threshold of pain and discomfort before they consider themselves ill enough to visit a doctor.

Medical definitions of health and illness

There is a distinction in most people's minds between those who *think* they are ill and those who *really are* ill. This 'sanctioning' of true or false illness is undertaken by doctors. If they say you really are ill, then a series of benefits flows – sympathy, medication, time off work and so on. If they decide that you are not really ill, then you receive no benefits and may in fact be open to accusations of **malingering**.

Doctors use a particular 'scientific' measure of health and illness in order to decide whether someone really is ill or not. This model is known as the **bio-medical model**, and it is the basis of all Western medicine. The various elements of this model are as follows:

- Illness is always based on an identifiable (physical or mental) cause.
- Illnesses and their causes can be identified, classified and measured.
- The cure usually lies in the physical body of the patient, not in their social relationships or their spiritual life.
- There is a reliance upon drugs or surgery.

Traditional and non-Western definitions of health and illness

The bio-medical model contrasts markedly with concepts of illness in traditional and non-Western societies, where illness is seen as the result of a wider range of factors than just the body itself.

In traditional societies, for example, these factors could include witchcraft – where the blame for the illness lies in the bad wishes of others, or possibly the 'will of God'. A more complex model of health exists in non-Western societies, where the body and the mind are seen as completely linked. Any understanding of the body must be linked with the person's mental state, and the two need to be treated together.

Defining disability

The dominance of medical definitions of health and ill health has had important implications for people with disabilities. The common perception of disability is that disabled people have some impediment that prevents them from operating 'normally'. This perception starts from the assumption that there is a clear definition of the 'normal' body, and a 'normal' range of activities associated with it.

However, it has been pointed out by critics such as Michael Oliver (1996) that the impediments imposed by society are at least as great as those imposed by the physical **impairment**. In other words, disability is a social construction, rather than just a physical one.

It is with this in mind that the World Health Organisation (WHO) has distinguished between impairment, disability and handicap:

- **Impairment** refers to the abnormality of, or loss of function of, a part of the body.
- **Handicap** refers to the physical limits imposed by the loss of function.
- **Disability** refers to the socially imposed restriction on people's abilities to perform tasks as a result of the behaviour of people in society.

Not everyone is able to do everything as well as others – for example, run, catch or throw a ball – yet we do not describe

---

Figure 6.1   From impairment to disability

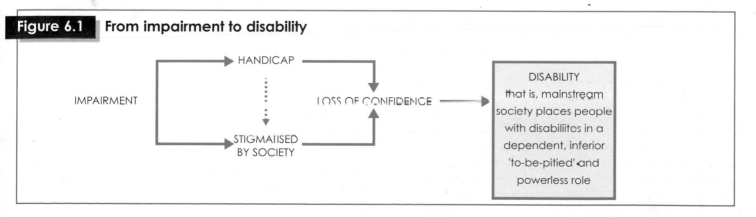

those who are less able as being 'disabled'. We just accept these differences as part of the normal range of human abilities. This range of normality could be extended to include those defined as 'disabled'. This could occur, it is argued, if physical facilities and social attitudes were adjusted to include those with disabilities – for example, by altering the way we construct buildings, and by regarding sport played by disabled people as equal to 'traditional' types of sport.

Stigma, illness and disability

Stigma is an important term in helping us to understand how people with disabilities are excluded from social activities. The idea of 'stigma' does not just apply to people with disabilities, but also to those with certain illnesses such as AIDS. The concept was first used in sociology by Erving Goffman (1963), who suggested that certain groups of people are defined as 'discredited' because of characteristics that are seen as 'negative'.

Types of stigma

Goffman suggested that there are two types of stigma:

- **Discrediting** – these are obvious types of stigma, such as being in a wheelchair. People find it awkward to have normal social relations with those who are 'discredited'. They may be embarrassed, avoid eye contact or ignore the 'obvious' disability.
- **Discreditable** – here the stigma is one of potential, dependent on whether other people find out about the discreditable illness or disability. Examples of this might include HIV status, or epilepsy. In this situation, the person with the illness may find it difficult to act 'normally' in case they are 'found out'.

The concept of 'master status'

When the discrediting or discreditable status becomes the main way in which people are seen by others, then Goffman calls this a 'master status'. The stigma then completely dominates the way the person is treated, and any other attributes are seen as less important. The person who is unable to walk unaided is seen simply as 'wheelchair bound' (not as an intelligent, articulate woman, for example); and the happy family man is seen as an 'AIDS victim'. Finally, Goffman points out that the individuals themselves may accept this master status and come to see themselves solely in terms of their stigmatised status.

CHECK YOUR UNDERSTANDING

1 How does the public define health?

2 Identify and explain any three factors that affect the definition of health and illness.

3 Who 'sanctions' illness, and what are the benefits of being 'sanctioned' as ill?

4 What is the difference between 'impairment' and 'disability'?

5 Explain the difference between stigma and disability.

KEY TERMS

Bio-medical model of health – the conventional Western model. It sees the body as very much like a biological machine, with each part of the body performing a function. The doctor's job is to restore the functions by solving the problem of what is wrong. Ideas about the environment or the spiritual health of the person are not relevant.

Disability – the socially imposed restriction on people's abilities to perform tasks as a result of the behaviour of people in society.

General practitioner (GP) – a local doctor who deals with general health issues.

Handicap – the physical limits imposed by a loss of function.

Health – a person's perception of the state of their body's wellbeing.

Illness - perception of feeling unacceptably worse than normal body state.

Impairment – the abnormality of, or loss of function of, a part of the body.

Malingering – pretending to be ill in order to avoid work or other responsibilities.

Sanction – officially approve.

Item A

The Ndembu ascribe all persistent or severe health problems to social causes, such as the secret malevolence of sorcerers or witches, or punishment by the spirits of ancestors. These spirits cause sickness in an individual if his or her family and kin are 'not living well together', and are involved in grudges or quarrelling.

The Ndembu traditional healer, the chimbuki, conducts a divinatory séance attended by the victim, his kin and neighbours. ... By questioning these people and by shrewd observation, he builds up a picture of the patient's social field and its various tensions. ... The diviner calls all the relatives of the patient before a sacred shrine to the ancestors, and induces them 'to confess any grudges ... and hard feelings they may nourish against the patient'. ... By this process all the hidden social tensions of the group are publicly aired and gradually resolved. ... Treatment involves rituals of exorcism to withdraw evil influences from the patient's body. It also includes the use of certain herbal and other medicines, manipulation and cupping and certain substances applied to the skin.

Adapted from C. Helman (2000) *Culture, Health and Illness*, Oxford: Butterworth/Heinemann, pp. 197–8

Item B

Medicine, like Western science generally, is based on scientific rationality; that is, all the assumptions and hypotheses must be capable of being tested and verified under objective, empirical and controlled conditions. Phenomena relating to health and sickness only become 'real' when they can be objectively observed and measured under these conditions. ... As Kleineman and colleagues put it, the modern Western doctor's view of clinical reality 'assumes that biological concerns are more basic, "real", clinically significant and interesting than psychological and sociocultural issues'.

The medical definition of ill health, therefore, is largely based on objectively demonstrable physical changes in the body's structure or function which can be quantified by reference to 'normal' physiological measurements. These abnormal changes, or diseases, are seen as 'entities', each with their own unique 'personality' of symptoms and signs. For example, tuberculosis is known to be caused by a particular bacillus, to reveal itself by certain characteristic symptoms, and ... to have a likely natural history depending on whether it is treated or not.

Adapted from C. Helman (2000) *Culture, Health and Illness*, Oxford: Butterworth/Heinemann, pp. 79–81

1 Explain what is meant by a 'medical definition of ill health' (Item B). (2)

2 Identify two characteristics of the medical model of health (Item B). (4)

3 Identify three factors that the Ndembu healer sees as being important in the diagnosis of illness (Item A). (6)

4 Identify and briefly explain two ways in which the Western model of health and illness (Item B) is different from the traditional model described in Item A. (8)

5 Discuss the view that societies themselves create 'disability'. (20)

6 Using information from the Items and elsewhere, assess the view that definitions of health and illness are social constructions. (20)

Extension activities

1 Visit the website of RADAR (www.radar.org.uk). (RADAR is an educational and campaigning organisation for people with disabilities.) The website has information sheets which are worth exploring for information on disability.

2 Conduct interviews with a small sample of your peers at school or college. Who sanctions their 'illness' when they feel too ill to come in to school or college? How does the process of 'negotiating' absence work?

3 Search the World Wide Web for more examples of traditional models of health and illness. Compare them with conventional Western models.

Getting you thinking

Year	I	II	III		IV	VRatio	V:I
			IIIN	IIIM			
1921–3	82	94		95	101	125	1.52
1930–2	90	94		97	102	111	1.23
1949–53	86	92		101	104	118	1.37
1959–63	76	81		100	103	143	1.91
1970–2	77	81	99	106	114	137	1.78
1979–80/ 1982–3	66	76	94	106	116	165	2.50
1991–3	66	72	100	117	116	189	2.86

SMRS BY SOCIAL CLASS FOR MEN AGED 15/20–64 (ENGLAND AND WALES)

Note: for 1921 to 1972, men aged 15–64 are included;
for 1979 to 1993, men aged 20–64 are included

Source: M. Shaw, D. Dorling, D. Gordon and G. Davey Smith
(1999) *The Widening Gap*, Bristol: Policy Press, p. 132

SMR stands for standardised mortality ratio. This is a guide to the relative chances of dying for specific age ranges (in this case men aged 15/20–64). In this model, average chances of death are 100 and any figures above this indicate above-average chances of death. Any figures below indicate below-average chances. The letters 'I' to 'V' stand for social classes, 'I' being the highest and 'V' the lowest.

Remember when answering these questions that SMRs are relative figures – that is, they show differences between groups. It is not possible to make any statements about the absolute figures over time.

1 In 1921–3, what was the SMR for social class I and social class V?

2 What changes happened in the relative SMRs of the social classes:
   (a) between 1921 and 1953?
   (b) after 1972?

3 What long-term impact, if any, did the introduction of the National Health Service in the late 1940s have on inequalities in the SMR?

4 What reasons can you suggest for all the changes you have identified from the table?

5 Look at the photographs above and make a list of the reasons why, in your opinion, people in the 'lower' social classes are more likely to die young. Do you think the government could do anything about these issues?

In 1979, the Labour government of the time commissioned a report on health and illness in Britain. Shortly afterwards they lost the election and a new Conservative government came into power. The following year, the committee reported back on their findings. The new government was so shocked at these findings that they only printed 260 copies, and gave the report no publicity, in the hope that no one would notice. Unfortunately for the government, they did, and what the press and the public read was quite shocking: after 35 years of a free health service, health and life expectation were still very closely linked to social class.

Despite this revelation, a further report (*Independent Inquiry into Inequalities in Health*), commissioned by the next Labour government almost 20 years later, found that the 'health gap' between the poorest and the richest had actually widened.

Research has shown that health is closely linked to a number of social factors. These include:

- Geography
- Social class
- Gender
- Ethnicity

| Figure 6.2 | Chances of early death in the UK, 1997 |

(SMR*)
- >110
- 105–109
- 100–104
- 95–99
- 90–94
- <90

*SMR stands for standardised mortality ratio (see the 'Getting you thinking' section opposite for an explanation of SMRs)

Source: *Regional Trends 34*, Office for National Statistics © Crown copyright 1999

Geographical differences

In 1999 a team of researchers led by Mary Shaw looked at the **parliamentary constituencies** in Britain and gathered information on the health of the people living in each constituency. They compared the one million people living in the constituencies that had the very worst health records with the one million people living in the constituencies that had the very best health records. The gap between these groups surprised even the researchers themselves.

The comparison showed that, in the worst health areas:

- children under the age of one year are twice as likely to die.
- There are ten times more women under the age of 65 who are permanently sick (including those who are disabled).
- Adults are almost three times as likely to state that they have a serious 'chronic' (long-term) illness or disability.
- Adults have a 70 per cent greater chance of dying before the age of 65.

These geographical differences generally reflect differences in income and levels of deprivation. However, they are not simply a reflection of these, because poorer people living in the richer areas tend to have higher standards of health. It seems that quality of life in poorer areas is generally lower and as a result health standards are worse.

Social class

Mortality

Over the last twenty years, **death rates** have fallen for both men and women, in all social classes. But they have fallen faster for those in the higher social classes, so that the difference in rates between those in the higher and those in the lower social classes has actually grown.

For example, in the early 1970s the death rate among men of working age was almost twice as high for those in class V (unskilled) as for those in class I (professional). By the 1990s, it was almost three times as high. Men in social class I can expect to live for almost nine years longer than men from social class V; whilst women in social class I can expect to live six years longer than their social class V counterparts.

Morbidity

Although death rates have fallen and life expectancy has increased, there is little evidence that the population is experiencing better health than 20 years ago. In fact, there has actually been a small increase in **self-reported** long-standing illness, and differences between the social classes are still quite clear. Before we look at these, though, we ought to remember that, as we saw in Topic 1, what is defined as health changes over time. So it may be that people are actually in better health but don't believe it.

Bearing this in mind, among the 45 to 64 age group, 17 per cent of professional men reported a limiting long-standing illness, compared to 48 per cent of unskilled men (1999). For women, the figures were 25 per cent for professional women and 45 per cent for unskilled women. In adulthood, being overweight is a measure of possible ill health, with **obesity** a risk factor for many chronic diseases. There is a noticeable social class gradient in obesity, which is greater for women than men. About 25 per cent of women in class V are classified as obese, compared to 14 per cent of women in class I.

Explanations for differences in health between social classes

Different ways of explaining class differences in **mortality** and **morbidity** have been suggested:

- The artefact approach
- Social selection
- Cultural explanations
- Structural explanations

The artefact approach
Illsley (1986) argues that the statistical connection between social class and illness exaggerates the situation. For example, he points out that the number of people in social class V has declined so much over the last 30 years that the membership is just too small to be used as the basis for comparisons with other social classes.

However, the recent *Independent Inquiry into Inequalities in Health* showed that, even when the classes were regrouped to include classes IV and V together, significant differences remained. For example, in the late 1970s, death rates were 53 per cent higher among men in classes IV and V, compared with those in classes I and II.

Social selection
This approach claims that social class does not cause ill health, but that ill health may be a significant cause of social class. For example, if a person is chronically ill (i.e. they have a long-term illness) or disabled in some way, it is usually difficult for them to obtain a secure, well-paid job. The fit and healthy are more likely to be successful in life and upwardly mobile in terms of social class.

The problem with this approach is that studies of health differences indicate that poor health is a result of poverty rather than a cause of it.

Cultural explanations
This approach stresses that differences in health are best understood as being the result of cultural choices made by individuals or groups in the population:

- **Diet** – manual workers consume twice as much white bread as professionals, and have higher sugar consumption and eat less fresh fruit.
- **Cigarette smoking** – whereas over 40 per cent of males and 35 per cent of females in social classes IV and V regularly smoke, only about 12 per cent of males and females in social class I smoke.
- **Leisure and lifestyle** – middle-class people are more likely to take exercise and to have a wider range of social activities than the working classes. These reduce levels of stress and help maintain a higher standard of health.
- **Alcohol** – alcohol consumption is directly related to social class, with much higher consumption amongst the 'lower' social classes.

The cultural approach, however, fails to ask why these groups have poor diets and high alcohol and cigarette consumption. Critics point out that there may be reasons why people are 'forced' into an unhealthy lifestyle. These critics have put forward an alternative 'structural' explanation.

Structural explanations
The final approach comes from those who see a direct relationship between differences in health and the unequal nature of British society. Supporters of this approach accept the behavioural differences pointed to earlier, but claim that this behaviour has to be seen within a broader context of inequality. So, poor health is the result of 'hazards to which some people have no choice but to be exposed given the present distribution of income and opportunity' (Shaw *et al.*, 1999).

- **Poverty** – poverty is the key factor that links a range of health risks. Poorer people have worse diets and worse housing conditions, and are more likely to be unemployed and generally to have a more highly stressed, lower quality of life. According to the British Regional Heart Survey (cited in Shaw *et al.*, 1999) – a study of 8,000 middle-aged men – over half of those who did not own a car or a home were reported to be in poor health, compared to a tenth of those who did own both.
- **Position at work** – workers with little power or control over their work are likely to experience worse health than those who are given more responsibility. Research on civil servants (Davey Smith *et al.*, 1990) has shown that routine clerical workers are much more likely to die young than workers in higher grades – if the lowest and highest grades are compared, those in the lowest grades are actually three times more likely to die before reaching the age of 65.
- **Unemployment** – according to Moser's long-term study of the relationship between income and wealth (Moser *et al.*, 1990), unemployed men and their wives are likely to die younger than those in employment.
- **Types of industry** – industries vary in how dangerous they are to their employees. For example, respiratory diseases are common amongst those working in road and building construction, as a result of the dust inhaled; while various forms of cancer are associated with chemical industries.

The structural approach has the advantage of explaining why there are cultural differences in behaviour between various groups in society. The argument advanced by those who support this approach is that people may make choices about their behaviour, but that the circumstances within which they make their choices are strongly affected by the extent of inequality existing in Britain.

Gender and health

Women live longer than men, but are more likely to visit their GPs for treatment. They also have higher levels of mental illness. This apparently contradictory pattern – higher morbidity combined with a longer life span – has led some observers to argue that it is not that women are more likely to be ill than men, but that they are more willing to visit the doctor. Yet MacIntyre (1993) shows that women are, in fact, no more likely than men to report symptoms. The answer perhaps lies in a combination of biological factors and social roles.

Explanations for the link between gender and health

Biology

There is some evidence to suggest that women are biologically stronger than men (for instance, female foetuses are less likely to die than male foetuses), and that they have a greater biological possibility of living longer. However, this does not mean that they are less immune to illness. In addition, they can suffer from a range of female-related health problems associated with reproduction and the menopause.

Social role

Women may also live longer because their social role tends to prevent them from taking risks. Their social role discourages them from violence, fast driving and excess alcohol consumption. Women are also less likely to smoke than men. However, the social role that limits their activities also places considerable stress upon women, by restricting opportunities in employment and in life in general. Furthermore, women are more likely than men to be living in poverty, and they are also more likely to be lone parents. Both place considerable burdens upon their health.

Work

According to Ellen Annandale (1998), women who go out to work have better levels of health than those who do not. Annandale argues that this is not just because of the financial benefits, but also because work gives women a sense of independence and a wider social network. Both of these have the effect of lowering stress levels – and stress is closely related to standards of health.

Ethnicity and health

Surprisingly, there is only limited information available on ethnicity and illness. This is partly because of the complex make-up of ethnic groups in the UK and the difficulty of making generalisations across these groupings. However, some specific health problems can be linked with particular groups – for example, those of Afro-Caribbean origin are much more likely to suffer from sickle cell disease.

The research that has been done (mainly by the Health Education Authority) shows that members of minority ethnic groups are more likely to define themselves as having poor health than the majority population. For example, just under 50 per cent of ethnic minority members described themselves as having fair or poor health. This compared with just under 30 per cent of the majority population.

As for mortality, all ethnic minority groups have a shorter life expectancy than the majority population. Patterns in the causes of death do seem to vary, with groups from the **'Indian subcontinent'** having the highest levels of coronary heart disease of the whole population; while those from the **'Caribbean commonwealth'** have the lowest levels of death from this cause. Although, overall, health levels are worse and life expectancy is lower, one striking difference is that all of the ethnic minority groups have lower levels of deaths from cancers than the majority population.

Figure 6.3 **People with limiting long-term illness, by ethnic group and sex, 1991**

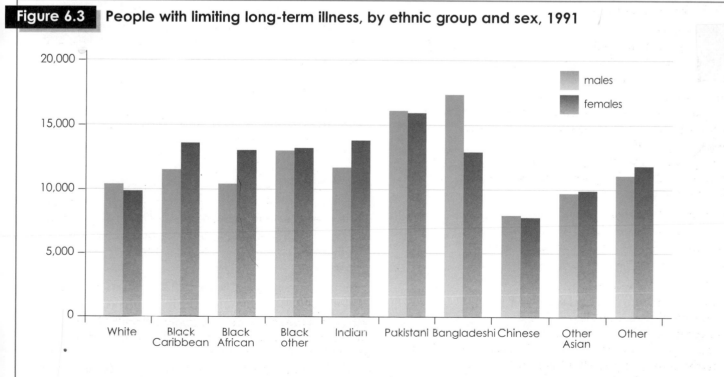

Source: E. Annandale (1998) *The Sociology of Health and Illness*, Cambridge: Polity Press

Explanations for the link between ethnicity and health

'Race' and inequality

We saw earlier the profound effects of inequality in helping to explain different levels of health. Minority ethnic groups have some of the lowest incomes, worst housing and highest unemployment rates in Britain. Even without any specific explanations related to 'race', the higher levels of morbidity and higher early mortality rates could largely be explained by their relative social deprivation.

'Race' as a specific factor

Some analysts have gone further than this, however, and have argued that 'race' is important by itself. First, much of the poverty and exclusion is actually caused by racism. Secondly, the experience of living in a racist society can place great stress upon people and this may impact upon health levels.

Culture and ethnicity

The final approach argues that cultural differences, in terms of diet and lifestyle, may influence health. For example, diets using large amounts of 'ghee' (clarified butter) can help cause heart disease amongst those of South Asian origin. Asian diets also tend to lack vitamin D. Long work hours and relatively little physical leisure activity may also lower the health levels of some ethnic minority groups.

CHECK YOUR UNDERSTANDING ✓✓✓

1 Identify four factors that are closely linked to health.

2 Why might some areas of Britain have worse health than others?

3 Give one example of health differences between the social classes.

4 What explanations have been suggested for health differences between the social classes?

5 Explain, in your own words, the meaning of the 'artefact approach'.

6 Do biological factors alone explain the differences in health between men and women?

7 What three explanations have been given for the differences in health between the various ethnic minorities and the majority of the population?

Exploring health inequalities

Item A

SMOKING AND SOCIAL CLASS (CURRENT SMOKERS[1] BY GENDER AND SOCIO-ECONOMIC GROUP[2])

Males

	1972	1982	1997	1999
Professional	33	20	12	15
Employers and managers	44	29	20	21
Intermediate and junior non-manual	45	30	24	23
Skilled manual	57	42	32	33
Semi-skilled manual	57	47	41	38
Unskilled manual	64	49	41	45
All aged 16 and over	52	38	29	28

Females

	1972	1982	1997	1999
Professional	33	21	11	14
Employers and managers	38	29	15	20
Intermediate and junior non-manual	38	30	28	24
Skilled manual	47	39	30	30
Semi-skilled manual	42	36	36	33
Unskilled manual	42	41	36	33
All aged 16 and over	42	33	28	26

[1] Adults aged 16 and over
[2] Classified by respondents' own job, or for those not currently working, their last job or their partner's job

Source: *Social Trends 2000*, Office for National Statistics (2000) © Crown copyright 1996

KEY TERMS

Artefact approach – an approach that believes that the statistics about class and health exaggerate the real situation.

Caribbean commonwealth – parts of the West Indies that are in the commonwealth, such as Barbados.

Cultural explanations – explanations that emphasise lifestyle and behaviour.

Death rate – the number dying per 1,000 of a population per year.

Indian subcontinent – the section of south Asia consisting of India, Pakistan and Bangladesh.

Morbidity – refers to statistics about illness.

Mortality – refers to statistics of death.

Obesity - a medical term for being overweight.

Item B

TRENDS IN PARTICIPATION IN SPORTS, GAMES AND PHYSICAL ACTIVITIES, BY SOCIAL CLASS (% PARTICIPATING, AGED 16 AND OVER)

Year	Occupational social class						
---	I	II	IIIN	IIIM	IV	V	Total
At least one activity (excluding walking)							
1987	65	52	45	48	34	26	45
1990	65	53	49	49	38	28	48
1993	63	52	47	45	37	23	46
1996	63	52	47	45	37	23	46
At least one activity							
1987	78	68	63	632	51	42	61
1990	79	71	67	66	55	46	65
1993	82	71	65	63	54	48	64
1996	80	69	66	63	55	45	64

Source: M. Shaw, D. Dorling, D. Gordon and G. Davey Smith (1999) *The Widening Gap*, Bristol: Policy Press, p. 97

Item C

Alongside these material and behavioural determinants, research is uncovering the psychosocial [social and psychological] costs of living in an unequal society. For example, perceiving oneself to be worse off relative to others may carry a health penalty, in terms of increased stress and risk-taking behaviour. Attention has also focused on the health effects of the work environment and particularly on the control that individuals exercise over the pace and content of work.

Material, behavioural and psychosocial factors cluster together: those in lower socio-economic groups are likely to be exposed to risks in all three domains. Health-damaging factors also accumulate together: children born into poorer circumstances clock up more by way of material, behavioural and psychosocial risks as they grow up and grow older. For example, girls and boys born into social classes 4 and 5 are more likely than those in higher social classes to grow up in overcrowded homes, to develop health-damaging habits like smoking and to be exposed to stressful life-events and work environments.

H. Graham (ed.) (2000) *Understanding Health Inequalities*, Buckingham: Open University Press

---

1 Explain what is meant by 'material factors' (Item C). (2)

2 Identify two trends in the table in Item B. (4)

3 Give three examples of 'risk-taking behaviour' (Item C). (6)

4 Identify and briefly explain two reasons why people from lower social classes may be more likely to smoke cigarettes (Item A). (8)

5 Using information from the Items and elsewhere, examine the links between health and inequality in society. (20)

6 Using information from the Items and elsewhere, assess the view that class inequalities in health are the result of cultural factors. (20)

Parliamentary constituency – an area that elects one MP. The country is divided into over 600.

Self-reported – the result of asking people themselves.

SMR (standardised mortality ratio) – a guide to the relative chances of dying for a specified age range (usually 20–65). Average chances of death are 100, and figures above and below indicate above-average and below-average chances.

Social selection – the idea that people with the best health are most likely to end up in higher social classes.

Structural explanations – explanations that focus on the make-up of society: for example, on inequalities of income and wealth.

Extension activities

1 Interview a small sample of male and female students about their health and lifestyle. Which gender engages in more 'risk-taking' behaviour? Does this appear to affect health? Which gender visits the doctor more? Why?

2 Find the government website that contains the 1998 Independent Inquiry into Inequalities in Health report (www.official-documents.co.uk/document/doh/ih/ih.htm). What are the key findings of this report?

3 Visit the 'Our Healthier Nation' website (at www.ohn.gov.uk/ohn/ohn.htm) which outlines government policy on health inequality issues. How successful do you think the government's strategy will be in improving general health and reducing inequalities in health?

Getting you thinking

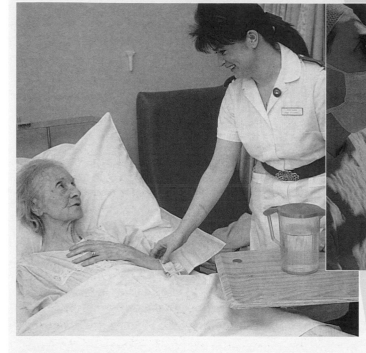

Look at the photographs above.

1 Which of these sorts of medical work do you think doctors would prefer to be involved in? Explain your answer.

Read the extract on the right.

2 Who do you think was right – the GP, or the parents?

3 On what grounds should a person be denied access to a GP?

4 How do people decide whether to visit a doctor or not?

5 How do you think this decision might be influenced by social class, gender or ethnicity?

Guardian, 27 January 1998

A CHESHIRE GP'S practice yesterday came under fire for striking off a family who called out an emergency doctor for their sick daughter – their first call-out in 25 years.

Michael and Janice O'Grady were told by Stephen Maxwell, a partner at the Kenmore Medical Centre in Wilmslow, that they had wasted resources and abused the system by calling out an emergency doctor when they feared that their 8-year-old daughter, Sara, had contracted meningitis.

… The dispute began on December 8th when Sara was sent home from school complaining of nausea and a headache. During the afternoon she also developed a temperature so her parents called the practice and were told to take Sara to the emergency surgery.

When they arrived to be told that they faced a 90-minute wait, they informed the receptionist that they would return in an hour. But as soon as they got home, Sara vomited, then fell asleep. Her parents decided to leave her in the hope that she would sleep off whatever she had been suffering from.

But when she awoke a few hours later, her condition appeared to have deteriorated. 'She was screaming for something to take away the pain in her head', said Mr O'Grady. 'We just panicked and called the doctor.'

An emergency locum attended and prescribed antibiotics for an infection – but only after Mr O'Grady received a phone call from Dr Maxwell, in which, he claims, the GP accused him of 'not being bothered' to wait at the practice.

Despite the National Health Service (NHS) being free to users, and despite taxpayers spending over £110 million each day on paying for the NHS, it remains a fact that some groups in the population are more likely to receive medical help than others. This occurs because the NHS fails to provide equal services for all those in need, and because certain groups are less likely to demand services than others.

Issues of provision

The NHS is the main provider of health care for the population, and it needs to plan how best to provide this care. Funding, which pays for the services, is influenced by:

- geographical inequalities
- the medical professions
- hospital competence

Geographical inequalities

Each area is allocated a certain amount of money by the government to provide health care for its residents. The amount of money given to each **health authority** is based on the principle of giving more money to poorer areas and less to richer areas. Unfortunately, this has never worked out as planned, and the poorer areas have never received adequate funding. Reasons for this include:

- **specialist teaching hospitals** – these are usually located in the richer areas of the country and have traditionally been given considerably higher levels of funding than other hospitals.
- **political pressures** – certain areas such as London have historically received more money than other regions. Over time the reasons for this extra funding have disappeared – with shifts in population, for example. Each time plans have been put forward to reallocate money to other areas, the politicians have blocked them for fear of losing votes.

The medical professions

The medical professions are extremely influential in determining which areas of health care receive funding. There are some areas that are seen as much more important and **prestigious**, whilst others are viewed as less important or less attractive. In general, chronic illness (that is, long-term illnesses for which there is no cure) is seen as a much less attractive area than surgery and high technology medicine.

Hospitals and competence

Different hospitals appear to be organised in very different ways, which results in great differences in the chances of survival from serious operations, and in the chances of catching some form of infection in hospital (**iatrogenesis**). In a study of all English hospitals in 2000, the researchers found that 17 people were likely to die in the worst hospitals for every 10 in the best.

Issues of demand

Social class variations

Although the health of the population as a whole has improved, there is no evidence to show that inequalities between the social classes have decreased. As we saw in Topic 2, despite the fact that members of the working class are more likely to be ill and to have accidents, they are actually less likely to attend doctors' surgeries. They are also less likely to take part in any form of **screening programme** that can discover disease (such as certain forms of cancer) at an early stage. They are, however, more likely to use accident and emergency services – often because conditions that have not been attended to have become acute.

The reasons for this are not that they care less about illness, but that there are more barriers to them accessing health care. They are less likely to be able to:

- afford to take time off work
- travel a considerable distance to a GP's surgery. This is a particular problem because there are far fewer GPs in poorer areas, in proportion to the population, than in more affluent areas.

Gender

Women live approximately seven years longer than men, but they do not necessarily do so in good health. In fact, on average, they have only two extra years of healthy life without significant chronic illness. During their lifetimes, too, women appear to have higher levels of illness and higher rates of attendance at doctors' surgeries. But this needs to be set against women's needs. Women give birth, and also take on the main childcare role, both of which put great strain upon their bodies.

Feminist sociologists argue that women actually under-use the health services, if their use is compared to their actual

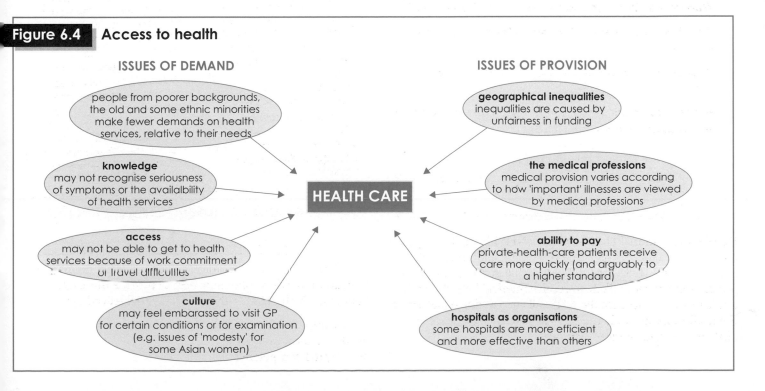

Figure 6.4   Access to health

needs. They argue that, instead, the health services spend much of their resources on controlling women, by turning many 'normal' physical activities, such as giving birth, into *medical* ones. This takes power away from women and hands it to men, who form the majority of doctors.

As a result of such concerns, a national screening programme for breast cancer was introduced in 1988, and for cervical cancer in 1995. However, within these programmes, considerable differences in attendance have occurred, related to social class and ethnicity. The take-up rates have been approximately 75 per cent, and the poorer the social group the less likely they are to attend. Similarly, the attendance rates for those of Bangladeshi and Pakistani origin are particularly low.

Ethnicity

There is a lower use of medical services by certain ethnic minority groups. The reasons for this, it has been suggested, are:

- **language barriers** – until recently there was little attempt to provide translation facilities or to publicise the NHS in minority languages.
- **cultural differences** – the traditional acceptance of male doctors has been challenged by many women from ethnic minorities, whose ideas of modesty have meant that many are unwilling to be seen by male doctors.
- **poverty** – ethnic minorities contain some of the lowest-income families in Britain, and so the factors that limit working-class use of health services (time off work and public transport difficulties) apply equally to them.

Age

Older people's approach to health care provision is different from that of middle-aged and younger people. Although they are the age group who are most in need of health services and who use them most, they tend to under-use them relative to their needs. Older people see themselves as 'wasting the doctor's time' if they consider that they may be consulting the doctor unnecessarily. What is more, **geriatric** medicine (the care of older people) is seen by doctors and nurses as an area of low prestige, and staffing and funding levels are extremely low. Therefore, both in terms of demand and provision, older people do particularly badly.

Private health care

Although there is much evidence of inequalities within the NHS, greater inequalities in access to health care exist between those who rely upon the NHS and those who use the private sector.

Private health care is used by those who pay directly for medical services or who have private health insurance. The total spending on private health care in Britain is about £2.5 billion each year, and those doctors who provide private health care earn about £550 million each year.

Private health care increase inequalities in health care by:

- allowing those who can pay to have treatment without waiting, whereas NHS patients have to join a waiting list
- giving private patients access to a range of medical services that may not be available on the NHS
- limiting the number of hours worked by doctors in the NHS, who prefer to earn more money in the private sector.

CHECK YOUR UNDERSTANDING

1 What do we mean by 'issues of provision and demand', when discussing inequalities in access to health care?

2 What impact can doctors and hospitals have on inequalities of provision?

3 What three factors help to restrict the use of health services by ethnic minorities?

4 How does the medical profession view geriatric medicine?

5 Explain what impact private medicine may have on health inequalities?

KEY TERMS

Geriatric – refers to older people.

Health authorities – the National Health Service is actually a system of local health services. Health authorities are the bodies responsible for ensuring that local people get adequate health services.

Iatrogenesis – illness caused by the medical professions (e.g. as a result of poor care or inaccurate diagnosis).

Prestigious – high-status.

Private health care – health care that is paid for.

Screening programmes – programmes where particular sections of the population are tested to see if they have signs of a particular disease.

Specialist teaching hospitals – very prestigious hospitals which train new doctors.

Exploring inequalities in health services

Strong evidence exists to support what might be called the 'Inverse Prevention Law' in primary care, in which those communities most at risk of ill health have least access to a range of effective preventive services including cancer screening programmes, health promotion and immunisation.

D. Gordon, M. Shaw, D. Dorling and G. Davey Smith (1999) *Inequalities in Health*, Bristol: Policy Press, p. 105

Item B

ADULTS WHO VISIT THE DENTIST FOR A REGULAR CHECK-UP, BY SOCIO-ECONOMIC GROUP AND GENDER (PERCENTAGES)				
	Males		Females	
	1985	1995–6	1985	1995–6
Professional	60	59	77	71
Employers and managers	54	55	70	70
Intermediate and junior non-manual	50	51	63	62
Skilled manual	34	40	51	57
Semi-skilled manual and personal service	29	37	46	49
Unskilled manual	26	38	35	52
All adults (average)	41	46	58	61

Source: *Social Trends 1998*, London: The Stationery Office

Item C

The way that [health] services are organised and offered is based on indigenous British culture and is often inflexible so that members of ethnic minority groups may find vital provision irrelevant, offensive, unhelpful or threatening.

Aspects of racism that are implicated here include the failure to provide health information in appropriate languages, the failure to make knowledge of religious, dietary and cultural imperatives basic to health professional training, and the failure to provide amenities to support cultural beliefs in the importance of running water for washing, death rites, prayer in hospital, visiting times, food in hospital, etc. as an automatic inclusion in health service budgets.

L. Culley and D. Dyson (1993) '"Race", inequality and health', *Sociology Review*, vol. 3, no. 1

1 Explain what is meant by the 'Inverse Prevention Law' (Item A). (2)

2 Give two reasons why members of ethnic minorities might find going into hospital an 'offensive, unhelpful or threatening' experience (Item C). (4)

3 Suggest three ways in which hospitals could be more sensitive towards ethnic minority patients (Item C). (6)

4 Identify two trends in the table in Item B, and suggest one possible reason for each. (8)

5 Discuss the sociological evidence that indicates that those social groups most in need of health services are least able to use them effectively. (20)

6 Using information from Items A and B and elsewhere, assess the view that inequalities of provision exist within the health service. (20)

Extension activities

1 Find the 'league tables' that measure the performance of health authorities across the country at www.doh.gov.uk/tables97/. What different ways of assessing 'performance' are used? How does your area compare with others? Do links appear to exist between the richer areas and 'better performance'? How useful do you think these tables are?

2 Interview a sample of older and younger men and women about their experiences of the health service. How do they feel they have been treated by the health service? Are they taking advantage of preventive services such as immunisation? Are there any differences between the experiences of older and younger people or males and females?

Getting you thinking

Go through the list of actions below and mark each on a scale of 1–4 according to how 'abnormal' you think the behaviour is ('1' being the least abnormal and '4' the most). If you think that the behaviour is evidence of mental illness, tick the separate box as well.

1–4   Mentally ill?

Action

- A woman who shouts abuse at nobody in particular while walking down the street
- A man using violence against his children
- A group of men chanting obscenities
- A woman drinking large amounts of alcohol every night
- A young woman singing loudly in the street
- A young man who refuses to talk to people he has just met
- A man who believes that he is the reincarnation of a Roman legionnaire
- A women who regularly feels depressed
- People who hear voices in their head, talking to them
- A man who claims to be sent from Heaven to redeem us
- A man who simply will not stop talking to you

Compare your results with those of others.

1 Which cases did you agree on, and which did you disagree on?

2 What problems did you face in identifying abnormality and mental illness?

3 How do you think someone can be identified as having a mental illness?

Mental illness has been the forgotten twin to physical illness, in terms of the attention paid to it and the funding provided by the NHS. The issue only comes into the open when a particularly spectacular event hits the headlines. However, mental health is a major problem in society, with about one in seven of the population claiming to have mental health problems at some point in their lives. But mental health is dogged with debates over definitions, and over the differences in the extent of mental health problems across different groups in society.

Defining mental illness

In Topic 1 we grappled with ways of defining health and illness in terms of physical states. The same problems occur when defining mental health and illness. The starting point for a common-sense definition of a mentally ill person is someone who acts in a way that is abnormal. But this varies over time and from society to society. For example, over time, alcohol consumption has been seen as normal, as morally wrong or even illegal, as a sign of being mentally ill, and as a central part of a religious ritual. In fact most of these different attitudes to alcohol can be found in Britain today!

Even greater extremes of behaviour have been seen as normal. For example, saying that you are possessed by the spirit of your ancestor would suggest madness in Western societies, but for native Americans, or in some West African religions, it would be a perfectly reasonable statement.

The following diagram is based on the explanation put forward by Helman (2000) for the complex relationship between madness and other forms of behaviour.

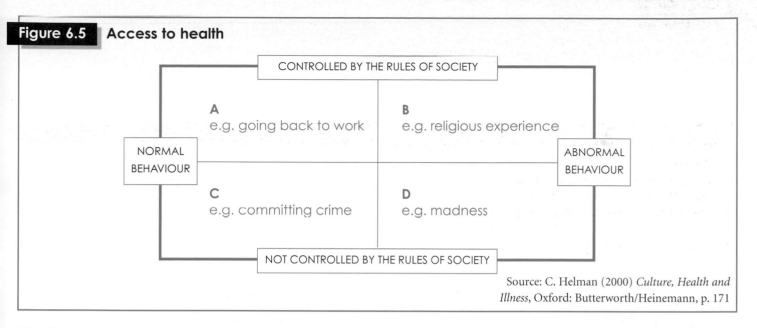

Figure 6.5 Access to health

CONTROLLED BY THE RULES OF SOCIETY

A
e.g. going back to work

B
e.g. religious experience

NORMAL BEHAVIOUR

ABNORMAL BEHAVIOUR

C
e.g. committing crime

D
e.g. madness

NOT CONTROLLED BY THE RULES OF SOCIETY

Source: C. Helman (2000) *Culture, Health and Illness*, Oxford: Butterworth/Heinemann, p. 171

The diagram has four sections. Section A refers to what is regarded as 'good' normal behaviour (e.g. going to work), and section C refers to 'bad' normal behaviour – such as committing crime. Section B includes all the sorts of abnormal behaviour that are seen as being controlled by the rules of society – for example, extreme religious acts, or 'naughty' behaviour at a party. What is left is behaviour that is seen as abnormal, and that is not controlled by social rules – this behaviour is regarded as a sign of mental illness. In every society, and over time, what falls into each of these four 'zones' will vary.

Mental illness: does it exist?

It is important to realise that there are forms of behaviour that cause considerable stress to the individual involved, and which prevent them from engaging in any meaningful participation in society. We need, therefore, to see mental health as a *continuum* – at one end there is little doubt that the behaviour is so extreme that it can be defined as 'mental illness', but, as we move away, the clarity of the mental illness becomes less and less clear.

Mental illness: the labelling perspective

This degree of flexibility about what constitutes normal and abnormal behaviour has been taken further by labelling theorists. Labelling theory (as we saw in Unit 1 Topic 4) examines how 'labelling' occurs in the first place and what effects it has on those who are labelled. Thomas Szasz (1973), for example, argues that the label 'mental illness' is simply a convenient way to deal with behaviour that people find disruptive.

The effects of labelling

According to Scheff (1966), whether someone becomes labelled or not is determined by the benefits that others might gain by labelling the person 'mentally ill'. So, those people who become a nuisance, or who prevent others from doing something they want to do, are far more likely to be defined as being mentally ill than those who pose no threat or inconvenience, and may be ignored.

Once labelled, there are a number of negative consequences for the person, because it is then assumed that all their behaviour is evidence of their mental state. A famous study by Rosenhan (1973) illustrates this. In the early 1970s in the USA, Rosenhan asked eight perfectly 'normal' researchers to enter a number of psychiatric institutions after phoning up and complaining that they were 'hearing voices'. Once in the institutions doctors and staff regarded the researchers as truly mentally ill and reinterpreted all their behaviour as proof of this. However, the researchers were under strict instructions to behave completely normally at all times.

In a later study, new staff in a psychiatric hospital were told that this experiment was to be repeated in their institution, and they were asked to uncover these researchers who were just pretending to be ill. In this study, staff routinely judged people who were 'genuinely ill' as merely pretending. It would seem, therefore, that there is some confusion as to how even experts can decide who is actually mentally ill.

Erving Goffman (1984) followed the **careers** of people who were genuinely defined as being mentally ill. He suggested that, once in an institution, people are stripped of their **presenting culture** – by which he means the image that we all choose to present to the world as 'us'. This may include a style of haircut, make-up, or the requirement that people address us as Mr or Mrs, rather than Michael or Sarah. The 'patient' may also lose their right to make decisions about their life, and they may be required to take medication which can disorientate them.

Quickly, the self-image that a patient has – perhaps of being a respectable, witty, middle-aged person – is stripped away, leaving her or him bewildered, vulnerable and ready to accept a new role. In this powerless situation, any attempts to reject the label of mental illness can actually be interpreted as further signs of illness, and perhaps as indicating a need for increased medication or counselling. In fact, accepting the role of being mentally ill is seen as the first sign of recovery.

Mental illness and ethnicity

As we have seen, the definition of mental illness varies across societies and time – but it also varies across groups in society.

A good illustration of this is the fact that members of ethnic minorities have significantly higher chances of being defined as mentally ill than the majority white population. There appear to be two main reasons for this:

1 There are variations in what is considered appropriate behaviour. It has been suggested that some of the behaviour of Afro-Caribbean adults, in particular, has been seen as inappropriate in British society, and it has therefore been labelled as a symptom of mental illness.

2 The sorts of pressures and stresses that can cause people to develop inappropriate behaviour – behaviour that would commonly be defined as a sign of being mentally ill – are more likely to be experienced by members of ethnic minorities, because they encounter racism and disadvantage throughout their lives.

Mental illness and gender

Women are more likely than men to exhibit behaviour defined as mental illness. There is considerable debate over the reasons for this. The first explanation, which is generally accepted, is that women are more likely to lead stressful lives – combining careers and the responsibility for childcare, for example, and being more likely to experience poverty and poor housing conditions. However, feminist writers go further and argue that the behaviour of women is more likely to be defined as evidence of mental illness, because the defining is done by a male-dominated profession. Rather than looking for the real reasons – which are most likely to be stress and poverty – psychiatrists are more interested in defining the problem in terms of an individual's mental state.

Inequality, social class and mental illness

The poorest groups in society are more likely to have higher levels of mental illness. Some writers argue that they are poor precisely because they have lower levels of mental health, but most sociologists argue instead that it is the stress of poverty that is likely to bring about mental illness.

Exploring mental health and mental illness

Item A *An Asian woman speaks about her experiences:*

'It affects your mind. If you feel depressed that you are not treated as other people are, or they look down on you, you will feel mentally ill won't you? It will depress you that you are not treated well racially, it will affect your health in some way. It will cause you depression, and that depression will cause the illness.'

E. Annandale (1998) *The Sociology of Health and Medicine*, Cambridge: Polity Press, p. 187

Item B Afro-Caribbeans are far more likely to reach the mental health system via the police, the courts, and prisons, and to experience the more harsh and invasive forms of treatment (such as electro-convulsive therapy), than others. It is also revealed in the analytic attention to threats to the white community, rather than the distress of those who experience mental health problems.

E. Annandale (1998) *The Sociology of Health and Medicine*, Cambridge: Polity Press, p. 186

CHECK YOUR UNDERSTANDING

1 How do people decide what mental illness is?

2 What is the relationship between power and mental illness?

3 How does the idea of 'labelling' help us to understand mental illness?

4 How is mental illness a 'career'?

5 Suggest two reasons why people from ethnic minorities are more likely to be defined as suffering from mental illness.

6 What argument do feminist writers use to explain why women are more likely to be defined as suffering from mental illness?

Item C

With regard to mental illness ... for all diagnoses combined, women's rate of admission to hospitals in England and Wales was 29 per cent above the rate for men.

E. Annandale (1998) *The Sociology of Health and Medicine*, Cambridge: Polity Press, p. 143

Item D

Katz ... examined the process of psychiatric diagnosis among both British and American psychiatrists. ... Groups of British and American psychiatrists were shown films of interviews with patients and asked to note down all the pathological symptoms and make a diagnosis. Marked disagreements in diagnosis between the two groups were found. ... The British saw less pathology [evidence of mental illness] generally. ... For example, one patient was diagnosed as 'schizophrenic' by one-third of the Americans, but by none of the British.

C. Helman (2000) *Culture, Health and Illness*, Oxford: Butterworth/Heinemann, p. 80

1 Explain what is meant by 'mental health' (Item B). (2)

2 Suggest two reasons why members of ethnic minorities might experience depression (Item A). (4)

3 Suggest three reasons why the British and American psychiatrists in Item D may have diagnosed the same individual differently. (6)

4 Identify and briefly explain two reasons that might explain why women's rate of admission to mental hospitals is higher then men's (Item C). (8)

5 Using information from the Items and elsewhere, discuss the possible reasons why rates of mental illness vary between different social groups. (20)

6 Assess the contribution of labelling theory to an understanding of mental illness. (20)

KEY TERMS

Career – refers, in this context, to the gradual changes in people as a response to a label (for example, 'mental patient').

Presenting culture – a term used by Goffman to refer to how people like to portray themselves to others.

Extension activities

1 Find the website of the mental health charity MIND (www.mind.org.uk). Use the 'links' section to explore the work of some of the organisations connected with mental health issues. Make a list of all the mental health issues covered. How important an issue is mental health in Britain today?

2 Watch the film *One Flew Over the Cuckoo's Nest* (or read the original book by Ken Kesey). What perspective on mental illness does this film (or book) illustrate?

Getting you thinking

THE SUN

Wednesday, January 31, 2001   30p   www.thesun.co.uk

THE SUN SAYS

IN the Alder Hey scandal, it is the professional ARROGANCE, the clinical ELITISM and the UNFORGIVABLE high-handedness that disgusts us.

BODY PARTS SCANDAL

My baby's body was on a dirty table in 36 jars...

Body plundered ... little Andrew O'Leary in hospital before he died

I put them in a carrier bag and ran sobbing into street

A WEEPING mother told yesterday how she found the organs of her dead baby in 36 glass jars in a dirty hospital basement.

Paula O'Leary, 42, said she gasped

Organ storage on huge scale uncovered by survey

About 105,000 human organs, body parts, stillbirths and foetuses are being held in medical schools and hospital pathology departments in England, the result of a common medical practice in which relatives were neither asked for permission nor told what was going on.

The finding is the result of a census of pathology departments and archives in the report of Prof. Liam Donaldson, the Chief Medical Officer, published yesterday. The snapshot, taken at the end of 1999, of pathology practice shows that since 1970 approximately 54,300 organs, body parts, stillbirths or foetuses were harvested. This figure includes 2,900 stillbirths or pre-viable foetuses.

... Prof. Donaldson said the practice of retaining organs, tissue and body parts after post-mortem examinations was commonplace. While some had been returned and others respectfully disposed of, it was clear that thousands of families remained unaware that organs and parts of their deceased children or relations were stored on shelves in pathology units and medical school laboratories.

Daily Telegraph, 31 January 2001

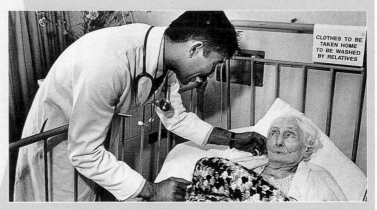

CLOTHES TO BE TAKEN HOME TO BE WASHED BY RELATIVES

1 What arguments can be put forward by doctors to justify their actions in retaining body parts without consent?

2 What arguments can be put forward against the retention of body parts without consent?

3 Which do you think is the more powerful set of arguments? Give your reasons.

4 Look at the photograph of the doctor. List five characteristics that you associate with the white coat – for example, being trustworthy.

5 Compare your list with those of others. What meanings are commonly attached to the white coat?

6 Why might these meanings be advantageous to doctors?

Members of the medical profession are among the most prestigious and well-paid groups in society. But how did they get this superior status? Was it really through their greater abilities, as they would have us believe? Sociologists are always suspicious of the claims groups make about themselves, and, as you might expect, their views are not always totally supportive of the caring, dedicated image the medical professions like to present.

There are five main sociological approaches to understanding the role of the medical professions. These are that the medical professions:

● benefit society – the functionalist argument
● are just an occupational strategy to get higher income and status
● are a means of controlling the majority of the population – the Marxist position
● can best be understood by seeing how they have controlled and marginalised women – a feminist position
● have emerged as a result of their ability to define knowledge – Foucault's approach

Professions as a benefit to society

The first approach to understanding the role of the professions developed from the functionalist school of sociology (see Unit 1 Topic 2) which attempts to show what functions the various parts of society play in helping society to exist.

Barber (1963) argued that professions, especially the medical professions, are very important for society because they deal with people when they are in particularly vulnerable positions. It is therefore in the interests of society to have the very best people, who maintain the highest standards, to provide medical care. Real professions can be recognised by the fact that they share a number of 'traits'. These are:

- that they have a theoretical basis to their knowledge – doctors have a full understanding of medical theories about the body
- that they are fully trained to the highest possible standards – only the most intelligent can enter
- that competence is tested by examination – so doctors have certificates to prove their ability
- that the profession has a strict code of ethics – this is particularly important for doctors because of the intimate nature of their work
- that they regulate themselves through a committee (Professional Council) of some sort, which decides who can enter and who can practise.

Critics of the functionalist approach argue that these traits merely *justify* the high status of doctors, because the profession uses them to exclude others from entering. This suspicion was for a long time supported by the fact that entry to medicine remained largely the preserve of males from higher social class backgrounds.

Professionalisation as a strategy

The second approach to understanding the power of the medical professions is that, rather than being constructed for the good of the community, they are, in fact, constructed for the good of the medical professions themselves. The main aim of these groups is to gain the status of a profession, which will ensure high status and good financial rewards.

This process has four important dimensions:

1 **The production of a body of esoteric knowledge** – this means creating an apparently complex body of knowledge which must be placed in the hands of experts.
2 **Educational barriers** – in order to interpret and apply this knowledge, a very high level of education and intelligence is required. Only the very best could possibly be allowed into the profession.
3 **Exclusion of competition** – the profession must wipe out any possible competitors – for example, faith healers, homeopaths and herbalists. They do this by claiming that only scientific medicine and surgery are effective.
4 **Maintenance of privilege** – the professional group will fight all attempts to have others impose any control over them. So doctors will demand **'clinical freedom'** – the right to do what they think best – and they will fight any attempts to hand over part of their work to others, such as allowing nurses to prescribe medicines.

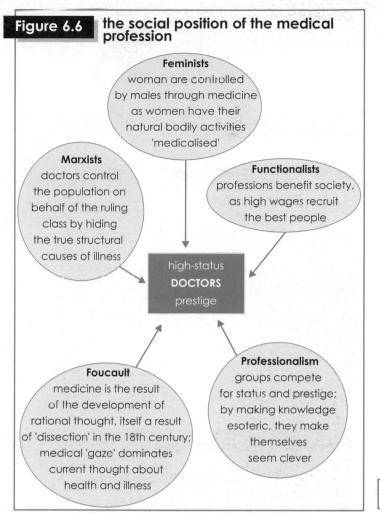

Figure 6.6 the social position of the medical profession

Feminists
woman are controlled by males through medicine as women have their natural bodily activities 'medicalised'

Marxists
doctors control the population on behalf of the ruling class by hiding the true structural causes of illness

Functionalists
professions benefit society, as high wages recruit the best people

high-status
DOCTORS
prestige

Foucault
medicine is the result of the development of rational thought, itself a result of 'dissection' in the 18th century; medical 'gaze' dominates current thought about health and illness

Professionalism
groups compete for status and prestige; by making knowledge esoteric, they make themselves seem clever

Marxist approaches

Marxists argue that in capitalist societies such as Britain a small ruling class exploits society for its own benefit. In order to hide this exploitation from people and to maintain its power, the ruling class employs a number of mechanisms, which involve distorting 'reality', so that people come to accept exploitation as 'natural'.

Medical professions play an important role in this by misleading the population as to the real cause of their illnesses. The medical professions explain health and illness in terms of individuals' actions and genetics – they point the finger away from the poor working conditions, poverty, poor housing and inequalities in society, which are the true, underlying causes of ill health. But what doctors do succeed in doing for the health of the population is to keep them fit enough to work.

Marxists also point out that health and illness in capitalist society are very carefully linked to being able to work or not. Doctors play a key role in deciding who is fit to work and who is sick enough to be eligible for state disability and sickness benefits.

Critics have pointed out that this perspective ignores the genuinely beneficial work that doctors do, and that to characterise their work as only misleading and controlling the population is inaccurate. Doctors do work very much within the framework of looking at individual problems, but stress in the workplace and the role of poverty are well known and recognised by doctors.

Feminist approaches

Feminist sociologists believe that doctors control women, both as patients and as medical practitioners. They point out that medicine has traditionally been a male occupation, with women excluded or marginalised into junior roles. This simply reinforces the subordinate position of women in society. (However, in the last 15 years, roughly equal numbers of men and women have been training to be doctors.)

Feminist sociologists also claim that the male-dominated profession of medicine has successfully **medicalised** a number of female problems. By this they mean that normal activities of women (such as childbirth and menopause), or problems faced more often by women (such as depression), have been taken over by the medical profession and turned into medical issues. So, for example, women are expected to give birth in the manner and in the place determined by 'the experts'.

When it comes to an 'illness' such as depression – which feminists argue is partly a result of the restricted role of women in society – the medical profession turns it into a *medical problem* that can be solved by prescribing medicines. This shifts the issue away from the position of women in general, to the particular medical condition of a single woman.

Foucault's approach

There is an old saying, 'knowledge is power', and in Foucault's analysis of society this is literally true. According to Foucault (1976), in every society, groups are 'battling' to look after their own interests. The best way of doing this is to get control of what is regarded as 'truth' or 'knowledge'. If other people believe that what you say is 'true' and what others say is 'false', then you have a high chance of getting them to do what you want. So you seek to create an overall framework of thought and ideas, within which all the more specific debates (what Foucault calls **'discourses'**) are conducted.

Foucault argues that, over time, doctors have led the way in helping to construct an idea of 'science', through their activities in dissecting bodies and demonstrating to people the ways in which bodies are constructed in the form of a 'biological machine'. This has resulted in a society where rational scientific thought is prized above all else, where other forms of thought are regarded as inferior, and where doctors have significant prestige and power.

So medicine has played a major part in constructing the way we think and act in contemporary society. In the process, the medical professions have gained considerable benefits in terms of prestige and financial rewards.

CHECK YOUR UNDERSTANDING

1 Give two examples of the 'traits' of a profession, according to the functionalists.

2 According to the 'professionalisation' approach, how do professions exclude other competing occupational groups?

3 How do the actions of doctors, in explaining why we are ill and then prescribing medicines, help capitalism?

4 Give one example of how doctors have 'medicalised' a normal activity of women?

5 According to Foucault, what is the relationship between knowledge and power over people?

KEY TERMS

Clinical freedom – the right of doctors to do what they think is best without other people having a say.

Discourse – a way of thinking about issues.

Esoteric – obscure and accessible only to a few.

Professionalisation – a tactic used by occupational groups to gain prestige and financial rewards.

Exploring the medical professions in society

It is commonly held that nursing, since becoming a profession (the first register was set up in 1919), has progressed to become a higher-status, centrally recognised health-care profession. Yet the crucial distinction between nursing and medicine remains: that of curing versus caring. Nursing's professional bodies are caught in a double-bind: in order to be of high status the profession must lay claim to clinical and curative skills, but in order to remain as 'nursing' the practice must be centred on caring for, not curing, patients.

This dilemma has been addressed in part by the conscious formation of a body of theoretical knowledge, the nursing process, which is particular to nursing and distinct from medicine. To some extent, this has also been the rationale behind the most recent developments in nurse education, for example, the creation of the new Project 2000 and the possibility of a degree in nursing, which superseded the old apprentice-style ward-based training of 'pupil' nurses.

I. Marsh (2000) *Sociology: Making Sense of Society*, Harlow: Prentice Hall

Item B Professional bodies (such as the General Medical Council) are charged with supervising the profession. But, being members of that profession, they usually whitewash or ignore cases of incompetence etc. Final sanctions, like striking a doctor off the medical register, are used only rarely and then more often for sexual misconduct than for gross incompetence.

P. Trowler (1996) *Investigating Health, Welfare and Poverty*, London: Collins Educational

Item C For functionalist sociologists the higher professions such as medicine are virtually beyond reproach. Professionals are seen as selfless individuals working for the good of the community, often making great personal sacrifices. They need to be of the highest intelligence and skill, have to undergo years of training and in their early careers earn very little. High levels of reward later, then, are necessary to attract, retain and motivate the best people into the professions.

P. Trowler (1996) *Investigating Health, Welfare and Poverty*, London: Collins Educational

1 Explain what is meant by a 'professional body' (Items A and B). (2)

2 Identify two ways in which nursing has attempted to improve its status in recent years (Item A). (4)

3 Suggest three reasons why professional bodies might 'ignore cases of incompetence' (Item B). (6)

4 Identify and briefly explain two reasons why functionalists argue that professionals deserve high rewards (Item C). (8)

5 Using information from Item A and elsewhere, examine the possible reasons why nurses have less status and pay than doctors. (20)

6 Using information from the Items and elsewhere, assess the view that professionalisation is simply a strategy for ensuring high status and rewards. (20)

Extension activities

1 Search the World Wide Web for information about complementary medical treatments such as herbal remedies, acupuncture and homeopathy. What ideas about 'the body' and healing lie behind these therapies and treatments? To what extent are they similar to, or different from, the conventional Western 'bio-medical model'?

2 Identify a small sample of people who have actually used some form of 'alternative' healing. Conduct unstructured interviews to uncover their motives in seeking the treatment, and the meaning they gave to their experiences.

3 Search on-line newspaper archives to find stories about the 'organ storage scandal' in various hospitals (see 'Getting you thinking' on p.172). Visit the website of the British Medical Association, the main organisation for doctors (www.bma.org.uk), and find out their views on medical ethics and 'professionalism'.

Unit 7

Research methods

Getting you thinking

The central objective of my research was to understand why and how women entered the world of prostitution: to discover the motivating factors, the dynamics of the introductory process, and how they learnt the skills, values, and codes of conduct of the

business. I wanted to explore the importance and impact of prostitution on their lifestyles and to put the 'deviance' of prostitution into context with other aspects of their criminality. I also wanted to discover how the women themselves and their families and friends, subjectively defined, perceived and rationalized their activities.

K. Sharpe (2000) 'Sad, bad and (sometimes) dangerous to know: street corner research with prostitutes, punters and the police' in R. D. King and E. Wincup, *Doing Research on Crime and Justice*, Oxford: Oxford University Press, p. 364

1 **What methods would it have been possible to use in this research? What are their advantages and disadvantages?**

2 **This research was conducted by a woman. What problems would have been faced by a male researcher?**

3 **Do you think that this research is justifiable? Explain your answer.**

Sociologists generally try to take a 'sideways' look at social life – seeking to provide insights into the social world that the ordinary person would never normally have. The best way to do this is to conduct research which uncovers patterns that would normally remain hidden. But the activities of sociologists do not stop there – for once they have uncovered these patterns they then seek explanations for the *relationships* between them. This process of constructing explanations for the social patterns is known as *theorising*.

So research leads – eventually – to theories.

But it does not stop there. For once theories exist, other sociologists are influenced by them and will use them as the starting point for their research.

So, research leads to theories, which lead to more research and – you can probably guess the next stage – yes, more theories!

But the process is even more complicated than this. For we need to know why some areas of social life are chosen and not others. Are they more interesting? Are they more important? Is someone paying for the research?

And we need to think very carefully about the moral or ethical issues involved in *choosing* what to study, in *doing research* itself and, finally, in *interpreting* and publicising the findings.

What does sociological research set out to do?

- Gather information – the first task of research is simply to gather information about the social world. This very basic function is the starting point for any kind of sociological understanding. Knowledge can take the form of statistical information, such as the numbers of marriages and divorces, and sociological 'facts', such as the attitudes of people in society towards marriage as an institution.

- Make correlations – research can go further than just gathering information. It can help us explore relationships between different elements of society. This can be in the form of simple **correlations** (showing that two things are linked in some way), such as the fact that there is a statistical relationship between drug use and crime. Statistics show that those who commit burglary are also likely to be heavy users of drugs. At this point all we know is that there is a link between burglary and drug consumption.

- Develop theories – the final role of research is to support or disprove a sociological **theory**. (A theory is simply an explanation of social events.) Researchers gather information and statistics which help sociologists to explain why certain social events occur. Often this involves providing an explanation for correlations. So, if a correlation exists between drug use and crime, various theories can be developed. One theory is that drug users are more likely to commit burglary because they need money to pay for their drug habit. An alternative is that burglars have a high income and so are more likely to have a pleasurable lifestyle that involves using drugs.

Research and ethics

Research can have a powerful impact on people's lives. It can do so in both harmful and beneficial ways, and so the researcher must always think very carefully about the impact of the research and how he/she ought to behave, so that no harm comes to the subjects of the research or to society in general. These sorts of concerns are generally discussed under the umbrella term **ethical issues**.

Most sociological researchers would agree that there are five areas of ethical concern:

- Choice of topic
- Choice of group to be studied
- Effects on the people being studied
- Effects on the wider society
- Issues of legality and immorality

Choice of topic

The first ethical issue relates to the decision about what to study. Merely by choosing an area, the researcher might be confirming some people's prejudices about a particular issue. For example, many sociologists are concerned about the extent of research into the 'negative' side of Afro-Caribbean life, with studies on school failure, lower levels of job success and even the claimed higher rate of criminality. Critics argue that merely by studying this a continued association is made between 'race' and criminality or race and failure.

Choice of group to be studied

One of the trickiest problems that sociologists face is gaining access to study particular groups. The more powerful the group, the less likely it is that the sociologist will manage to obtain agreement to study its members. The result, as you will see, is that the groups most commonly studied by sociologists are the least powerful – so students, petty criminals and less skilled workers are the staple diet of sociological research. The really powerful evade study. Does sociology have a duty to explore the lives of the powerful?

Effects on the people being studied

Research can often have an effect on the people being studied, and so, before setting out to do the research, the sociologist must think carefully about what these effects will be. One of the reasons that sociologists rarely use experiments, for example, is that these may lead to the subjects being harmed by the experiment. In participant observational studies, where the researcher actually joins in with the group being studied (see pp. 186–7), the researcher can often become an important member of the group and may influence other members to engage in behaviour they might not otherwise have engaged in.

Effects on the wider society

But it is not only the people being studied who are potentially affected by the research. The families of those being researched may have information given about them that they wish to keep secret. Also, victims of crime may be upset by the information that researchers obtain about the perpetrators, as they may prefer to forget the incident.

Issues of legality and immorality

Finally, sociologists may be drawn into situations where they may commit crimes or possibly help in or witness deviant acts. For example, in Howard Parker's study of young men in Liverpool he actually acted as a lookout when they went out to steal car radios. Later they asked him to give them advice on how they should deal with the police and the courts – and he agreed.

The relationship between theories and methods

Earlier we saw that research findings could be used either to generate new sociological theories or to confirm or challenge existing theories. But the relationship between research and theory is even more complicated than this. If a sociologist has a particular interest in a theoretical approach, then this may well influence his or her research methodology. There are areas in which theory has a strong influence on research:

1   The theoretical approach often directs people to explore certain areas of research.
2   The theoretical approach often influences the actual techniques chosen.
3   The theoretical approach may influence how the researcher interprets the research findings.

Theory and choice of an area of research

One of the great joys of studying sociology is that the variety of different views and theories generates so many different opinions about society. However, when reading sociological research, the student must always be aware that sociologists who hold strong theoretical beliefs about society are bound to

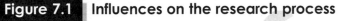

Figure 7.1   Influences on the research process

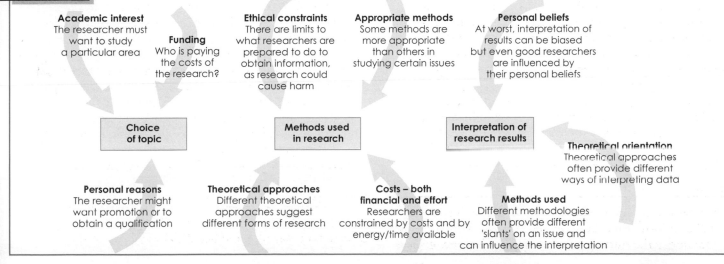

Academic interest
The researcher must want to study a particular area

Funding
Who is paying the costs of the research?

Ethical constraints
There are limits to what researchers are prepared to do to obtain information, as research could cause harm

Appropriate methods
Some methods are more appropriate than others in studying certain issues

Personal beliefs
At worst, interpretation of results can be biased but even good researchers are influenced by their personal beliefs

Choice of topic

Methods used in research

Interpretation of research results

Theoretical orientation
Theoretical approaches often provide different ways of interpreting data

Personal reasons
The researcher might want promotion or to obtain a qualification

Theoretical approaches
Different theoretical approaches suggest different forms of research

Costs – both financial and effort
Researchers are constrained by costs and by energy/time available

Methods used
Different methodologies often provide different 'slants' on an issue and can influence the interpretation

study the topics that, in their eyes, are the most important, and to be less interested in other areas. **Feminist sociologists** see it as their role to examine the position of women in society, and to uncover the ways in which **patriarchy**, or the power of men, has been used to control and oppress women. Consequently their choice of research projects will be influenced by this. **Marxist or 'critical' sociologists** argue that the most important area of study is the question of how a relatively small group of people exploit the vast majority of the population – and they will study issues such as the concentration of power and wealth and the importance of social class divisions. **Functionalist**-oriented sociologists, who think that society is based on a general consensus of values, will be interested in looking at the ways in which society maintains agreement on values and solves social problems – and they will therefore look at the role of religion or schools in passing on values.

Theory and techniques of study

Various theories may point to different areas of interest, but theories also nudge sociologists into different ways of study-ing society. Theories in sociology usually fall into two camps – top-down and bottom-up theories.

Top-down approaches
Top-down approaches, such as functionalism and Marxism, say that the best way to understand society is to view it as a real 'thing' which exists above and beyond us all as individuals. It shapes our lives and provides us with a social world in which we live. Our role is generally to conform.

These sorts of theoretical approaches emphasise that any research ought to bear this in mind and that the researcher should be looking for general patterns of behaviour – which the individuals may not even be aware of. The favoured research methods used by these sociologists tend to be those that generate sets of statistics, such as questionnaires – known as *quantitative* methods (see pp. 182–5).

Bottom-up approaches
Bottom-up approaches, such as interactionism, stress that the only way to understand society is to look at the world through the eyes of individuals, for it is their activities and

---

Exploring methods, theories and ethics

Item A — *Suicide: an example of the relationship between theory and method*

In 1897 Emile Durkheim published his study on the issue of suicide. Durkheim wanted to show how the cultures of different (European) societies could help explain the individual decision to commit suicide. The research was intended to prove that individual action can best be understood by examining social rather than individual differences; and in doing so it aimed to promote sociology as a science on a par with biology or chemistry. Durkheim gathered suicide statistics across various groups, religions and societies. He then interpreted these statistics as showing that the chances of individuals committing suicide vary according to the social group to which they belong. In particular, certain societies have higher rates of 'social cohesion' – that is, people feel a greater sense of belonging in some societies or groups than in others. For example, married people had lower rates of suicide, and so too did people in Catholic societies (Catholicism provided a greater sense of belonging, he claimed). Durkheim's analysis was regarded by many as an excellent example of sociological research – in gathering statistics across different countries to provide the basis for a clear theory.

However, in the 1960s and 1970s, sociologists who believed that the only way to understand society was by trying to see into the minds of individuals – the bottom-up theorists – began to criticise Durkheim's acclaimed study. They argued that the statistics on which Durkheim had based his research were fundamentally flawed. These sociologists said that in only a few cases can one know for certain if the death was suicide or not, as there are rarely suicide notes. Usually, a death is a 'suicide' when a coroner says it is. The real research, they argued, was in studying how coroners go about making their decision as to whether or not to classify a death as suicide.

Item B — *Feminist perspectives*

The topic of Catrin's [research] very much evolved out of two fundamental concerns: women's health and women's imprisonment.

Emma's interest, similarly, developed when she began to read a number of highly critical accounts of women's imprisonment. ...

Both pieces of research were primarily influenced by what could loosely be termed a 'feminist' criminological perspective. In the 1970s and for some time after, feminist concern was directed at the misrepresentation and/or absence of women in conventional criminological research. ... We were aware of the incomplete nature of this knowledge and were keen to address some of the gaps.

Adapted from C. Smith and E. Wincup (2000) 'Breaking in: researching criminal justice institutions for women' in R. D. King and E. Wincup, *Doing Research on Crime and Justice*, Oxford: Oxford University Press, pp. 332–3

Item C — *Ethical dilemmas*

Carolyn Hoyle conducted research into domestic violence.

... victims were told who I was, what the research was about, how it was funded and how I would use the data. ... However ... this rigorous approach to consent did not rule out ethically dubious practice and, furthermore, it was not extended to perpetrators.

Hoyle goes on to describe how the violent husband and the victims were interviewed in separate rooms of their homes. The husbands were told that they were being asked the same questions as their wives. This was not true – they were misled as to the true nature of the questions asked of the wives – but Hoyle argued that it allowed the victims to speak freely and be assured that the husband/perpetrator would not know what they were really asked.

I believe that minimising the risk of further violence to the victim and having the opportunity to talk openly and honestly to a victim ... justified this duplicity [deliberate misleading]. But this is an ethical question. All social scientists 'have a responsibility to ensure that the physical, social and psychological well-being of research participants is not adversely affected by their research'.

Principles are not absolutes, but have to be given a weight. The weighting should not be based on a researcher's desire to progress her own career, but could

beliefs that make up the social world. Research must start at 'the bottom' and work upwards. The sorts of research favoured by these sociologists tend to be those that allow the researcher to see the world from the same perspective as those being studied – known as *qualitative* methods. A good example is participant observation (see pp. 186–7).

The interpretation of research findings

The final impact of theory on research comes when interpreting the research findings. The research is completed and the results are all there in the computer. How does the researcher make sense of the results? This will depend, of course, on what he or she is looking for, and that, in turn, depends upon what theoretical approach the researcher sympathises with. This is very different from bias or personal values – rather it
is a matter of choosing which results are more important than others, and this will always depend upon what best fits the theoretical framework of the researcher. A feminist researcher will be keen to understand the position of women; the Marxist will be looking for signs of class struggle; the functionalist will be looking at the key indicators to prove that a set of common beliefs exists.

be based, for example, on the social desirability of obtaining reliable evidence on a controversial topic. This may be especially so if the evidence can help to bring about changes which could improve the lot of the research subjects. The greater the social problem, the more it may be justified to attach less weight to particular methodological principles.

Adapted from C. Hoyle (2000) 'Being "a nosy bloody cow": ethical and methodological issues in researching domestic violence' in R. D. King and E. Wincup, *Doing Research on Crime and Justice*, Oxford: Oxford University Press, pp. 401–2

1 Give one example of a 'bottom-up' perspective that believes sociology should 'see into the minds of individuals' (Item A). (2)

2 Identify two reasons why Durkheim chose to study suicide in the way he did (Item A). (4)

3 Explain briefly what is meant by a 'feminist perspective' and suggest two ways in which the feminist beliefs of the researchers may have had an influence on how they carried out the research and interpreted the findings (Item B). (6)

4 Identify and briefly describe two situations (other than that described in Item C) where misleading or withholding information from respondents might be justified. (8)

5 Using information from the Items and elsewhere, discuss the influence of theory on sociologists' choice of methods. (20)

6 Using information from the Items and elsewhere, assess the importance of ethical issues in sociological research. (20)

CHECK YOUR UNDERSTANDING

1 Name the three main aims that sociological researchers set out to achieve.

2 Explain in your own words what we mean by ethical issues.

3 Illustrate how ethical issues may emerge in:
   (a) the choice of topic to be studied.
   (b) the effects on the people being studied

4 How can a theoretical approach influence:
   (a) the area of study?
   (b) the methodological techniques chosen?

KEY TERMS

Bottom-up theories (generally called 'micro' or 'interpretive' approaches) – sociological theories that analyse society by studying the ways in which individuals interpret the world.

Correlation – a statistical relationship between two things. It does not necessarily mean that one causes the other. For example, over 70 per cent of burglars drink coffee, but this does not mean that drinking coffee causes someone to commit burglary.

Ethical issues – refers to moral concerns about the benefits and potential harm of research – to the people being researched, to the researcher her/himself and to society.

Feminist sociology – an approach within sociology that concerns itself with studying the way in which women are oppressed by men.

Functionalism – an approach within sociology that stresses that society is based on a general agreement of values.

Marxist or critical sociology – an approach within sociology that stresses the exploitation of the majority of the population by a small and powerful 'ruling class'.

Patriarchy – the oppression of women by men.

Sociological theory – an explanation of how different parts of society or different events relate to one another.

Top-down theories (often called 'macro' or 'structural' approaches) – sociological theories that believe it is important to look at society as a whole when studying it.

Extension activities

1 Search the World Wide Web to find examples of codes of ethics used by psychologists and sociologists.

2 Look in your school or college library for resources about alcohol. Whose views do the resources represent? What views do they put across? Then conduct some interviews with friends about the meaning of alcohol to them. Compare your friends' views with the other sources. Are they similar or different? How might any differences be explained?

3 Use a sociology textbook to find out how feminism has influenced research on the family.

Getting you thinking

Ten per cent of Year 10 boys and 7 per cent of Year 10 girls have probably taken an illegal drug during the previous week, according to the latest data collected using the Health Related Behaviour Questionnaire ... in the majority of cases the drug concerned will be cannabis.

Perhaps it is not surprising to find that smoking cigarettes and using illegal drugs go together. The data for Year 10 boys show that:

- 51 per cent of those who smoke and don't want to stop have used an illegal drug within the past week.
- 3 per cent of those who have never smoked at all have tried an illegal drug.

J. Balding and D. Regis (1998) 'Cannabis: getting safer as the years go by?' *Education and Health*, vol. 16, no. 1 (produced by Schools Health Education Unit, School of Education, St Lukes, Heavitree Rd, Exeter EX1 2LU)

1 **How can anyone make these claims? Did they ask every Year 10 student in Britain? If they didn't, how is it possible to arrive at these figures?**

2 **How honestly do you think pupils will answer these questions?**

Sociologists choose different methods of research depending upon what method seems most appropriate in the circumstances, and the resources available to them. The approach covered in this Topic is quantitative research. This stresses the importance of gathering statistical information which can be checked and tested. Quantitative research usually involves one or more of the following:

- **social surveys**
- **comparative research**
- **experiments**
- **case studies**

Surveys

A social survey involves obtaining information in a standardised manner from a large group of people. Surveys usually obtain this information through questionnaires or, less often, through interviews. The information is then analysed using statistical techniques. There are three possible aims of social surveys. They can be used:

- to find out 'facts' about the population
- to uncover differences in beliefs, values and behaviour
- to test 'a hypothesis'

A good example of a survey is the British Crime Survey, which takes place every two years and asks people about their experience of being a victim of crime. This survey has helped sociologists gain a fuller understanding of patterns of crime.

Before a full social survey is carried out, it is usual for a researcher to carry out a **pilot survey**. This is a small-scale version of the full survey, which is intended:

- to help evaluate the usefulness of the larger survey
- to test the quality and the accuracy of the questions
- to test the accuracy of the sample
- to find out if there are any unforeseen problems

Longitudinal surveys

Social surveys are sometimes criticised for providing us with only a 'snapshot' of social life at any one time. **Longitudinal surveys** get around this problem by studying the same people over a long period of time (as the name suggests) – sometimes over as long as 20 years. Such surveys provide us with a clear, moving image of the changes in attitudes and actions over time. The National Child Development Study began with 40,000 children all born in one week in March 1958. Follow-up surveys have tracked the group at 16, 23 and 33, and have provided fascinating insights into the importance of class, education and family in our lives.

Longitudinal surveys suffer from a number of problems, but the main one is that respondents drop out of the survey because they get bored with answering the questions, or they move and the researchers lose track of them. If too many people 'drop out', this may make the survey unreliable, as the views of those who remain may well be significantly different from the views of those who drop out.

Sampling

It is usually impossible for sociologists to study the entire population, on the grounds of cost and practicality. Instead they have to find a way of studying a smaller proportion of the population whose views will exactly mirror the views of the whole population. There are two main ways of ensuring that the smaller group studied (the sample) is typical – or representative – of the entire population:

1 Some form of **random sampling**
2 **Quota sampling**

There are also other forms of sampling which are not representative but are sometimes used. These include:

3 Snowball sampling
4 Theoretical sampling

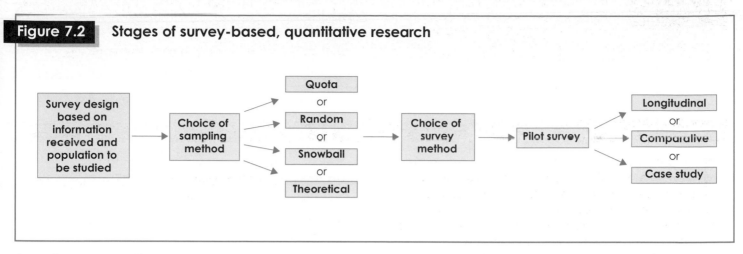

Random sampling

This is based on the idea that, by choosing randomly, each person has an equal chance of being selected and so those chosen are likely to be a cross-section of the population. A simple random sample involves selecting names randomly from a list, known as a **sampling frame**. A sampling frame is some form of list from which the sample can be drawn. If the sampling frame is inaccurate, this can lead to great errors in the final findings. Therefore it needs to be a true reflection of the sort of people whom the researcher wishes to study. Examples of commonly used sampling frames are electoral registers or GPs' patient records.

A simple random sample does not guarantee a representative sample – you may, for instance, select too many young people, too many males or too many from some other group. For this reason many sociologists break down their list of names into separate categories (for example, males and females) and then select from those lists.

Types of random sampling

There are a number of commonly used types of random sampling which aim to guarantee a representative sample. These include:

- **Systematic sampling** – where every nth name (for example, every tenth name) on a list is chosen. It is not truly random – but it is close enough.
- **Stratified sampling** – where the population under study is divided according to known criteria (for example, it could be divided into 52 per cent women and 48 per cent men, to reflect the sex composition of the UK). Within these broad strata people are then chosen at random. The strata can become quite detailed – for example, with further divisions into age, social class, geographical location.
- **Cluster sampling** – where the researcher selects a series of different places and then chooses a sample at random within the cluster of people within these areas. This method is sometimes used where the population under study is spread over a wide area and it is impossible for the researcher to cover the whole area.

Quota sampling

This form of sampling is often used by market research companies and is used purely as the basis for interviews. Since the main social characteristics of the UK population (age, income, occupation, location, ethnicity, etc.) are known,

researchers can give interviewers a particular quota of individuals whom they must find and question – for example, a certain proportion of women of different ages and occupations, and a certain proportion of men of different ages and occupations. The results, when pieced together, should be an accurate reflection of the population as a whole. This form of sampling can only be used where accurate information about the major characteristics of the population is available.

The major advantage of quota sampling over random sampling is the very small number of people needed to build up an accurate picture of the whole. For example, the typical surveys of voting preferences in journals and newspapers use a quota sample of approximately 1,200 to represent the entire British electorate.

Non-representative sampling

Sometimes researchers either do not want a cross-section of the population, or are unable to obtain one.

Snowball sampling

This method is used when it is difficult to gain access to a particular group of people who are the subjects of study, or where there is simply no sampling frame available. It involves making contact with one member of the population to be studied and then asking them to name one or more possible contacts. An example was Martin Plant's study (1975) of drug users, in which he simply asked if they would tell him of other drug users they knew who would agree to be interviewed.

Theoretical sampling

Glaser and Strauss (1967) argue that sometimes it is more helpful to study non-typical people, who may help generate theoretical insights. Feminist sociologists have deliberately studied very untypical societies where women occupy non-traditional roles in order to show that gender roles are socially constructed – if they were based on biology we would expect to see the same roles in every society.

Experiments

Experiments are very commonly used in the natural sciences. An experiment is basically research in which all the variables are closely controlled, so that the effect of changing one or more of the variables can be understood. Experiments are widely used in psychology, but much less so in sociology.

This is because:

- It is impossible to recreate normal life in the artificial environment of an experiment.
- There are many ethical problems in performing experiments on people.
- There is the possibility of the experimenter effect, where the awareness of being in an experiment affects the behaviour of the person undertaking the experiment.

Occasionally sociologists use field experiments, where a form of experiment is undertaken in the community. Rosenhahn (1982) sent 'normal' people to psychiatric institutions in the USA in the late 1960s to see how they were treated by the staff. (Rather worryingly, the staff treated ordinary behaviour in institutions as evidence of insanity!)

Comparative research

The sociological version of an experiment is the comparative method. When a sociologist is interested in explaining a particular issue, one way of doing so is by comparing differences across groups or societies, or across one society over time. By comparing the different social variables in the different societies and their effects upon the issue being studied, it is sometimes possible to identify a particular social practice or value which is the key factor in determining that issue. Emile Durkheim used the comparative method in his classic study of the different levels of suicide in societies – concluding that specific cultural differences motivated people to commit suicide. In order to arrive at this conclusion, Durkheim collected official statistics from a number of different countries and then compared the different levels of suicide, linking them to cultural differences, including religion and family relationships, which varied across the different countries.

Case studies

A **case study** is a detailed study of one particular group or organisation. Instead of searching out a wide range of people via sampling, the researcher focuses on one group. The resulting studies are usually extremely detailed and provide a depth of information not normally available. However, there is always the problem that this intense scrutiny may miss wider issues by its very concentration. An example of a case study is Grieshaber's work (1997), where she conducted case studies of how families ate their meals, and the rules that the parents and their children negotiated.

CHECK YOUR UNDERSTANDING ✓✓✓✓

1 What do we mean by quantitative research?

2 Explain in your own words the importance of sampling.

3 What is 'quota' sampling? What is the main drawback of this method?

4 Identify and explain, in your own words, three types of random sampling.

5 Why don't sociologists use experiments?

6 What is a case study?

7 Give one example of a research project that used the comparative method.

KEY TERMS

Case study – a highly detailed study of one or two social situations or groups.

Comparative research – a comparison across countries or cultures; sociology's version of an experiment.

Experiment – a highly controlled situation where the researchers try to isolate the influence of each variable. Rarely used in sociology.

Longitudinal survey – a survey that is carried out over a considerable number of years on the same group of people.

Pilot survey – a small-scale survey carried out before the main one, to iron out any problems.

Quota sampling – where a representative sample of the population is chosen using known characteristics of the population.

Random sampling – where a representative sample of the population is chosen by entirely random methods.

Sampling frame – a list used as the source for a random sample.

Snowball sampling – where a sample is obtained using a series of personal contacts. Usually used for the study of deviant behaviour.

Survey – a large-scale piece of quantitative research aiming to make general statements about a particular population.

Theoretical sampling – where an untypical sample of the population is chosen to illustrate a particular theory.

Item A *A longitudinal study*

The North-West Longitudinal Study involved following several hundred young people from Year 1 when they were 14 years old for five years until they were 18. The overall aim of this study was to assess how 'ordinary' young people, growing up in England in the 1990s, developed attitudes and behaviours in relation to the unprecedented ready availability of drugs, alongside other consumption options such as alcohol and tobacco.

The primary technique was a self-report questionnaire initially administered personally by the researchers (and then by post) to several hundred young people within eight state secondary schools in two, non-inner-city boroughs of metropolitan north-west England.

In Year 1 the sample was representative of those areas in terms of gender, socio-economic status and ethnicity. However, attrition partly reduced this over time with the disproportionate loss of some 'working-class' participants and some from Asian and Muslim backgrounds.

A longitudinal study is able to address issues of validity and reliability far more extensively than one-off snapshot surveys, but in turn must also explain inconsistent reporting that occurs over the years.

This analysis provides a sophisticated conceptualisation of how young people develop attitudes and behaviours through time.

Adapted from H. Parker, J. Aldrige and F. Measham (1998) *Illegal Leisure*, London: Routledge, pp. 48–9

Item B *Research in Northern Ireland*

Brewer and his colleagues studied the way in which local communities managed to control and limit crime, given that the police were often not welcome in certain areas of Belfast.

... research in hardline loyalist areas of East Belfast and Republican ones in West Belfast, which touches on issues such as policing and the paramilitary organisations, fits the templates of sensitive research, and because of this we worked through local community-based agencies and organisations in order to access general members of the public. Initial contact with the organisations was facilitated by the network of contacts possessed by the authors and by the snowball technique.

... Our research design allowed us to ensure that organisations selected were an accurate political and social representation of the locality.

J. D. Brewer, B. Lockhart and P. Rodgers (1998) 'Informal social control and crime management in Belfast', *British Journal of Sociology*, vol. 49, December.

1 Explain in your own words what is meant by a 'longitudinal study' (Item A). (2)

2 Identify two problems the North West Longitudinal Study (Item A) would be likely to face (Item A). (4)

3 Explain briefly what is meant by the 'snowball technique' and suggest two reasons why the sample in Item B may not have been representative of the people of Belfast. (6)

4 Identify and briefly describe two situations in which it may not be possible and/or desirable to choose a representative sample. (8)

5 Examine the arguments for and against the use of experiments in sociological research. (20)

6 Using information from Item A and elsewhere, assess the advantages and disadvantages of longitudinal studies. (20)

Extension activities

1 Work out the proportions needed in your sample if you were to do a quota sample of your school or college.

2 Conduct a small survey to discover the extent of alcohol use among students at your school or college. Compare their use of alcohol with the use of illegal drugs identified in the exercise at the beginning of this Topic.

3 Find the website of the polling organisation MORI (Market and Opinion Research International) at www.mori.com. Look at some of their recent polls and assess the strengths and weaknesses of their survey techniques.

Getting you thinking

At shortly after five o'clock on a weekday evening, four men enter a public rest room in the city park. One wears a well-tailored business suit; another wears tennis shoes, shorts and teeshirt; the third man is still clad in the khaki uniform of his filling station; the last, a salesman, has loosened his tie and left his sports coat in the car. What has caused these men to leave the company of other homeward-bound commuters on the freeway? What common interest brings these men, with their divergent backgrounds, to this public facility?

They have come here not for the obvious reason, but in search of sex. Many men – married and unmarried, those with heterosexual identities and those whose self-image is a homosexual one – seek such impersonal sex, shunning involvement, desiring kicks without commitment.

L. Humphreys (1970) *Tearoom Trade: Impersonal Sex in Public Places*, Chicago: Aldine Publishing, pp. 1–2

This is the introduction to a book that studies sexual activity between men in public toilets. The researcher wanted to find out as much as possible about men who wanted sex from other men, even if they were not gay. How did the men know where to go? What to do? How to behave? The result is a detailed study of the activities of the men and the views of some of them on why they did what they did.

1 **Why do you think the men went to public toilets for sex?**

2 **How do you think they indicated to other men that they wanted sex?**

3 **How could a researcher best find this out?**

4 **If you wanted to study an activity that is illegal, or one that people are ashamed of, what drawbacks do you think questionnaires or interviews might have?**

Have you ever watched a sporting event on television and heard the commentator saying what a fantastic atmosphere there is? Yet, at home, you remain outside of it. You know there is a fantastic atmosphere, you hear the roar of the crowd, yet you are not part of it. For the people actually in the stadium the experience of the (same) sporting event is quite different. The heat, the closeness of thousands of others, the emotional highs and lows of the actual event, and the noise, all combine to give a totally different sense of what is happening.

Well, many sociologists argue that a similar sort of division exists among sociologists. On the one hand there is research which uses questionnaires, interviews and surveys to obtain a clear, overall view of the 'event'. On the other hand, there are sociologists who are more interested in experiencing the emotions and sense of 'being-there'. These sociologists set out to 'immerse' themselves in the lifestyle of the group they wish to study.

Because this form of research is less interested in statistics to prove its point (that is, *quantitative research*), and more interested in the qualities of social life, it is sometimes known as **qualitative research**. Qualitative approaches are based on the belief that it is not appropriate or possible to accurately measure and categorise the social world – all that is possible is to observe and describe what is happening and offer possible explanations.

The most common form of qualitative research consists of observational studies in which a particular group of people is closely observed and their activities noted. The belief is that, by exploring the lives of people in detail, insights may be gained which can be applied to the understanding of society in general. Observational studies derive from **ethnography**, which is the term used to describe the work of anthropolo-

gists who study simple, small-scale societies by living with the (usually tribal) people and observing their daily lives. However, strictly speaking, qualitative research can include a wide variety of other approaches, such as video and audio recording, in-depth interviews, analysis of the internet, or even analysis of books, magazines and journals.

Types of observational research

Observational (or ethnographic) research is a general term which covers a range of different research techniques.

Observational studies vary according to:

(a) the extent to which the researcher joins in the activities of the group – the researcher may decide to be a participant or not. The choice is between **non-participant observation** and **participant observation**.

(b) whether the researcher is honest and tells the group what he or she is actually doing, or prefers to pretend to be one of the group. The choice is between **overt** and **covert** research.

Participant observation

The most common form of observational study is participant observation, where the researcher joins the group being studied.

The advantages of participant observation

- *Experience* – participant observation allows the researcher to fully join the group and see things through the eyes (and actions) of the people in the group. The researcher is placed in exactly the same situation as the group under study, fully experiencing what is happening. This results in the researcher seeing social life from the same perspective as the group.
- *Generating new ideas* – often this can lead to completely new insights and generate new theoretical ideas, unlike

QUALITATIVE RESEARCH	QUANTITATIVE RESEARCH
Consists mainly of observational methods	Consists mainly of survey work
Researchers join groups as full members or as observers	Uses mainly questionnaires and interviews to obtain information
Rejects the idea that research should attempt to copy the natural sciences	Is based on the belief that the best model for research is the one used in natural sciences, such as biology or chemistry
Research is carried out to generate ideas which might become theories	Most research is set up to test a hypothesis

traditional research which undertakes the study in order to explore an existing theory or hypothesis.

- *Getting the truth* – one of the problems with questionnaires, and to a lesser extent with interviews, is that the respondent can lie. Participant observation prevents this because the researcher can see the person in action – it may also help them understand why the person would lie in a questionnaire or interview.
- *Digging deep* – participant observation can create a close bond between the researcher and the group under study, and individuals in the group may be prepared to confide in the researcher on issues and views that would normally remain hidden.
- *Dynamic* – questionnaires and interviews are 'static' – they are only able to gain an understanding of a person's behaviour or attitudes at the precise moment of the interview. Participant observation takes place over a period of time and allows an understanding of how changes in attitudes and behaviour take place.
- *Reaching into difficult areas* – participant observation is normally used to obtain research information on hard-to-reach groups, such as religious sects and young offenders.

The disadvantages of participant observation
- *Bias* – the main problem lies with bias, as the observer can be drawn into the group and start to see things through their eyes. This may blind him or her to the insights that would otherwise be available.
- *Influence of the researcher* – the presence of the researcher may make the group act less 'naturally' as they are aware

of being studied. Of course, this is less likely to happen if the researcher is operating 'covertly'.

- *Ethics* – even if the group members do not know that they are being studied, the researcher may still have an impact on the activities of the group. The researcher's behaviour will inevitably influence others, or at least have an impact on how they behave. This leads to an ethical problem for the covert researcher, of just how far it is possible to be drawn into the activities of the group – particularly if these activities are immoral or illegal.
- *Proof* – critics have pointed out that there is no way of knowing 'objectively' whether the findings of the researcher are actually true or not, since there is no possibility of replicating the research. In quantitative research, however, other researchers may be able to replicate the research to challenge (or support) the original research findings.
- *Too specific* – participant observation is usually used to study small groups of people who are not typical of the wider population. It is therefore difficult to claim that the findings can be generalised across the population as a whole.
- *Studying the powerless* – finally, almost all participant observational studies are concerned with the least powerful groups in society – typically groups of young males or females who engage in deviant activities. Some critics argue that the information obtained is therefore relatively trivial and does not help us to understand the more important issues in society.

Non-participant observation

Often the researcher will prefer to withdraw from participation and merely be an observer.

Advantages over participant observation
- *Bias* – as the researcher is less likely to be drawn into the group, he or she will also be less likely to be biased in his or her views.
- *Influencing the group* – as the researcher is not making any decisions or joining in activities, the group may be less influenced than in participant observation.

Disadvantages of non-participant observation
- *Superficial* – the whole point of participant observation is to be a member of the group and experience life as they experience it. Merely observing leaves the researcher on the outside and may limit understanding.
- *Altering behaviour* – people may well act differently if they know they are being watched.

Figure 7.3 Types of Observational Research

Observational research varies (a) in the extent to which researchers participate in the activities of the group being studied and (b) according to whether they tell the group of their research role (overt or covert)

covert

Humphreys studies homosexual activity in public toilets. He pretended to be a gay voyeur.

James Patrick's study of a violent Glasgow gang. Patrick joined in the activities.

non-participant ————————————————————————— **participant**

Parker's study of youths who stole from cars. They knew he was a researcher, but also he refused to become involved.

Whyte's study of a group of poor, US, inner-city males. Whyte 'hung around' with them, but they knew he was a researcher.

overt

Covert and overt methods

Observational research is usually carried out amongst deviant groups or other groups who are unusual in some way – such as religious cults. Usually these groups will not be very welcoming to a researcher. Before the researcher begins their work, therefore, they must decide whether they wish to conduct the research in a covert or overt way.

The advantages of covert research

- *Forbidden fruit* – the researcher can enter forbidden areas, be fully accepted and trusted, and immerse him/herself totally in the group to be studied. This can generate a real sense of understanding of the views of the group.
- *Normal behaviour* – the group will continue to act 'naturally', unaware that they are being studied.

The disadvantages of covert research

- *Danger!* – if the researcher's true role is uncovered, the researcher may place him/herself in danger.
- *Ethical dilemmas* – if the group engages in illegal or immoral activities, then the researcher may have to engage in these activities as well. The researcher may find him/herself in possession of knowledge which it may be immoral to withhold from the authorities.

The advantages of overt observation

- *The confidante* – as someone who has no role within the group, the researcher may be in the position of the trusted outsider and receive confidences from group members.
- *Honest* – the researcher is also able to play an open, clear and honest role which will help minimise ethical dilemmas.

The disadvantage of overt observation

- *Outsider* – there will be many situations where only a trusted insider will be let into the secrets. Anyone else, even a sympathetic observer, will be excluded.

Doing ethnographic research

The process of doing ethnographic research involves solving some key problems. These are:

- *Joining the group* – usually observational studies are of groups of people on the margins of society, and the first problem is to actually contact and join the group. The sociologist has to find a place where the group goes and a situation in which they would accept the researcher. Shane Blackman studied a group of young homeless people, whom he met at an advice centre for young people.

- *Recording information* – when researchers are actually hanging around with a group, it is difficult to make notes – particularly if the researcher is engaged in covert research. Even if the group members are aware of the research, someone constantly making notes would disrupt normal activity – and, of course, the researcher would also be unable to pay full attention to what was going on. In participant observational studies, therefore, researchers generally use a **field diary**. This is simply a detailed record of what happened, which the researcher writes up as often as possible. However, the research diary can also be a real weakness of the research.

- *Research diaries* – usually research is carried out on groups with erratic lifestyles. It can be difficult to write a diary up each night. Therefore there is plenty of time to forget things and to distort them. Most observational studies include quotes – yet it is impossible to remember the exact words. So the quotes reflect what the researcher thinks the people said. This may be inaccurate.

- *Maintaining objectivity* – in observational research, it is hard to remain objective. Close contact with the group under study means that feelings almost always emerge. Pryce (1979) studied a group of politically active people of Caribbean descent and really enjoyed their company: 'Increasingly, I had no choice but to abdicate my role as researcher and become a real participant. I shared many interests with the "in-betweeners" [the group], I found real participation with most of them enjoyable.'

- *Influencing the group* – the more involved the researcher is with the group, the greater the chance of influencing what happens. Howard Parker, in his study of young males who stole from cars, actually got as far as giving legal advice.

CHECK YOUR UNDERSTANDING

1 What forms of observational studies are there?

2 What advantages does observational research have over quantitative methods?

3 Name three problems of participant observation.

4 Suggest two examples of research situations where it would be better to use observational methods, and two examples where it would be better to undertake a survey.

KEY TERMS

Covert observation – where the sociologist does not admit to being a researcher.

Ethnography – is the term used to describe the work of anthropologists who study simple, small-scale societies by living with the people and observing their daily lives. The term has been used by sociologists to describe modern-day observational studies.

field diary – a detailed record of events, conversations and thoughts kept by participant observers, written up as often as possible.

Non-participant observational studies – where the sociologist simply observes the group but does not seek to join in their activities.

Overt observation – where the sociologist is open about the research role.

Participant observational studies – where the sociologist joins a group of people and studies their behaviour.

Qualitative research – a general term for approaches to research that are less interested in collecting statistical data, and more interested in observing and interpreting the ways in which people behave.

Item A

Youth homelessness in Brighton

In 1992 Shane Blackman spent several months with a group of young homeless people in Brighton.

As the study proceeded my research role expanded to also include that of action researcher, drinking partner, friend, colleague and football player. In terms of techniques, I found that the conventional social research interview was an impossibility with the individuals in the study, due to their suspicion of such forms of enquiry. The main research instrument was the field diary.

Where social research focuses on individuals and groups who are on the margins of society, the method through which data is collected is often of a highly intimate nature. The researcher is drawn into the lives of the researched and the fieldworker feels emotions while listening to respondents' accounts of their own lives.

… Ethnographic descriptions are able to convey experience from the perspective of the subject of the research and to develop theories based on feeling.

Adapted from S. Blackman (1997) 'An ethnographic study of youth underclass' in R. McDonald, *Youth, the Underclass and Social Exclusion*, London: Routledge

Item B

Covert participant observation

Humphreys defended his covert study of sex acts in public lavatories. … He claimed that he didn't openly advertise his true interests in the rest rooms because the subjects gave tacit [implied] consent. They had, it seems, trusted him enough to ask that he signal when a stranger approached. 'In that setting', Humphreys maintained, 'I misrepresented my identity no more than anyone else. Furthermore, my activities were intended to gain entrance not to a "private domain", but to a public rest room. The only sign on the door said "Men" which makes me quite eligible for entering.

Later Humphreys traced the addresses of a handful of these patrols from their motor vehicle records. In disguise, he visited their homes to ask questions [about their lives].

C. D. Herrera (1999) 'Two arguments for "covert methods" in social research', *British Journal of Sociology*, vol. 50, no. 2

1 Explain in your own words what is meant by a 'field diary' (Item A). (2)

2 Identify two reasons why Blackman found it impossible to use conventional social research interviews for his research (Item A). (4)

3 Suggest two ethical criticisms of Humphrey's research and one way in which he defends his use of covert methods (Item B). (6)

4 Identify and briefly explain two problems in keeping a 'field diary' while undertaking participant observation. (8)

5 Using information from Item B and elsewhere, discuss arguments for and against the use of a covert approach in sociological research. (20)

6 Using information from the Items and elsewhere, assess the usefulness of participant observation to sociologists. (20)

Extension activities

1 Copy the two axes of the diagram on p. 187. Within each of the four squares, where we have given examples of the types of observational research, write a short summary of the advantages of that form of research.

2 Go to your local library. Spend one hour there watching how people behave.

Write down as accurate a description of their behaviour as you can. Spend an evening at home 'observing' your family. Write down as accurate a description of home behaviour that evening as you can.

Which study is likely to be more biased? Why? Does this make it any less accurate? Are you able to get greater 'depth' studying your family? Why? Do you think it would make a difference if you operated in a covert rather than an overt way with your family?

Getting you thinking

The 1998–9 Youth Lifestyles Survey was a detailed study of young people in Britain. One section focused on offending. Amongst the many conclusions was the following:

Almost a fifth of 12- to 30-year-olds admitted having committed one or more offences in the last twelve months. Females were less likely to have offended (11 per cent), compared to males (26 per cent).

The information was obtained by administering a questionnaire, which young people had to complete themselves. Part of the questionnaire is shown here on the right.

1 **Complete the questionnaire ANONYMOUSLY, writing only male or female at the top. Check the results – do your results coincide with the statement at the beginning?**

2 **Can you suggest any other ways in which you could have got this information?**

In the last 12 months, have you:

Criminal damage

		yes	no
1	damaged or destroyed, purposely or recklessly, something belonging to someone else (e.g. a telephone box, bus shelter, car, window of a house, etc.)?	☐	☐
2	set fire, purposely or recklessly, to something not belonging to you? It might be to paper or furniture, a barn, a car, a forest, a basement, a building or something else.	☐	☐

Property offences

		yes	no
3	stolen money from a gas or electricity meter, public telephone, vending machine, video game or fruit machine?	☐	☐
4	stolen anything from a shop, supermarket or department store?	☐	☐
5	stolen anything in school worth more than £5?	☐	☐
6	stolen anything from the place where you work worth more than £5?	☐	☐
7	taken away a bicycle without the owner's permission, not intending to give it back?	☐	☐
8	taken away a motorbike or moped without the owner's permission, not intending to give it back?	☐	☐
9	taken away a car without the owner's permission, not intending to give it back?	☐	☐
10	stolen anything from a car?	☐	☐
11	pickpocketed anything from anybody?	☐	☐
12	sneaked into someone's garden or house or a building, intending to steal something (not meaning an abandoned or ruined building)?	☐	☐
13	stolen anything worth more than £5, not mentioned already (e.g. from a hospital, youth club, sports centre, pub, building site, etc.)?	☐	☐
14	bought something that you knew, or believed at the time, was stolen?	☐	☐

The most obvious way of finding out something is to ask questions. There are two ways of doing this:

1 asking the questions face-to-face – the interview
2 writing the questions down and handing them to someone to complete – the questionnaire

Sociologists use both methods, depending upon which way of asking questions seems to best fit the circumstances and to have the best chance of gaining the information required.

Questionnaires

The essence of a good questionnaire

When constructing a questionnaire, the sociologist has to ensure:

- that it asks the *right questions* which unearth exactly the information wanted
- that the questions are asked in a *clear and simple* manner which can be understood by the people completing the questionnaire
- that it is *as short as possible*, since people usually cannot be bothered to spend a long time completing questionnaires

When to use questionnaires

Questionnaires are used for reaching a *large number* of people, since the forms can just be handed out, or a *widely dispersed* group of people, where they can simply be mailed out. Questionnaires are also *less time-consuming* for researchers than interviewing, as they do not require the researcher to actually go and meet people face-to-face and talk to them.

Anonymous questionnaires are also very useful if the researcher wishes to *ask embarrassing questions* about such things as sexual activities or illegal acts. People are more likely to tell the truth if they can do so anonymously than if they have to face an interviewer.

Types of questionnaires

There is a wide variety of different types of questionnaires. They vary in the way in which they expect the person to answer the questions set. At one extreme are 'closed' questionnaires, which have a series of questions with a choice of answers – all the respondent has to do is tick the box next to the most appropriate answer. At the other extreme are 'open' questionnaires that seek the respondent's opinion.

Figure 7.4 — The relationship between questionnaires and interviews

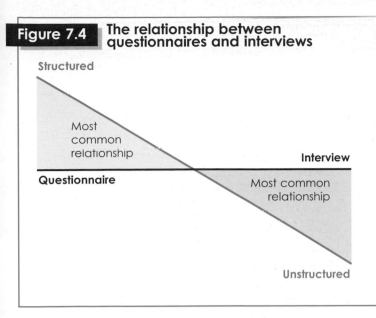

The differences between interviews and questionnaires are not as clear-cut as would first appear. Questionnaires are most commonly 'structured' with **'closed' questions** – that is, they have clear questions and boxes for answers. But sometimes they ask people to express their views and opinions rather than just restricting them to a tick in a box. These types of 'unstructured' questionnaires with **'open' questions** can be quite like interviews,

The same thing happens with interviews: they can often be simply a questionnaire which is administered by the interviewer, and each reply could be only one of a series of options.

The diagram illustrates this complex relationship. Questionnaires are more likely to be structured, while interviews are more likely to be unstructured (see shaded areas). But there is a whole range of possibilities for various degrees of unstructured questionnaires and structured interviews (see unshaded areas).

Issues in undertaking questionnaires

- Unfortunately many people cannot be bothered to reply to questionnaires – that is, unless there is some benefit to them, such as the chance to win a prize. This is a serious drawback of questionnaires in research.
- A low **response rate** (the proportion of people who reply) makes a survey useless, as you do not know if the small number of replies is representative of all who were sent the questionnaire. Those who reply might have strong opinions on an issue, for example, whereas the majority may have much less firm convictions – without an adequate number of replies, you will never know.
- It is difficult to *go into depth* in a questionnaire, because the questions need to be as clear and simple as possible.
- You can never be sure that *the correct person answers*. If you mail a questionnaire to one member of a household, how do you know that that person answers it?
- You can never be sure that the person who replies to the questionnaire *interprets* the questions in the way that the researcher intended. So their replies might actually mean something different from what the researcher believes they mean.
- Lying is also a danger. People may simply not tell the truth when answering questionnaires. There is little that the researcher can do, apart from putting in 'check questions' – which are questions that ask for the same information, but are phrased differently.

Questionnaires and scientific method

Questionnaires – particularly closed questionnaires – are a favourite method used by positivist sociologists (see pp. 00–00), as they can be used in large numbers and the answers can be codified and subjected to statistical tests.

Interviews

An interview is a series of questions asked directly by the researcher to the respondent, or it can be conducted as a discussion.

When to use interviews

- Sociologists generally use interviews if the subject of enquiry is *complex*, and a questionnaire would not allow the researcher to probe deeply.

Figure 7.5 — Types of survey questions

1 Quantity or information
In which year did you enrol on the part-time degree? _____

2 Category
Have you ever been, or are you now, involved almost full-time in domestic duties (i.e. as a housewife/househusband)?
☐ yes (currently)   ☐ yes (in the past)   ☐ never

3 List or multiple choice
Do you view the money spent on your higher education as any of the following?
☐ a luxury   ☐ an investment   ☐ a necessity
☐ a gamble   ☐ a burden   ☐ a right
☐ none of these

4 Scale
How would you describe your parents' attitude to higher education at that time? Please tick one of the options below:

very positive	positive	mixed/ neutral	very negative	very negative	not sure
☐	☐	☐	☐	☐	☐

5 Ranking
What do you see as the main purpose(s) of your degree study? Please rank all those relevant in order from 1 downwards:
☐ personal development   ☐ career advancement
☐ subject interest   ☐ recreation
☐ fulfil ambition   ☐ keeping stimulated
☐ other (please write) _____

6 Complex grid or table
How would you rank the benefits of your degree study for each of the following? Please rank each item.

for:	very positive	positive	mixed/ neutral	negative	very negative	not sure
you						
your family						
your employer						
the country						
your community						
your friends						

7 Open-ended
We would like to hear from you if you have any further comments.
_____
_____

Source: L. Blaxter, C. Hughes and M. Tight (1996)
How to Research, Buckingham: Open University Press, p. 161

- Interviews are also used when researchers want to *compare their observations with the replies given by the respondents*, to see if they appear true or not – and, of course, in an interview researchers are also sure that they are getting information from the right person.
- Because they can be organised virtually on the spot – as opposed to preparing a questionnaire, finding a sampling frame and posting the questionnaires out – one advantage of interviews is that they can be done *immediately*.
- Finally, there is *a much higher response rate* with interviews than with questionnaires, as the process is more personal and it is difficult to refuse a researcher when approached politely.

Types of interviews

Interviews fall between two extremes: **structured** and **unstructured**. At their most structured, they can be very tightly organised, with the interviewer simply reading out questions from a prepared questionnaire. At the other extreme, they can be unstructured, where the interviewer simply has a basic area for discussion and asks any questions that seem relevant.

There are also individual and group interviews. Most people assume that an interview is between just two people, but in sociological research a group of people may get together to discuss an issue, rather than simply giving an answer to a question. Group interviews are commonly used where the researcher wants to explore the dynamics of the group, believing that a 'truer' picture emerges when the group are all together, creating a 'group dynamic'. An example of this is Mairtin Mac an Ghaill's *The Making of Men: Masculinities, Sexualities and Schooling* (1994), in which a group of gay students discuss their experiences of school.

Issues in undertaking interviews

Influencing the replies
Interviews are a form of conversation between people and, as in any conversation, likes and dislikes emerge. The problem is to ensure that the interviewer does not influence the replies provided by the respondent in any way – known as **interviewer bias**. For example, respondents may want to please the interviewer and so give the replies they think the interviewer wants. Influences that can affect the outcome of the interview include such things as manner of speech, ethnic origin, sex or personal habits.

Lying
There is no reason why people should tell the truth to researchers, and this is particularly true when a sensitive issue is being researched. When questioned about sexual activities or numbers of friends, for example, people may well exaggerate in order to impress the interviewer.

Interview reliability
The aim of the research process is to conduct enough interviews for the researcher to be able to make an accurate generalisation. But if interviews are actually different from each other as a result of the interaction, then it is wrong to make generalisations.

Recording the information
Unstructured interviews are generally recorded and usually require **transcribing** (writing up), which is time-consuming. Tizard and Hughes (1991) recorded interviews with students to find out how they went about learning – and every hour of interview took 17 hours to transcribe and check! But writing down the replies at the time is slow and can disrupt the flow of an interview.

Questions and values

Both questionnaires and interviews share the problem of the values of the researcher creeping into the questions asked. Two problems are particularly important – using leading questions and using loaded words.

Leading questions
Here researchers write or ask questions that suggest what the appropriate answer is. For example, 'Wouldn't you agree that …?'

Loaded words and phrases
Here researchers use particular forms of language that either indicate a viewpoint or will generate a particular positive or negative response. For example, 'termination of pregnancy' (a positive view) or 'abortion' (a negative view); 'gay' or 'homosexual'.

Interviews and scientific methods

Interviews are used by all kinds of sociologists. The more structured the interviews, the more likely they are to be used in a quantitative way to produce statistics. The more unstructured the interviews (including group interviews), the more likely they are to be of use to 'qualitative' sociologists.

Issues of validity and reliability

Validity

We have discussed the importance of ensuring that the questions asked actually produce the information that is required. This is a crucial issue in sociological research and is known as the issue of **validity** (i.e. getting at the truth). The type of questions asked in the questionnaire or interview must allow the respondent to give a true and accurate reply.

Reliability

The researcher must ensure not only that the design of the question gets to the truth of the matter, but also that it does so *consistently*. If the question means different things to different people, or can be interpreted differently, then the research is not reliable. **Reliability**, then, refers to the fact that all completed questionnaires and interviews are exactly the same.

CHECK YOUR UNDERSTANDING

1 **What are the three elements of a good questionnaire?**

2 **What do we mean when we talk about loaded questions and leading questions? Illustrate your answer with an example of each and show how the problem could be overcome by writing a 'correct' example of the same questions.**

3 **Why are 'response rates' so important?**

4 **When is it better to use questionnaires rather than interviews?**

5 **When would it be more appropriate to use 'open' questions? Give an example of an open question.**

6 **What do we mean by 'transcribing'?**

Exploring questionnaires and interviews

Gaining trust

From my own experience in researching white British and Caribbean people with diabetes, I would argue that there is evidence suggesting that my own Caribbean background was a distinct advantage. .... Rapport [a good relationship] with the Caribbeans developed fairly spontaneously. ... We traded stories about how we ended up in England, what part of Jamaica or the Caribbean we are from and generally how we coped with the cold weather and lack of sunshine.

... The interviews with the white British sub-sample differed significantly. Initial conversations were polite and were confined to matters relating to the interview .... Generally, there was no sharing of personal details and the interviewees did not elaborate on the issues of the research in the way that the Caribbean sample had.

P. Scott (1999) 'Black people's health: ethnic status and research issues' in S. Hod, B. Mayall and S. Oliver, *Critical Issues in Social Research*, Buckingham: Open University Press

Item B **Telling the truth?**

'The first time we had this questionnaire, I thought it was a bit of a laugh. That's my memory of it. I can't remember if I answered it truthfully or not. ... It had a list of drugs and some of them I'd never heard of, and just the names just cracked me up.'

H. Parker, J. Aldrige and F. Measham (1998) *Illegal Leisure*, London: Routledge, pp. 46–7

1 Explain in your own words what is meant by 'interviewer bias'. (2)

2 Identify one advantage and one disadvantage of the rapport identified in Item A. (4)

3 Suggest three problems of using questionnaires to collect sensitive information. (6)

4 Identify and explain two advantages and two disadvantages of the researcher in Item A using a questionnaire rather than an interview. (8)

5 Using information from Item A and elsewhere, examine the ways in which different types of interviews have been used in sociological research. (20)

6 Using information from Item B and elsewhere, assess the usefulness of questionnaires in sociological research. (20)

KEY TERMS

Closed questions – questions that require a very specific reply, such as 'yes' or 'no'.

Interviewer bias – the influence of the interviewer (e.g. their age, 'race', sex) on the way the respondent replies.

Open questions – questions that allow the respondent to express themselves fully.

Reliability – refers to the need for all interviews to be exactly the same, so that they can be compared. Not a great problem with structured/closed question interviews, but a major problem with unstructured/open questions where interviewer bias may occur.

Response rate – the proportion of the questionnaires that are returned (could also refer to the number of people who agree to be interviewed).

Structured interview – where the questions are delivered in a particular order and no explanation or elaboration of the questions is allowed by the interviewer.

Transcribing – the process of writing up interviews that have been recorded.

Unstructured interview – where the interviewer is allowed to explain and elaborate on questions.

Validity – refers to the problem of ensuring that the questions actually measure what the researcher intends them to.

Extension activities

1 Your aim is to find out about a sample of young people's experience of schooling. Draft a closed questionnaire to collect this data. Collect and analyse the data quantitatively. Now draft guide questions for an unstructured interview to find out about the same issue. Conduct two or three of these interviews, either taping or making notes of the responses.

Compare the two sorts of data. What differences are there? Why do those differences occur? Which method do you think was most effective for that particular purpose? Why? *(This task is particularly suitable as a pair or group activity.)*

2 Search the world wide web and/or some magazines for examples of questionnaires. Print them off and assess the strengths and weaknesses of the question design.

3 Working with a partner of the opposite sex, draft guide questions for an unstructured interview with young men about their attitudes to homosexuality. Each partner should then conduct three of these interviews.

Discuss the different ways interviewees responded. Are the young men more honest and open with a male or female interviewer or is there no difference? Which interviewer gained the more valid results? Why?

Getting you thinking

far left: *A Congolese villager contemplates the hand and foot of his 5-year-old daughter after his family were killed and eaten by Leopold's rubber collectors, 1904*

left: *'Impongi', a boy mutilated in King Leopold's Congo as a punishment for his village's 'failure' to meet rubber production quotas*

Source: A. Mitchell (1999) 'New light on the "Heart of Darkness"', *History Today*, December, pp. 20–1

The photos above were taken in the early part of the twentieth century and used to illustrate an article in the magazine *History Today*. The article explores the way in which European colonialists exploited Africans around this period, and describes how Belgian colonialists would chop limbs off children if they failed to collect enough rubber. Below is the list of sources quoted by the writer which he used for his article.

- Joseph Conrad, *Heart of Darkness* (edited by D. D. R. A. Goonetilleke) (1995)
- Broadway Literary Texts 1
- Frederick Karl and Laurence Davies, *The Collected Letters of Joseph Conrad*, Cambridge University Press
- Marvin Swartz (1971) *The Union of Democratic Control in British Politics During the First World War*, Oxford: Clarendon Press
- Wm. Roger Louis, *The Triumph of the Congo Reform Movement 1905–1908*, Boston University Papers on Africa
- Roger Anstey (1971) 'The Congo rubber atrocities – a case study', *African Historical Studies*, Vol. IV, 1

1 **List the variety of sources used by the author (e.g. academic articles, novels, etc.).**

2 **Why do you think that he used this range of material?**

3 **If you wanted to study something that happened in 1904, what would you do?**

4 **Can you think of any problems that might result from using the range of sources mentioned above?**

Not all research uses primary sources – that is, observing people in real life, sending out questionnaires or carrying out interviews. Many sociologists prefer to use material collected and published by other people. This material is known as **secondary data**.

Secondary data consist of a very wide range of material collected by organisations and individuals for their own purposes, and include sources as complex as official government statistics at one extreme, and, at the other extreme, sources such as personal diaries. These data include written material, sound and visual images. Such material can be from the present day or historical data. Finally, and most commonly, secondary sources include the work of other sociologists which is read, analysed and commented on by other sociologists.

Secondary sources are invaluable to sociologists, both on their own and in combination with primary sources. It is unheard of for a researcher not to refer to some secondary sources in research.

Why sociologists use secondary sources

Some of the main reasons are:

- The information required already exists as secondary data.
- Historical information is needed, but the main participants are dead or too old to be interviewed.
- The researcher is unable for financial or other reasons to visit places to collect data firsthand.
- The subject of the research concerns illegal activities and it is unsafe for the researcher to go to collect data.
- Data need to be collected about groups who are unwilling to provide accounts of their activities – such as extreme religious sects.

Some general problems with secondary sources

Whenever a sociologist uses a secondary source, they must be aware that the person who first created the source did so for a specific reason, and this could well create **bias**. A diary, for example, gives a very one-sided view of what happened and is bound to be sympathetic to the writer. Official statistics may have been constructed to shed a good light on the activities of the government – so that they can claim they are 'winning the war against crime', for example. Even the work of previous sociologists may contain errors and biases.

Types of secondary data

The most common types of secondary data used by sociologists include:

- Previous sociological research
- Official publications, including statistics and reports
- Diaries and letters
- Novels and other works of fiction
- Oral history and family histories
- The media

Previous sociological research

Previous studies as a starting point

Whenever a sociologist is undertaking a study, the first thing they do is to undertake a **literature search** – that is, go to the library or the internet and look up every available piece of sociological research on the topic of interest. The sociologist can then see the ways in which the topic has been researched before, the conclusions reached and the theoretical issues thrown up. Armed with this information, the researcher can then construct the new research study to explore a different 'angle' on the problem or simply avoid the mistakes made earlier.

But there are sometimes methodological errors in published research, as well as possible bias in the research findings. There have been many examples of research that has formed the basis for succeeding work and that only many years later has been found to be faulty. A famous piece of anthropological research which was used for 40 years before it was found to be centrally flawed was Mead's *Coming of Age in Samoa* (1945).

Reinterpreting previous studies

Often sociologists do not want to carry out a new research project, but prefer instead to examine previous research in great detail in order to find a new interpretation of the original research results. So the secondary data provide all the information that is needed.

Official publications

Statistics

Statistics compiled by governments and reputable research organisations are particularly heavily used by sociologists. These statistics often provide far greater scale and detail than a sociologist could manage, and it is much cheaper to work on statistics already collected than repeating the work.

Usually, the government will produce these statistics over a number of years (for example, the government statistical publication *Social Trends* has been published for 30 years), and so comparisons can be made over a long period of time.

Figure 7.6   The use of secondary sources in research

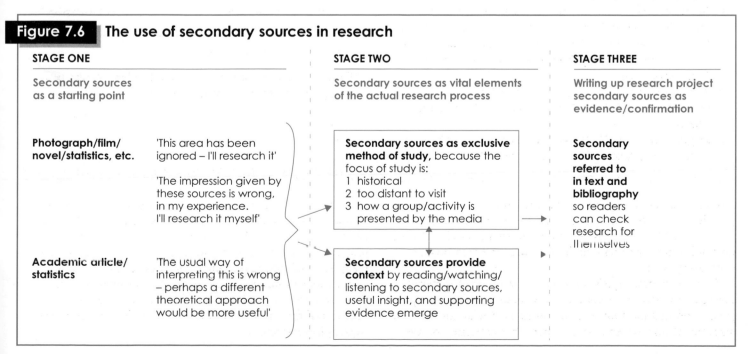

STAGE ONE	STAGE TWO	STAGE THREE
Secondary sources as a starting point	Secondary sources as vital elements of the actual research process	Writing up research project secondary sources as evidence/confirmation

STAGE ONE

Photograph/film/novel/statistics, etc.

'This area has been ignored – I'll research it'

'The impression given by these sources is wrong, in my experience. I'll research it myself'

Academic article/statistics

'The usual way of interpreting this is wrong – perhaps a different theoretical approach would be more useful'

STAGE TWO

Secondary sources as exclusive method of study, because the focus of study is:
1 historical
2 too distant to visit
3 how a group/activity is presented by the media

Secondary sources provide context by reading/watching/listening to secondary sources, useful insight, and supporting evidence emerge

STAGE THREE

Secondary sources referred to in text and bibliography so readers can check research for themselves

However, although these official statistics have many advantages, there are also some pitfalls that researchers have to be aware of. The statistics are collected for administrative reasons and the classifications used may omit crucial information for sociologists. For example, sociologists may be interested in exploring issues of 'race' or gender, but this information might be missing from the official statistics.

Official statistics may be affected by political considerations, such as when they are used to assist the image of the government of the day. They may also reflect a complex process of interaction and negotiation – as is the case with crime statistics – and may well need to be the focus of investigation themselves!

Reports and government inquiries

The civil service and other linked organisations will often produce official reports which investigate important problems or social issues. However, although they draw together much information on these issues, they are constrained by their 'remit', which states the limits of their investigations. The government and other powerful bodies are therefore able to exclude discussion of issues that they do not want to become the centre of public attention. Government discussions on issues related to drugs, for example, are usually carefully controlled by the government so that legalisation of drugs is simply not discussed.

Diaries and letters

It is difficult to understand a historical period or important social events if the researcher has no way of interviewing the people involved. Usually, only the official information or media accounts are available. Using such things as letters and diaries helps to provide an insight into how participants in the events felt at the time.

However, problems can occur, as the writers may have distorted views of what happened, or they may well be justifying or glorifying themselves in their accounts. Almost any politician's memoirs prove this.

Novels

Novels can give an insight into the attitudes and behaviour of particular groups, especially if the author is drawn from one of those groups. However, they are fiction and will exaggerate actions and values for the sake of narrative. Also, writing books is typically a middle- or upper-class activity, which may limit the insight that can be gained about the particular group featured.

Oral history and family histories

Often the events to be studied took place some considerable time ago, but there may be older people alive who can recall the events, or who themselves were told about them. There may be recordings available of people (now dead) talking of their lives. Often people have old cine-film or family photos of events of interest. All of these can be collected and used by the researcher to help understand past events. Of course, the best of all these methods is the interview, with the older person recalling events of long ago (although quite where the line can be drawn between this as secondary research and as a simple interview is rather unclear).

These approaches do all share the usual problems that events are reinterpreted by older people or by families to throw a positive light on their actions, and of course to hide any harm they did to others.

The media and content analysis

A huge amount of material is available from newspapers, the internet, magazines and television. In fact so much material is available that one of the major problems of using the mass media as secondary data lies with the selection of material – on exactly what grounds are items included or excluded? Researchers have to be very careful to include all relevant material and not to be biased in their selection in order to 'prove' their point. Two of the best-known studies using **content analysis** have been strongly criticised for just this. Critics of the Glasgow Media Group's publications such as *Bad News* and *More Bad News* (which were critical appraisals of how television news provided only one interpretation of political events) claim that they were selective in their choice of material and that they applied their own interpretations to the selections.

However, trying to understand and interpret accurately the printed and broadcast media is not just a matter of watching out for bias – there is also the issue of *how* to interpret the material. When we look at pictures or read a story in a magazine, different people find different *meanings* in the material. There are many factors influencing this, but one crucial factor is our own beliefs and attitudes towards the subject that we are reading about. The importance of this for research using secondary data is that we must not assume that what we read or see is the same as it was for the original readers or viewers.

CHECK YOUR UNDERSTANDING ✓ ✓ ✓ ✓

1 **What are secondary data?**

2 **Why do sociologists use secondary sources?**

3 **What are the disadvantages of using secondary sources?**

4 **What are the advantages and disadvantages of using official statistics and other government documents?**

5 **What are the advantages and disadvantages of using qualitative secondary data such as diaries?**

KEY TERMS

Bias – where the material reflects a particular viewpoint to the exclusion of others. This may give a false impression of what happened. This is a particularly important problem for secondary sources.

Content analysis – exploring the contents of the various media in order to find out how a particular issue is presented.

Literature search – the process whereby a researcher finds as much published material as possible on the subject of interest. Usually done through library catalogues or the internet.

Secondary data – data already collected by someone else for their own purposes.

Item A — Policing the working-class city

In an article entitled 'Policing the working-class city', Phil Cohen discusses how the working class in cities have always been in conflict with the police, and how the police have in fact managed to exclude them from large parts of the city. The idea of the police 'no-go zone' is nothing new. Cohen wrote the article for the National Deviancy Conference/Conference of Socialist Economists – both 'left-wing' academic organisations.

For nearly half a century (from the 1880s) Popham Street and Packington Street off Essex Road ... saw numerous affrays between constabulary and local populace. The local press records 146 such incidents in these areas between 1880 and 1920. ... This ancient tradition of collective self-defence still existed in this area two generations later, as shown by a report ('Islington Gazette', June 1924) from the 1920s. A policeman arrested a local woman, when a hostile crowd ... gathered round to rescue her. ...

Even arrest might not be the end of the story. One Islington resident (Mr Malone: oral testimony) recalled how in his youth, before the First World War ....

P. Cohen (1981) 'Policing the working-class city' in M. Fitzgerald, G. McLennan and J. Pawson (eds) *Crime and Society: Readings in History and Theory*, London: Routledge

Item B — My Aunt Esther

Stephen Bourne grew up in London in the 1960s and his family was regularly visited by his Aunt Esther, a black woman. Stephen Bourne thought nothing about this until he saw a television programme about black people in Britain and he also found some old family photos showing his aunt and his mother's family when they were young.

The point of departure for me came in 1974 when I watched ... *The Black Man in Britain 1550–1950*. This documented the history of black people in Britain over 400 years. ... By this time I had discovered a shoe box in Mum's wardrobe which was full of old family photographs. Several featured Aunt Esther. ... Hungry for information, I was disappointed to find that, apart from the slave trade there was no mention of black people in our school history books. ... However, through ... inter-library loans, I accessed two books then available on the subject: James Walvin's *Black and White: The Negro and English Society 1555–1945* (1973) and Folarin Shyllon's *Black People in Britain 1555-1833* (1977). ... I realised that my quest for knowledge would have to come from first-hand accounts, so I began to ask Aunt Esther questions. ... Aunt Esther – who worked as a seamstress – gave me first-hand accounts of what life was like for a working class black Londoner throughout the century. ... In 1992 we published her life story .... For this we received the Raymond Williams Prize for Community Publishing. ... However, although the black

media and women's press gave the book excellent coverage ... book editors on the broadsheet newspapers completely ignored us.

S. Bourne (2000) 'My Aunt Esther', *History Today*, February, pp. 62–3

1 Explain what is meant by 'personal documents'. (2)

2 Identify two types of data used by Phil Cohen in Item A. (4)

3 Identify three criticisms of the claim that the data gathered from Aunt Esther represents an accurate picture of 'life for a working-class black Londoner throughout the century'. (Item B) (6)

4 Identify and briefly explain two problems the author of Item B may have experienced in interviewing Aunt Esther. (8)

5 Discuss the advantages and disadvantages of using official statistics in sociological research. (20)

6 Using material from the Items and elsewhere, evaluate the usefulness of personal and historical documents for sociologists. (20)

Top left: Esther (second left) and family in Dieppe Street, Fulham, 1947

Above: Aunt Esther with author Stephen Bourne, 1991

Left: Esther and Joseph Bruce (her father), 1918

Extension activities

1 Search the World Wide Web for the website of the British government's Office of National Statistics. What statistics are there and how accurate do you think they are? Are there any that you think have the potential for distortion? Why?

2 Find some home pages on the World Wide Web that belong to particular individuals. How useful are these in giving us a true picture of those individuals? Explain your answer.

Two organisations, or awarding bodies, offer qualifications in AS-level sociology.

NAME OF AWARDING BODY	INITIALS	AS-LEVEL SOCIOLOGY COURSE CODE
Assessment and Qualifications Alliance	AQA	5191
Oxford, Cambridge and RSA Examinations	OCR	3878

You will be following one of these two courses. This means you only need to read about the specifications that apply to you in this unit. Check with your teacher if you are not sure which course you are following.

A table linking the units in this book to the two specifications can be found at the start of this book (on p. v).

The AQA specifications *Joan Garrod, Chair of Examiners, AQA AS/A-level sociology*

What will I study?

Aims of the course

The AQA specification in AS-/A-level sociology offers you the opportunity to acquire knowledge and understanding of key aspects of sociological thought, a sound introduction to sociological research methods and the opportunity to study a number of different areas of social life in depth. The AS course is both a sound introduction to the study of sociology leading to a qualification in its own right, and also an essential grounding for those wishing to continue for a further year of A-level study.

The AS course is sufficiently flexible to allow a choice of topic areas within Units 1 and 2 and the choice of a written examination or a coursework task based on a research proposal for Unit 3. It also ensures a thorough coverage of sociological perspectives and of the two core themes:

● socialisation, culture and identity, and
● social differentiation, power and stratification.

These core themes are required elements of any AS/A-level sociology specification.

The knowledge and skills acquired in this course should enable you to take a more informed and critical look at many aspects of your own society and how they relate to your own life, while at the same time enabling you to develop and practise the skills of informed debate and critical analysis. The skills acquired in a sociology course can be of life-long benefit.

Modules of study and units of assessment

The AQA AS course is divided into three modules of study, which lay out what you should know. When you enter for an examination, the module becomes a unit of assessment. Modules 1 and 2 each contain three topic areas, and each topic area forms the basis of a question in the written examination for the first two units of assessment. Module 3 covers only one area of study, namely: sociological methods. You are given a choice regarding the assessment of this unit.

MODULE OF STUDY	TOPICS	UNIT OF ASSESSMENT	FORMS OF ASSESSMENT
1	• Families and households • Health • Mass media	1	Written examination of 1.25 hours; one data-response question per topic area
2	• Education • Wealth, poverty and welfare • Work and Leisure	2	Written examination of 1.25 hours; one data-response question per topic area
3	• Sociological methods	3	**Either**: written examination of one hour consisting of one data-response question, **or**: coursework task based on structured proposal for a piece of research

How will I be assessed?

Skills

The skills you will acquire and develop in your AS course are tested in the examination by two assessment objectives, each of which counts for half of the available marks.

Assessment objective 1 (AO1): knowledge and understanding

This requires you to demonstrate your knowledge and understanding of the chosen topic area which forms the basis of the assessment. It covers knowledge and understanding of relevant sociological theories and perspectives, concepts, studies and social policies. You should also be able to make reference to relevant issues and events. Also included in AO1 is the skill of communication. While this is not assessed separately, and therefore does not carry a particular mark weighting, it is an important skill, as poor communication will prevent you from showing the examiner clearly what you mean.

Assessment objective 2 (AO2): identification, analysis, interpretation and evaluation

This range of skills together counts for half of the available marks. To demonstrate them successfully you will need to be able to identify perspectives, reasons, examples, criticisms and so on, as required by the particular question. The skill of interpretation covers your ability to work out and respond to what the question is requiring you to do and to interpret different types of evidence, including research studies and statistical data, by discussing what they can tell us. Good analysis is shown by presenting an informed, detailed and accurate discussion of a particular theory, perspective, study or event, and also by the ability to present your arguments and evidence in a clear and logically structured manner. Evaluation refers to your ability to recognise and discuss the strengths and weaknesses of theories and perspectives, studies, sociological methods and data presented in a variety of forms.

Exams

The basic structure of the units of assessment is shown in the diagram below and the question structure is discussed in more detail in the next section. The weighting given to each of the three AS units is given in the following table, which shows the percentage of the marks allocated to each unit in terms of both the AS and the full A level.

UNIT OF ASSESSMENT	AS-LEVEL WEIGHTING	A-LEVEL WEIGHTING
Unit 1	35% of the total AS-level marks	17.5% of the total A-level marks
Unit 2	35% of the total AS-level marks	17.5% of the total A-level marks
Unit 3	30% of the total AS-level marks	15% of the total A-level marks

Coursework

The AS coursework task is offered in Unit 3 as an alternative to the written examination. It takes the form of a highly-structured research proposal which may, if you wish, form the basis of an actual research project in the second year of the course. Further details of the AS coursework are given in the *How can I do well in the coursework task?* section (p. 202).

How can I do well in the written exams?

Question style and structure

AS-level questions are data-response questions. Each question has typically two Items of information. The Items have a dual purpose. They provide the basis for some of the shorter questions, for example when you are asked to *explain the meaning of* a concept or phrase which occurs in the Item or to *interpret* some statistical data from a graph or table, and they also provide helpful information to assist you in answering the longer, higher-mark questions.

Each question is marked out of 60, and it might be helpful to think of the 60 marks being allocated in three groups of 20 marks.

Short-answer questions (a), (b), (c) and (d)

The first 20 marks are awarded for a series of short-answer questions, namely (a), (b), (c) and (d) – typically carrying 2, 4, 6 and 8 marks respectively.

- The 2-mark question will usually ask you to *explain the meaning of* a concept or phrase taken from one of the Items.
- The 4- and 6-mark questions will ask you to do two or three things, each of which will carry 2 marks. Typical questions would be:
  - *give two reasons why …*
  - *give three examples of …*
  - *suggest two explanations of …*
  - *identify three criticisms which could be made of ….*
- The 8-mark question will typically carry the instruction: *identify and briefly explain* **two** …. The *two* could refer to criticisms, reasons why, disadvantages of, etc. As you have been asked to do two things (identify and briefly explain), and you have been asked to do these for each of two different things (criticisms, reasons why, disadvantages of, etc.), the marks are awarded as 2 + 2 + 2 + 2 (assuming that you do everything correctly!). In other words, you get 2 marks for each of the two 'things' correctly identified, and a further 2 marks for each of these successfully explained.

Longer-answer questions (e) and (f)

- The (e) question carries 20 marks, and will typically ask you to *discuss* or *examine* something. It is important to understand that this question carries 14 of the 20 available marks for knowledge and understanding (AO1) and the remaining 6 marks for the AO2 skills. This question will usually not be based on one of the Items, but will focus on a different aspect of the topic area than that covered in the Items, allowing you to demonstrate a breadth of knowledge.
- The (f) question also carries 20 marks, and will typically ask you to *assess* something. It is important to understand that this question carries 14 of the 20 available marks for the AO2 skills, particularly analysis and evaluation, and the remaining 6 marks for knowledge and understanding.

The two longer-answer questions do not allocate specific marks for each of the two assessment objectives, that is, you do not get a mark out of 14 and a mark out of 6. Marks are allocated between three broad bands, and are awarded on the basis of descriptions of typical answers. The greater focus of the (e) mark scheme is on the relevant knowledge and understanding displayed, while in the (f) mark scheme the emphasis is on the AO2 skills shown in the answer.

Exam tips

● Read both the Items and the whole question very carefully before you begin to answer. The Items will contain information that is essential, helpful or both, and reading the whole question will give you an understanding of which aspects of the topic have been covered.

● Keep an eye on the time. Remember that the (e) and (f) questions together count for 40 of the 60 marks available, so it is very important that you allow sufficient time for these, and are able to write more than just a few paragraphs. It is quite acceptable, in questions in which you are asked to *give two reasons*, or *give three examples*, to do just that, using bullet points if you wish. There is no need in such questions to write a long paragraph.

● In the 8-mark (d) questions, separate out your answer into two parts, so that you *identify and briefly explain* one thing, and then leave a line and go on to *identify and briefly explain* a second thing. This makes it less likely that you will forget to do both parts of the question.

● Particularly in the 20-mark questions, refer to appropriate theories, perspectives, studies and evidence to support and inform your answer. Where possible, bring in examples of recent or current events or social policies to illustrate the points you are making. Make quite sure that in the (f) question you have given sufficient demonstration of the AO2 skills, particularly analysis and evaluation.

● Finally, make sure that you answer the question that the examiner has set, rather than the one that you wished had been set! This is a serious point – many candidates fail to achieve marks because they have not kept to the focus of the question. No question is likely to ask you simply to *write everything you know about …*, and yet this is what some students do.

How can I do well in the coursework task?

Requirements

The AS-level coursework task requires you to submit a proposal for a piece of sociological research, based on the collection of primary or secondary data. Your proposal has to be presented under four set headings, as shown in the table. There is an overall word limit of 1200 words, and each of the four sections has its own word limit, which has to be shown on the proposal. Your proposal does not have to be for research that would be capable of being conducted by a 17-year-old student. However, if you think that you may wish to develop your AS proposal

and use it as the basis for an actual research project in A2, then you would have to bear in mind when framing your AS proposal the obvious limitations of time, cost, access to informants, data and so on that you would have to deal with at A2. The table below shows you in outline what you have to do.

SECTION	OUTLINE REQUIREMENTS	MAXIMUM NO. OF WORDS	TOTAL MARKS FOR THAT SECTION
Hypothesis/ aim	Identify an appropriate sociological area or issue and develop a hypothesis or aim to form the basis of your research, explaining its sociological significance.	100	8
Context and concepts	Identify and briefly describe two pieces of material that would form appropriate contexts for the proposed research. Choose two concepts that would be useful in the collection and/or analysis of the data.	400	20
Main research method and reasons	Choose a single research method for the collection of data, saying why you think it is appropriate to test/explore your hypothesis or aim. Give supporting information regarding the implementation of the method.	400	20
Potential problems	Identify some problems of which a sociologist would need to be aware if the proposed research were carried out, explaining why these problems might arise.	300	12
Total		1200	60

What will the A2 course be like?

Modules of study and units of assessment

The A2 part of the course is also divided into three modules of study/units of assessment.

● Module 4 contains three topics: *power and politics*, *religion*, and *world sociology*. Each of these will form the basis of a question in the written examination. This unit carries 15% of the total A-level marks.

● Module 5 is based on *theory and methods*, and you have a choice between a written examination of this topic, and submitting a piece of coursework with a maximum word length of 3500 words. This unit carries 15% of the total A-level marks.

● Module 6 is the synoptic module (see below) and is assessed by a written examination. This unit carries 20% of the total A-level marks.

Coursework tips

- Make sure that your research has a clear sociological focus.
- Do not be over-ambitious and do not make your hypothesis or aim too broad – this will lead to problems in the later sections.
- Keep referring back to your hypothesis or aim – all the other sections should show a clear link to this.
- Make sure that you spend time choosing appropriate pieces of context and show how and why these provide an appropriate context for the proposed research.

- Choose only one method to use as the main method of data collection.
- Remember to give clear reasons for all your choices and decisions.
- Allow sufficient time to draft and redraft your proposal – it is seldom possible to get everything right the first time. Make sure that you are aware of, and meet, the set deadline.
- Stick to the word limit!

Synoptic assessment

Unit 6 is the synoptic unit, which will test your knowledge and understanding of the links between all the sections of the course that you have studied. The two topic areas that form the basis of synoptic assessment are: *crime and deviance*, and *stratification and differentiation*. There will be a question on each of these on the examination paper. You will answer a question on one of these topics only. The questions on this paper will require you to show an informed and critical knowledge and understanding of your chosen synoptic topic and its links with sociological theory, sociological methods, and the other topic areas you have studied over the two years of the course.

The OCR specifications *Steve Chapman, Chief Examiner, OCR AS/A-level sociology*

What will I study?

Aims of the course

The OCR A-level specification aims to offer you a sound introduction to sociology regardless of whether you are only interested in gaining the AS award or aiming for the full A level. In particular, it aims to develop a knowledge and understanding of social processes, structures and theories which are both contemporary and relevant to your life. You are positively encouraged by this specification to reflect on your social identity and experience of the social world and to apply your knowledge and understanding of sociology to everyday life. Your experience of this specification should equip you with the necessary skills to engage in sociological debate and to be able to interpret, apply and evaluate relevant evidence and to construct convincing sociological arguments. Finally, this specification is designed to offer you choice and flexibility in terms of its content, its varied assessment system and its coursework options.

Themes of the course

The AS specification has three inter-linked themes:

- examining how and to what extent individuals shape, and are shaped by, social structures – this underpins the entire specification and offers progression to the other AS units and to A2
- exploring the agencies that make up the cultural institutions of our society and especially those with which we

have daily contact – a good deal of the sociology explored looks at how we are socialised into our identities and culture by such agencies
- examining how sociologists collect information about the social world and whether their views are truthful and worthwhile.

Modules

There are three modules at AS level:

- Module 2532 : The individual and society
- Module 2533 : Culture and socialisation
- Module 2534 : Sociological research skills **or** Module 2535: Research report (sociology).

Topics

- The *individual and society* module involves a basic introduction to sociological theories aimed at understanding human behaviour, an examination of how culture is formed, the role of primary and secondary agents of socialisation and identity in relation to gender, ethnicity, nationality and social class.
- The *culture and socialisation* module covers the family, mass media, religion, and youth and culture.
- The *sociological research skills* module involves basic concepts in research design such as reliability and validity, sampling, primary research methods and secondary data.

How will I be assessed?

Skills

For AS-level sociology, you will be tested by the following assessment objectives.

Assessment objective 1 (AO1): knowledge and understanding

After studying this specification, you should be able to demonstrate knowledge and understanding of sociological theories, methods, concepts and different types of evidence, how these are inter-linked and how they relate to both social-life and social problems. It is important to stress that you are not expected or required to have an advanced understanding of sociological theory. Rather, at this level, you should be 'conceptually confident', meaning that you will have to demonstrate that you understand important concepts and are able to apply these when constructing a sociological argument. It is also a good idea to know some sociological studies because these often count as evidence in support of a particular view.

Assessment objective 2 (AO2): interpretation and analysis, and evaluation

(a) *Interpretation and analysis*

This skill essentially involves showing the ability to select and analyse different types of evidence and data. In particular, it involves the ability to apply and link sociological evidence to specific sociological arguments. It also involves the ability to interpret quantitative and qualitative data, i.e. to work out what it is saying and/or put it into your own words.

(b) *Evaluation*

It is important to be able to evaluate specific sociological arguments. This normally involves assessing the available evidence or critically examining the methods used to collect that evidence.

Exams

UNIT CODE	TITLE	EXAM	% OF AS-LEVEL	% OF FULL A LEVEL
Unit 2532	The individual and society	You answer one from two data-response questions in 1 hour	30	15
Unit 2533	Culture and socialisation	You answer two two-part structured essay questions, chosen from the same or different options in 1.5 hours	40	20
Unit 2534	Sociological research skills	You answer one data-response question in 1 hour	30	15

Coursework

Unit 2535 Research report is offered as an alternative to the written examination in Unit 2534 and represents 30% of the AS level and 15% of the full A level.

How can I do well in the exams?

Timing

It is important that you use your time effectively in exams.

The individual and society

The examination lasts one hour. The data-response question is divided into four parts worth 90 marks in all. You should spend at least five minutes reading through the data material and the questions. Questions (a) and (b) are worth 12 marks each and it is recommended that you spend approximately 15 minutes in total on these two parts. Question (c) is worth 26 marks and it is recommended that you spend approximately 15 minutes on this. Aim for about a page of writing. Finally, part (d) is worth 40 marks. It is recommended that you spend about 25 minutes on this – your response should aim for one to two sides of writing.

Culture and socialisation

You have to answer two questions in one hour and 30 minutes. These are organised into two parts; part (a) is worth 20 marks and part (b) is worth 40 marks. You should aim to spend about 15 minutes on the former and 30 minutes on the latter. Aim for about a half to two thirds of a side for part (a) and about two sides or more for part (b).

Sociological research skills

The examination lasts an hour and is a data-response organised into four questions and worth 90 marks in all. It is recommended that you spend approximately 30 minutes on questions (a) and (b), worth 8 marks and 35 marks respectively. Don't make the mistake of overdoing part (a). About five minutes and a paragraph should suffice in answering this question effectively. You should spend approximately 30 minutes on parts (c) and (d). Again, most of this time should be spent on organising and writing part (d).

Style of questioning

OCR has decided to use the same action or trigger words and phrases for every examination session so that you can respond in the most effective fashion to the question set.

The individual and society

- Question (a) will always be geared to asking about the data in the Item. This data may take a number of forms. It may be pictorial (e.g. a magazine cover, newspaper headline, cartoon, etc.), numerical (e.g. in the form of statistical tables, graphs, charts, etc.) or textual (e.g. an extract from a textbook). The action words are likely to be *identify and briefly explain* and these will be accompanied by an instruction to use the data.
- Question (b) also uses the action phrase *identify and briefly explain* and is likely to ask for two ways or examples.
- Question (c) will normally ask you to *outline and comment on* two ways that something happens. Note that the word *outline* means explain or describe. The word *comment* is often misinterpreted. In this context, it means to assess or evaluate.
- Question (d) will always begin *discuss...* and most probably focus on a particular view (e.g. 'discuss the view that gender identities have become confused in the 21st

century'). You should be aware of two things when answering a question like this. First, you don't have to accept the view in the question. You can question it but you should outline it before you do. Second, *discuss* implies both sides of an argument. In other words, it has an evaluative component because it should involve looking at both the strengths and weaknesses of the view.

Culture and socialisation

● Part (a) of these questions will always ask you to *identify and explain two* ways or examples or aspects of a sociological problem or issue. Part (b) will always begin *outline and discuss the view…* . (See the discussion above.)

Sociological research skills

● Question (a) will always ask you to *define*, in your own words, a sociological concept related to research design and is likely to use the action words, *briefly explain*.

● Question (b) will always ask you to *identify and explain two strengths and two weaknesses* of the research design in Item A.

● Question (c) will always ask you to summarise, in your own words, the data provided in Item B. You should approach this data with care and pay special attention to how it is organised in terms of scale and proportion. Candidates often throw away marks because they rush this section and do not pay enough attention to detail.

● Question (d) will always ask you to *outline in detail and briefly assess one method of collecting data* relating to a specific sociological problem. You must explain clearly and in detail how your method might practically work in terms of sampling and how you intend to operationalise the sociological problem so that your research method measures it effectively. The strengths and weaknesses of your chosen research method must be discussed with specific reference to the practicalities of investigating this sociological problem.

Exam tips

● Do read the instructions on the front of the examination paper. Too many candidates waste time or throw away marks because they have answered too many questions or not enough or they've answered from the wrong sections.

● Plan your response to any question worth over 20 marks.

● Try to avoid writing down all you know about a particular topic, regardless of the question asked. Think about how what you do know relates to the question set. Be prepared to think on your feet.

● Don't fall into the trap of mistaking your own opinion for sociology. Always support what you say with evidence.

● A coherent, logical presentation of argument and evidence is necessary to achieve a good A-level standard.

How do I do well in coursework?

Requirements

The Research Report requires you to choose and report on a short piece of sociological research (1000 words). The research could be a well-known sociological study, a piece of research taken from the magazine, *Sociology Review*, or even a personal study completed by another student in your centre. You should aim to complete:

1 a summary of the research objectives (10–30 words)
2 an outline of the research methodology (200–270 words)
3 reasons for the selection of the methodology (250–300 words)
4 an outline and evaluation of the findings of the research (350–400 words).

Coursework tips

● Choose an accessible study that uses straightforward research methods and on which there is plenty of information available in textbooks, etc. to help you evaluate its effectiveness.

● There is no advantage to be gained by exceeding the word limit.

What will the A2 course be like?

Modules and topics

If you decide to continue into A2, you can expect to study the following modules:

● Module 2536: *power and control* – this includes six topic areas: crime and deviance; education; health; protest and social movements; popular culture; and social policy and welfare
● Module 2537: *applied sociological research skills*

Synoptic assessment

Unit 2539 is the synoptic unit, *social inequality and difference*. This involves looking at inequalities relating to social class, gender and ethnic minorities. Synoptic means being assessed on how well you understand the links between social inequality, sociological theory and research methods. You would also be expected to know how social inequality impacts on other units studied throughout AS and A2.

Coursework

OCR offers students the option of a personal study at A2. This is an extended piece of work (2500 words) on a sociological topic chosen by the candidate that0 involves practical research and the analysis of any primary and/or secondary data.

References

Althusser, L. (1971) 'Ideology and ideological state apparatuses' in *Lenin and Philosophy and Other Essays*, London: New Left Books.

Anderson, M. (1971) 'Family, household and the Industrial Revolution' in M. Anderson (ed.) *The Sociology of the Family*, Harmondsworth: Penguin.

Annandale, E. (1998) *The Sociology of Health and Illness*, Cambridge: Polity Press.

Anwar, M. (1981) *Between Two Cultures: A Study of Relationships between Generations in the Asian Community*, London: CRE.

Aries, P. (1962) *Centuries of Childhood*, London: Random House

Ball, S. *et al.* (1994) 'Market forces and parental choice' in S. Tomlinson (ed.) *Educational Reform and its Consequences*, London: Rivers Oram Press.

Bandura, A., Ross, D. and Ross, S. A. (1963) 'The imitation of film mediated aggressive models', *Journal of Abnormal and Social Psychology*, vol. 66, no.1, pp. 3–11.

Barber, B. (1963) 'Some problems in the sociology of professions', *Daedalus*, vol. 92, no. 4.

Bauman, Z. (1990) *Thinking Sociologically*, Oxford: Blackwell.

Baxter, J. and Western, M. (1998) 'Satisfaction with housework: examining theparadox', *Sociology*, vol. 30, no.1.

Beck, U. (1992) *Risk Society: Towards a New Modernity*, London: Sage.

Becker, H. (1963) *Outsiders: Studies in the Sociology of Deviance*, London: Macmillan.

—— (1971) 'Social class variations in the teacher pupil relationship' in B. Cosin (ed.) *School and Society*, London: Routledge & Kegan Paul.

Benston, M. (1972) 'The political economy of women's liberation' in N. Glazer-Malbin and H. Y. Waehrer (eds) *Women in a Man-Made World*, Chicago: Rand McNally.

Bernardes, J. (1997) *Family Studies: An Introduction*, London: Routledge.

Billington, R. *et al.* (1998) *Exploring Self and Society*, Basingstoke: Macmillan.

Blaxter, M. (1990) *Health and Lifestyles*, London: Tavistock.

Blumler, J. G. and McQuail, D. (1968) *Television in Politics: Its Uses and Influence*, London: Faber and Faber.

Bordieu, P. and Passeron, J. (1977) *Reproduction in Education, Society and Culture*, London: Sage.

Bowles, S. and Gintis, H. (1976) *Schooling in Capitalist America: Educational Reform and the Contradictions of Economic Life*, New York: Basic Books.

Bradshaw, J. and Ernst, J. (1990) *Establishing a Modest but Adequate Budget for a British Family*, Family Budget Unit.

Buckingham, D. (ed.) (1993) *Reading Audiences: Young People and the Media*, Manchester: Manchester University Press.

Burghes, L. (1997) *Fathers and Fatherhood in Britain*, London: Policy Studies Institute.

Buswell, C. (1987) *Training for Low Pay*, Basingstoke: Macmillan.

Butler, C. (1995) 'Religion and gender: young Muslim women in Britain', *Sociology Review*, vol. 4, no.3, pp. 21–2.

Coard, B. (1971) *How the West-Indian Child is Made Educationally Sub-normal in the British School System*, London: New Beacon Books.

Cohen, P. (1984) 'Against the new vocationalism' in L. Bates, J. Clarke, P. Cohen, R. Moore and P. Willis, *Schooling for the Dole*, Basingstoke: Macmillan.

Connell, R. (1995) *Masculinities*, Cambridge: Polity Press.

Davey Smith, G., Shipley, M. J. and Rose, G. (1990) 'The magnitude and causes of socio-economic differentials in mortality: further evidence from the Whitehall study', *Journal of Epidemiology and Community Health*, vol. 44, pp. 265–70.

Delphy, C. (1984) *Close to Home*, London: Hutchinson.

Downing, J. (1988) 'The Cosby Show and American racial discourse' in G. Smitherman-Donaldson and T. van Dijk (eds) *Discourse and Discrimination*, Detroit: Wayne State University Press.

Drew, D. (1995) *Race, Education and Work: The Statistics of Inequality*, Aldershot: Avebury.

Edgell, S. (1980) *Middle-class Couples*, London: Allen & Unwin.

Elias, N. (1978) *The Civilising Process*, Oxford: Blackwell.

Essex University Study (2000) *Family Formation in Multicultural Britain: Three Patterns of Diversity*, Institute for Social and Economic Research, Essex University (author: Richard Berthoud).

Ferguson, M. (1983) *Forever Feminine: Women's Magazines and the Cult of Femininity*, London: Heinemann.

Fesbach, S. and Sanger, J. L (1971) *Television and Aggression*, San Francisco: Jessey-Bass.

Field, F. (1989) *Losing Out: The Emergence of Britain's Underclass*, Oxford: Blackwell.

Finn, D. (1987) *Training without Jobs*, Basingstoke: Macmillan.

Foster, J. (1990) *Villains: Crime and Community in the Inner City*, London: Routledge.

Foucault, M. (1976) *The Birth of the Clinic*, London: Tavistock.

Fuller, M. (1984) 'Black girls in a London comprehensive' in R. Deem (ed.) *Schooling for Women's Work*, London: Routledge.

Future Foundation Survey (2000) 'Complicated lives' (conducted by William Nelson).

Galtung, J. and Ruge, M. (1973) 'Structuring and selecting news' in S. Cohen and J. Young, *The Manufacture of News, Social Problems, Deviance and the Mass Media*, London: Constable.

Ghaill, M. Mac an (1988) *Young, Gifted and Black*, Milton Keynes: Open University Press.

—— (1992) 'Coming of age in 80s England: reconceptualising black students' educational experience', in D. Gill, B. Mayor and M. Blair (eds) *Racism and Education: Structures and Strategies*, London: Sage.

—— (1994) *The Making of Men: Masculinities, Sexualities and Schooling*, Milton Keynes: Open University Press.

—— (1996) 'What about the boys? Schooling, class and the crisis of masculinity', *Sociological Review*, vol. 44, no. 3.

Gilborn, D. (1990) *'Race', Ethnicity and Education: Teaching and Learning in Multi-ethnic Schools*. London: Unwin Hyman.

Gillborn, D. and Gipps, B. (1996) *Recent Research in the Achievement of Ethnic Minority Pupils*, London: HMSO.

Gilroy, P. (1993) *The Black Atlantic: Modernity and Double Consciousness*, London: Verso.

Glaser, B. and Strauss, A. (1967) *The Discovery of Grounded Theory*, Chicago: Aldine.

Goffman, E. (1963) *Stigma: Notes on the Management of Spoiled Identity*, New York: Prentice Hall.

—— (1984) *Asylums*, Harmondsworth: Penguin (first published 1961).

Gordon, D. et al. (2000) *Poverty and Social Exclusion in Britain*, York: Joseph Rowntree Foundation.

Grieshaber, S. (1997) 'Mealtime rituals: power and resistance in the construction of mealtime rules', *British Journal of Sociology*, vol. 48, no. 4.

Griffin, C. (1985) *Typical Girls: Young Women from School to the Job Market*, London: Routledge & Kegan Paul.

Guibernau, M. and Goldblatt, D. (2000) 'Identity and nation' in K. Woodward (ed.) *Questioning Identity: Gender, Class, Nation*, London: Routledge/Open University.

Hakim, C. (1996) *Key Issues in Women's Work*, London: Athlone.

Hall, S. and Jefferson, S. (1976) *Resistance through Rituals: Youth Subcultures in Post-war Britain*, London: Hutchinson.

Hargreaves, D. H. (1967) *Social Relations in a Secondary School*, London: Routledge & Kegan Paul.

Helman, C. (2000) *Culture, Health and Illness*, Oxford: Butterworth/Heinemann.

Himmelweit, H. (1958) *TV and the Child*, Oxford: Oxford University Press.

Illsley, R. (1986) 'Occupational class, selection and the production of inequalities in health', *Quarterly Journal of Social Affairs*, vol. 2, no. 2, pp. 151–64.

Independent Inquiry into Inequalities in Health (1998) London: HMSO.

Jacobson, J. (1997) 'Religion and ethnicity: dual and alternative sources of identity among young British Pakistanis', *Ethnic and Racial Studies*, vol. 20, no. 2.

Jhally, S. and Lewis, J. (1992) *Enlightened Racism. The Cosby Show, Audiences and the Myth of the American Dream*, Oxford: Westview Press.

Johal, S. (1998) 'Brimful of Brasia', *Sociology Review*, vol. 8, no. 1.

Jordan, B. (1992) *Trapped in Poverty? Labour Market Decisions in Low Income Households*, London: Routledge.

Joseph Rowntree Foundation Survey (1999) *Monitoring Poverty and Social Exclusion*, York: Joseph Rowntree Foundation (authors: C. Howarth, P. Kenway, G. Palmer and R. Miorelli).

Klapper, J. T. (1960) *The Effects of Mass Communication*, New York: The Free Press.

Krause, I. B. (1989) 'Sinking heart: a Punjabi communication of distress', *Social Science Medicine*, vol. 29, pp. 563–75.

Lees, S. (1986) *Losing Out: Sexuality and Adolescent Girls*, London: Hutchinson.

Legal & General Survey (2000) 'The value of a mum'.

Leighton, G. (1992) 'Wives' paid and unpaid work and husbands' unemployment', *Sociology Review*, vol. 1, no. 3.

Lewis, O. (1966) *La Vida*, New York: Random House.

McGlone, F., Park, A. and Smith, K. (1998) *Families and Kinship*, London: Family Policy Studies Centre.

MacIntyre, S. (1993) 'Gender differences in the perceptions of common cold symptoms', *Social Science and Medicine*, vol. 36, no. 1, pp. 15–20.

Mack, J. and Lansley, S. (1993) *Breadline Britain*, London: Unwin Hyman.

Mackintosh, M. and Mooney, G. (2000) 'Identity, inequality and social class' in K. Woodward (ed.) *Questioning Identity: Gender, Class, Nation*, London: Routledge/Open University.

McRobbie, A. (1991) 'Romantic individualism and the teenage girl' in A. McRobbie (ed.) *Feminism and Youth Culture*, Basingstoke: Macmillan.

Marshall, G. et al. (1988) *Social Class in Modern Britain*, London: Hutchinson.

Marsland, D. (1996) 'From cradle to grave mistake', *Times Higher Education Supplement*, 17 May.

Mason, D. (2000) *Race and Ethnicity in Modern Britain*, Oxford: Oxford University Press.

Mirza, H. (1992) *Young, Female and Black*, London: Routledge.

Modood, T. (1997) *Ethnic Minorities in Britain: Diversity and Disadvantage*, London: Policy Studies Institute.

Morley, D. (1980) *The Nationwide Audience*, London: BFI.

Morrison, D. E. (1999) *Defining Violence: The Search for Understanding*, Luton: University of Luton Press.

Moser, K., Goldblatt, P., Fox, J. and Jones, D. (1990) 'Unemployment and mortality' in P. Goldblatt (ed.) *Longitudinal Study: Mortality and Social Organisation*, London: HMSO.

Mulvey, L. (1975) 'Visual pleasures and narrative cinema', *Screen*, vol. 16, no. 3.

Murray, C. (1994) *Underclass: The Crisis Deepens*, London: IEA.

Newsom, E. (1994) 'Video violence and the protection of children', *The Psychologist*, June.

Oakley, A. (1982) *Subject Women*, London: Fontana.

O'Donnell, M. (1991) *Race and Ethnicity*, Harlow: Longman.

Oliver, M. (1996) *Understanding Disability*, London: Macmillan.

Orbach, S. (1991) *Fat is a Feminist Issue*, London: Hamlyn.

Pahl, R. E. (1988) 'Some remarks on informal work, social polarisation and the class structure', *International Journal of Urban and Regional Research*, vol. 12, no. 2, pp. 247–67.

Parsons, T. and Bales, R. F. (eds) (1955) *Family, Socialization and Interaction Process*, New York: The Free Press.

Plant, M. (1975) *Drug Takers in an English Town*, London: Tavistock.

Pryce, K. (1979) *Endless Pressure*, Harmondsworth: Pelican.

Rapoport, R. N., Fogarty, M. P. and Rapoport, R. (eds) (1982) *Families in Britain*, London: Routledge.

Riseborough, G. (1993) 'The gobbo barmy army: one day in the life of YTS boys' in I. Bates (ed.) *Youth and Inequality*, Milton Keynes: Open University Press.

Rosenhahn, D. L. (1973/1982) 'On being sane in insane places', *Science*, vol. 179, pp. 250–8; also in M. Bulmer (ed.) (1982) *Social Research Ethics*, London: Holmes and Meier.

Rosenthal, R. and Jacobson, L. (1968) *Pygmalion in the Classroom*, New York: Holt, Rinehart & Winston.

Said, E. (1985) *Orientalism*, Harmondsworth: Penguin.

Saunders, P. (1990) *Social Class and Stratification*, London: Routledge.

Savage, M. (1995) 'The middle classes in modern Britain', *Sociology Review*, vol. 5, no. 2.

Scheff, T. (1966) *Being Mentally Ill: A Sociological Theory*, Chicago: Aldine.

Schlesinger, P. (1978) *Putting Reality Together*, London: Constable.

Schudsen, M. (1994) 'Culture and integration of national societies' in D. Crane (ed.) *The Sociology of Culture*, Oxford: Blackwell.

Sharpe, S. (1976) *Just Like a Girl*, Harmondsworth: Penguin (2nd edn published 1994).

—— (1994) *Sugar and Spice*, Harmondsworth: Penguin.

Shaw, M., Dorling, D., Gordon, D. and Davey Smith, G. (1999) *The Widening Gap*, Bristol: Policy Press.

Smith, J. (1989) *Mysogenies*, London: Faber and Faber.

Statham, J. (1986) *Daughters and Sons: Experiences of Non-sexist Child-raising*, Oxford: Blackwell.

Stone, M. (1981) *The Education of the Black Child in Britain*, Glasgow: Fontana.

Strinati, D. (1995) *An Introduction to Theories of Popular Culture*, London: Routledge.

Swann Report (1985) *Education for All*, London: HMSO.

Swingewood, A. (2000) *A Short History of Sociological Thought*, Basingstoke: Macmillan.

Szasz, T. (1973) *The Myth of Mental Illness*, London: Paladin (first published 1962).

Taylor, S. (1999) 'Postmodernism: a challenge to sociology', *'S' Magazine*, no. 4.

Tizard and Hughes (1991) 'Reflections on young people learning' in G. Walford (ed.) *Doing Educational Research*, London: Routledge.

Troyna, B. (1978) 'Race and streaming: a case study', *Educational Review*, vol. 30, no. 1.

Tuchman, G. *et al.* (eds) (1978) *Hearth and Home: Images of Women in the Mass Media*, New York: Oxford University Press.

van Dijk, T. (1991) *Racism and the Press*, London: Routledge.

Viewing the World: A Study of British Television Coverage of Developing Countries (2000) Department for International Development.

Vogler, C. (1994) 'Money in the household' in M. Anderson, F. Bechofer and J. Gershuny (eds) *The Social and Political Economy of the Household*, Oxford: Oxford University Press.

Waters, M. (1995) *Globalization*, London: Routledge.

Willis, P. (1977) *Learning to Labour*, Aldershot: Ashgate.

Winship, J. (1987) *Inside Women's Magazines*, London: Pandora Press.

Wolf, N. (1990) *The Beauty Myth*, London: Vintage.

Wood, J. (1993) 'Repeatable pleasures: notes on young people's use of video' in D. Buckingham (ed.) *Reading Audiences: Young People and the Media*, Manchester: Manchester University Press.

Woods, P. (1983) *Sociology and the School: An Interactionist Viewpoint*, London: Routledge & Kegan Paul.

Wright, C. (1992) 'Early education: multi-racial primary classrooms' in D. Gill, B. Mayor and M. Blair (eds) *Racism and Education: Structures and Strategies*. London: Sage.

Young, M. and Willmott, P. (1957) *Family and Kinship in East London*, Harmondsworth: Penguin.

—— (1973) *The Symmetrical Family*, Harmondsworth: Penguin.

Index

Note: page numbers in **bold** denote key terms and their definitions.